Astrology Unlocked

By

Philip F. Young, PhD

BALBOA.
PRESS

A DIVISION OF HAY HOUSE

Balboa Press books may be ordered through booksellers or by contacting:

Balboa Press
A Division of Hay House
1663 Liberty Drive
Bloomington, IN 47403
www.balboapress.com
1 (877) 407-4847

ISBN: 978-1-4525-8783-7 (sc)
ISBN: 978-1-4525-8784-4 (e)

Library of Congress Control Number: 2013921590

Printed in the United States of America.

Balboa Press rev. date: 8/12/2014

Dedication

This book is dedicated to spiritual truth seekers. May this work offer you some help along your journey.

Forward

Philip is an astrological colleague and longtime friend who is a Renaissance man with varied interests and an open-minded, progressive view of astrology. I have known him since 2003 and have followed his evolution in life and as a professional astrologer. He studied for years, combining astrology with his practice of tarot. He has warmth and sensitivity for people, making him an excellent counselor. At the same time, he is a "questioner," wanting to challenge the status quo to provide fresh insights into traditional views of astrology. These insights are exemplified in this book, *Astrology Unlocked*.

Self-understanding is the first step toward spiritual evolution and this book is a catalyst for this step. Philip states in the book, "Astrology is health care for the soul, spirit, and personality." I recommend this book for anyone seeking that kind of health care.

Randy Wasserstrom, MSW
Professional Astrologer

Given the great complexity of human lives and human nature, all of us have the same goal: understand ourselves and our story the best we can. But after work, family, and day-to-day mundane life circumstances, how do we have the time to really focus energy on getting answers to the broad and specific questions related to our personal lives? We all want answers, clues, and insight but the dilemma is whether or not we can take the time to search for those answers and balance that with our daily schedules. With this very dilemma in mind, Philip Young has constructed this book to encourage you toward a more meaningful consideration of the questions you ask and the way in which you can search for the answers. I know no other astrology book that comes close to providing the interesting and applicable ways of understanding our independent and interdependent aspects of life. He offers us a way to apply the well-known but under-used tool of astrology to help us identify what is and isn't "working" for us—within any life category. Simply, he facilitates our own abilities in understanding the misunderstood and enigmatic aspects of our lives.

But I don't want you to think that this will happen overnight, or that this is easy. It's not. I learned this the hard way over the many conversations I have had with Philip. Given my background in psychology, I am naturally interested in our behaviors, thoughts, and emotions. I am intrigued by people's stories, as well as my own, and I desire to learn from them. My conversations with Philip are thoughtful and intense, never lacking a head tilt or "hmm…" somewhere during our time together. What I enjoy and admire most about Philip is that he is extremely well-read and educated on astrology. It is not a hobby. It is not a side dish in his meal of existence, but the main course. Fortunately for you, he has taken all of his knowledge and experience with astrology, prioritized the most meaningful elements, and developed a path for those of us that don't really know where to start. Or where to go. He has presented a compass that allows us the freedom to develop perspective on all aspects of our lives. It is not an exhaustive manual on using astrology but, as the title denotes, a way to unlock the meaning behind and power of astrology. Fortunately, Philip has given us a key.

Julie A. Thompson, PhD
Developmental Research Scientist
Professor of Research Methods and Applied Statistics
Duke University

Contents

Astrology Unlocked by Philip Young, PhD

Astrology Unlocked by Philip Young, PhD

Preface

This book has been created to help you discover and appreciate the complexity and elegance that is the practice of astrology. I have written this book because astrology positively impacted my life at many important junctures and helped me understand and get through some very difficult times. Astrology has been a salve to my spiritual and emotional wounds, a gift to help me appreciate my life treasures, and a tool for problem-solving on my life journey.

After almost 20 years as a college-level English instructor and another six as a stay-at-home father, I have found many ways to transform students and successfully parent my daughter. I know what useful thinking strategies look like and how they have to perform to produce successful results and sought-after outcomes. Some very useful thinking strategies include writing about your interests instead of writing to a formula; practical life learning through Montessori education instead of memorizing and testing for facts; and collaborative writing, which produces higher-quality stories and ideas than standalone thinking and efforts.

Astrology is another thinking strategy that, when applied at a high level, moves people forward in remarkable and dramatic ways that can truly improve their lives. For those people who want to learn the skill themselves, this book is meant to prime you for the real effort involved, no sugar coating or promises of "made easy." This field of study is immense and its application powerful. For those people who are skeptical or dismissive, this book should give you pause to consider the subject with a bit more appreciation or, on the other hand, a lot less derision. For those of you just curious, perhaps thinking about getting a reading from a professional, this book should help you recognize the effort and skill professionals must have to make a living doing the work – as professional as a doctor, lawyer, or engineer. In the end, if any writer is truly honest, I've written this book for myself, to be the book I wish I had started with when I first got interested in the subject. And hopefully this book can fill that role in your astrological journey.

Acknowledgements

I want to acknowledge everyone who let me have their birth information, from free readings while I was learning to the paid readings after I attained enough mastery. In many ways this book is a collaboration of all those who have touched my life in a significant way; without each life lesson I could not have become the astrologer who would write this book, so thank you! I want to specifically thank my manuscript readers: Betsy Yenner (John Deere Global Toy Manager); Darrell Steen (Professional Astrologer); Randy Wasserstram, MSW (Professional Astrologer); Julie Thompson, PhD (Research Psychologist); Ina Britz (Homemaker); Jim Lyda (Mankind Project Warrior, Magician, and Priest); and Nancy Kress (University Librarian).

Introduction

Astrology is a fascinating subject to read about and study. But if you want to learn to "do" astrology you may find, as I did, that learning to read a chart effectively is a process both frustrating and exciting, alternating between fits of confusion and starts of epiphany. This book provides a deeper starting point than most other beginning books by offering a formula that can be used to put together the three essential data points that are calculated when a chart is cast (Energy Point[1], Sign[2], and House[3]). This data is combined in a specific way to move into the first layer of complexity required for interpreting your chart in a truly meaningful way. Most other beginner's books will give examples of each Energy Point in a Sign and each Energy Point in a House; and maybe, but not always a few examples of the meaning of the Energy Point in the Sign and the House (all together). I am going to give you the formula and every example (144 per Energy Point) of every combination for each energy point I use in client charts. Having this formula and all the examples will allow you to enter the study of astrology in a particular place of the learning process that will help you to experience more epiphanies with regularity.

You see, the confusion, in my experience, lies between memorizing the necessary discrete elements and seeing a complex and complete human spirit in the meaningful interweaving of all this data. To get to the complex human being, and his or her dominant spiritual and life themes, you have to go through a series of unlocking efforts, starting with the unlocking of the meanings of the individual and specific Energy Points, the Signs, and the Houses. These first "locks" are simple and unlocking them is mostly a matter of memorization. But as you encounter more and more complicated locks (Energy Point in a Sign, Energy Point in a House, Energy Point in a Sign AND House, Energy Point in a Sign and House IN RELATION TO (called Aspects[4]) another Energy Point in a Sign and House, and so on), you will have to develop more sophisticated unlocking techniques; memorization will not be enough.

---

[1] I will break with tradition on several occasions throughout this book and this will be one that resolves a particular pet peeve of mine, imprecise identification. I know it is common practice to refer to all astronomical bodies in astrology as "planets," but they are not. The Sun is a star, the Moon is a satellite, and Pluto is no longer a planet. There are also points that are not astronomical bodies, but rather calculated points, like the Part of Fortune or the Dark Moon Lilith. These astronomical bodies and calculated points are representative of energy captured in the human body at the time of birth and so I refer to them as Energy Points.

[2] I will be capitalizing common terms that are part of astrological jargon to highlight their special use in astrology. The break with grammatical rules is intentional.

[3] Refer to footnote 2.

[4] Refer to footnote 2.

You will have to learn to MAKE interpretive meaning out of the simpler meanings of the many data points (Energy Point, Sign, House, and Aspects) found in the chart. Even this book only breaks through the surface; but instead of scratching the surface, I am attempting to give you a solid first shovel-full that will allow you start digging deep with the more advanced books and techniques, so you can learn faster and with more confidence.

I will tell you right now that if you want to read astrology charts effectively, then you will simply have to memorize the meanings of the Energy Points, Signs, Houses, and later (not covered in this book) the Aspects. You will have to know them cold; otherwise you will have trouble seeing the nuances of an Energy Point in a Sign in a House. To even attempt to understand the full meaning of "your Sun is in Taurus in the 3rd House" or "your Juno is in Virgo in your 7th House," you will need to be able to know what the Sun represents, how Taurus expresses itself, what area of your life the 3rd House manages, and the meanings of Juno, Virgo, and the 7th House. And then you will need to be able to convey what that astrological sentence means without using any astrological terminology: "your life path manifests through your persistent and steady quest for reliable and practical understanding of and communication with the world around you" and "your sense of duty manifests through your methodical and critical quest for skillful and capable guides."

Now, let me officially welcome you to astrology. I have written this book to accomplish two tasks: providing an accessible introduction to the complexity of professional astrology for beginners and offering a desk reference for other professional astrologers. The first part of the book will attempt to layer definitions and simple meaning-making formulas onto the basic sophisticated formula that is the foundation for interpretation of the birth chart datum. The second part of the book is a set of tables using the formulas to provide one-sentence interpretations of the combined birth chart datum (Energy Point, Sign, and House) for every Energy Point I use in my chart readings for clients.

As I noted above, most beginner's books provide the simple formula of Energy Point in Sign and Energy Point in House and then a few examples combining all three (Energy Point in Sign in House). This book provides every possible configuration (144 for each Energy Point) for 25 different Energy Points, starting with the Sun and ending with the Part of Fortune (a whopping 1728 interpretations). The book also includes interpretations for the Ascendant, Descendant, Midheaven, and Imum Coeli (another 96 interpretations). If you are new to astrology, do not worry. By the time you finish reading this book, you will know what all the unknown terms in this paragraph mean.

Astrology and the Spiritual Narrative

What is your story? Right now, holding this book in your hand at this time in your life, what is your story? Are you single, involved, married, divorced, or widowed? Do you like, love, or tolerate your job? Do you need one? Is the world an amazing place, going to hell in a hand basket, an endless drudgery, a temporary stop on the way to spiritual enlightenment, or all of the above? Are you young, middle-aged, old, young at heart, old at heart, an excited old soul, or a weary youthful soul? Do you have children? In essence, we are the stories we tell others and ourselves, interacting in a world full of stories, some directly impacting us and many we will never know. When people come to me for an astrology reading, they come with their stories.

Most of the story starting points I encounter revolve around location/relocation/travel, relationship, work, family, and self-discovery or self-fulfillment. For one client, the relationship question has to do with a new relationship, and another client will see me about one that is ending. The astrology reading people come to get from me is also a story, one based on the time of birth, the date of birth, and the location of birth, marking the arrangement of the astronomical bodies in the solar system at the moment they took their first breath. People arrive at my office because they are experiencing a dramatic change in their story, they want to make a change in their story, or they want a deeper understanding of their story. They seek and need an alternative narrative to hold up against their current narrative, in order to evaluate who they are, why they are, and where they want to go next.

So here is the key question for you: "Is your current story working for you?" Are certain stories within your larger story working, while others are failing? Is your romantic relationship fantastic but your career struggling? Maybe you have unresolved issues regarding the family you grew up with, while the family you have created is doing wonderfully. Astrology recognizes the complexity of the human spirit/consciousness and is sophisticated enough to help you appreciate what is working for you in life, understand what is not, and offer explanations that can help you improve your strengths and overcome your weaknesses. Astrology is simply one of the most powerful explanatory models regarding human behavior, spirituality, and life purpose available to you!

Every philosophy, political position, social framework, psychology, and "ism" (capitalism, socialism, communism, and so on) offers a model to explain life. Some are quite narrow, like

Astrology Unlocked by Philip Young, PhD

fundamentalism and racism, while others are much broader, like liberalism and utilitarianism, and the world accommodates them all. But they are not all equally successful, useful, or morally defensible. Racism continually fails every time a member of the denigrated race excels. Feminism has effectively shone light on the dehumanization and objectification of women in the media, religion, literature, the workforce, and on and on in every world culture. And science, with the scientific method, has had more enduring and positive outcomes in a short period of time than any other explanatory model in existence.

Astrology, at its best, is one of the most useful explanatory models for life purpose, spiritual direction, and soul growth, because it offers both a broad and deep world view, continuing to adapt and grow with new astronomical discoveries and new innovations in chart interpretation. Astrology is not the explanatory model for engineering a building or testing new medication; it is not a scientific tool. Instead, astrology is a narrative strategy, one that relies on astronomical data to construct the skeleton of a story as shown in the symbols of the astrology chart that makes certain meanings and knowledge available for use during your spiritual journey. The astrology chart and its spiritual narrative unlock the "whys" behind actual events that come to make up the lived narrative of your physical, psychological, and emotional experiences in this lifetime. The "whys" generally reflect two energies that apply to your life: 1) why you feel compelled to act, feel, and think in certain ways that affect outcomes in life (asserting your will in life) and 2) why you attract certain experiences, people, and situations to you for spiritual and life lessons (encountering your fate).[5]

Since astrology uses the Earth and your geographic point of birth as the centermost point of the chart display, the practice is egocentric, focusing entirely on your unique existence. Based on the date and time of your birth event, the location of all astronomical bodies (and various calculated points) is identified and marked by glyphs (or symbols)in the chart. Imagine a working three-dimensional, holographic model of the solar system in front of you that is synced up with the actual movements and placements of the astronomical bodies the year of your birth. The model of the Earth is your focal point. Then, on the day you were born, at the time you took your first breath, you see a red dot light up on the holographic Earth image at the

---

[5] Real life is not a lock step of predetermined outcomes, nor is it a wild "free will"-for-all. Chaos Theory is the scientific exploration of choice/event interactions, showing that there are moments of choice that set in motion predictable and determined outcomes that lead to new moments of choice that lead to new outcomes and so on ad infinitum. In life, you get to choose, you get choices made for you, and you have no-choice situations.

location you were born. At that moment, the holographic model stops, giving you a three-dimensional snapshot of the solar system when you were born. You have your holographic-model generator hooked up to your printer, which does not print in 3D, so when you print your chart, the three-dimensional snapshot is compressed down to a two-dimensional representation that is the astrology chart you get from a computer program or professional astrologer. Every glyph in the chart represents a meaning, including the numbers assigned to the Houses and the actual degrees on the wheel of the chart.[6] These meanings provide the rich details that make up the particular narrative that is the foundation of your astrological story. Once the snapshot has been taken, the solar system continues its movements, and its story continues to unfold. Only now you have entered the cosmic drama and will have a part in the larger story that will unfold as your particular life unfolds.

Since we are naturally egocentric creatures, we enhance our understanding of ourselves when we compare narratives from the world outside with our own internal narratives as a way to reinforce, challenge, explore, explain, and create the meanings in our lives so we can find purposes, joys, accomplishments, and satisfaction. Consider the music you listen to regularly or the movies you prefer to watch. Think about the news you prefer to read or the art you are willing to purchase. Reflect on the clothes you wear or the medicine you need to take or the food you dislike or enjoy. They all play a part in the construction and action of your life narrative. Astrology is an outside narrative system that uses real-world reference points based on the most significant event of your life, your birth, to invite you toward the idea that your life has a meaningful purpose bound up in the configuration of the universe at the time, date, and place you were born.

Now blend in your non-astrological factors: gender, race, and class (a few examples) and you have the makings of a powerful and very interesting story, one that adapts and evolves as you grow. The energy of the solar system moves and interacts with the energy signature tattooed on your soul at birth. If you are skeptical about having a soul, then refer to your psychological composition as your self-image. You do not have to have or believe in a soul to use astrology any more than you need to believe in a deity to appreciate and be affected by art or a beautiful sunset. A spiritual belief or no spiritual belief is just another context that leads you to certain kinds of interpretations. My most enjoyable conversations are often with

---

[6] Assigned meaning by Dr. Marc Edmund Jones in his book *The Sabian Symbols in Astrology* (ISBN: 094335840X).

skeptics, and non-believers do get readings from me as a form of entertainment. For many of them, the entertainment is profoundly transformative.

Successful practice with and use of astrology depends on building your astrological knowledge foundation. What will keep you moving forward with astrology is new and better discoveries about yourself, your lovers, your friends, your family, your coworkers, where you live, what you will excel at, what you should avoid, and on and on. Astrology can make a confusing time in your life clear, help you see things about yourself you do not even yet know you need to see, and make sense out of a life that too often does not make sense. In essence, your birth chart contains many coded messages that will help you enjoy and manage your journey in this lifetime and appreciate your role in the cosmic drama of life on this planet. You only need to have a passion to learn about both the symbolism of astrology and the deeper layers you and others possess.

My Journey to Astrology

My journey to astrology was hardly straightforward, occurring in fits and starts, with periods of intense study and years of inactivity. Unlike my academic education, which proceeded in a traditional linear fashion from 1st grade to 22nd grade (PhD), my astrological education developed almost entirely as a lifelong independent study, which is still unfolding. The spark to study astrology ignited in 1989 when I was in a mall bookstore in Greensboro[7] and picked up *Linda Goodman's Sun Signs* (ISBN: 0553278827) and read about my Sun Sign, Aries. The initial flame that ignited that day was rather small but it never died, eventually becoming a blaze almost 20 years later. Fortunately, the material in Goodman's book was interesting enough for me to enjoy, but unfortunately too mass market for me to be deeply impressed.

I was already on my way as a trained critical thinker and determined that the Sun Sign book was too general to be of much use to me, since I did not see most of the traits assigned to Aries in my own behavior and outlook in life. As I read through other parts of the book, I found myself aligned more with Scorpio and Libra. I put the book back on the shelf thinking, "Interesting subject, but this book is not very accurate." Instead, I bought a tarot deck, *The Mythic Tarot* by Juliet Sharman-Burke (ISBN: 1572817364), that day and pursued the study of those tarot cards with intense vigor from 1989 until 1991, when I started reading cards professionally. The card descriptions in Juliet Sharman-Burke's book were more useful than the Sun Sign descriptions in Linda Goodman's, and *The Mythic Tarot* card set came with a workbook, which was the perfect tool for an academically-minded person like me.

I did not "rediscover" astrology until I found White Rabbit Books on the edge of the University of North Carolina at Greensboro's (UNCG) campus in 1992, after I started my PhD program. This alternative bookstore carried multiple tarot decks, runes, crystals, and other spiritual talismans and tools, as well as a number of astrology books that went far beyond the daily horoscope and Sun Signs. There I found *Alan Oken's Complete Astrology* (ISBN: 0553345370) and learned how to cast my own chart, without the aid of a computer! Reading his book I discovered the Rising Sign and the placement of the traditional ten Energy Points (Sun, Moon, Mercury, Venus, Mars, Jupiter, Saturn, Uranus, Neptune, and Pluto). I came to

---

[7] Walden books, the grandfather of online bookstores and the father of the standalone retail bookstore.

understand why so much of Scorpio, which was my Rising Sign, and Libra, which was where my Moon was in my chart, sounded more like me than Aries (in Linda Goodman's book). Oken's book also introduced me to Aspects, or the relationship of one Energy Point to another based on certain degrees apart from each other on the horoscope circle. I could begin to see the immense complexity of the astrological system even if I could not yet see its simple elegance. It would be many more years (from 1992 to 2003) of on-and-off research and fun forays into the charts of friends before I would truly understand and appreciate the power and usefulness of the tool.

In 2002 I separated from my wife and finalized our divorce in early 2004. North Carolina law requires a year of separation before a married couple can file for divorce. A year to the day of my separation, I met Betsy, who would become my romantic life partner until early 2013. She had a love for the esoteric and was thrilled to discover that I read tarot cards professionally. Our first date included several tarot card readings, all favorable (smile). With her high interest in New Age and ancient fields of study, I once again started studying astrology deeply, making a push in the direction of doing charts for people for money. Before asking for payment, I created my own astrology meetup through meetup.com and did astrology presentations for free using chart information collected from members. I was able to work with and practice on over 200 charts from 2004 to 2006. Once I felt comfortable with my knowledge and happy with my reading technique, I began to charge for my services, slowly building a positive reputation through individual clients and the people they recommended to see me.

Astrology's role in my personal life increased exponentially, beginning with relationship readings about my connection to Betsy and the karmic nature of our pairing. We enjoyed and still enjoy our Trine Moons, which is a *Fancy Nancy* astrological way of saying we give and receive love in a similar energetic fashion, through communication. Her Moon is in Gemini and mine is in Libra, meaning that talking and listening to people we care about is how we show affection and convey emotions – giving us tremendous benefits so long as we use our communication skills openly. Many, many more elements of our charts showed beneficial energetic connections, while the more challenging points were readily identifiable and easily manageable. When we first considered having our child, we researched astrological Signs to determine the best potential positive outcome in a household with an Aries Sun/Scorpio

11

Ascendant father and Scorpio Sun/Capricorn Ascendant mother. We planned for a Sagittarius, Capricorn, or Aquarius child and managed to conceive in May of 2004, resulting in an Aquarius daughter (January 30, 2005). She was also born with Mars and Pluto merged in Sagittarius, so she's a powerhouse in her own right, which any child would need to be in our family dynamic — especially now that she has a Scorpio Sun/Leo Rising stepfather-to-be in her life (at the time of this writing).

But the most profound benefits from astrology study came during a series of spiritual crises beginning with an awakening/breakdown in 2009 that literally leveled me to my core. This was followed by more core work in 2011 when I had to accept my need for anti-anxiety medicine. And in 2013, my partnership with Betsy transformed as she fell in love with my brother-friend James, leading her heart to pull her romantic love away from me. You will have to reserve judgment until you read all the way through this paragraph. With my insight into their charts, I was the one to encourage their exploration of their feelings. I had an inside track, knowing their astrology; I knew their connection would be undeniable and intense. With energy so intense, I can honestly say it is best to support such energy rather than stand in its way. To complicate matters just a bit more, we all live together and share parenting responsibilities. Our successful living situation and transformation of relationships was made possible with the help of insights from each of our astrological charts.

And finally, the last, most profound crisis during this time in my life was my final and complete acceptance that I have been called to perform this service in this lifetime. I did try to become a college professor and did well enough at the task; but my heart, as they say, was not in it. I made one last grasp for the security of the academic world and a reliable paycheck by applying to the University of North Carolina at Chapel Hill (UNC) School of Social Work for a Master's Degree. I put together an outstanding application and, I think, reasonably expected that holding a PhD would suffice to prove my ability and worthiness to enter and complete the program. My letters of recommendation were stellar and my personal narrative was tightly written and edited by a published professional, and my interview was spot on. However, I did not get in and I knew, spiritually speaking, that path was closed to me for good.

I could see that I needed to make one final effort to go with what felt most secure and most comfortable by applying once again to graduate school. And by making a great effort (and failing) I came to know, deep in my heart, that I had left nothing behind that would allow me to

12

Astrology Unlocked by Philip Young, PhD

second guess the outcome and the astrological profession I had to pursue wholeheartedly. Throughout each trauma (which included three visits to the emergency room and two extended but temporary uses of anti-anxiety medicine), I was able to turn to my own chart and the advice of fellow professional astrologers Randy Wasserstram and Darrell Steen for guidance and reassurance along the way. Not only did the medical and psychological communities help me with the nuts-and-bolts ailments of my mind and body – astrology helped me understand the spiritual nature and need for each crisis and how best to use each experience to enhance my soul growth. In the best of times astrology can be wings for flight and in the worst of times, a lifesaving buoy in a raging storm!

Professional Introduction

Allow me to introduce myself properly. My name is Philip Young and I am a professional astrologer and tarot reader who was a college English instructor for almost 15 years. My PhD is in English, with a concentration in Rhetoric and Composition. As a result of my teaching background and my academic training, I felt compelled to write this astrology book to address a common shortcoming I found in most beginning astrology books, as well as a common problem they unknowingly present to the profession. The work I do for clients requires quite a bit of preparation time, aided by years of intense study and practice. Thanks to *Astrology for Dummies* (ISBN: 0470098406), *The Complete Idiot's Guide to Astrology* (ISBN: 1592575811), *Astrology Made Simple* (ISBN: 1477677755), and *The Everything Astrology Book* (ISBN: 1580620620) the idea of paying someone to "do astrology for you" must obviously be a waste of money since it is so easy to learn and anyone can do it.

I know it sounds all "rainbows and unicorns"[8] to offer up the idea that anyone can learn anything, but the realities of being a doctor, astronaut, physicist, architect, nuclear submarine engineer, college professor, or professional astrologer do not bear out the claim any more than *Nuclear Submarine Design for Dummies* will actually teach you how to design nuclear submarines or *College Teaching Made Easy* will give you the tools to become a college professor. But that is the implied message to people picking up almost any beginner's book in the mass market. The real message of beginner's books, for those of you who want to learn what astrology can really do, should be, "this is the tip of iceberg and you need to dive beneath the surface to see how big this iceberg really is."

I know from experience that when students hit a wall in their learning process – because they feel mislead – they usually lose any interest in the subject and do not give it the necessary time and attention to be successful and access the value of the subject. When I do workshops, attendees often approach me afterwards and ask about learning the craft because they are so impressed with the results I show them in the presentation. The first thing I tell them, knowing they want to get the same quality of results I show in my workshops, is how much commitment it takes at the beginning to get to point where the full chart that appears

---

[8] A phrase that my friend Heather used in a conversation we were having about life paths and recent experiences.

14

Astrology Unlocked by Philip Young, PhD

later in this book reveals itself and makes sense as something whole, and not just a confusing collection of data points.

What level of commitment does it take? PhD level. I am writing this book in the hopes that it inspires you to take the full journey, from *Astrology for Dummies* (if that is the first book you bought) to a library filled with other more advanced astrology books, as well as books on psychology, history, symbolism, religion, and spirituality. Even if you decide not to read charts for other people, this long journey into astrology can help you unlock the various layers of your identity and appreciate all your life lessons (even the most difficult ones).

Once I got to the deeper meanings offered by Alan Oken's book, I discovered that astrology could deliver what it fundamentally advertises, a better and more fulfilling understanding of myself, at my core, and over the course of my entire lifetime. Astrology is the ultimate "personality test," but with much greater complexity than Myers-Briggs[9] or the Enneagram[10] and far more elegance than different philosophies of psychology. I only wish I had a better understanding of the subject earlier in my life. But, not ironically, such understanding had to wait to occur until after I had a lot more life under me. It is something of the paradox of astrology, namely that learning the craft requires not only devotion to the study but years of full-tilt life experience, which can only accrue with age. Call it the "*Good Will Hunting* effect".[11]

---

[9] *Please Understand Me II: Temperament, Character, Intelligence* (ISBN: 1885705026)
[10] *The Wisdom of the Enneagram: The Complete Guide to Psychological and Spiritual Growth for the Nine Personality Types* (ISBN: 0553378201)
[11] In the movie *Good Will Hunting* a young, raw genius played by Matt Damon (as Will Hunting) has a test-of-wills encounter with a psychologist played by Robin Williams (as Sean Maguire). Will gets the better of Sean and they part with Will thinking he has bested Sean and will not see him again. But Sean meets with him again and reengages Will by acknowledging that Will is a genius, but he lacks life experience. Unlike Sean, Will has never known the love of a woman for 30 years (as was the case with Sean for his wife). Genius cannot supplant experience and experience is absolutely necessary to understand certain issues in life at the proper depth.

New to Astrology

If you are brand new to astrology and this book is your first, or among your first, that you have pulled off the bookshelf or ordered online, then you are my target audience. To get off the ground with astrology, even if it is only a small leap, you must start with a printout of your birth chart. Here is a copy of mine:

Philip Young
Natal Chart
Apr 12 1968, Fri
9:39 pm EST +5:00
Lynchburg, Virginia
37°N24'49" 079°W08'33"
Geocentric
Tropical
Whole Signs
Mean Node
Rating: A

Compliments of:
Philip Young, PhD
Black Unykorn Tarot and Astrology
919-971-6818
http://www.blackunykorn.com
blackunykorn@gmail.com

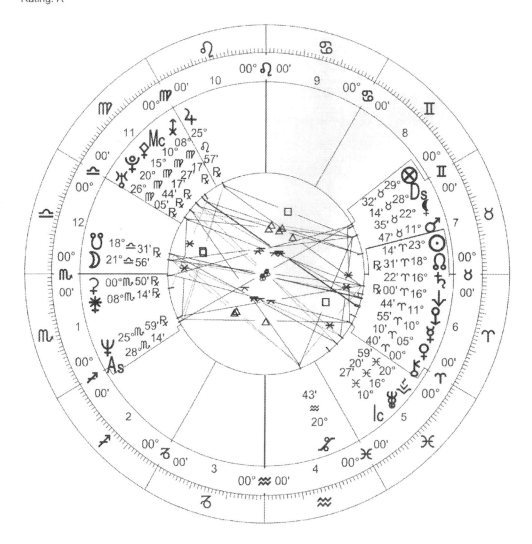

As you can see from the cast chart above, there is a lot of data that makes up the picture you see and all of it is shown through symbols. On the outermost ring you have glyphs[12] for the Signs of the Zodiac. You have numerical symbols in the second most outer ring representing the Houses (1 to 12). And you have glyphs placed inside each House representing astronomical bodies and calculated points, which are connected by lines representing particular geometric relationships (known as Aspects) based on the location of the bodies and the calculations at the time of your birth. More numbers appear next to these glyphs indicating the degree location of each point in terms of degrees and minutes. The chart is basically a visual circuit board, revealing the interactions of discrete data points in meaningful combinations. Lastly, you will see a symbol that looks like ℞ next to the minutes' number of certain Energy Point glyphs degree location (18° ♎ 56' ℞), which represents Retrograde Motion, a term I will define and explain in the definitions section later in the book.

Now, let's locate an Energy Point symbol from my chart and unlock its meaning, just to give you a taste of what this book is intended to help you do. We want to find the Energy Point glyph first, and then determine which Sign it is "in" (the glyph on the outer ring and between the degree and minutes of the Energy Point) and identify its House location (the numeric symbol). The Moon in the chart above should be fairly easy to find since the glyph looks like a crescent moon (☽). You will see the Moon glyph on the left side of the chart image with 21d ♎ 56' next to it. The ♎ glyph represents the Sign Libra. You will also note that the symbol is in the 12th House. The combination of the Energy Point in Sign in House creates a symbolic sentence shown on the next page.

---

[12] Glyphs defined: stylized figures that impart information nonverbally.

Astrology Unlocked by Philip Young, PhD

The symbolic sentence looks like this:

$$\text{☽} \; \underline{\Omega} \;_{12}$$

The astrological verbal sentence reads like this:

This individual (me) has his "Moon in Libra in the Twelfth House."

The astrological, meaning-filled verbal sentence reads like this:

My "Soul Path (Moon) manifests through my analytical and balanced (Libra) quest for and attraction to harmonious and logical (Libra) spirituality (12th House)."

What I come to understand about myself (and would say to a client) might read like this:

You believe in fairness above all else and are a born peacemaker. You rely on your spiritual beliefs to help you make life decisions.

The last two examples show the meaning embedded in the symbolic language that the astrologer learns how to unlock for himself or herself first, and later for lovers, friends, family, and paying clients (if he or she decides to go beyond just personal use and help others learn about themselves). The meaning-filled verbal sentence is an example of the formulaic sentence I have created to interpret all the Energy Points in all the Signs in all the Houses in the second part of this book.

To get started you will need to get a copy of your own chart. There are several different ways to get your chart. You can do so by searching out a website that offers free astrology charts, purchase an astrology program to use to cast the chart (like the one I used to cast this chart), or search for and pay a professional astrologer to cast your chart. No matter which method you use, you will need to provide the website, the computer program, or the astrologer with:

- your birth date,
- your birth location, and
- your birth time.

Keep in mind that most sites that offer free charts will usually only provide the most common Energy Points in the chart image (anywhere from 10 to 15 points) and you will have to know how to add points through the program in order to get all the points I interpret in Part Two. If you decide you want to contact me to get your chart with all the Energy Points used in this book, I will be happy to provide you a copy of your chart for a small processing fee (http://www.blackunykorn.com/orderbirthchart/).

Birth time is important and can be a barrier to getting your chart done if you do not know your birth time offhand. The best place to find it is your birth certificate. Unfortunately not all hospitals and birth centers record the time on the certificate. If that is your case, then check with family members to see if they recorded or remember your birth time. It may seem obvious to ask your mother, but I have encountered more than a few mothers who not only did not remember the time, but remembered it incorrectly (at night 3:00 a.m. was actually at night 10:00 p.m.). If you are relying on someone's memory, be sure to ask a number of people, especially anyone that was present at the birth (father, aunt, uncle, or even an older sibling). If it turns out, and it does happen, that you cannot find out your birth time, you can still get started by casting your chart for noon on your birthday.

An unknown birth time is something astrologers have encountered enough times over the history of astrology to have developed a technique to determine the best approximation of the birth time for an individual; the technique is called Rectification. Professional astrology programs and professional astrologers can perform this technique; I would recommend contacting a professional astrologer before trying to use an astrology program. The birth time is significant since it is used in the calculations of the chart to determine the Signs of the Houses in the chart, thus determining where the Energy Points will reside and have their most important role.

Once you have your birth chart in hand, you are ready to begin the exploration of astrology and start unlocking its immense power. I know from experience that people like to "dabble" in the field and still end up having profound discoveries and reactions; but if you really want to see how useful and powerful the tool is, then you will need to dig deep and devote some serious time to your studies. This book is really a quick immersion into astrology so you feel excited enough by your discoveries about yourself to keep studying and learning as much as possible!

19

Why Study Astrology

Astrology is a tool for self-examination: one of the oldest and still one of the best. By studying astrology seriously, reading as many books on the subject as you can, you will make profound discoveries about your identity, life purpose, and role in the cosmic drama. We humans strive to do more than simply survive and reproduce, to learn more than how to survive and reproduce – we create, discover, and explore. We make and find meaning. True human potential magnifies when we meet and exceed our survival needs, allowing us to put a person in space or destroy an entire city with a single bomb. At our best and worst, we range far beyond instinct and the restrictions of our physical bodies, especially with help from the technologies that spring from our creative and dreaming minds. We can travel under the sea and through the skies, correct physical deformities, cure most illnesses, and enjoy great happiness or endure immense sorrow.

We are most amazing creatures. And when we are truly honest with ourselves, we find nothing more fascinating than our own lives and how we journey through our existence. For many of the most significant parts of our journey – our identity, our values, our interactions with others, our family, our creative self-expression, our skills, our partnerships, our loves, our purpose, our career, our role in community, and our spirituality – astrology is a tool you can use over and over again to help you through difficulties and take full advantage of the good times, understand "whys" (why do I love this person but cannot make a relationship with them work; why am I not happy where I live; why do I feel so different from my family), and learn how to make the most of the life you have lived, are living, and want to live in the future. While most people encounter and enjoy (or dismiss) astrology by way of the daily horoscope, found in the Lifestyle section of the newspaper or online, the real power of astrology is as complex and elegant as any profound system of thought – scientific, philosophical, or psychological – and intensely particular to you, the individual. You must look at the individual chart to understand the particular flavor of each Sign and expression of each House as they apply to your lived life.

If, after reading this book or other beginner's books, you realize that the study of astrology is a field you want to pursue further, then consider visiting a professional astrologer and forming a long-term relationship with him or her. A professional astrologer can help

Astrology Unlocked by Philip Young, PhD

nurture your interest and help you unlock the deeper mysteries of your own chart until you feel comfortable recognizing them yourself. Astrology is health care for the soul, spirit, and personality. Yearly visits with a professional can help keep you attuned to and on your best spiritual path the same way yearly physical checkups can help you assess your current state of bodily health and avoid sudden, catastrophic illnesses. Your birth chart is only the beginning and a professional astrologer, like a physician, can provide helpful consulting about your spiritual condition throughout your life.

You carry and pulse a specific spiritual energy signature that was created and stored within your physical body at birth. Since astrology is based on the astronomical workings of the solar system and those workings operate in cyclical patterns, each Energy Point continues its movement after your birth applying to and affecting the matrix of your Energy Points in certain ways and at certain times in your life. In essence, you carry the energetic spiritual blueprint of the solar system at the time of your birth and your energy reacts to the ongoing motion of the chart points as they move into and out of various geometric positions with your birth points. The relationships of the Energy Points-in-motion with your birth Energy Points are known as Transits, which are used as an advanced interpretation technique in astrology.

A professional astrologer will be able to cast and interpret your birth chart along with a host of other types of charts, all aimed at overcoming difficulties and maximizing benefits in your life; helping you make meaning and find direction in your life; understanding reoccurring themes in your life; and on and on. The field of astrology is immense and creative astrologers continue to develop new techniques and calculations that other astrologers can use to help clients better understand themselves and the world around them. Seeing astrology as an ongoing and ever-available resource will help you pursue the craft with the commitment necessary to reach the high level of understanding that will yield the most powerful and helpful results. Should you find that the study of the field is not for you, but you do want to still get help from the tool, then definitely seek out a professional astrologer and give him or her the chance to help you with your spiritual and life development through their work.

Astrology Unlocked by Philip Young, PhD

What Astrology Is ... and Is Not

Astrology – as both a subject and practice – is complicated. I share this thought with you at the beginning of your astrology journey because there is no single correct way to study or practice astrology and the simplifications found in this book and other introductory books are merely starting points for a never-ending journey into the subject and practice. And the more you read on the subject, the more you will find exceptions and derivations. Bear with me while I try to summarize, using astrology jargon. Please note that this book and the books I recommend are all focused on Western instead of Eastern (Vedic) astrology. I, and the authors of the other Western astrology books, use Tropical instead of Sidereal astrology. Unlike my fellow authors, except Demetra George, I use the Whole Sign House system to construct my charts instead of the Placidus House system, which is the default House system in astrology software and the majority of books on Astrology. Unlike the first two categories (Western/Eastern and Tropical/Sidereal), there happen to be over ten different House systems you can choose from to cast your charts. And one path of astrology, Cosmobiology, eliminates the house system in favor of a 90 degree dial and midpoints, conveniently bypassing the House system confusion.

With the discovery of the asteroid belt, new astronomical bodies are now available for use and interpretation in the chart. Where there were once only seven Energy Points in use (Sun, Moon, Mercury, Venus, Mars, Jupiter, and Saturn), the ones visible to the naked eye, there is now an ever-expanding number coming out of the asteroid belt and long-range astronomy. Most books and software, even the ones recently published, still only focus on the primary 10 Energy Points of the last half of the 20th century (the original seven plus Uranus, Neptune, and Pluto). Even beginner's books published as recently as 2007 fail to include Chiron, Juno, Ceres, Vesta, and Pallas (major asteroids that have books written about them). I have chosen to stretch even farther and added the Part of Fortune, the North Node, the South Node, Lilith, Urania, Eris, Vulcan, Astraea, Hygeia, and Zeus (for reasons that will be made apparent later in the book).

I am not trying to scare you away from the subject, really, but I do think you need to know what you are "getting into" if you want to be serious about astrology and get the powerful benefits the tool has to offer! If you realize the study and practice is not for you, but you do want the knowledge you can access by having your chart read professionally, you will be able to appreciate the prices professional astrologers charge for their services after reading this book. In other words: if you think the information in this book is a lot, keep in mind that I am only showing you the "tip of the iceberg." 90 percent of the "mass" of astrology's iceberg is below the surface and requires a deep dive to see the truly massive size of this field of study. And so, by design, this book and other beginner's books attempt to offer you insights that will fuel your thirst for more and more knowledge about astrology – just not to the depths that further study or a professional reading will provide.

Because astrology has so many different avenues and systems, the practice is highly individualistic, which is probably why it attracts nonconformists to the field. I can almost say that astrology is as varied and unique as each astrologer, but that would be going just a bit too far. The field has enough core ideas that it cannot be whatever anyone wants to make of it; I cannot, for instance, make the explanation for Aries the explanation for Taurus any more than I can put diesel fuel in a car that runs on unleaded. However, the astrology practice is an interaction of humans using narrative as the basis for the experience. The narrative is shaped in certain ways by the meanings of the different components of the chart, the dialogue with the client and astrologer, and the worldviews of the client and astrologer.

In fact, I would argue that astrology's enduring quality is the imaginative and creative narrative. My clients respond intensely to their astrological narrative, especially if they have had any long-term psychological counseling. From these clients I often hear that their astrology reading identifies their personality, struggles, advantages, negative behavior patterns, and strengths more clearly and deeply for them, in one session, than years of therapy. I do not think this claim indicates that the narratives of psychology have failed, but is rather a testament to power of the astrological narrative. I, myself, have experienced two extended periods working with psychologists, finding one rather unhelpful and another lifesaving. I have also observed that people are more willing to make real changes in their lives from an astrological (or tarot) reading.

Clients freely admit to failing to take action that their psychologists, close friends, self-help books, and religious counselors provide to help them make necessary changes and attack negative patterns. However, the astrology reading often results in the needed awakening to activate change. I am sure some of the reason psychological counseling fails, when it fails, has to do with people's resistance to its narrative. It strives to be scientific, which is often defined as "not spiritual," giving it a rather cold and calculating narrative that is far less appealing than the creative language of astrology.

Case in point: you have a child or adult that is highly sensitive to what is going on around them all the time. A visit to a psychologist yields a *diagnosis*, which turns out to be attention deficit hyperactivity disorder (ADHD). The offered solution will depend on the behavior being identified as a type of mental illness, from mild in form to severe. A visit to an astrologer yields an *explanation*, which attempts to put the child's or adult's behavior into a spiritual context involving his/her life purpose and how to integrate what is a natural phenomenon into the larger context of the world around them. The offered solution depends on seeing the behavior as something the cosmic drama WANTS from this child/adult. Their spiritual quest/responsibility is then to figure out how to integrate an ingrained quality successfully into his/her environment and interactions in the world.

To be fair, astrology fails too. When it does, it is usually because people are seeking, and an astrologer is giving, a fate "full" reading with specific outcomes that cannot be accurately predicted within the dynamic flow of current and future life events. If the spectrum of counseling ranges from friendly advice to psychiatric medication, I would argue that astrology offers a "not illness" approach to understanding one's way through life. If work with an astrologer fails to help, then perhaps the situation does call for the corrective efforts offered by psychology. And, perhaps the best approach in many situations is a combination of the two. Psychology wants and strives to be scientific; astrology wants and strives to be spiritual.

For this reason, and many others, I would not argue that the practice of astrology is scientific, even though it uses astronomical data; and trying to promote it as a science, even a cosmic one, is rather like poking a hornets' nest for no particularly good reason. I do not want one of my fellow astrologers performing a bone marrow transplant or building a deck on my House any more than I want my surgeon or my carpenter giving me life purpose counseling. Astrology is an imaginative, creative, sometimes intuitive, and useful tool for problems of human consciousness, not feats of mechanical engineering or scientific problem-solving. It can be used to help you determine the best time and location to build a home or business, but not to design the architecture and do the calculations for load-bearing walls. And for what is designed to do, it is downright amazing.

At the end of the day and the end of the discussion, all that really matters is whether or not astrology works for you, the individual, on a problem or problems in your life. For me, astrology is a pragmatic, imaginative problem-solving tool that helps me get outside my own thinking by offering a system of meaning grounded in astronomical behaviors that are cyclical, measurable, and outside my personal perception. Since astrology proposes a story "out there" that interacts with my story "in here," I am given the opportunity to reflect on my own narrative and life journey in a creative and powerful way. Ultimately this helps me and my clients understand, and if necessary, reinterpret life events so that we feel more empowered about life's gifts and less overwhelmed by life's struggles.

Let's Get Started

To get started you need several beginner's astrology books. Yes, you did read the sentence correctly – I did say several. Astrology is a complex practice and no single book or series of books will be enough for you to learn how to read a chart, even if you only plan to read your own chart and no one else's. Most people I talk to who express a desire to learn astrology stop dead in their tracks when I tell them how much information they will have to memorize (over 20 Energy Points, 12 Signs, 12 Houses, and at least 6 Aspects). On top of that work, at the beginning of your studies, you need to "touch" astrology by reading books and casting charts at least a few hours a day, every day.

You cannot be casually engaged in this practice and expect to get all the value you may want from the tool and that is available to you. If you decide to share partial insights before getting deep enough into the study, you can actually lead others astray. So, as much as I loved and got great information out of *The Only Way to Learn Astrology* series by Marion D. March and Joan McEvers (ISBN: 1934976016, 1934976024, 1934976032, and 1934976040), those books do not represent the only way to learn (or even enough to learn) astrology. They are a great starting point. My astrology library consists of over 100 books and numerous websites at the time of this writing. I usually add five to 10 books a year.

To drive this point home, I want to refer you to the second chapter of Malcolm Gladwell's book *Outliers* (HC ISBN: 978-0-316-03669-6). The title of the chapter is "The 10,000-Hour Rule." We love to believe, romantically, that innate talent can somehow supersede practice and effort, but the research does not bear out any such result. Gladwell writes about the research of psychologist K. Anders Ericsson and two of his colleagues at Berlin's elite Academy of Music, who studied violinists at the school, looking at the stars who could become world-class professionals, the "merely good" who would have professional performing careers, and those likely to teach music in the public school system without attaining professional performing status.

All the students began playing at roughly the same age (five), but distinct differences began to emerge around eight, and it was not talent; it was the desire of certain students to increase their practice time. The best students became the best because they began to practice more than their peers, working from six hours a week at age nine to 30 hours a week at age

20. "In fact, by the age of twenty, the elite performers had each totaled ten thousand hours of practice. By contrast, the merely good students had totaled eight thousand hours, and the future music teachers had totaled just over four thousand hours" (*Outliers*, p.39). To achieve excellence performing a complex task, which reading an astrology chart is, much in the same vein as playing a musical instrument, requires a critical minimum level of practice that continues to come up in studies about expertise.

Gladwell's essay includes examples debunking the idea of genius without dedicated effort, including a critical look at Mozart (composer) and Bobby Fisher (grandmaster chess player). Their greatest achievements occurred not at the start of their respective careers, but well into them, at least nine years in with dedicated devotion, 30 or more hours a week. From the studies of expertise it has been determined that "ten thousand hours is the magic number of greatness" (*Outliers*, p.41). Basically to become not just competent, or pretty good, but great, you must have talent *and* put in 10,000 hours. If you want to be reading your own chart expertly and share competent insights with friends and family, 4,000 hours would certainly be enough. Gladwell does not mince words about what it takes to get to the highest levels, and concentrated, uninterrupted chunks of time are necessary for building the foundation that allows experts in any field to achieve at the level required to do the work professionally at different levels of pay and recognition.

So, are you ready to dive in, knowing that real proficiency will require years of study, a lot of reading, and a passion for what the practice can reveal about yourself and life around you? If so, the starting points are numerous and excellent and I am going to list several of my favorites below. Keep in mind that this book is meant to extend the main idea of every beginner's book, synthesizing data into a coherent and meaningful concept by giving you an example of EVERY possible combination for 25 Energy Points, starting with the Sun and ending with the Part of Fortune. Also, I have added a chapter for the four angular points, which I cast as individual Energy Points instead of House cusps (another sentence that will make more sense once you have finished the first part of the book).

Beginner's Books

There are plenty of beginner's books available to you, including *Astrology for Dummies* (ISBN: 0470098406) and *The Only Astrology Book You Will Ever Need* (ISBN: 1589796535). Of course, the second book is NOT the only book you will ever need, but it is as good as any to get the basic information to get started. Many good beginners' astrology books are out-of-print and will require finding a used reseller to get a copy; fortunately, the World Wide Web offers numerous resources for out-of-print books and inexpensive used copies of books still in print. I prefer Amazon.com and Alibris.com. If you feel like starting out by "kickin' it old school," you can track down a copy of *The Principles of Astrology* (most recent reprint ISBN: 1933303263) or *A Beginner's Guide to Practical Astrology* (most recent reprint ISBN: 1933303360). The first print for *The Principles of Astrology* was 1925 and the first print for *A Beginner's Guide to Practical Astrology* was 1931. The information is solid, but dated.

I do, however, have my own favorites and will share the ones I think will best compliment this book. At the top of the list is *The Inner Sky* (ISBN: 0979067715) by Steven Forrest, who has written many outstanding astrology books which are all worth reading and adding to your astrology library. *The Inner Sky* is the touchstone or litmus test for all other traditional beginner's books and Forrest is one of those rare writers who can make complex ideas clear without oversimplification. *The Inner Sky* is for intelligent people who want to learn the terms of astrology from another intelligent person who understands how to introduce jargon without requiring you to have years of experience reading academic tomes. Forrest hits the magical sweet spot – complex and accessible – that is really the best way to make an inroad into any new subject.

Other good beginner's books include *Astrology for Beginners* (ISBN: 0738711063) and *Take Control with Astrology: A Teach Yourself Guide* (ISBN: 0071665048). The writers of these two books also have Forrest's deft touch and make the getting-started process enjoyable. They too have created helpful resource books you can revisit even after you have mastered the basic information you need to read a chart in full. Lastly, if you do enjoy academic writing and want to start with more theory, then I can suggest the following three books: *Horoscope Symbols* (ISBN: 0914918168); *Astrology, Psychology, and the Four Elements: An Energy Approach to Astrology and Its Use in the Counseling Arts* (ISBN: 0916360016); and *Astrology and the Authentic Self:*

Integrating Traditional and Modern Astrology to Uncover the Essence of the Birth Chart (ISBN: 0892541490). These last three are rather like jumping in the deep end of the pool to learn to swim instead of walking gradually from the shallow end until your feet no longer touch. A beginner can drown in one of those books and never enjoy swimming in the knowledge and practice of astrology again. It helps to tackle the "deep end" books of astrology if you have experience reading "deep end" books in other subjects or a natural penchant for learning by being "thrown in the deep end" with your study material! There are many, many more beginners' books I did not mention and will be coming out after this book has been written and published. They are referred to as beginner's books for a reason; they only offer you a starting place and the necessary foundational knowledge you absolutely must have to be able to access the more complex and truly useful applications of the practice. That said, let us keep moving along.

How to Read this Book (and Any Beginner's Book)

Beginner's astrology books are not always best digested by reading them from cover-to-cover, especially once you reach the cookbook section which lists the Energy Point in House 1, then 2, then 3 and so on, usually followed by the Energy Point in Sign, starting with Aries and ending with Pisces. If you read straight through, without any context (your chart in hand), you are likely to either get bored by the repetition or disinterested because the descriptions do not apply to you or anyone you know. Once you get past this introduction, most of the book will be pure data that you use to build a chart interpretation. Like other beginner's books, it is organized to walk you through the data in a methodical way, starting, almost always, with the Energy Points (Sun, Moon, Mercury, and so on); then the Signs in their accepted order (Aries, Taurus, Gemini and so on); and then the Houses (1st, 2nd, 3rd, and so on). At this point, I would like to offer you a *reading strategy* that will help you learn the data more effectively and with more enjoyment. Once you have this reading strategy, you can leap into the middle of any beginner's or astrology reference book, perform the specific task of the strategy and then return your linear reading path.

First and foremost, you must have your chart in hand and have learned all the symbols and the data points they reference (or have a cheat sheet handy until you do learn them all; I have provided tables near the end of this first part of the book that you can use). Take any and all of your beginner's books and flip to the cookbook sections and find your specific Energy Points in Sign and Energy Points in House. Write your name or initials next to the examples that apply to your chart. In my case, I have my name in all my books next to Sun in Aries and Sun in the 6th House. Once I finished with my chart, I started using my girlfriend's chart, then my close friends', and then my parents'. By working with the charts of people you know, you will have a deeply vested interest to learn the data and a desire to understand how all the pieces fit together.

I know it is common practice to use celebrity charts, but I never found a single celebrity chart as interesting as a person I know in real life. Working with charts from people you spend quality time with, have a deep personal connection to, or who have had a strong impact on your life is the best way to learn the definitions and interpretations that make up a chart reading. You can use this technique for any astrology book you buy, including more advanced ones (like those dealing with Aspects and other advanced information). As you annotate more books with the charts of people you know, you will probably discover, as I did, certain patterns in the people in your life, especially the ones you choose, like your friendships and the people you end up dating. Among my significant romantic relationships, I have consistently dated women with Suns in Aquarius, Cancer, Sagittarius, and Scorpio and Moons in Aries, Sagittarius, Libra, and Scorpio; and I have never dated ones with a Sun in Taurus, Gemini, Virgo, and Libra – or a Moon in Pisces, Libra, Aquarius, or Cancer. One of my best relationships was with a woman who has a Gemini Moon, which by Sign and degree, forms a mutually-supportive Aspect (Trine) with my Libra Moon. My lovers, my friends, and my family members all have their initials in my beginning and advanced astrology books.

The Jargon of Astrology

Every field of knowledge has its own jargon: terms making up the language of that subject that practitioners use to communicate information, explain ideas, and distinguish one field of knowledge from another. Astrology has a good number of terms you will need to learn to make sense of the birth chart, the relationship of one piece of information to another piece of information, and the code of interpretation. You will see the terms below used throughout the rest of the book. Each term represents various data with specific meaning that, when combined in certain ways, yields knowledge you can learn about yourself or share with another, if you are reading someone else's chart. Since this book focuses on foundation knowledge, only select terms will be defined and explained. For an extensive list of astrology terms, I recommend getting and adding *Astrology*, edited by Kim Farnell (ISBN: 1568525044) to your library.

The very phrase, "reading the birth chart," reveals that the symbol configuration of the chart is shorthand for the narrative of a person's spirit or soul. The narrative is open, not closed; free will and fate interplay in the astrological world view. The birth chart is a dynamic representation of qualities ingrained and available for use in our life journey. We can embrace or resist our qualities but, spiritually speaking, they are as determined as our biological features, only far more flexible and variable in their uses and lessons. In the tables that follow in the second half of this book, you will find the symbols associated with each Energy Point and each Sign.

Definitions and Examples

Element – One of four types (Fire, Earth, Air, and Water) used to represent the Quality of human behavior (Creating, Acting, Thinking, and Feeling). Energy Points, Signs, and Houses all have a ruling Element. For example: Mars is a Fire Energy Point, Gemini is an Air Sign, and the 2nd House is an Earth House.

Rulership – Each Energy Point Rules a Sign and House, and each Sign and House is Ruled by one or two Energy Points[13], indicating in which Sign and House the Energy Point is strongest. Each House is Ruled by a Sign. In classical astrology, before the

---

[13] The Sun Rules Leo and the 5th House and the Moon, Cancer and the 4th House. They do not share Sign or House Rulership with any other Energy Point. All other Houses have co-Rulers (masculine and feminine).

discovery of the outer planets and the asteroids, several Energy Points did double duty: Mars Ruled Aries and Scorpio; Venus Ruled Taurus and Libra; Mercury Ruled Gemini and Virgo; Jupiter Ruled Sagittarius and Pisces; and Saturn Ruled Capricorn and Aquarius. Rulership is a reminder that astrology is not a stagnant practice and the arrival of new Energy Points can herald a change in Rulership.

Energy Point – An astronomical body in our solar system (Sun, Moon, Mercury, and so on); a calculated point based on the movement of an astronomical body (Nodes of the Moon, Black Moon Lilith, and so on); or a point-in-space relationship between astronomical bodies (Part of Fortune). Energy Points represent Aspects of spiritual direction (Primary Drive, Soul Path, and so on) and personality (Way of Communicating, Way of Relating, and so on). They work in two ways, either attracting necessary energy/situations to you, and/or causing you to initiate the energy from within to do necessary work.

Direct/Stationary/Retrograde – Terms used to describe the movement of an Energy Point in relation to the Earth. Direct refers to the more common forward motion of the Energy Points; Stationary describes the transition from Direct to Retrograde and Retrograde to Direct (when the Energy Point "stands still" before going in its new direction); and Retrograde refers to the *apparent* backward motion of the Energy Points. Astrology is Earth-centric rather than Helio(Sun)centric. Since astrologers look at the sky "from the Earth" instead of the Sun, Energy Points can appear to move backwards in the sky during certain times of year. Energy Points that are Stationary or Retrograde have modified meanings to reflect the change in status of their movement. A Stationary position at the time of birth concentrates the Energy, and Retrograde positions turn the Energy inward. In simple terms, a person with Venus Direct (most people) seeks to relate by searching out in the world. A person with Venus Retrograde (a good number of people) seeks to relate by waiting for the world to approach. And a person with Venus Stationary (the rarest), can relate in both ways as circumstances and desires dictate.

Astrology Unlocked by Philip Young, PhD

Sign – One of twelve energetic signifiers (Aries, Taurus, Gemini, and so on) based on constellations that ring our solar system and apply generally between the dates of the 21st and 21st of each month (with Aries starting March 21 to April 21). Signs represent human behavior. All Energy Points reside in one of the twelve Signs at any given time. All Signs have an Elemental type (Fire, Earth, Air, or Water) and Quality (Cardinal, Fixed, or Mutable). Example: Gemini is a Mutable Air Sign.

> **Quality** (as applied to a Sign and its Element) – One of three types (Cardinal, Fixed, and Mutable) used to describe human action and reaction (Initiation, Organization, and Adaptability). Aries is a Cardinal Fire Sign; it initiates action. Leo is a Fixed Fire Sign; it organizes action. Sagittarius is a Mutable Fire Sign; it adapts action.

House – One of twelve sections (1st House, 2nd House, 3rd House, and so on) calculated with the first section delineated at the point where the Sun crossed or would cross the horizon at a certain time of day on the day of a person's birth; they represent areas of human experience (identity, values, learning, and so on). Because this method of calculation is used to determine which Sign Rules the first House of a person's chart, Signs ruling Houses vary from chart to chart (one person may have the Sun cross the horizon in Leo while another might have it cross Scorpio). Also there are numerous House "systems" that perform the calculation in such a way that the size of the House varies (Placidus, Koch, and so on) while others keep House sizes equal (Equal and Whole). As I wrote earlier, I use the Whole House system as written about by Demetra George in her book *Astrology and the Authentic Self*.

> **Quality** (as applied to a House and its Element) – One of three types (Angular, Succedent, and Cadent) used to describe the approach in a given area of the chart (Initiation, Organization, and Adaptability). The 4th House is Angular; it is where a person initiates his/her roots. The 2nd House is Succedent; it is where a person organizes his/her values. The 9th House is Cadent; it is where a person adapts his/her expertise.

Cusp – The lines where the House begins and ends.

House System – The order of the Houses based on the point where the Sun crossed or would have crossed the horizon (if you were born before dawn). Several different systems exist; the most commonly used is Placidus.

What You Have to Memorize

There are core data points you must memorize to get from a chart to an interpretation. There is no shortcut for this foundation knowledge. You must know all the Energy Points and their symbols you intend to use to cast a chart, the Signs and their symbols, and the Houses. You must know certain common terms (like Rulership and Retrograde). You must know the Qualities and Elements for Signs and Houses. Like any truly professional interpretive counseling skill, you must master, and know cold, the basic terminology that informs the complex practice. Then you must perform, rigorously and repetitively, the practice until you can make it look simple to the uninitiated (your clients, friends, or family). Following this section, there are tables of all the basic data points arranged in different ways to help with the learning and memorization process.

In the particular combination of my chart I am able to uncover and see narratives about my career, family, love life, identity, values, community, spirituality, and so on. Like real life I have to navigate what I want, what I can achieve, what I need, what I cannot have, what I can have for a limited amount of time in a certain way, what comes easy, what is hard, and what I must learn to grow. The narrative of my chart, when held up against my lived life, becomes a tool to help me cope, adjust to, progress, accept, excel at, and appreciate all my experiences.

Astrology Unlocked by Philip Young, PhD

Energy Points

Energy Points can be arranged in a number of different ways and I am going to present them in three different tables, one based on the order of use from classical to modern astrology, another based on the concepts of Rulership, and the last one grouping feminine and masculine separately.

Classical to Modern

Energy Point	Symbol	Key Words	Meaning	Element	Rules Sign	Rules House
Classical Seven						
Sun	☉	Primary Drive	Energy of Life	Fire	Leo	5th
Moon	☽	Soul Path	Emotions in Life	Water	Cancer	4th
Mercury	☿	Way of Communicating	Intellect in Life	Air	Gemini	3rd
Venus[14]	♀	Way of Relating	Connection to Others in Life	Water	Pisces	12th
Mars	♂	Way of Wanting	Desire in Life	Fire	Aries	1st
Jupiter	♃	Way of Expanding	Exploration in Life	Fire	Sagittarius	9th
Saturn	♄	Way of Accomplishing	Structure and Limitations in Life	Earth	Capricorn	10th
Additional Three Added to Solar System as Primary Bodies						
Uranus	♅	Way of Awakening	Epiphanies in Life	Air	Aquarius	11th

---

[14] Venus has been traditionally placed as the Ruler for Taurus and Libra, and I fully expect to get plenty of push back for reassigning Venus to Pisces. My reasons are not arbitrary. I have long felt and observed in readings that Mercury (Communication) and Venus (Love) can both easily Rule any Sign and House, so why not leave Venus as a single Ruler for one its traditional Signs and Houses? Two reasons: first, the origin/birth of Aphrodite/Venus occurs in the ocean from the sea foam that was the blood and semen of Ouranos/Uranus, who was castrated by his Titan son Kronos/Cronos and second, Venus, as a personal planet, is the conduit for universal love manifest in the physical world. Pisces as the Ruler of the 12th House of Spirituality has and needs both an expression of idealistic (Neptune) and realistic (Venus) love. Neptune in the chart shows the spiritual consciousness of a generation while Venus shows the individual's spiritual consciousness through the particulars of relating to others in life.

Astrology Unlocked by Philip Young, PhD

Neptune	♆	Way of Surrendering and Dreaming	Mystery in Life	Water	Pisces	12th
Pluto	♇	Way of Transforming	Death and Rebirth in Life	Water	Scorpio	8th

Asteroids and Calculated Point based on The Asteroid Ephemeris by Rique Pottenger (2008)						
Chiron	⚷	Way of Wounding and Healing	Struggle of Life	Earth	Virgo	6th
Ceres	⚳	Way of Gathering	Necessities of Life	Earth	Capricorn	10th
Pallas	⚴	Way of Problem Solving	Strategy in Life	Air	Libra	7th
Juno	⚵	Way of Sacrificing (Duty)	Responsibilities to Others in Life	Fire	Sagittarius	9th
Vesta	⚶	Way of Hearth and Home	Place of Sanctuary in Life	Earth	Taurus	2nd
Lilith	⚸	Way of Unyielding	Fortitude in Life	Fire	Aries	1st

Newly Applied Asteroids and Calculated Points to Balance Masculine/Feminine Rulership of Houses						
Astraea	⚺	Way of Community	Connections in Life	Air	Aquarius	11th
Hygeia	⚕	Way of Health	The Body in Life	Earth	Virgo	6th
Urania	U	Way of Understanding	Thirst for Knowledge in Life	Air	Gemini	3rd
Zeus	⚡	Way of Judgment	Decisions and Authority in Life	Air	Libra	7th
Eris	⚷	Way of Disrupting	Drama of Life	Water	Scorpio	8th
Vulcan	↓	Way of Producing	Work in Life	Earth	Taurus	2nd

Calculated Points from Classical Astrology						
Part of Fortune	⊗	Way of Good Luck	Unexpected Gifts in Life	Any	None	None

North Node	☊	Way of Soul Growth	Purpose in Life (Dharma)	Any	None	None
South Node	☋	Way of the Worn Path	Lesson in Life (Karma)	Any	None	None
Ascendant	A^SC	Way of Presenting	What You Offer Others in Life	Fire	None[15]	None
Descendant	D^SC	Way of Partnering	What You Need from Others in Life	Air	None	None
Midheaven	M^C	The Way Outward	The Public Life	Earth	None	None
Imum Coeli (Nadir)	I^C	The Way Inward	The Private Life	Water	None	None

---

[15] The Angular Points are fixed to the 1st, 7th, 3rd/4th/5th/, and 9th/10th/11th Houses and do not represent Rulers of the Houses even though they are defined by Elements.

Astrology Unlocked by Philip Young, PhD

Rulerships

Rulership is a term applied to the Energy Point that "Rules" a certain Sign and a certain House. The Energy Point is most powerful if it is in the Sign or House it Rules. Keep in mind that powerful expression does not equate to good expression, but such placement does require you to focus on the Energy Point in the chart. Below is the table for Rulerships.

Energy Point	Symbol	Key Words	Meaning	Element	Rules Sign	Rules House
Lilith	⚸	Way of Unyielding	Fortitude in Life	Fire	Aries	1st
Mars	♂	Way of Wanting	Desire in Life	Fire	Aries	1st
Vesta	⚶	Way of Hearth and Home	Place of Sanctuary in Life	Earth	Taurus	2nd
Vulcan	↓	Way of Producing	Work in Life	Earth	Taurus	2nd
Urania	U	Way of Understanding	Thirst for Knowledge in Life	Air	Gemini	3rd
Mercury	☿	Way of Communicating	Intellect in Life	Air	Gemini	3rd
Moon	☽	Soul Path	Emotions in Life	Water	Cancer	4th
Sun	☉	Primary Drive	Energy of Life	Fire	Leo	5th
Hygeia	⚕	Way of Health	The Body in Life	Earth	Virgo	6th
Chiron	⚷	Way of Wounding and Healing	Struggle of Life	Earth	Virgo	6th
Pallas	⚴	Way of Problem Solving	Strategy in Life	Air	Libra	7th
Zeus	⚡	Way of Judgment	Decisions and Promises in Life	Air	Libra	7th
Eris	⯰	Way of Disrupting	Drama of Life	Water	Scorpio	8th
Pluto	⯓	Way of Transforming	Death and Rebirth in Life	Water	Scorpio	8th
Jupiter	♃	Way of Expanding	Exploration in Life	Fire	Sagittarius	9th

Astrology Unlocked by Philip Young, PhD

Juno	⚹	Way of Sacrificing (Duty)	Responsibilities to Others in Life	Fire	Sagittarius	9th
Saturn	♄	Way of Accomplishing	Structure and Limitations in Life	Earth	Capricorn	10th
Ceres	⚳	Way of Gathering	Necessities of Life	Earth	Capricorn	10th
Astraea	⚕	Way of Community	Connections in Life	Air	Aquarius	11th
Uranus	⛢	Way of Awakening	Epiphanies in Life	Air	Aquarius	11th
Venus[16]	♀	Way of Relating	Connection to Others in Life	Water	Pisces	12th
Neptune	♆	Way of Surrendering and Dreaming	Mystery in Life	Water	Pisces	12th
Part of Fortune	⊗	Way of Good Luck	Unexpected Gifts in Life	Any	None	None
North Node	☊	Way of Soul Growth	Purpose in Life (Dharma)	Any	None	None
South Node	☋	Way of the Worn Path	Lesson in Life (Karma)	Any	None	None
Ascendant	ASC	Way of Presenting	What You Offer Others in Life	Fire	Aries	1st
Descendant	DSC	Way of Partnering	What You Need from Others in Life	Air	Libra	7th
Midheaven	MC	The Way Outward	The Public Life	Earth	Capricorn	10th
Imum Coeli (Nadir)	IC	The Way Inward	The Private Life	Water	Cancer	4th

Rulerships of Signs and Houses have been evolving with each new astronomical discovery and study of the behavior of the Energy Point. Uranus was the first addition, taking Rulership of Aquarius and the 11th House from Saturn. It does take time for an Energy Point to become accepted as a Ruler by the larger astrological community. But somewhere in the process, practicing astrologers started using new Energy Points as new Rulers. For quite some time the

---

[16] Refer to footnote 3.

Astrology Unlocked by Philip Young, PhD

masculine/feminine energy has been woefully out of balance, favoring masculine energy five (Sun, Mercury, Mars, Jupiter, and Saturn) to two (Moon and Venus). The imbalance increased with the addition of three more masculine bodies (Uranus, Neptune, and Pluto). And then Chiron became another strong influence, adding yet another masculine energy to the casting of charts. Finally, with the work of Demetra George in *Asteroid Goddesses: The Mythology, Psychology, and Astrology of the Re-Emerging Feminine* (ISBN: 0892540826) and *Mysteries of the Dark Moon: The Healing Power of the Dark Goddess* (ISBN: 0062503707) five new feminine energies arrived: Ceres, Vesta, Pallas Athena, Juno, and Lilith. I have decided to push the envelope by adding the additional bodies necessary to give all Houses co-Rulers, one masculine and one feminine, except for the 4th and 5th, which are Ruled by the Moon and Sun respectively and are the gender match for each other. In my chart castings I have 22 Rulers and seven additional calculated points for a total of 29 points.

Feminine and Masculine Energy Points

Energy Point	Symbol	Key Words	Meaning	Element	Rules Sign	Rules House
Feminine Energy Points						
Lilith	☽	Way of Unyielding	Fortitude in Life	Fire	Aries	1st
Vesta	⚶	Way of Hearth and Home	Place of Sanctuary in Life	Earth	Taurus	2nd
Urania	U	Way of Understanding	Thirst for Knowledge in Life	Air	Gemini	3rd
Moon	☽	Soul Path	Emotions in Life	Water	Cancer	4th
Hygeia	⚕	Way of Health	The Body in Life	Earth	Virgo	6th
Pallas	⚴	Way of Problem Solving	Strategy in Life	Air	Libra	7th
Eris	⚴	Way of Disrupting	Drama of Life	Water	Scorpio	8th
Juno	⚵	Way of Sacrificing (Duty)	Responsibilities to Others in Life	Fire	Sagittarius	9th
Ceres	⚳	Way of Gathering	Necessities of Life	Earth	Capricorn	10th
Astraea	⚷	Way of Community	Connections in Life	Air	Aquarius	11th
Venus[17]	♀	Way of Relating	Connection to Others in Life	Water	Pisces	12th
Masculine Energy Points						
Mars	♂	Way of Wanting	Desire in Life	Fire	Aries	1st
Vulcan	↓	Way of Producing	Work in Life	Earth	Taurus	2nd
Mercury	☿	Way of Communicating	Intellect in Life	Air	Gemini	3rd

---

[17] Refer to footnote 3.

Sun	☉	Primary Drive	Energy of Life	Fire	Leo	5th
Chiron	⚷	Way of Wounding and Healing	Struggle of Life	Earth	Virgo	6th
Zeus	⚡	Way of Judgment	Decisions and Promises in Life	Air	Libra	7th
Pluto	♇	Way of Transforming	Death and Rebirth in Life	Water	Scorpio	8th
Jupiter	♃	Way of Expanding	Exploration in Life	Fire	Sagittarius	9th
Saturn	♄	Way of Accomplishing	Structure and Limitations in Life	Earth	Capricorn	10th
Uranus	♅	Way of Awakening	Epiphanies in Life	Air	Aquarius	11th
Neptune	♆	Way of Surrendering and Dreaming	Mystery in Life	Water	Pisces	12th
Neutral Energy Points						
Part of Fortune	⊗	Way of Good Luck	Unexpected Gifts in Life	Any	None	None
North Node	☊	Way of Soul Growth	Purpose in Life (Dharma)	Any	None	None
South Node	☋	Way of the Worn Path	Lesson in Life (Karma)	Any	None	None
Ascendant	ASC	Way of Presenting	What You Offer Others in Life	Fire	Aries	1st
Descendant	DSC	Way of Partnering	What You Need from Others in Life	Air	Libra	7th
Midheaven	MC	The Way Outward	The Public Life	Earth	Capricorn	10th
Imum Coeli (Nadir)	IC	The Way Inward	The Private Life	Water	Cancer	4th

Astrology Unlocked by Philip Young, PhD

Signs

The Signs set the energetic and Elemental parameters for the Energy Points and Houses. An Energy Point in a certain Sign expresses its own energy within the "container" energy of the Sign.

Sign	Symbol	Quality	Element	Ruler(s)	Attributes	Rules
Aries	♈	Cardinal	Fire	Mars, Lilith	Independent, Heroic, Maverick, Pioneering	1st House
Taurus	♉	Fixed	Earth	Vulcan, Vesta	Secure, Steadfast, Persistent, Reliable	2nd House
Gemini	♊	Mutable	Air	Mercury, Urania	Inquisitive, Social, Communicative, Mentally Agile	3rd House
Cancer	♋	Cardinal	Water	Moon	Nurturing, Empathetic, Protective, Emotional	4th House
Leo	♌	Fixed	Fire	Sun	Creative, Romantic, Dramatic, Expressive	5th House
Virgo	♍	Mutable	Earth	Chiron, Hygeia	Practical, Meticulous, Methodical, Deductive	6th House
Libra	♎	Cardinal	Air	Zeus, Pallas	Decisive, Analytical, Neutral, Balanced	7th House
Scorpio	♏	Fixed	Water	Pluto, Eris	Transformative, Intense, Disruptive, Penetrating	8th House
Sagittarius	♐	Mutable	Fire	Jupiter, Juno	Authoritative, Worldly, Exploratory, Expansive	9th House
Capricorn	♑	Cardinal	Earth	Saturn, Ceres	Disciplined, Accomplished, Goal-Oriented, Responsible	10th House
Aquarius	♒	Fixed	Air	Uranus, Astraea	Unconventional, Original, Authentic, Idealistic	11th House
Pisces	♓	Mutable	Water	Neptune, Venus	Imaginative, Spiritual, Loving, Emotionally Aware	12th House

An Energy Point with a natural Elemental expression of Fire (Mars, Lilith, Sun, Jupiter, and Juno) in a Fire Sign (Aries, Leo, and Sagittarius) is "at home" in the Sign because the Elemental alignment is merged. An Energy Point with a natural Elemental expression of Air (Mercury, Urania, Pallas, Zeus, Astraea, and Uranus) in a Fire Sign is "comfortable visiting" in the Sign because the Elemental alignment is complimentary. An Energy Point with a natural Elemental

45

expression of Earth or Water (Vesta, Vulcan, Chiron, Hygeia, Ceres, and Saturn – or the Moon, Pluto, Eris, Venus, and Neptune) in a Fire Sign is "working to enjoy its stay" in the Sign because the Elemental alignment is compromising.   Like Energy Points, the Houses have default Elemental expressions.   Sometimes the Signs and Houses align mutually (if Leo, a Fire Sign, applies to the 1st House, which is a Fire House, then all other Signs and Houses mutually align). The Signs and Houses can align in a complimentary way when an Air Sign is applying to the 1st House.   The Signs and Houses compromise when either a Water Sign or Earth Sign applies to the 1st House.

Astrology Unlocked by Philip Young, PhD

Houses

Houses represent areas of Focus in the human experience, starting with identity and ending with spirituality. When an Energy Point occupies a House, it "lives" there for the duration of the person's life, manifesting and evolving most and strongest in that area of human development. The Houses also have natural Elemental resonance that influence and are influenced by the relationships with the Energy Points occupying the House and the Sign applying to the House.

House	Quality	Element	Focus on	Ruling Sign	Ruling Energy Point(s)
1st	Angular	Fire	Identity	Aries	Mars/Lilith
2nd	Succedent	Earth	Resources and Values	Taurus	Vulcan/Vesta
3rd	Cadent	Air	Communication	Gemini	Mercury/Urania
4th	Angular	Water	Roots and Family	Cancer	Moon
5th	Succedent	Fire	Creative Self-Expression	Leo	Sun
6th	Cadent	Earth	Service and Skills	Virgo	Chiron/Hygiea
7th	Angular	Air	Partnerships and Guides	Libra	Zeus/Pallas
8th	Succedent	Water	Transformation	Scorpio	Pluto/Eris
9th	Cadent	Fire	Mastership	Sagittarius	Jupiter/Juno
10th	Angular	Earth	Ambition and Accomplishments	Capricorn	Saturn/Ceres
11th	Succedent	Air	Community	Aquarius	Uranus/Astraea
12th	Cadent	Water	Spirituality	Pisces	Neptune/Venus

Formulas of Meaning

The interpretation of the Energy Point in Sign and House is an integration of layers of Meaning, starting with the simplest formulas for individual data points.

Simplest formulas:

Formula	Example
Energy Point (EP) = Meaning (M)	The Sun represents the Primary Drive.
Sign (S) = Meaning (M)	Aries is independent and heroic.
House (H) = Meaning (M)	The 6th House is your House of Service and Skills.
Element (E) = Meaning (M)	Fire is energetic and creative.
Quality of Element (QE) = Meaning (M)	Cardinal Signs takes charge.
Quality of House (QH) = Meaning (M)	Succedent Houses organize.
Aspect (A) between two Energy Points (EP) = Meaning (M)	A Conjunction merges energy.

Basic Formulas

$S = QE$	Aries is a Cardinal Fire Sign.
$H = QH$	The 6th House is a Cadent Earth House.

Advanced formulas:

$EP + S = M/I$[18]	(Sun) in [Aries] means, "(The Primary Drive) is [Independence]" *because* the Sun is in the Cardinal Fire Sign (of Aries).
$EP + H = M/I$	(Sun) in {6th} House means, "(The Primary Drive) focuses on the {Quest for Service and Skills}" *because* the Sun is the Cadent Earth House.

---

[18] I = Interpretation

Interpretation formulas:

EP + S + H = M/I	(Sun) in [Aries] in the {6th House} means, "(Your Primary Drive) manifests through your [independent and heroic] {quest for and attraction to} [maverick and individualistic] {skills for your day-to-day work}."

Since the Sign influences the Energy Point **and** the House, descriptors apply to the Primary Drive **and** the way the individual pursues the expression in an Area of Life. So the abbreviated formula would be:

$$(EP + S) + (H + S) = \text{Interpretation (I)}.$$

Also, it is important to understand the Elemental and Quality matrix of the Energy Point in Sign and House, so, "The Sun, a Fire Energy Point, is in a Cardinal Fire Sign in a Cadent Earth House (Fire/Fire/Earth)."

Just to give you a preview of the next two levels of Interpretation. Here is the formula for two Aspected Energy Points.

$(EP_1 + S_1 + H_1) + A_1 + (EP_2 + S_2 + H_2) = M/I$	Sun (EP_1) in Aries (S_1) in the 6th House (H_1) Opposes (A_1) Moon (EP_2) in Libra (S_2) in the 12th House (H_2) means, "Your Primary Drive (EP_1) manifests through your independent and heroic (S_1) quest for and attraction to maverick and individualistic (S_1) skills for your day-to-day work (H_1) seeks balance with (A_1) Your Soul Path (EP_2), which manifests through your analytical and balanced (S_2) quest for and attraction to harmonious and logical (S_2) spirituality (H_2).

So the abbreviated formula would be:

$$[(EP_1 + S_1) + (H_1 + S_1)] + A_1 + [(EP_2 + S_2) + (H_2 + S_2)] = I.$$

49

When Energy Points form a patterned circuit (three or more Energy Points forming a geometric shape), they create a formula that looks like this (for a Grand Trine):

$$\{[(EP_1 + S_1) + (H_1 + S_1)] + A_1 + [(EP_2 + S_2) + (H_2 + S_2)] + A_2 + [(EP_3 + S_3) + (H_3 + S_3)]$$
$$+ A_3 + [(EP_1 + S_1) + (H_1 + S_1)\} = 1$$

where Energy Point 1 Trines Energy Point 2 which Trines Energy Point 3 which Trines (back to) Energy Point 1.

Astrology Unlocked by Philip Young, PhD

Nuancing, the Real Goal of Interpretation

While it is a necessity to learn all the meanings of all the Energy Points you choose to use in a chart – as well as all the Signs, Houses, and Aspects – the mechanical knowledge of the data will not be enough to invoke the true power within the chart. To access the full richness of your chart and anyone else's chart, you will have to put enough time and study into charts to begin to see the nuances in the wholeness of a chart. For beginners (and I was one once too!) the first look at a full chart requires focusing on discrete data and building an understanding through repetition. After many years of practice, research, and chart readings, I now see a chart in its totality and work backwards to break out the significant themes that I want share with a client when I do a reading and look for answers to their session questions. The deeper you go into your studies the more nuances you will find, and find useful, when researching your own chart or those of other people.

Nuancing is the practice of identifying and appreciating subtle but important degrees of difference in the multiplicity of information in the chart. "Chiron in Aries" with no chart context is like a solid block of wood. In someone's chart Chiron is a detailed sculpture. As you learn more ideas in astrology and apply them to an actual Energy Point in a person's chart you begin to "get to" the sculpture in the block of wood. With each piece of new information you "nuance" the data point until it is fully realized. And so, Chiron in Aries in the 6th House is more nuanced than plain old Chiron in Aries. Chiron with the Sun sitting side-by-side Chiron in a chart gives more nuance, and so on. I want to "nuance" this point as much as possible for you, so you can see the impact additional astrological meanings have on the understanding of the Energy Point in an actual chart. I am going to use the Chiron in the chart at the beginning of the book.

Chiron was in Aries from 1968 to 1976, so bluntly, without nuancing, this generation of people experience their wounding and healing when they assert their independence or fail to do so. The generation before this group (1960 to 1968) had Chiron in Pisces and experience their wound and healing when they connect to/deny their role in higher consciousness and the pursuit of their dreams. So by adding the first layer of additional information, that Chiron in my chart is in my 6th House, I am able to realize that my wound/healing will occur most often and intensely in my quest for skills and the type of work I will do in service to others.

51

Here is where the tip of the iceberg above the water ends and the rest of the knowledge expands below the water line. My Chiron is a 0°40' and is direct (not retrograde); I was born with "a new Chiron in Aries." In a sense, I am on the front line of Chiron in Aries and will feel some of the Chiron in Pisces energy due to my proximity to that Sign. As a result, I can expect to be wounded by being a dreamer (Pisces) who struggles to assert himself (Aries), as different from a person with Chiron in Aries in a later degree, who is more likely to be wounded and have to heal from over-asserting himself or herself. Were Chiron retrograde, I would carry my wounding/healing burden/responsibility internally and be more likely to wait until much later in life to do the healing work. The direct energy is more readily manifest and active.

Moving forward with even more nuance, the Signs are made up of 30 degrees, which have been broken down into 10° zones called decans, ranging from 0° to 9° (1st decan), 10° to 19° (2nd decan), and 20° to 29° (3rd decan). Each zone has an energetic Ruler from among the Signs that Rule that Element. Thus, my Chiron is not just in Aries, but also in the Aries zone of Aries. I have an Aries/Aries 1st zone Chiron, which makes my wounding actions and healing attempts quite impulsive. Were my Chiron at 12° it would be an Aries/Leo Chiron and at 25° an Aries/Sagittarius Chiron. Even the very degree adds nuance thanks to the work of Dr. Marc Edmund Jones, who with the aid of psychic/medium/clairvoyant Elsie Wheeler, assigned a specific meaning to all 360 degrees. The 0° to 1° meaning for a point on Aries is "a woman rises out of water, a seal rises and embraces her" and the keyword is "realization."[19] Also, there are two essential expressions for an Energy Point: healthy/positive and unhealthy/negative. The negative expression even has a special term … the shadow. I can improve my healing process if I address my wounds openly, with "realization," or I can "fester" my wounds by obsessing over my failures.[20] When I follow the negative path of an Energy Point's spiritual lesson, I end up living in its "shadow."

We still have plenty of "Chiron iceberg" to go. My Chiron has seven Aspects with other Energy Points in my chart. The Aspects I choose to use are the Conjunction, Square,

---

[19] *The Sabian Symbols in Astrology* (ISBN: 094335840X), page 150.
[20] Ibid.

Opposition, Trine, Sextile, and Quincunx[21]. I can always add more nuance by seeing if my Chiron Aspects other Energy Points through some of the less common, but still viable Aspects like the Quintile, Semi-Square, Decile, and so on. At that point you are looking at the details of the sculpture with a magnifying glass. Each Aspect brings its own set of nuances. I am going to write about just one just to show the effect. Keep in mind that the Energy Point in Aspect with Chiron has to be understood in all the same ways I just wrote about Chiron, then related to Chiron so its impact can be fully understood.

Determining the power of an Aspect is not as simple as proximity or type of Aspect. The proximity of one Energy Point to another in Aspect is determined by the orb of influence, within six degrees higher or lower of exact alignment. My Chiron is 0°40' in Aries and my Venus is at 5°10' of Aries, forming a Conjunction and merging the two energies. They are "within orb" by 4°30', but not particularly close, thus reducing the intensity of the impact measurably. Now my Chiron at 0°40' in Aries and my Ceres at 0°50' of Scorpio are Aspected as Quincunx and are within 0°10' orb of each other, which is an almost exact angular relationship. In terms of Aspect power, the Conjunction is the most intense since energies merge; the Quincunx is often used as a second-tier Aspect (the top-tier Aspects include the Conjunction, Square, Trine, and Opposition). So in the case of these two Aspected Energy Points to Chiron the Venus Conjunction, weaker in terms of orb of influence is still stronger overall because Venus, as a personal planet, is stronger than Ceres and the Conjunction is much stronger than the Quincunx.

Now let us look at all the influences associated with the Chiron/Venus Conjunction by nuancing Venus. Venus in Aries in the 6th House indicates a preference for independence in relationships, both for myself and among the people I know. More specifically, with its placement in the 6th House, I prefer to work with/for people who allow me to be autonomous and who, they themselves, take care of their own work responsibilities. I have no real desire to manage people or be managed myself (unless it is very hands-off, results-oriented management). At 5° Venus is in the 1st Decan, and thus an Aries/Aries Venus, meaning I can be impulsive and maverick with the people I choose to relate to. The Sabian phrase is "a square brightly lighted

---

[21] The Conjunction Aspect occurs when Energy Points are within 0 to 6 degrees of one another, Square when 84 to 90 degrees of one another, Trine when 114 to 126, Opposing when 174 to 186, Sextile when 54 to 66, and Quincunx when 144 to 156.

on one side" and the Sabian keyword is "set."[22] When positive, the energy of my Venus helps me be absolutely clear with people in relationships with me. If I am in the shadow of this Venus placement I can surrender to frustration with my relationships, especially in my day-to-day work.[23] Since these energies merge, they pull each other in a positive or negative direction together. I can either get help healing my wound through positive, maverick, and heroic relationships or suffer greater wounding when my relationships are restrictive and limiting to my freedom. I must also be wary of asserting my independence in impulsive and selfish ways, causing me to suffer long-term detriment for short-term gain. As you can read, my Chiron gets more nuanced, more personal, and more unique the more I apply to its meaning with additional and related information. We are, believe it or not, nowhere near the bottom of the "Chiron iceberg," but we have reached a deep enough depth to get a true sense of what we are dealing with.

I offer these examples so you understand that the information in this book needs additional knowledge and techniques to unlock the full potential of the chart. The purpose of this book remains foundational, with a lot of repetition used to solidify the core data you must store in your mind and at the ready to broach the more advanced techniques used to do the profound work possible with astrology. For this reason I have created a worksheet to help you study and practice the astrology written about in this book so far, which can be found at the very end. The worksheet will only offer you a skeletal picture of your spiritual identity, soulful goals, personality traits, and energy expressions and should not be taken as a comprehensive and integrated interpretation of your chart.

---

[22] The Sabian Symbols in Astrology by Dr. Marc Edmond Jones, page 154.
[23] Ibid.

Practice, Practice, Practice!

Now, let's start practicing. You will need a copy of the worksheet, the table for the Energy Points, and the table for the Signs. Use the Energy Point table to locate and match the symbols in the Houses of the chart below to start filling in your worksheet. The first chart I am going to show you, on the next page, has just the classical seven Energy Points and the Angular House points (11 points in all). "Read" the first chart below and enter all the requested data into the worksheet. Then go to Part Two and look up the interpretation for the Energy Point, starting with the Sun in the chart Sign/House placement. Write that interpretation into your worksheet.

The second chart below adds the three bodies discovered in our solar system in 1781 (Uranus), 1846 (Neptune), and 1930 (Pluto), as well as the Nodes of the Moon and the Part of Fortune. The third chart adds the asteroids that have received enough attention from astrologers to have books written about them (Chiron, Pallas, Vesta, Juno, and Ceres), as well as the Black Moon Lilith (also with substantial written material). The final chart includes all the Energy Points I use in my chart readings, which will hopefully lead to new learning for you: this chart provides valuable and essential new interpretations in a chart. These additional points address the lack of feminine energy and add important energetic details to the chart reading.

If you have made it this far, then you are ready to make the attempt to see the shape of the soul or personality in the chart. Once you have filled out your worksheet, read through all the information and see if you get a sense of the individual in the chart or if you notice any dominant themes (locations in the chart where a number of Energy Points share the same House and Sign). Keep in mind the Rulerships and dominant energy of the Signs and Houses. You may discover a "theme of communication" if several Energy Points are in the 3rd House and in Gemini or a "theme of nurturing and caretaking" if several Energy Points are in the 4th House and Cancer. Remember, the Signs and Houses usually do not align, so Gemini might be applying to the 2nd House in one chart and the 8th House in another. Cancer could be on the 1st House or the 11th. Hint: in the chart below, watch for the "theme of transformation" (Pluto/Eris, Scorpio, 8th) and communication/learning (Urania/Mercury, Gemini, 3rd).

Jane Doe
Natal Chart
Nov 3 1974, Sun
10:15 am JST -9:00
Okinawa, Japan
26°N20' 127°E50'
Geocentric
Tropical
Whole Signs
Mean Node

Compliments of:
Philip Young, PhD
Black Unykorn Tarot and Astrology
919-971-6818
http://www.blackunykorn.com
blackunykorn@gmail.com

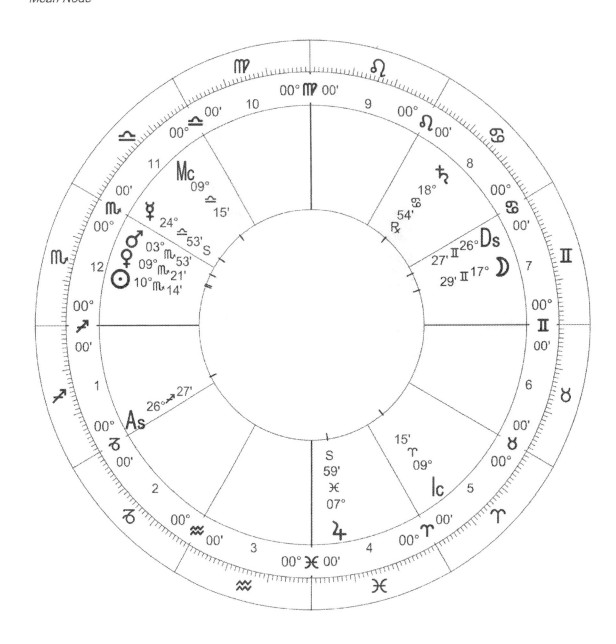

Astrology Unlocked by Philip Young, PhD

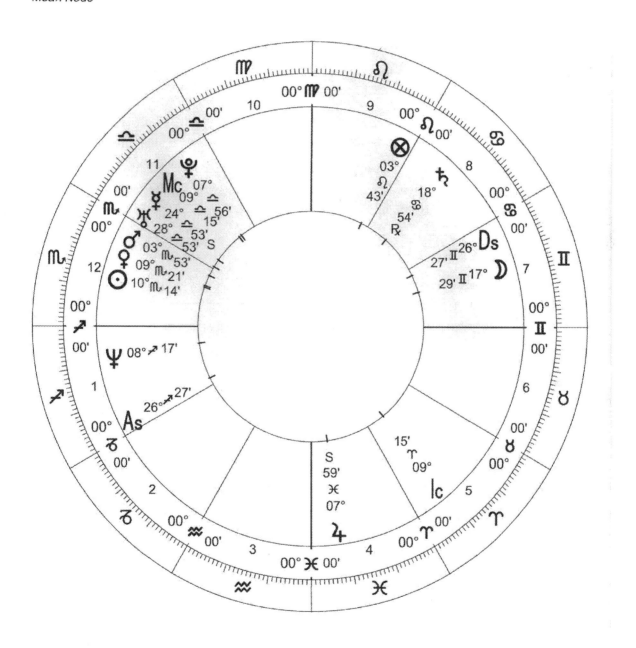

Jane Doe
Natal Chart
Nov 3 1974, Sun
10:15 am JST -9:00
Okinawa, Japan
26°N20' 127°E50'
Geocentric
Tropical
Whole Signs
Mean Node

Compliments of:
Philip Young, PhD
Black Unykorn Tarot and Astrology
919-971-6818
http://www.blackunykorn.com
blackunykorn@gmail.com

57

Jane Doe
Natal Chart
Nov 3 1974, Sun
10:15 am JST −9:00
Okinawa, Japan
26°N20' 127°E50'
Geocentric
Tropical
Whole Signs
Mean Node

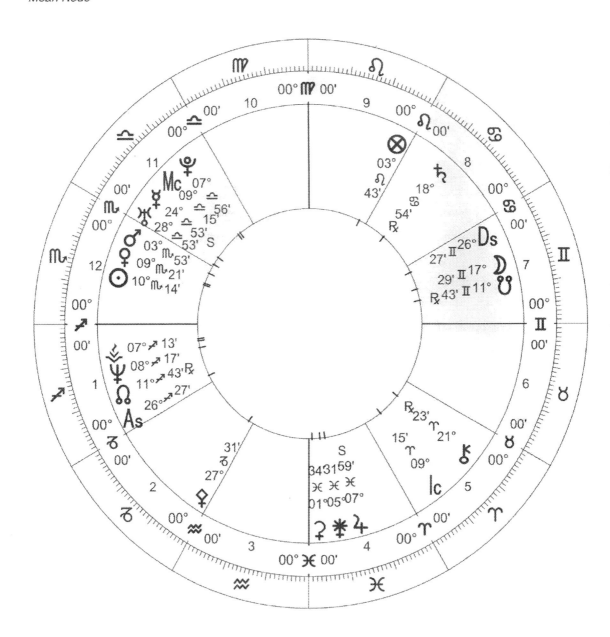

Compliments of:
Philip Young, PhD
Black Unykorn Tarot and Astrology
919−971−6818
http://www.blackunykorn.com
blackunykorn@gmail.com

Astrology Unlocked by Philip Young, PhD

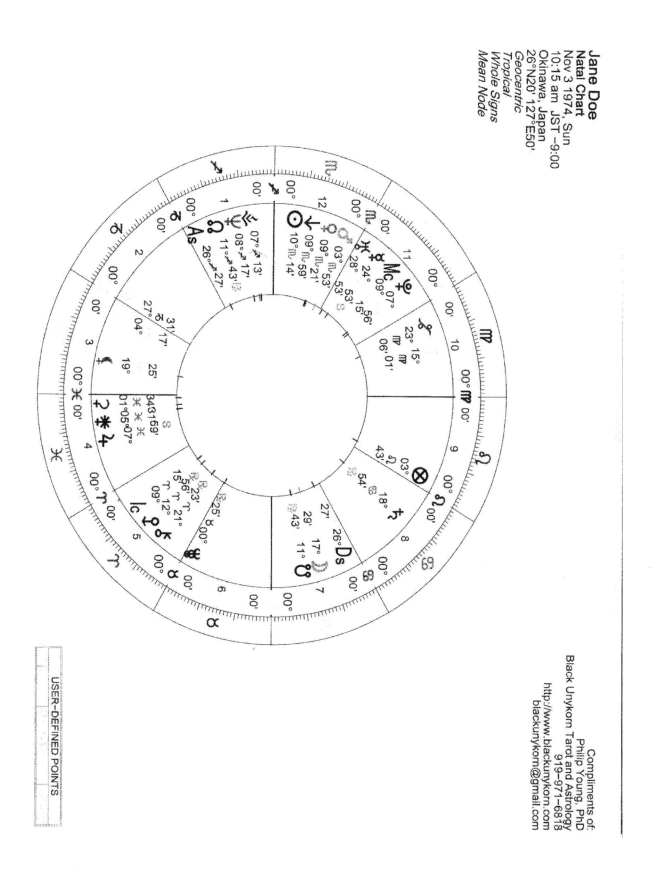

Jane Doe
Natal Chart
Nov 3 1974, Sun
10:15 am JST –9:00
Okinawa, Japan
26°N20′ 127°E50′
Geocentric
Tropical
Whole Signs
Mean Node

Compliments of:
Philip Young, PhD
Black Unykorn Tarot and Astrology
919-971-6818
http://www.blackunykorn.com
blackunykorn@gmail.com

USER–DEFINED POINTS

59

Part Two: Energy Point/Sign/House Interpretations

In the following section of the book you will find the written interpretations for all the Energy Points used in the final chart from part one, sample of each House meaning with each of the 12 Ascendants, and the worksheet. Remember, once you have your chart in hand, apply the reading strategy from part one and go directly to the Energy Point interpretations for the points in your chart and write your initials or name next to the interpretation. After you have done your chart, start gathering the charts of your significant other(s), friends, family, and so on and do the same with their charts. Make sure to make copies of the blank worksheet before filling it in so you can fill in all the information for all the additional charts you want to study. By the time you complete just five charts you will be well on your way to memorizing and absorbing the necessary foundational knowledge to help you access more advanced techniques and knowledge. The interpretation tables have been arranged so that the classical Energy Points are listed first, then the 19th and 20th century expanded solar system points, then the principle Asteroids, and then the remaining astronomical bodies and calculated points.

Astrology Unlocked by Philip Young, PhD

Sun | ☉

Energy Point Type: **Star**

Rules Sign: **Leo**

Rules House: **5**th

Element: **Fire**

Key Phrase: **Primary Drive**

The Sun represents our Primary Drive in life. Its placement in Sign and House reveals our lifelong energetic identity through the *Quality* of the Sign's influence and the *quest* of the House. In my case my Primary Drive is expressed through Fire (Aries) in my *quest* to serve (6th House). Fire's expression is pioneering, creative, and exploratory. In Aries the Element acts independently, heroically, and aggressively. So, my key phrase is "*Your Primary Drive manifests through your independent and heroic quest for and attraction to maverick and individualistic service for others.*" In short, I have to be my own boss.

When you look up your Sun in the Sign and House formula, think about how and where you feel you need to direct most of your energy. Much of life, especially early adulthood, usually reflects partial or even blocked efforts on the path to greater fulfillment and appropriate expression. Consider a Sun in Scorpio in the 11th House, "*Your Primary Drive manifests through your intense and truth seeking quest for and attraction to penetrating and emotionally transformative community.*" If this combination is your Primary Drive, you would find your best expression as a community leader or community healer, perhaps a physician, counselor, activist, shaman, priest, or guru. Since this Sun resides in one of the later Houses, the full realization of this Primary Drive may not occur until later in life, after 50 or 60. Regardless of the level of fulfillment or the timing of the best expression, this individual would likely be more mature than his or her peer group and a resource people in need would naturally or professionally seek out.

For more in depth reading about the Sun, I recommend purchasing and reading:

- *Alan Oken's Complete Astrology* by Alan Oken (ISBN: 9780892541256)
- *Astrology for Beginners* by Joann Hampar (ISBN: 9780738711065)

- *Horoscope Symbols* by Robert Hand (ISBN: 0914918168)

- *The Inner Planets* by Liz Green & Howard Sasportas (ISBN: 0877287414)

- *The Inner Sky* by Steven Forrest (ISBN: 9780979067716)

- *The Luminaries* by Liz Greene & Howard Sasportas (ISBN: 08778287503)

- *Mythic Astrology Applied* by Ariel Guttman & Kenneth Johnson (ISBN: 0738704253)

- *Planets in Play* by Laurence Hillman (ISBN: 9781585425877)

- *Sun Signs & Past Lives: Your Soul's Evolutionary Path* by Bernie Ashman (ISBN: 9780738721071)

- *Take Control with Astrology* by Lisa Tenzin-Dolma (ISBN: 9780071665049)

☉	Sun	Aries	♈	1	Your Primary Drive manifests through your independent and heroic quest for and attraction to maverick and individualistic identity development.
☉	Sun	Aries	♈	2	Your Primary Drive manifests through your independent and heroic quest for and attraction to maverick and individualistic values and ways to meet your needs.
☉	Sun	Aries	♈	3	Your Primary Drive manifests through your independent and heroic quest for and attraction to maverick and individualistic understanding of the world around you.
☉	Sun	Aries	♈	4	Your Primary Drive manifests through your independent and heroic quest for and attraction to maverick and individualistic emotional caretaking and traditions.
☉	Sun	Aries	♈	5	Your Primary Drive manifests through your independent and heroic quest for and attraction to maverick and individualistic creative expression.
☉	Sun	Aries	♈	6	Your Primary Drive manifests through your independent and heroic quest for and attraction to maverick and individualistic service for others.
☉	Sun	Aries	♈	7	Your Primary Drive manifests through your independent and heroic quest for and attraction to maverick and individualistic life teachers.
☉	Sun	Aries	♈	8	Your Primary Drive manifests through your independent and heroic quest for and attraction to maverick and individualistic intimate relationships.
☉	Sun	Aries	♈	9	Your Primary Drive manifests through your independent and heroic quest for and attraction to maverick and individualistic mastership of a body of knowledge.
☉	Sun	Aries	♈	10	Your Primary Drive manifests through your independent and heroic quest for and attraction to maverick and individualistic accomplishments.
☉	Sun	Aries	♈	11	Your Primary Drive manifests through your independent and heroic quest for and attraction to maverick and individualistic community.
☉	Sun	Aries	♈	12	Your Primary Drive manifests through your independent and heroic quest for and attraction to maverick and individualistic spirituality.

☉	Sun	Taurus	♉	1	Your Primary Drive manifests through your steadfast and persistent quest for and attraction to enduring and secure identity development.
☉	Sun	Taurus	♉	2	Your Primary Drive manifests through your steadfast and persistent quest for and attraction to enduring and secure values and ways to meet your needs.
☉	Sun	Taurus	♉	3	Your Primary Drive manifests through your steadfast and persistent quest for and attraction to enduring and secure understanding of the world around you.
☉	Sun	Taurus	♉	4	Your Primary Drive manifests through your steadfast and persistent quest for and attraction to enduring and secure emotional caretaking and traditions.
☉	Sun	Taurus	♉	5	Your Primary Drive manifests through your steadfast and persistent quest for and attraction to enduring and secure creative expression.
☉	Sun	Taurus	♉	6	Your Primary Drive manifests through your steadfast and persistent quest for and attraction to enduring and secure service for others.
☉	Sun	Taurus	♉	7	Your Primary Drive manifests through your steadfast and persistent quest for and attraction to enduring and secure life teachers.
☉	Sun	Taurus	♉	8	Your Primary Drive manifests through your steadfast and persistent quest for and attraction to enduring and secure intimate relationships.
☉	Sun	Taurus	♉	9	Your Primary Drive manifests through your steadfast and persistent quest for and attraction to enduring and secure mastership of a body of knowledge.
☉	Sun	Taurus	♉	10	Your Primary Drive manifests through your steadfast and persistent quest for and attraction to enduring and secure accomplishments.
☉	Sun	Taurus	♉	11	Your Primary Drive manifests through your steadfast and persistent quest for and attraction to enduring and secure community.
☉	Sun	Taurus	♉	12	Your Primary Drive manifests through your steadfast and persistent quest for and attraction to enduring and secure spirituality.

☉	Sun	Gemini	♊	1	Your Primary Drive manifests through your inquisitive and mentally agile quest for and attraction to ever changing and adaptable identity development.
☉	Sun	Gemini	♊	2	Your Primary Drive manifests through your inquisitive and mentally agile quest for and attraction to ever changing and adaptable values and ways to meet your needs.
☉	Sun	Gemini	♊	3	Your Primary Drive manifests through your inquisitive and mentally agile quest for and attraction to ever changing and adaptable understanding of the world around you.
☉	Sun	Gemini	♊	4	Your Primary Drive manifests through your inquisitive and mentally agile quest for and attraction to ever changing and adaptable emotional caretaking and traditions.
☉	Sun	Gemini	♊	5	Your Primary Drive manifests through your inquisitive and mentally agile quest for and attraction to ever changing and adaptable creative expression.
☉	Sun	Gemini	♊	6	Your Primary Drive manifests through your inquisitive and mentally agile quest for and attraction to ever changing and adaptable service for others.
☉	Sun	Gemini	♊	7	Your Primary Drive manifests through your inquisitive and mentally agile quest for and attraction to ever changing and adaptable life teachers.
☉	Sun	Gemini	♊	8	Your Primary Drive manifests through your inquisitive and mentally agile quest for and attraction to ever changing and adaptable intimate relationships.
☉	Sun	Gemini	♊	9	Your Primary Drive manifests through your inquisitive and mentally agile quest for and attraction to ever changing and adaptable mastership of a body of knowledge.
☉	Sun	Gemini	♊	10	Your Primary Drive manifests through your inquisitive and mentally agile quest for and attraction to ever changing and adaptable accomplishments.
☉	Sun	Gemini	♊	11	Your Primary Drive manifests through your inquisitive and mentally agile quest for and attraction to ever changing and adaptable community.
☉	Sun	Gemini	♊	12	Your Primary Drive manifests through your inquisitive and mentally agile quest for and attraction to ever changing and adaptable spirituality.

Astrology Unlocked by Philip Young, PhD

☉	Sun	Cancer	♋	1	Your Primary Drive manifests through your emotional and caring quest for and attraction to nurturing and supportive identity development.
☉	Sun	Cancer	♋	2	Your Primary Drive manifests through your emotional and caring quest for and attraction to nurturing and supportive values and ways to meet your needs.
☉	Sun	Cancer	♋	3	Your Primary Drive manifests through your emotional and caring quest for and attraction to nurturing and supportive understanding of the world around you.
☉	Sun	Cancer	♋	4	Your Primary Drive manifests through your emotional and caring quest for and attraction to nurturing and supportive emotional caretaking and traditions.
☉	Sun	Cancer	♋	5	Your Primary Drive manifests through your emotional and caring quest for and attraction to nurturing and supportive creative expression.
☉	Sun	Cancer	♋	6	Your Primary Drive manifests through your emotional and caring quest for and attraction to nurturing and supportive service for others.
☉	Sun	Cancer	♋	7	Your Primary Drive manifests through your emotional and caring quest for and attraction to nurturing and supportive life teachers.
☉	Sun	Cancer	♋	8	Your Primary Drive manifests through your emotional and caring quest for and attraction to nurturing and supportive intimate relationships.
☉	Sun	Cancer	♋	9	Your Primary Drive manifests through your emotional and caring quest for and attraction to nurturing and supportive mastership of a body of knowledge.
☉	Sun	Cancer	♋	10	Your Primary Drive manifests through your emotional and caring quest for and attraction to nurturing and supportive accomplishments.
☉	Sun	Cancer	♋	11	Your Primary Drive manifests through your emotional and caring quest for and attraction to nurturing and supportive community.
☉	Sun	Cancer	♋	12	Your Primary Drive manifests through your emotional and caring quest for and attraction to nurturing and supportive spirituality.

☉	Sun	Leo	♌	1	Your Primary Drive manifests through your energetic and dramatic quest for and attraction to creative and romantic identity development.
☉	Sun	Leo	♌	2	Your Primary Drive manifests through your energetic and dramatic quest for and attraction to creative and romantic values and ways to meet your needs.
☉	Sun	Leo	♌	3	Your Primary Drive manifests through your energetic and dramatic quest for and attraction to creative and romantic understanding of the world around you.
☉	Sun	Leo	♌	4	Your Primary Drive manifests through your energetic and dramatic quest for and attraction to creative and romantic emotional caretaking and traditions.
☉	Sun	Leo	♌	5	Your Primary Drive manifests through your energetic and dramatic quest for and attraction to creative and romantic creative expression.
☉	Sun	Leo	♌	6	Your Primary Drive manifests through your energetic and dramatic quest for and attraction to creative and romantic service for others.
☉	Sun	Leo	♌	7	Your Primary Drive manifests through your energetic and dramatic quest for and attraction to creative and romantic life teachers.
☉	Sun	Leo	♌	8	Your Primary Drive manifests through your energetic and dramatic quest for and attraction to creative and romantic intimate relationships.
☉	Sun	Leo	♌	9	Your Primary Drive manifests through your energetic and dramatic quest for and attraction to creative and romantic mastership of a body of knowledge.
☉	Sun	Leo	♌	10	Your Primary Drive manifests through your energetic and dramatic quest for and attraction to creative and romantic accomplishments.
☉	Sun	Leo	♌	11	Your Primary Drive manifests through your energetic and dramatic quest for and attraction to creative and romantic community.
☉	Sun	Leo	♌	12	Your Primary Drive manifests through your energetic and dramatic quest for and attraction to creative and romantic spirituality.

☉	Sun	Virgo	♍	1	Your Primary Drive manifests through your critically-minded and methodical quest for and attraction to meticulous and practical identity development.
☉	Sun	Virgo	♍	2	Your Primary Drive manifests through your critically-minded and methodical quest for and attraction to meticulous and practical values and ways to meet your needs.
☉	Sun	Virgo	♍	3	Your Primary Drive manifests through your critically-minded and methodical quest for and attraction to meticulous and practical understanding of the world around you.
☉	Sun	Virgo	♍	4	Your Primary Drive manifests through your critically-minded and methodical quest for and attraction to meticulous and practical emotional caretaking and traditions.
☉	Sun	Virgo	♍	5	Your Primary Drive manifests through your critically-minded and methodical quest for and attraction to meticulous and practical creative expression.
☉	Sun	Virgo	♍	6	Your Primary Drive manifests through your critically-minded and methodical quest for and attraction to meticulous and practical service for others.
☉	Sun	Virgo	♍	7	Your Primary Drive manifests through your critically-minded and methodical quest for and attraction to meticulous and practical life teachers.
☉	Sun	Virgo	♍	8	Your Primary Drive manifests through your critically-minded and methodical quest for and attraction to meticulous and practical intimate relationships.
☉	Sun	Virgo	♍	9	Your Primary Drive manifests through your critically-minded and methodical quest for and attraction to meticulous and practical mastership of a body of knowledge.
☉	Sun	Virgo	♍	10	Your Primary Drive manifests through your critically-minded and methodical quest for and attraction to meticulous and practical accomplishments.
☉	Sun	Virgo	♍	11	Your Primary Drive manifests through your critically-minded and methodical quest for and attraction to meticulous and practical community.
☉	Sun	Virgo	♍	12	Your Primary Drive manifests through your critically-minded and methodical quest for and attraction to meticulous and practical spirituality.

☉	Sun	Libra	♎	1	Your Primary Drive manifests through your analytical and balanced quest for and attraction to harmonious and logical identity development.
☉	Sun	Libra	♎	2	Your Primary Drive manifests through your analytical and balanced quest for and attraction to harmonious and logical values and ways to meet your needs.
☉	Sun	Libra	♎	3	Your Primary Drive manifests through your analytical and balanced quest for and attraction to harmonious and logical understanding of the world around you.
☉	Sun	Libra	♎	4	Your Primary Drive manifests through your analytical and balanced quest for and attraction to harmonious and logical emotional caretaking and traditions.
☉	Sun	Libra	♎	5	Your Primary Drive manifests through your analytical and balanced quest for and attraction to harmonious and logical creative expression.
☉	Sun	Libra	♎	6	Your Primary Drive manifests through your analytical and balanced quest for and attraction to harmonious and logical service for others.
☉	Sun	Libra	♎	7	Your Primary Drive manifests through your analytical and balanced quest for and attraction to harmonious and logical life teachers.
☉	Sun	Libra	♎	8	Your Primary Drive manifests through your analytical and balanced quest for and attraction to harmonious and logical intimate relationships.
☉	Sun	Libra	♎	9	Your Primary Drive manifests through your analytical and balanced quest for and attraction to harmonious and logical mastership of a body of knowledge.
☉	Sun	Libra	♎	10	Your Primary Drive manifests through your analytical and balanced quest for and attraction to harmonious and logical accomplishments.
☉	Sun	Libra	♎	11	Your Primary Drive manifests through your analytical and balanced quest for and attraction to harmonious and logical community.
☉	Sun	Libra	♎	12	Your Primary Drive manifests through your analytical and balanced quest for and attraction to harmonious and logical spirituality.

	Sun	Scorpio	♏	1	Your Primary Drive manifests through your intense and truth seeking quest for and attraction to penetrating and emotionally transformative identity development.
	Sun	Scorpio	♏	2	Your Primary Drive manifests through your intense and truth seeking quest for and attraction to penetrating and emotionally transformative values and ways to meet your needs.
	Sun	Scorpio	♏	3	Your Primary Drive manifests through your intense and truth seeking quest for and attraction to penetrating and emotionally transformative understanding of the world around you.
	Sun	Scorpio	♏	4	Your Primary Drive manifests through your intense and truth seeking quest for and attraction to penetrating and emotionally transformative emotional caretaking and traditions.
	Sun	Scorpio	♏	5	Your Primary Drive manifests through your intense and truth seeking quest for and attraction to penetrating and emotionally transformative creative expression.
	Sun	Scorpio	♏	6	Your Primary Drive manifests through your intense and truth seeking quest for and attraction to penetrating and emotionally transformative service for others.
	Sun	Scorpio	♏	7	Your Primary Drive manifests through your intense and truth seeking quest for and attraction to penetrating and emotionally transformative life teachers.
	Sun	Scorpio	♏	8	Your Primary Drive manifests through your intense and truth seeking quest for and attraction to penetrating and emotionally transformative intimate relationships.
	Sun	Scorpio	♏	9	Your Primary Drive manifests through your intense and truth seeking quest for and attraction to penetrating and emotionally transformative mastership of a body of knowledge.
	Sun	Scorpio	♏	10	Your Primary Drive manifests through your intense and truth seeking quest for and attraction to penetrating and emotionally transformative accomplishments.
	Sun	Scorpio	♏	11	Your Primary Drive manifests through your intense and truth seeking quest for and attraction to penetrating and emotionally transformative community.
	Sun	Scorpio	♏	12	Your Primary Drive manifests through your intense and truth seeking quest for and attraction to penetrating and emotionally transformative spirituality.

	Sun	Sagittarius	♐	1	Your Primary Drive manifests through your wide-ranging and open-minded quest for and attraction to experiential and risk-taking identity development.
	Sun	Sagittarius	♐	2	Your Primary Drive manifests through your wide-ranging and open-minded quest for and attraction to experiential and risk-taking values and ways to meet your needs.
	Sun	Sagittarius	♐	3	Your Primary Drive manifests through your wide-ranging and open-minded quest for and attraction to experiential and risk-taking understanding of the world around you.
	Sun	Sagittarius	♐	4	Your Primary Drive manifests through your wide-ranging and open-minded quest for and attraction to experiential and risk-taking emotional caretaking and traditions.
	Sun	Sagittarius	♐	5	Your Primary Drive manifests through your wide-ranging and open-minded quest for and attraction to experiential and risk-taking creative expression.
	Sun	Sagittarius	♐	6	Your Primary Drive manifests through your wide-ranging and open-minded quest for and attraction to experiential and risk-taking service for others.
	Sun	Sagittarius	♐	7	Your Primary Drive manifests through your wide-ranging and open-minded quest for and attraction to experiential and risk-taking life teachers.
	Sun	Sagittarius	♐	8	Your Primary Drive manifests through your wide-ranging and open-minded quest for and attraction to experiential and risk-taking intimate relationships.
	Sun	Sagittarius	♐	9	Your Primary Drive manifests through your wide-ranging and open-minded quest for and attraction to experiential and risk-taking mastership of a body of knowledge.
	Sun	Sagittarius	♐	10	Your Primary Drive manifests through your wide-ranging and open-minded quest for and attraction to experiential and risk-taking accomplishments.
	Sun	Sagittarius	♐	11	Your Primary Drive manifests through your wide-ranging and open-minded quest for and attraction to experiential and risk-taking community.
	Sun	Sagittarius	♐	12	Your Primary Drive manifests through your wide-ranging and open-minded quest for and attraction to experiential and risk-taking spirituality.

71

☉	Sun	Capricorn	♑	1	Your Primary Drive manifests through your goal-driven and focused quest for and attraction to results-oriented and successful identity development.
☉	Sun	Capricorn	♑	2	Your Primary Drive manifests through your goal-driven and focused quest for and attraction to results-oriented and successful values and ways to meet your needs.
☉	Sun	Capricorn	♑	3	Your Primary Drive manifests through your goal-driven and focused quest for and attraction to results-oriented and successful understanding of the world around you.
☉	Sun	Capricorn	♑	4	Your Primary Drive manifests through your goal-driven and focused quest for and attraction to results-oriented and successful emotional caretaking and traditions.
☉	Sun	Capricorn	♑	5	Your Primary Drive manifests through your goal-driven and focused quest for and attraction to results-oriented and successful creative expression.
☉	Sun	Capricorn	♑	6	Your Primary Drive manifests through your goal-driven and focused quest for and attraction to results-oriented and successful service for others.
☉	Sun	Capricorn	♑	7	Your Primary Drive manifests through your goal-driven and focused quest for and attraction to results-oriented and successful life teachers.
☉	Sun	Capricorn	♑	8	Your Primary Drive manifests through your goal-driven and focused quest for and attraction to results-oriented and successful intimate relationships.
☉	Sun	Capricorn	♑	9	Your Primary Drive manifests through your goal-driven and focused quest for and attraction to results-oriented and successful mastership of a body of knowledge.
☉	Sun	Capricorn	♑	10	Your Primary Drive manifests through your goal-driven and focused quest for and attraction to results-oriented and successful accomplishments.
☉	Sun	Capricorn	♑	11	Your Primary Drive manifests through your goal-driven and focused quest for and attraction to results-oriented and successful community.
☉	Sun	Capricorn	♑	12	Your Primary Drive manifests through your goal-driven and focused quest for and attraction to results-oriented and successful spirituality.

☉	Sun	Aquarius	♒	1	Your Primary Drive manifests through your unconventional and idealistic quest for and attraction to authentic and non-traditional identity development.
☉	Sun	Aquarius	♒	2	Your Primary Drive manifests through your unconventional and idealistic quest for and attraction to authentic and non-traditional values and ways to meet your needs.
☉	Sun	Aquarius	♒	3	Your Primary Drive manifests through your unconventional and idealistic quest for and attraction to authentic and non-traditional understanding of the world around you.
☉	Sun	Aquarius	♒	4	Your Primary Drive manifests through your unconventional and idealistic quest for and attraction to authentic and non-traditional emotional caretaking and traditions.
☉	Sun	Aquarius	♒	5	Your Primary Drive manifests through your unconventional and idealistic quest for and attraction to authentic and non-traditional creative expression.
☉	Sun	Aquarius	♒	6	Your Primary Drive manifests through your unconventional and idealistic quest for and attraction to authentic and non-traditional service for others.
☉	Sun	Aquarius	♒	7	Your Primary Drive manifests through your unconventional and idealistic quest for and attraction to authentic and non-traditional life teachers.
☉	Sun	Aquarius	♒	8	Your Primary Drive manifests through your unconventional and idealistic quest for and attraction to authentic and non-traditional intimate relationships.
☉	Sun	Aquarius	♒	9	Your Primary Drive manifests through your unconventional and idealistic quest for and attraction to authentic and non-traditional mastership of a body of knowledge.
☉	Sun	Aquarius	♒	10	Your Primary Drive manifests through your unconventional and idealistic quest for and attraction to authentic and non-traditional accomplishments.
☉	Sun	Aquarius	♒	11	Your Primary Drive manifests through your unconventional and idealistic quest for and attraction to authentic and non-traditional community.
☉	Sun	Aquarius	♒	12	Your Primary Drive manifests through your unconventional and idealistic quest for and attraction to authentic and non-traditional spirituality.

73

☉	Sun	Pisces	♓	1	Your Primary Drive manifests through your imaginative and faithful quest for and attraction to consciousness-raising and soulful identity development.
☉	Sun	Pisces	♓	2	Your Primary Drive manifests through your imaginative and faithful quest for and attraction to consciousness-raising and soulful values and ways to meet your needs.
☉	Sun	Pisces	♓	3	Your Primary Drive manifests through your imaginative and faithful quest for and attraction to consciousness-raising and soulful understanding of the world around you.
☉	Sun	Pisces	♓	4	Your Primary Drive manifests through your imaginative and faithful quest for and attraction to consciousness-raising and soulful emotional caretaking and traditions.
☉	Sun	Pisces	♓	5	Your Primary Drive manifests through your imaginative and faithful quest for and attraction to consciousness-raising and soulful creative expression.
☉	Sun	Pisces	♓	6	Your Primary Drive manifests through your imaginative and faithful quest for and attraction to consciousness-raising and soulful service for others.
☉	Sun	Pisces	♓	7	Your Primary Drive manifests through your imaginative and faithful quest for and attraction to consciousness-raising and soulful life teachers.
☉	Sun	Pisces	♓	8	Your Primary Drive manifests through your imaginative and faithful quest for and attraction to consciousness-raising and soulful intimate relationships.
☉	Sun	Pisces	♓	9	Your Primary Drive manifests through your imaginative and faithful quest for and attraction to consciousness-raising and soulful mastership of a body of knowledge.
☉	Sun	Pisces	♓	10	Your Primary Drive manifests through your imaginative and faithful quest for and attraction to consciousness-raising and soulful accomplishments.
☉	Sun	Pisces	♓	11	Your Primary Drive manifests through your imaginative and faithful quest for and attraction to consciousness-raising and soulful community.
☉	Sun	Pisces	♓	12	Your Primary Drive manifests through your imaginative and faithful quest for and attraction to consciousness-raising and soulful spirituality.

Moon | ☽

Energy Point Type: **Satellite to Earth**
Rules Sign: **Cancer**
Rules House: **4**th
Element: **Water**
Key Phrase: **Soul Path**

The Moon represents your Soul Path, your emotional drive in life. Its placement in Sign and House reveals how we give and receive love, give and seek emotional nourishment, and try to manifest our spiritual and soulful purpose alongside our primary drive (Sun). In my case my Soul Path is expressed through Air (Libra) in my spiritual quest (12th House). Air's expression is analytical, strategic, and curious. In Libra the Element acts judgmentally, decisively, and neutrally. So, my key phrase is "*Your Soul Path manifests through your analytical and balanced quest for and attraction to harmonious and logical spirituality.*" In short, I believe in and follow a spiritual path of moderation and make most of my decisions based on ideals of fairness, right judgment, and negotiation.

When you look up your own Moon in the Sign and House formula, think about how you act and react emotionally, what excites you on an emotional level, in what situations and around what kinds of people do you experience joy or sorrow, and how do you prefer to give and receive love. Consider a Moon in Sagittarius in the 4th House, "*Your Soul Path manifests through your wide-ranging and open-minded quest for and attraction to experiential and risk-taking emotional caretaking and traditions.*" An individual with this Moon prefers emotional adventure in the most personal sense. He or she will give love by showing a partner his or her willingness to try new experiences (Sagittarius), but only if they remain largely private to the two of them (4th House). He or she will enjoy receiving love from a partner who understands his or her desire for new experiences (Sagittarius) that happen "close to home" rather than out in public (4th House). This individual will generally be an adventurous lover and appreciate emotional situations that stretch him or her in some way.

75

For more in depth reading about the Moon, I recommend purchasing and reading:

- *Alan Oken's Complete Astrology* by Alan Oken (ISBN: 9780892541256)

- *Astrology for Beginners* by Joann Hampar (ISBN: 9780738711065)

- *Horoscope Symbols* by Robert Hand (ISBN: 0914918168)

- *The Inner Planets* by Liz Green & Howard Sasportas (ISBN: 0877287414)

- *The Inner Sky* by Steven Forrest (ISBN: 9780979067716)

- *The Luminaries* by Liz Greene & Howard Sasportas (ISBN: 08778287503)

- *Mythic Astrology Applied* by Ariel Guttman & Kenneth Johnson (ISBN: 0738704253)

- *Planets in Play* by Laurence Hillman (ISBN: 9781585425877)

- *Take Control with Astrology* by Lisa Tenzin-Dolma (ISBN: 9780071665049)

☽	Moon	Aries	♈	1	Your Soul Path manifests through your independent and heroic quest for and attraction to maverick and individualistic identity development.
☽	Moon	Aries	♈	2	Your Soul Path manifests through your independent and heroic quest for and attraction to maverick and individualistic values and ways to meet your needs.
☽	Moon	Aries	♈	3	Your Soul Path manifests through your independent and heroic quest for and attraction to maverick and individualistic understanding of the world around you.
☽	Moon	Aries	♈	4	Your Soul Path manifests through your independent and heroic quest for and attraction to maverick and individualistic emotional caretaking and traditions.
☽	Moon	Aries	♈	5	Your Soul Path manifests through your independent and heroic quest for and attraction to maverick and individualistic creative expression.
☽	Moon	Aries	♈	6	Your Soul Path manifests through your independent and heroic quest for and attraction to maverick and individualistic service for others.
☽	Moon	Aries	♈	7	Your Soul Path manifests through your independent and heroic quest for and attraction to maverick and individualistic life teachers.
☽	Moon	Aries	♈	8	Your Soul Path manifests through your independent and heroic quest for and attraction to maverick and individualistic intimate relationships.
☽	Moon	Aries	♈	9	Your Soul Path manifests through your independent and heroic quest for and attraction to maverick and individualistic mastership of a body of knowledge.
☽	Moon	Aries	♈	10	Your Soul Path manifests through your independent and heroic quest for and attraction to maverick and individualistic accomplishments.
☽	Moon	Aries	♈	11	Your Soul Path manifests through your independent and heroic quest for and attraction to maverick and individualistic community.
☽	Moon	Aries	♈	12	Your Soul Path manifests through your independent and heroic quest for and attraction to maverick and individualistic spirituality.

☽	Moon	Taurus	♉	1	Your Soul Path manifests through your steadfast and persistent quest for and attraction to enduring and secure identity development.
☽	Moon	Taurus	♉	2	Your Soul Path manifests through your steadfast and persistent quest for and attraction to enduring and secure values and ways to meet your needs.
☽	Moon	Taurus	♉	3	Your Soul Path manifests through your steadfast and persistent quest for and attraction to enduring and secure understanding of the world around you.
☽	Moon	Taurus	♉	4	Your Soul Path manifests through your steadfast and persistent quest for and attraction to enduring and secure emotional caretaking and traditions.
☽	Moon	Taurus	♉	5	Your Soul Path manifests through your steadfast and persistent quest for and attraction to enduring and secure creative expression.
☽	Moon	Taurus	♉	6	Your Soul Path manifests through your steadfast and persistent quest for and attraction to enduring and secure service for others.
☽	Moon	Taurus	♉	7	Your Soul Path manifests through your steadfast and persistent quest for and attraction to enduring and secure life teachers.
☽	Moon	Taurus	♉	8	Your Soul Path manifests through your steadfast and persistent quest for and attraction to enduring and secure intimate relationships.
☽	Moon	Taurus	♉	9	Your Soul Path manifests through your steadfast and persistent quest for and attraction to enduring and secure mastership of a body of knowledge.
☽	Moon	Taurus	♉	10	Your Soul Path manifests through your steadfast and persistent quest for and attraction to enduring and secure accomplishments.
☽	Moon	Taurus	♉	11	Your Soul Path manifests through your steadfast and persistent quest for and attraction to enduring and secure community.
☽	Moon	Taurus	♉	12	Your Soul Path manifests through your steadfast and persistent quest for and attraction to enduring and secure spirituality.

☽	Moon	Gemini	♊	I	Your Soul Path manifests through your inquisitive and mentally agile quest for and attraction to ever changing and adaptable identity development.
☽	Moon	Gemini	♊	2	Your Soul Path manifests through your inquisitive and mentally agile quest for and attraction to ever changing and adaptable values and ways to meet your needs.
☽	Moon	Gemini	♊	3	Your Soul Path manifests through your inquisitive and mentally agile quest for and attraction to ever changing and adaptable understanding of the world around you.
☽	Moon	Gemini	♊	4	Your Soul Path manifests through your inquisitive and mentally agile quest for and attraction to ever changing and adaptable emotional caretaking and traditions.
☽	Moon	Gemini	♊	5	Your Soul Path manifests through your inquisitive and mentally agile quest for and attraction to ever changing and adaptable creative expression.
☽	Moon	Gemini	♊	6	Your Soul Path manifests through your inquisitive and mentally agile quest for and attraction to ever changing and adaptable service for others.
☽	Moon	Gemini	♊	7	Your Soul Path manifests through your inquisitive and mentally agile quest for and attraction to ever changing and adaptable life teachers.
☽	Moon	Gemini	♊	8	Your Soul Path manifests through your inquisitive and mentally agile quest for and attraction to ever changing and adaptable intimate relationships.
☽	Moon	Gemini	♊	9	Your Soul Path manifests through your inquisitive and mentally agile quest for and attraction to ever changing and adaptable mastership of a body of knowledge.
☽	Moon	Gemini	♊	10	Your Soul Path manifests through your inquisitive and mentally agile quest for and attraction to ever changing and adaptable accomplishments.
☽	Moon	Gemini	♊	11	Your Soul Path manifests through your inquisitive and mentally agile quest for and attraction to ever changing and adaptable community.
☽	Moon	Gemini	♊	12	Your Soul Path manifests through your inquisitive and mentally agile quest for and attraction to ever changing and adaptable spirituality.

Astrology Unlocked by Philip Young, PhD

☽	Moon	Cancer	♋	1	Your Soul Path manifests through your emotional and caring quest for and attraction to nurturing and supportive identity development.
☽	Moon	Cancer	♋	2	Your Soul Path manifests through your emotional and caring quest for and attraction to nurturing and supportive values and ways to meet your needs.
☽	Moon	Cancer	♋	3	Your Soul Path manifests through your emotional and caring quest for and attraction to nurturing and supportive understanding of the world around you.
☽	Moon	Cancer	♋	4	Your Soul Path manifests through your emotional and caring quest for and attraction to nurturing and supportive emotional caretaking and traditions.
☽	Moon	Cancer	♋	5	Your Soul Path manifests through your emotional and caring quest for and attraction to nurturing and supportive creative expression.
☽	Moon	Cancer	♋	6	Your Soul Path manifests through your emotional and caring quest for and attraction to nurturing and supportive service for others.
☽	Moon	Cancer	♋	7	Your Soul Path manifests through your emotional and caring quest for and attraction to nurturing and supportive life teachers.
☽	Moon	Cancer	♋	8	Your Soul Path manifests through your emotional and caring quest for and attraction to nurturing and supportive intimate relationships.
☽	Moon	Cancer	♋	9	Your Soul Path manifests through your emotional and caring quest for and attraction to nurturing and supportive mastership of a body of knowledge.
☽	Moon	Cancer	♋	10	Your Soul Path manifests through your emotional and caring quest for and attraction to nurturing and supportive accomplishments.
☽	Moon	Cancer	♋	11	Your Soul Path manifests through your emotional and caring quest for and attraction to nurturing and supportive community.
☽	Moon	Cancer	♋	12	Your Soul Path manifests through your emotional and caring quest for and attraction to nurturing and supportive spirituality.

Astrology Unlocked by Philip Young, PhD

☽	Moon	Leo	♌	1	Your Soul Path manifests through your energetic and dramatic quest for and attraction to creative and romantic identity development.
☽	Moon	Leo	♌	2	Your Soul Path manifests through your energetic and dramatic quest for and attraction to creative and romantic values and ways to meet your needs.
☽	Moon	Leo	♌	3	Your Soul Path manifests through your energetic and dramatic quest for and attraction to creative and romantic understanding of the world around you.
☽	Moon	Leo	♌	4	Your Soul Path manifests through your energetic and dramatic quest for and attraction to creative and romantic emotional caretaking and traditions.
☽	Moon	Leo	♌	5	Your Soul Path manifests through your energetic and dramatic quest for and attraction to creative and romantic creative expression.
☽	Moon	Leo	♌	6	Your Soul Path manifests through your energetic and dramatic quest for and attraction to creative and romantic service for others.
☽	Moon	Leo	♌	7	Your Soul Path manifests through your energetic and dramatic quest for and attraction to creative and romantic life teachers.
☽	Moon	Leo	♌	8	Your Soul Path manifests through your energetic and dramatic quest for and attraction to creative and romantic intimate relationships.
☽	Moon	Leo	♌	9	Your Soul Path manifests through your energetic and dramatic quest for and attraction to creative and romantic mastership of a body of knowledge.
☽	Moon	Leo	♌	10	Your Soul Path manifests through your energetic and dramatic quest for and attraction to creative and romantic accomplishments.
☽	Moon	Leo	♌	11	Your Soul Path manifests through your energetic and dramatic quest for and attraction to creative and romantic community.
☽	Moon	Leo	♌	12	Your Soul Path manifests through your energetic and dramatic quest for and attraction to creative and romantic spirituality.

☽	Moon	Virgo	♍	1	Your Soul Path manifests through your critically-minded and methodical quest for and attraction to meticulous and practical identity development.
☽	Moon	Virgo	♍	2	Your Soul Path manifests through your critically-minded and methodical quest for and attraction to meticulous and practical values and ways to meet your needs.
☽	Moon	Virgo	♍	3	Your Soul Path manifests through your critically-minded and methodical quest for and attraction to meticulous and practical understanding of the world around you.
☽	Moon	Virgo	♍	4	Your Soul Path manifests through your critically-minded and methodical quest for and attraction to meticulous and practical emotional caretaking and traditions.
☽	Moon	Virgo	♍	5	Your Soul Path manifests through your critically-minded and methodical quest for and attraction to meticulous and practical creative expression.
☽	Moon	Virgo	♍	6	Your Soul Path manifests through your critically-minded and methodical quest for and attraction to meticulous and practical service for others.
☽	Moon	Virgo	♍	7	Your Soul Path manifests through your critically-minded and methodical quest for and attraction to meticulous and practical life teachers.
☽	Moon	Virgo	♍	8	Your Soul Path manifests through your critically-minded and methodical quest for and attraction to meticulous and practical intimate relationships.
☽	Moon	Virgo	♍	9	Your Soul Path manifests through your critically-minded and methodical quest for and attraction to meticulous and practical mastership of a body of knowledge.
☽	Moon	Virgo	♍	10	Your Soul Path manifests through your critically-minded and methodical quest for and attraction to meticulous and practical accomplishments.
☽	Moon	Virgo	♍	11	Your Soul Path manifests through your critically-minded and methodical quest for and attraction to meticulous and practical community.
☽	Moon	Virgo	♍	12	Your Soul Path manifests through your critically-minded and methodical quest for and attraction to meticulous and practical spirituality.

	Moon	Libra	♎	1	Your Soul Path manifests through your analytical and balanced quest for and attraction to harmonious and logical identity development.
	Moon	Libra	♎	2	Your Soul Path manifests through your analytical and balanced quest for and attraction to harmonious and logical values and ways to meet your needs.
	Moon	Libra	♎	3	Your Soul Path manifests through your analytical and balanced quest for and attraction to harmonious and logical understanding of the world around you.
	Moon	Libra	♎	4	Your Soul Path manifests through your analytical and balanced quest for and attraction to harmonious and logical emotional caretaking and traditions.
	Moon	Libra	♎	5	Your Soul Path manifests through your analytical and balanced quest for and attraction to harmonious and logical creative expression.
	Moon	Libra	♎	6	Your Soul Path manifests through your analytical and balanced quest for and attraction to harmonious and logical service for others.
	Moon	Libra	♎	7	Your Soul Path manifests through your analytical and balanced quest for and attraction to harmonious and logical life teachers.
	Moon	Libra	♎	8	Your Soul Path manifests through your analytical and balanced quest for and attraction to harmonious and logical intimate relationships.
	Moon	Libra	♎	9	Your Soul Path manifests through your analytical and balanced quest for and attraction to harmonious and logical mastership of a body of knowledge.
	Moon	Libra	♎	10	Your Soul Path manifests through your analytical and balanced quest for and attraction to harmonious and logical accomplishments.
	Moon	Libra	♎	11	Your Soul Path manifests through your analytical and balanced quest for and attraction to harmonious and logical community.
	Moon	Libra	♎	12	Your Soul Path manifests through your analytical and balanced quest for and attraction to harmonious and logical spirituality.

	Moon	Scorpio	♏	1	Your Soul Path manifests through your intense and truth seeking quest for and attraction to penetrating and emotionally transformative identity development.
	Moon	Scorpio	♏	2	Your Soul Path manifests through your intense and truth seeking quest for and attraction to penetrating and emotionally transformative values and ways to meet your needs.
	Moon	Scorpio	♏	3	Your Soul Path manifests through your intense and truth seeking quest for and attraction to penetrating and emotionally transformative understanding of the world around you.
	Moon	Scorpio	♏	4	Your Soul Path manifests through your intense and truth seeking quest for and attraction to penetrating and emotionally transformative emotional caretaking and traditions.
	Moon	Scorpio	♏	5	Your Soul Path manifests through your intense and truth seeking quest for and attraction to penetrating and emotionally transformative creative expression.
	Moon	Scorpio	♏	6	Your Soul Path manifests through your intense and truth seeking quest for and attraction to penetrating and emotionally transformative service for others.
	Moon	Scorpio	♏	7	Your Soul Path manifests through your intense and truth seeking quest for and attraction to penetrating and emotionally transformative life teachers.
	Moon	Scorpio	♏	8	Your Soul Path manifests through your intense and truth seeking quest for and attraction to penetrating and emotionally transformative intimate relationships.
	Moon	Scorpio	♏	9	Your Soul Path manifests through your intense and truth seeking quest for and attraction to penetrating and emotionally transformative mastership of a body of knowledge.
	Moon	Scorpio	♏	10	Your Soul Path manifests through your intense and truth seeking quest for and attraction to penetrating and emotionally transformative accomplishments.
	Moon	Scorpio	♏	11	Your Soul Path manifests through your intense and truth seeking quest for and attraction to penetrating and emotionally transformative community.
	Moon	Scorpio	♏	12	Your Soul Path manifests through your intense and truth seeking quest for and attraction to penetrating and emotionally transformative spirituality.

☽	Moon	Sagittarius	♐	1	Your Soul Path manifests through your wide-ranging and open-minded quest for and attraction to experiential and risk-taking identity development.
☽	Moon	Sagittarius	♐	2	Your Soul Path manifests through your wide-ranging and open-minded quest for and attraction to experiential and risk-taking values and ways to meet your needs.
☽	Moon	Sagittarius	♐	3	Your Soul Path manifests through your wide-ranging and open-minded quest for and attraction to experiential and risk-taking understanding of the world around you.
☽	Moon	Sagittarius	♐	4	Your Soul Path manifests through your wide-ranging and open-minded quest for and attraction to experiential and risk-taking emotional caretaking and traditions.
☽	Moon	Sagittarius	♐	5	Your Soul Path manifests through your wide-ranging and open-minded quest for and attraction to experiential and risk-taking creative expression.
☽	Moon	Sagittarius	♐	6	Your Soul Path manifests through your wide-ranging and open-minded quest for and attraction to experiential and risk-taking service for others.
☽	Moon	Sagittarius	♐	7	Your Soul Path manifests through your wide-ranging and open-minded quest for and attraction to experiential and risk-taking life teachers.
☽	Moon	Sagittarius	♐	8	Your Soul Path manifests through your wide-ranging and open-minded quest for and attraction to experiential and risk-taking intimate relationships.
☽	Moon	Sagittarius	♐	9	Your Soul Path manifests through your wide-ranging and open-minded quest for and attraction to experiential and risk-taking mastership of a body of knowledge.
☽	Moon	Sagittarius	♐	10	Your Soul Path manifests through your wide-ranging and open-minded quest for and attraction to experiential and risk-taking accomplishments.
☽	Moon	Sagittarius	♐	11	Your Soul Path manifests through your wide-ranging and open-minded quest for and attraction to experiential and risk-taking community.
☽	Moon	Sagittarius	♐	12	Your Soul Path manifests through your wide-ranging and open-minded quest for and attraction to experiential and risk-taking spirituality.

	Moon	Capricorn	♑	1	Your Soul Path manifests through your goal-driven and focused quest for and attraction to results-oriented and successful identity development.
	Moon	Capricorn	♑	2	Your Soul Path manifests through your goal-driven and focused quest for and attraction to results-oriented and successful values and ways to meet your needs.
	Moon	Capricorn	♑	3	Your Soul Path manifests through your goal-driven and focused quest for and attraction to results-oriented and successful understanding of the world around you.
	Moon	Capricorn	♑	4	Your Soul Path manifests through your goal-driven and focused quest for and attraction to results-oriented and successful emotional caretaking and traditions.
	Moon	Capricorn	♑	5	Your Soul Path manifests through your goal-driven and focused quest for and attraction to results-oriented and successful creative expression.
	Moon	Capricorn	♑	6	Your Soul Path manifests through your goal-driven and focused quest for and attraction to results-oriented and successful service for others.
	Moon	Capricorn	♑	7	Your Soul Path manifests through your goal-driven and focused quest for and attraction to results-oriented and successful life teachers.
	Moon	Capricorn	♑	8	Your Soul Path manifests through your goal-driven and focused quest for and attraction to results-oriented and successful intimate relationships.
	Moon	Capricorn	♑	9	Your Soul Path manifests through your goal-driven and focused quest for and attraction to results-oriented and successful mastership of a body of knowledge.
	Moon	Capricorn	♑	10	Your Soul Path manifests through your goal-driven and focused quest for and attraction to results-oriented and successful accomplishments.
	Moon	Capricorn	♑	11	Your Soul Path manifests through your goal-driven and focused quest for and attraction to results-oriented and successful community.
	Moon	Capricorn	♑	12	Your Soul Path manifests through your goal-driven and focused quest for and attraction to results-oriented and successful spirituality.

Astrology Unlocked by Philip Young, PhD

☽	Moon	Aquarius	♒	1	Your Soul Path manifests through your unconventional and idealistic quest for and attraction to authentic and non-traditional identity development.
☽	Moon	Aquarius	♒	2	Your Soul Path manifests through your unconventional and idealistic quest for and attraction to authentic and non-traditional values and ways to meet your needs.
☽	Moon	Aquarius	♒	3	Your Soul Path manifests through your unconventional and idealistic quest for and attraction to authentic and non-traditional understanding of the world around you.
☽	Moon	Aquarius	♒	4	Your Soul Path manifests through your unconventional and idealistic quest for and attraction to authentic and non-traditional emotional caretaking and traditions.
☽	Moon	Aquarius	♒	5	Your Soul Path manifests through your unconventional and idealistic quest for and attraction to authentic and non-traditional creative expression.
☽	Moon	Aquarius	♒	6	Your Soul Path manifests through your unconventional and idealistic quest for and attraction to authentic and non-traditional service for others.
☽	Moon	Aquarius	♒	7	Your Soul Path manifests through your unconventional and idealistic quest for and attraction to authentic and non-traditional life teachers.
☽	Moon	Aquarius	♒	8	Your Soul Path manifests through your unconventional and idealistic quest for and attraction to authentic and non-traditional intimate relationships.
☽	Moon	Aquarius	♒	9	Your Soul Path manifests through your unconventional and idealistic quest for and attraction to authentic and non-traditional mastership of a body of knowledge.
☽	Moon	Aquarius	♒	10	Your Soul Path manifests through your unconventional and idealistic quest for and attraction to authentic and non-traditional accomplishments.
☽	Moon	Aquarius	♒	11	Your Soul Path manifests through your unconventional and idealistic quest for and attraction to authentic and non-traditional community.
☽	Moon	Aquarius	♒	12	Your Soul Path manifests through your unconventional and idealistic quest for and attraction to authentic and non-traditional spirituality.

Astrology Unlocked by Philip Young, PhD

	Moon	Pisces	♓	1	Your Soul Path manifests through your imaginative and faithful quest for and attraction to consciousness-raising and soulful identity development.
	Moon	Pisces	♓	2	Your Soul Path manifests through your imaginative and faithful quest for and attraction to consciousness-raising and soulful values and ways to meet your needs.
	Moon	Pisces	♓	3	Your Soul Path manifests through your imaginative and faithful quest for and attraction to consciousness-raising and soulful understanding of the world around you.
	Moon	Pisces	♓	4	Your Soul Path manifests through your imaginative and faithful quest for and attraction to consciousness-raising and soulful emotional caretaking and traditions.
	Moon	Pisces	♓	5	Your Soul Path manifests through your imaginative and faithful quest for and attraction to consciousness-raising and soulful creative expression.
	Moon	Pisces	♓	6	Your Soul Path manifests through your imaginative and faithful quest for and attraction to consciousness-raising and soulful service for others.
	Moon	Pisces	♓	7	Your Soul Path manifests through your imaginative and faithful quest for and attraction to consciousness-raising and soulful life teachers.
	Moon	Pisces	♓	8	Your Soul Path manifests through your imaginative and faithful quest for and attraction to consciousness-raising and soulful intimate relationships.
	Moon	Pisces	♓	9	Your Soul Path manifests through your imaginative and faithful quest for and attraction to consciousness-raising and soulful mastership of a body of knowledge.
	Moon	Pisces	♓	10	Your Soul Path manifests through your imaginative and faithful quest for and attraction to consciousness-raising and soulful accomplishments.
	Moon	Pisces	♓	11	Your Soul Path manifests through your imaginative and faithful quest for and attraction to consciousness-raising and soulful community.
	Moon	Pisces	♓	12	Your Soul Path manifests through your imaginative and faithful quest for and attraction to consciousness-raising and soulful spirituality.

Astrology Unlocked by Philip Young, PhD

Mercury[24] | ☿

Energy Point Type: **Planet**

Co-Rules Sign: **Gemini**

Co-Rules House: **3rd**

Element: **Air**

Key Phrase: **Way of Communicating**

Mercury represents your Way of Communicating. Its placement in Sign and House reveals how we try to make sense of the world around us and develop our own internal dialogue, which we then try to communicate back into the world as we navigate our interactions. In my case my Way of Communicating is expressed through Fire (Aries) in my quest to serve (6th House). Fire's expression is pioneering, creative, and exploratory. In Aries the Element acts independently, heroically, and aggressively. So, my key phrase is *"Your Way of Communicating manifests through your independent and heroic quest for and attraction to maverick and individualistic service for others."* In short, I am direct and forthright in my communications, especially when applying my skills and doing my day-to-day work.

When you look up your own Mercury in the Sign and House formula, think about the style of your communication and how you tend to interpret others and your experiences in daily life. Consider Mercury in Cancer in the 9th House, *"Your Way of Communicating manifests through your emotional and caring quest for and attraction to nurturing and supportive mastership of a body of knowledge."* A person with this Mercury interprets and expresses through the Element of Water, through feelings. He or she listens for and communicates with emotion, particularly emotion imbued with Cancer's focus on nurturing and caring. He or she will enjoy conversations about health and well-being (Cancer) that go in depth and explore expert knowledge about the subjects (9th House).

---

[24]Since the planet represents communication; it could easily Rule any sign and house. Traditionally, and for most of the modern era, Mercury has Ruled Gemini/3rd house and Virgo/6th house. Now Chiron is being used more and more as the Ruler for Virgo and the 6th house, leaving Mercury to Rule just Gemini and the 3rd House. I have found Chiron to be a perfect fit for the Rulership of Virgo and the 6th house and use that Rulership in my chart interpretations.

For more in depth reading about Mercury, I recommend purchasing and reading:

- *Alan Oken's Complete Astrology* by Alan Oken (ISBN: 9780892541256)
- *Astrology for Beginners* by Joann Hampar (ISBN: 9780738711065)
- *Horoscope Symbols* by Robert Hand (ISBN: 0914918168)
- *The Inner Planets* by Liz Green & Howard Sasportas (ISBN: 0877287414)
- *The Inner Sky* by Steven Forrest (ISBN: 9780979067716)
- *Mythic Astrology Applied* by Ariel Guttman & Kenneth Johnson (ISBN: 0738704253)
- *Planets in Play* by Laurence Hillman (ISBN: 9781585425877)
- *Take Control with Astrology* by Lisa Tenzin-Dolma (ISBN: 9780071665049)

	Mercury	Aries	♈	1	Your Way of Communicating manifests through your independent and heroic quest for and attraction to maverick and individualistic identity development.
☿	Mercury	Aries	♈	2	Your Way of Communicating manifests through your independent and heroic quest for and attraction to maverick and individualistic values and ways to meet your needs.
☿	Mercury	Aries	♈	3	Your Way of Communicating manifests through your independent and heroic quest for and attraction to maverick and individualistic understanding of the world around you.
☿	Mercury	Aries	♈	4	Your Way of Communicating manifests through your independent and heroic quest for and attraction to maverick and individualistic emotional caretaking and traditions.
☿	Mercury	Aries	♈	5	Your Way of Communicating manifests through your independent and heroic quest for and attraction to maverick and individualistic creative expression.
☿	Mercury	Aries	♈	6	Your Way of Communicating manifests through your independent and heroic quest for and attraction to maverick and individualistic service for others.
☿	Mercury	Aries	♈	7	Your Way of Communicating manifests through your independent and heroic quest for and attraction to maverick and individualistic life teachers.
☿	Mercury	Aries	♈	8	Your Way of Communicating manifests through your independent and heroic quest for and attraction to maverick and individualistic intimate relationships.
☿	Mercury	Aries	♈	9	Your Way of Communicating manifests through your independent and heroic quest for and attraction to maverick and individualistic mastership of a body of knowledge.
☿	Mercury	Aries	♈	10	Your Way of Communicating manifests through your independent and heroic quest for and attraction to maverick and individualistic accomplishments.
☿	Mercury	Aries	♈	11	Your Way of Communicating manifests through your independent and heroic quest for and attraction to maverick and individualistic community.
☿	Mercury	Aries	♈	12	Your Way of Communicating manifests through your independent and heroic quest for and attraction to maverick and individualistic spirituality.

☿	Mercury	Taurus	♉	1	Your Way of Communicating manifests through your steadfast and persistent quest for and attraction to enduring and secure identity development.
☿	Mercury	Taurus	♉	2	Your Way of Communicating manifests through your steadfast and persistent quest for and attraction to enduring and secure values and ways to meet your needs.
☿	Mercury	Taurus	♉	3	Your Way of Communicating manifests through your steadfast and persistent quest for and attraction to enduring and secure understanding of the world around you.
☿	Mercury	Taurus	♉	4	Your Way of Communicating manifests through your steadfast and persistent quest for and attraction to enduring and secure emotional caretaking and traditions.
☿	Mercury	Taurus	♉	5	Your Way of Communicating manifests through your steadfast and persistent quest for and attraction to enduring and secure creative expression.
☿	Mercury	Taurus	♉	6	Your Way of Communicating manifests through your steadfast and persistent quest for and attraction to enduring and secure service for others.
☿	Mercury	Taurus	♉	7	Your Way of Communicating manifests through your steadfast and persistent quest for and attraction to enduring and secure life teachers.
☿	Mercury	Taurus	♉	8	Your Way of Communicating manifests through your steadfast and persistent quest for and attraction to enduring and secure intimate relationships.
☿	Mercury	Taurus	♉	9	Your Way of Communicating manifests through your steadfast and persistent quest for and attraction to enduring and secure mastership of a body of knowledge.
☿	Mercury	Taurus	♉	10	Your Way of Communicating manifests through your steadfast and persistent quest for and attraction to enduring and secure accomplishments.
☿	Mercury	Taurus	♉	11	Your Way of Communicating manifests through your steadfast and persistent quest for and attraction to enduring and secure community.
☿	Mercury	Taurus	♉	12	Your Way of Communicating manifests through your steadfast and persistent quest for and attraction to enduring and secure spirituality.

Astrology Unlocked by Philip Young, PhD

☿	Mercury	Gemini	♊	1	Your Way of Communicating manifests through your inquisitive and mentally agile quest for and attraction to ever changing and adaptable identity development.
☿	Mercury	Gemini	♊	2	Your Way of Communicating manifests through your inquisitive and mentally agile quest for and attraction to ever changing and adaptable values and ways to meet your needs.
☿	Mercury	Gemini	♊	3	Your Way of Communicating manifests through your inquisitive and mentally agile quest for and attraction to ever changing and adaptable understanding of the world around you.
☿	Mercury	Gemini	♊	4	Your Way of Communicating manifests through your inquisitive and mentally agile quest for and attraction to ever changing and adaptable emotional caretaking and traditions.
☿	Mercury	Gemini	♊	5	Your Way of Communicating manifests through your inquisitive and mentally agile quest for and attraction to ever changing and adaptable creative expression.
☿	Mercury	Gemini	♊	6	Your Way of Communicating manifests through your inquisitive and mentally agile quest for and attraction to ever changing and adaptable service for others.
☿	Mercury	Gemini	♊	7	Your Way of Communicating manifests through your inquisitive and mentally agile quest for and attraction to ever changing and adaptable life teachers.
☿	Mercury	Gemini	♊	8	Your Way of Communicating manifests through your inquisitive and mentally agile quest for and attraction to ever changing and adaptable intimate relationships.
☿	Mercury	Gemini	♊	9	Your Way of Communicating manifests through your inquisitive and mentally agile quest for and attraction to ever changing and adaptable mastership of a body of knowledge.
☿	Mercury	Gemini	♊	10	Your Way of Communicating manifests through your inquisitive and mentally agile quest for and attraction to ever changing and adaptable accomplishments.
☿	Mercury	Gemini	♊	11	Your Way of Communicating manifests through your inquisitive and mentally agile quest for and attraction to ever changing and adaptable community.
☿	Mercury	Gemini	♊	12	Your Way of Communicating manifests through your inquisitive and mentally agile quest for and attraction to ever changing and adaptable spirituality.

☿	Mercury	Cancer	♋	1	Your Way of Communicating manifests through your emotional and caring quest for and attraction to nurturing and supportive identity development.
☿	Mercury	Cancer	♋	2	Your Way of Communicating manifests through your emotional and caring quest for and attraction to nurturing and supportive values and ways to meet your needs.
☿	Mercury	Cancer	♋	3	Your Way of Communicating manifests through your emotional and caring quest for and attraction to nurturing and supportive understanding of the world around you.
☿	Mercury	Cancer	♋	4	Your Way of Communicating manifests through your emotional and caring quest for and attraction to nurturing and supportive emotional caretaking and traditions.
☿	Mercury	Cancer	♋	5	Your Way of Communicating manifests through your emotional and caring quest for and attraction to nurturing and supportive creative expression.
☿	Mercury	Cancer	♋	6	Your Way of Communicating manifests through your emotional and caring quest for and attraction to nurturing and supportive service for others.
☿	Mercury	Cancer	♋	7	Your Way of Communicating manifests through your emotional and caring quest for and attraction to nurturing and supportive life teachers.
☿	Mercury	Cancer	♋	8	Your Way of Communicating manifests through your emotional and caring quest for and attraction to nurturing and supportive intimate relationships.
☿	Mercury	Cancer	♋	9	Your Way of Communicating manifests through your emotional and caring quest for and attraction to nurturing and supportive mastership of a body of knowledge.
☿	Mercury	Cancer	♋	10	Your Way of Communicating manifests through your emotional and caring quest for and attraction to nurturing and supportive accomplishments.
☿	Mercury	Cancer	♋	11	Your Way of Communicating manifests through your emotional and caring quest for and attraction to nurturing and supportive community.
☿	Mercury	Cancer	♋	12	Your Way of Communicating manifests through your emotional and caring quest for and attraction to nurturing and supportive spirituality.

☿	Mercury	Leo	♌	1	Your Way of Communicating manifests through your energetic and dramatic quest for and attraction to creative and romantic identity development.
☿	Mercury	Leo	♌	2	Your Way of Communicating manifests through your energetic and dramatic quest for and attraction to creative and romantic values and ways to meet your needs.
☿	Mercury	Leo	♌	3	Your Way of Communicating manifests through your energetic and dramatic quest for and attraction to creative and romantic understanding of the world around you.
☿	Mercury	Leo	♌	4	Your Way of Communicating manifests through your energetic and dramatic quest for and attraction to creative and romantic emotional caretaking and traditions.
☿	Mercury	Leo	♌	5	Your Way of Communicating manifests through your energetic and dramatic quest for and attraction to creative and romantic creative expression.
☿	Mercury	Leo	♌	6	Your Way of Communicating manifests through your energetic and dramatic quest for and attraction to creative and romantic service for others.
☿	Mercury	Leo	♌	7	Your Way of Communicating manifests through your energetic and dramatic quest for and attraction to creative and romantic life teachers.
☿	Mercury	Leo	♌	8	Your Way of Communicating manifests through your energetic and dramatic quest for and attraction to creative and romantic intimate relationships.
☿	Mercury	Leo	♌	9	Your Way of Communicating manifests through your energetic and dramatic quest for and attraction to creative and romantic mastership of a body of knowledge.
☿	Mercury	Leo	♌	10	Your Way of Communicating manifests through your energetic and dramatic quest for and attraction to creative and romantic accomplishments.
☿	Mercury	Leo	♌	11	Your Way of Communicating manifests through your energetic and dramatic quest for and attraction to creative and romantic community.
☿	Mercury	Leo	♌	12	Your Way of Communicating manifests through your energetic and dramatic quest for and attraction to creative and romantic spirituality.

☿	Mercury	Virgo	♍	1	Your Way of Communicating manifests through your critically-minded and methodical quest for and attraction to meticulous and practical identity development.
☿	Mercury	Virgo	♍	2	Your Way of Communicating manifests through your critically-minded and methodical quest for and attraction to meticulous and practical values and ways to meet your needs.
☿	Mercury	Virgo	♍	3	Your Way of Communicating manifests through your critically-minded and methodical quest for and attraction to meticulous and practical understanding of the world around you.
☿	Mercury	Virgo	♍	4	Your Way of Communicating manifests through your critically-minded and methodical quest for and attraction to meticulous and practical emotional caretaking and traditions.
☿	Mercury	Virgo	♍	5	Your Way of Communicating manifests through your critically-minded and methodical quest for and attraction to meticulous and practical creative expression.
☿	Mercury	Virgo	♍	6	Your Way of Communicating manifests through your critically-minded and methodical quest for and attraction to meticulous and practical service for others.
☿	Mercury	Virgo	♍	7	Your Way of Communicating manifests through your critically-minded and methodical quest for and attraction to meticulous and practical life teachers.
☿	Mercury	Virgo	♍	8	Your Way of Communicating manifests through your critically-minded and methodical quest for and attraction to meticulous and practical intimate relationships.
☿	Mercury	Virgo	♍	9	Your Way of Communicating manifests through your critically-minded and methodical quest for and attraction to meticulous and practical mastership of a body of knowledge.
☿	Mercury	Virgo	♍	10	Your Way of Communicating manifests through your critically-minded and methodical quest for and attraction to meticulous and practical accomplishments.
☿	Mercury	Virgo	♍	11	Your Way of Communicating manifests through your critically-minded and methodical quest for and attraction to meticulous and practical community.
☿	Mercury	Virgo	♍	12	Your Way of Communicating manifests through your critically-minded and methodical quest for and attraction to meticulous and practical spirituality.

☿	Mercury	Libra	♎	1	Your Way of Communicating manifests through your analytical and balanced quest for and attraction to harmonious and logical identity development.
☿	Mercury	Libra	♎	2	Your Way of Communicating manifests through your analytical and balanced quest for and attraction to harmonious and logical values and ways to meet your needs.
☿	Mercury	Libra	♎	3	Your Way of Communicating manifests through your analytical and balanced quest for and attraction to harmonious and logical understanding of the world around you.
☿	Mercury	Libra	♎	4	Your Way of Communicating manifests through your analytical and balanced quest for and attraction to harmonious and logical emotional caretaking and traditions.
☿	Mercury	Libra	♎	5	Your Way of Communicating manifests through your analytical and balanced quest for and attraction to harmonious and logical creative expression.
☿	Mercury	Libra	♎	6	Your Way of Communicating manifests through your analytical and balanced quest for and attraction to harmonious and logical service for others.
☿	Mercury	Libra	♎	7	Your Way of Communicating manifests through your analytical and balanced quest for and attraction to harmonious and logical life teachers.
☿	Mercury	Libra	♎	8	Your Way of Communicating manifests through your analytical and balanced quest for and attraction to harmonious and logical intimate relationships.
☿	Mercury	Libra	♎	9	Your Way of Communicating manifests through your analytical and balanced quest for and attraction to harmonious and logical mastership of a body of knowledge.
☿	Mercury	Libra	♎	10	Your Way of Communicating manifests through your analytical and balanced quest for and attraction to harmonious and logical accomplishments.
☿	Mercury	Libra	♎	11	Your Way of Communicating manifests through your analytical and balanced quest for and attraction to harmonious and logical community.
☿	Mercury	Libra	♎	12	Your Way of Communicating manifests through your analytical and balanced quest for and attraction to harmonious and logical spirituality.

Astrology Unlocked by Philip Young, PhD

☿	Mercury	Scorpio	♏	1	Your Way of Communicating manifests through your intense and truth seeking quest for and attraction to penetrating and emotionally transformative identity development.
☿	Mercury	Scorpio	♏	2	Your Way of Communicating manifests through your intense and truth seeking quest for and attraction to penetrating and emotionally transformative values and ways to meet your needs.
☿	Mercury	Scorpio	♏	3	Your Way of Communicating manifests through your intense and truth seeking quest for and attraction to penetrating and emotionally transformative understanding of the world around you.
☿	Mercury	Scorpio	♏	4	Your Way of Communicating manifests through your intense and truth seeking quest for and attraction to penetrating and emotionally transformative caretaking and traditions.
☿	Mercury	Scorpio	♏	5	Your Way of Communicating manifests through your intense and truth seeking quest for and attraction to penetrating and emotionally transformative creative expression.
☿	Mercury	Scorpio	♏	6	Your Way of Communicating manifests through your intense and truth seeking quest for and attraction to penetrating and emotionally transformative service for others.
☿	Mercury	Scorpio	♏	7	Your Way of Communicating manifests through your intense and truth seeking quest for and attraction to penetrating and emotionally transformative life teachers.
☿	Mercury	Scorpio	♏	8	Your Way of Communicating manifests through your intense and truth seeking quest for and attraction to penetrating and emotionally transformative intimate relationships.
☿	Mercury	Scorpio	♏	9	Your Way of Communicating manifests through your intense and truth seeking quest for and attraction to penetrating and emotionally transformative mastership of a body of knowledge.
☿	Mercury	Scorpio	♏	10	Your Way of Communicating manifests through your intense and truth seeking quest for and attraction to penetrating and emotionally transformative careers
☿	Mercury	Scorpio	♏	11	Your Way of Communicating manifests through your intense and truth seeking quest for and attraction to penetrating and emotionally transformative community.
☿	Mercury	Scorpio	♏	12	Your Way of Communicating manifests through your intense and truth seeking quest for and attraction to penetrating and emotionally transformative spirituality.

	Mercury	Sagittarius	♐	1	Your Way of Communicating manifests through your wide-ranging and open-minded quest for and attraction to experiential and risk-taking identity development.
☿	Mercury	Sagittarius	♐	2	Your Way of Communicating manifests through your wide-ranging and open-minded quest for and attraction to experiential and risk-taking values and ways to meet your needs.
☿	Mercury	Sagittarius	♐	3	Your Way of Communicating manifests through your wide-ranging and open-minded quest for and attraction to experiential and risk-taking understanding of the world around you.
☿	Mercury	Sagittarius	♐	4	Your Way of Communicating manifests through your wide-ranging and open-minded quest for and attraction to experiential and risk-taking emotional caretaking and traditions.
☿	Mercury	Sagittarius	♐	5	Your Way of Communicating manifests through your wide-ranging and open-minded quest for and attraction to experiential and risk-taking creative expression.
☿	Mercury	Sagittarius	♐	6	Your Way of Communicating manifests through your wide-ranging and open-minded quest for and attraction to experiential and risk-taking service for others.
☿	Mercury	Sagittarius	♐	7	Your Way of Communicating manifests through your wide-ranging and open-minded quest for and attraction to experiential and risk-taking life teachers.
☿	Mercury	Sagittarius	♐	8	Your Way of Communicating manifests through your wide-ranging and open-minded quest for and attraction to experiential and risk-taking intimate relationships.
☿	Mercury	Sagittarius	♐	9	Your Way of Communicating manifests through your wide-ranging and open-minded quest for and attraction to experiential and risk-taking mastership of a body of knowledge.
☿	Mercury	Sagittarius	♐	10	Your Way of Communicating manifests through your wide-ranging and open-minded quest for and attraction to experiential and risk-taking accomplishments.
☿	Mercury	Sagittarius	♐	11	Your Way of Communicating manifests through your wide-ranging and open-minded quest for and attraction to experiential and risk-taking community.
☿	Mercury	Sagittarius	♐	12	Your Way of Communicating manifests through your wide-ranging and open-minded quest for and attraction to experiential and risk-taking spirituality.

☿	Mercury	Capricorn	♑	1	Your Way of Communicating manifests through your goal-driven and focused quest for and attraction to results-oriented and successful identity development.
☿	Mercury	Capricorn	♑	2	Your Way of Communicating manifests through your goal-driven and focused quest for and attraction to results-oriented and successful values and ways to meet your needs.
☿	Mercury	Capricorn	♑	3	Your Way of Communicating manifests through your goal-driven and focused quest for and attraction to results-oriented and successful understanding of the world around you.
☿	Mercury	Capricorn	♑	4	Your Way of Communicating manifests through your goal-driven and focused quest for and attraction to results-oriented and successful emotional caretaking and traditions.
☿	Mercury	Capricorn	♑	5	Your Way of Communicating manifests through your goal-driven and focused quest for and attraction to results-oriented and successful creative expression.
☿	Mercury	Capricorn	♑	6	Your Way of Communicating manifests through your goal-driven and focused quest for and attraction to results-oriented and successful service for others.
☿	Mercury	Capricorn	♑	7	Your Way of Communicating manifests through your goal-driven and focused quest for and attraction to results-oriented and successful life teachers.
☿	Mercury	Capricorn	♑	8	Your Way of Communicating manifests through your goal-driven and focused quest for and attraction to results-oriented and successful intimate relationships.
☿	Mercury	Capricorn	♑	9	Your Way of Communicating manifests through your goal-driven and focused quest for and attraction to results-oriented and successful mastership of a body of knowledge.
☿	Mercury	Capricorn	♑	10	Your Way of Communicating manifests through your goal-driven and focused quest for and attraction to results-oriented and successful accomplishments.
☿	Mercury	Capricorn	♑	11	Your Way of Communicating manifests through your goal-driven and focused quest for and attraction to results-oriented and successful community.
☿	Mercury	Capricorn	♑	12	Your Way of Communicating manifests through your goal-driven and focused quest for and attraction to results-oriented and successful spirituality.

Astrology Unlocked by Philip Young, PhD

☿	Mercury	Aquarius	♒	1	Your Way of Communicating manifests through your unconventional and idealistic quest for and attraction to authentic and non-traditional identity development.
☿	Mercury	Aquarius	♒	2	Your Way of Communicating manifests through your unconventional and idealistic quest for and attraction to authentic and non-traditional values and ways to meet your needs.
☿	Mercury	Aquarius	♒	3	Your Way of Communicating manifests through your unconventional and idealistic quest for and attraction to authentic and non-traditional understanding of the world around you.
☿	Mercury	Aquarius	♒	4	Your Way of Communicating manifests through your unconventional and idealistic quest for and attraction to authentic and non-traditional emotional caretaking and traditions.
☿	Mercury	Aquarius	♒	5	Your Way of Communicating manifests through your unconventional and idealistic quest for and attraction to authentic and non-traditional creative expression.
☿	Mercury	Aquarius	♒	6	Your Way of Communicating manifests through your unconventional and idealistic quest for and attraction to authentic and non-traditional service for others.
☿	Mercury	Aquarius	♒	7	Your Way of Communicating manifests through your unconventional and idealistic quest for and attraction to authentic and non-traditional life teachers.
☿	Mercury	Aquarius	♒	8	Your Way of Communicating manifests through your unconventional and idealistic quest for and attraction to authentic and non-traditional intimate relationships.
☿	Mercury	Aquarius	♒	9	Your Way of Communicating manifests through your unconventional and idealistic quest for and attraction to authentic and non-traditional mastership of a body of knowledge.
☿	Mercury	Aquarius	♒	10	Your Way of Communicating manifests through your unconventional and idealistic quest for and attraction to authentic and non-traditional accomplishments.
☿	Mercury	Aquarius	♒	11	Your Way of Communicating manifests through your unconventional and idealistic quest for and attraction to authentic and non-traditional community.
☿	Mercury	Aquarius	♒	12	Your Way of Communicating manifests through your unconventional and idealistic quest for and attraction to authentic and non-traditional spirituality.

☿	Mercury	Pisces	♓	1	Your Way of Communicating manifests through your imaginative and faithful quest for and attraction to consciousness-raising and soulful identity development.
☿	Mercury	Pisces	♓	2	Your Way of Communicating manifests through your imaginative and faithful quest for and attraction to consciousness-raising and soulful values and ways to meet your needs.
☿	Mercury	Pisces	♓	3	Your Way of Communicating manifests through your imaginative and faithful quest for and attraction to consciousness-raising and soulful understanding of the world around you.
☿	Mercury	Pisces	♓	4	Your Way of Communicating manifests through your imaginative and faithful quest for and attraction to consciousness-raising and soulful emotional caretaking and traditions.
☿	Mercury	Pisces	♓	5	Your Way of Communicating manifests through your imaginative and faithful quest for and attraction to consciousness-raising and soulful creative expression.
☿	Mercury	Pisces	♓	6	Your Way of Communicating manifests through your imaginative and faithful quest for and attraction to consciousness-raising and soulful service for others.
☿	Mercury	Pisces	♓	7	Your Way of Communicating manifests through your imaginative and faithful quest for and attraction to consciousness-raising and soulful life teachers.
☿	Mercury	Pisces	♓	8	Your Way of Communicating manifests through your imaginative and faithful quest for and attraction to consciousness-raising and soulful intimate relationships.
☿	Mercury	Pisces	♓	9	Your Way of Communicating manifests through your imaginative and faithful quest for and attraction to consciousness-raising and soulful mastership of a body of knowledge.
☿	Mercury	Pisces	♓	10	Your Way of Communicating manifests through your imaginative and faithful quest for and attraction to consciousness-raising and soulful accomplishments.
☿	Mercury	Pisces	♓	11	Your Way of Communicating manifests through your imaginative and faithful quest for and attraction to consciousness-raising and soulful community.
☿	Mercury	Pisces	♓	12	Your Way of Communicating manifests through your imaginative and faithful quest for and attraction to consciousness-raising and soulful spirituality.

Venus[25] | ♀

Energy Point Type: **Planet**
Co-Rules Sign: **Pisces**
Co-Rules House: **12**th
Element: **Water**
Key Phrase: **Way of Relating**

Venus represents your Way of Relating. Its placement in Sign and House reveals how we appreciate pleasure, beauty, art, creativity, our interactions with our environment, and our interactions with the people in our lives. In my case my Way of Relating is expressed through Fire (Aries) in my quest to serve (6th House). Fire's expression is pioneering, creative, and exploratory. In Aries the Element acts independently, heroically, and aggressively. So, my key phrase is *"Your Way of Relating manifests through your independent and heroic quest for and attraction to maverick and individualistic service for others."* In short, I prefer to work with and relate to people who are my equals and who can manage themselves, eschewing the role of manager and employee.

When you look up your own Venus in the Sign and House formula, think about the art you love, the music you prefer to listen to, the movies you spend your money on, and the kinds of people you find attractive and the kinds of people you attract. Consider Venus in Aquarius in the 8th House, *"Your Way of Relating manifests through your unconventional and idealistic quest for and attraction to authentic and non-traditional intimate relationships."* This configuration is perfect for a dominatrix, if a woman's chart, or a monk in a man's chart. With Aquarius ruling, any

---

[25] My Rulership placement of Venus breaks with astrological tradition, which places Venus as the ancient and modern Ruler of Taurus and Libra. Instead, I harken back to the origin myth of Aphrodite, which did not change when the Romans assigned the new name for the Goddess of Love. In her origin story, Aphrodite/Venus emerges from sea foam and is associated with the Element of Water. For this reason I have paired her with Neptune as the co-Ruler of Pisces. Like Mercury/Communication, Venus/Love is an energy that could easily hold Rulership in any sign and house. As we most often associate Love with emotions, the Water Rulership makes more sense and has born more fruitful results in my readings for clients. As Neptune represents the more ambiguous and mysterious power of universal love, I find Venus a reflection of Love manifest through the physical body. As a result of my reimagining the Rulership, the books I offer as references for additional reading will only reflect the traditional Rulership definitions. Regardless, the interpretation of Venus and its role as an Energy Point in the chart remains aligned to its assigned function even with this Elemental change.

Astrology Unlocked by Philip Young, PhD

kind of direction can be taken in terms of intimate relationships (8th House). If there is a desire for the conventional relationship, this individual will still find a way to make it unconventional and authentic. They may actually fall in love with their grade school sweetheart, date them in high school, then college, marry, and live happily ever after; certainly not the norm in reality, but an 8th House Aquarius Venus would be just the type to manifest Disney in the real world.

For more in depth reading about Venus, I recommend purchasing and reading:

- *Alan Oken's Complete Astrology* by Alan Oken (ISBN: 9780892541256)
- *Astrology for Beginners* by Joann Hampar (ISBN: 9780738711065)
- *Horoscope Symbols* by Robert Hand (ISBN: 0914918168)
- *The Inner Planets* by Liz Green & Howard Sasportas (ISBN: 0877287414)
- *The Inner Sky* by Steven Forrest (ISBN: 9780979067716)
- *Mythic Astrology Applied* by Ariel Guttman & Kenneth Johnson (ISBN: 0738704253)
- *Planets in Play* by Laurence Hillman (ISBN: 9781585425877)
- *Take Control with Astrology* by Lisa Tenzin-Dolma (ISBN: 9780071665049)

♀	Venus	Aries	♈	1	Your Way of Relating manifests through your independent and heroic quest for and attraction to maverick and individualistic identity development.
♀	Venus	Aries	♈	2	Your Way of Relating manifests through your independent and heroic quest for and attraction to maverick and individualistic values and ways to meet your needs.
♀	Venus	Aries	♈	3	Your Way of Relating manifests through your independent and heroic quest for and attraction to maverick and individualistic understanding of the world around you.
♀	Venus	Aries	♈	4	Your Way of Relating manifests through your independent and heroic quest for and attraction to maverick and individualistic emotional caretaking and traditions.
♀	Venus	Aries	♈	5	Your Way of Relating manifests through your independent and heroic quest for and attraction to maverick and individualistic creative expression.
♀	Venus	Aries	♈	6	Your Way of Relating manifests through your independent and heroic quest for and attraction to maverick and individualistic service for others.
♀	Venus	Aries	♈	7	Your Way of Relating manifests through your independent and heroic quest for and attraction to maverick and individualistic life teachers.
♀	Venus	Aries	♈	8	Your Way of Relating manifests through your independent and heroic quest for and attraction to maverick and individualistic intimate relationships.
♀	Venus	Aries	♈	9	Your Way of Relating manifests through your independent and heroic quest for and attraction to maverick and individualistic mastership of a body of knowledge.
♀	Venus	Aries	♈	10	Your Way of Relating manifests through your independent and heroic quest for and attraction to maverick and individualistic accomplishments.
♀	Venus	Aries	♈	11	Your Way of Relating manifests through your independent and heroic quest for and attraction to maverick and individualistic community.
♀	Venus	Aries	♈	12	Your Way of Relating manifests through your independent and heroic quest for and attraction to maverick and individualistic spirituality.

♀	Venus	Taurus	♉	1	Your Way of Relating manifests through your steadfast and persistent quest for and attraction to enduring and secure identity development.
♀	Venus	Taurus	♉	2	Your Way of Relating manifests through your steadfast and persistent quest for and attraction to enduring and secure values and ways to meet your needs.
♀	Venus	Taurus	♉	3	Your Way of Relating manifests through your steadfast and persistent quest for and attraction to enduring and secure understanding of the world around you.
♀	Venus	Taurus	♉	4	Your Way of Relating manifests through your steadfast and persistent quest for and attraction to enduring and secure emotional caretaking and traditions.
♀	Venus	Taurus	♉	5	Your Way of Relating manifests through your steadfast and persistent quest for and attraction to enduring and secure creative expression.
♀	Venus	Taurus	♉	6	Your Way of Relating manifests through your steadfast and persistent quest for and attraction to enduring and secure service for others.
♀	Venus	Taurus	♉	7	Your Way of Relating manifests through your steadfast and persistent quest for and attraction to enduring and secure life teachers.
♀	Venus	Taurus	♉	8	Your Way of Relating manifests through your steadfast and persistent quest for and attraction to enduring and secure intimate relationships.
♀	Venus	Taurus	♉	9	Your Way of Relating manifests through your steadfast and persistent quest for and attraction to enduring and secure mastership of a body of knowledge.
♀	Venus	Taurus	♉	10	Your Way of Relating manifests through your steadfast and persistent quest for and attraction to enduring and secure accomplishments.
♀	Venus	Taurus	♉	11	Your Way of Relating manifests through your steadfast and persistent quest for and attraction to enduring and secure community.
♀	Venus	Taurus	♉	12	Your Way of Relating manifests through your steadfast and persistent quest for and attraction to enduring and secure spirituality.

♀	Venus	Gemini	♊	1	Your Way of Relating manifests through your inquisitive and mentally agile quest for and attraction to ever changing and adaptable identity development.
♀	Venus	Gemini	♊	2	Your Way of Relating manifests through your inquisitive and mentally agile quest for and attraction to ever changing and adaptable values and ways to meet your needs.
♀	Venus	Gemini	♊	3	Your Way of Relating manifests through your inquisitive and mentally agile quest for and attraction to ever changing and adaptable understanding of the world around you.
♀	Venus	Gemini	♊	4	Your Way of Relating manifests through your inquisitive and mentally agile quest for and attraction to ever changing and adaptable emotional caretaking and traditions.
♀	Venus	Gemini	♊	5	Your Way of Relating manifests through your inquisitive and mentally agile quest for and attraction to ever changing and adaptable creative expression.
♀	Venus	Gemini	♊	6	Your Way of Relating manifests through your inquisitive and mentally agile quest for and attraction to ever changing and adaptable service for others.
♀	Venus	Gemini	♊	7	Your Way of Relating manifests through your inquisitive and mentally agile quest for and attraction to ever changing and adaptable life teachers.
♀	Venus	Gemini	♊	8	Your Way of Relating manifests through your inquisitive and mentally agile quest for and attraction to ever changing and adaptable intimate relationships.
♀	Venus	Gemini	♊	9	Your Way of Relating manifests through your inquisitive and mentally agile quest for and attraction to ever changing and adaptable mastership of a body of knowledge.
♀	Venus	Gemini	♊	10	Your Way of Relating manifests through your inquisitive and mentally agile quest for and attraction to ever changing and adaptable accomplishments.
♀	Venus	Gemini	♊	11	Your Way of Relating manifests through your inquisitive and mentally agile quest for and attraction to ever changing and adaptable community.
♀	Venus	Gemini	♊	12	Your Way of Relating manifests through your inquisitive and mentally agile quest for and attraction to ever changing and adaptable spirituality.

♀	Venus	Cancer	♋	1	Your Way of Relating manifests through your emotional and caring quest for and attraction to nurturing and supportive identity development.
♀	Venus	Cancer	♋	2	Your Way of Relating manifests through your emotional and caring quest for and attraction to nurturing and supportive values and ways to meet your needs.
♀	Venus	Cancer	♋	3	Your Way of Relating manifests through your emotional and caring quest for and attraction to nurturing and supportive understanding of the world around you.
♀	Venus	Cancer	♋	4	Your Way of Relating manifests through your emotional and caring quest for and attraction to nurturing and supportive emotional caretaking and traditions.
♀	Venus	Cancer	♋	5	Your Way of Relating manifests through your emotional and caring quest for and attraction to nurturing and supportive creative expression.
♀	Venus	Cancer	♋	6	Your Way of Relating manifests through your emotional and caring quest for and attraction to nurturing and supportive service for others.
♀	Venus	Cancer	♋	7	Your Way of Relating manifests through your emotional and caring quest for and attraction to nurturing and supportive life teachers.
♀	Venus	Cancer	♋	8	Your Way of Relating manifests through your emotional and caring quest for and attraction to nurturing and supportive intimate relationships.
♀	Venus	Cancer	♋	9	Your Way of Relating manifests through your emotional and caring quest for and attraction to nurturing and supportive mastership of a body of knowledge.
♀	Venus	Cancer	♋	10	Your Way of Relating manifests through your emotional and caring quest for and attraction to nurturing and supportive accomplishments.
♀	Venus	Cancer	♋	11	Your Way of Relating manifests through your emotional and caring quest for and attraction to nurturing and supportive community.
♀	Venus	Cancer	♋	12	Your Way of Relating manifests through your emotional and caring quest for and attraction to nurturing and supportive spirituality.

Astrology Unlocked by Philip Young, PhD

♀	Venus	Leo	♌	1	Your Way of Relating manifests through your energetic and dramatic quest for and attraction to creative and romantic identity development.
♀	Venus	Leo	♌	2	Your Way of Relating manifests through your energetic and dramatic quest for and attraction to creative and romantic values and ways to meet your needs.
♀	Venus	Leo	♌	3	Your Way of Relating manifests through your energetic and dramatic quest for and attraction to creative and romantic understanding of the world around you.
♀	Venus	Leo	♌	4	Your Way of Relating manifests through your energetic and dramatic quest for and attraction to creative and romantic emotional caretaking and traditions.
♀	Venus	Leo	♌	5	Your Way of Relating manifests through your energetic and dramatic quest for and attraction to creative and romantic creative expression.
♀	Venus	Leo	♌	6	Your Way of Relating manifests through your energetic and dramatic quest for and attraction to creative and romantic service for others.
♀	Venus	Leo	♌	7	Your Way of Relating manifests through your energetic and dramatic quest for and attraction to creative and romantic life teachers.
♀	Venus	Leo	♌	8	Your Way of Relating manifests through your energetic and dramatic quest for and attraction to creative and romantic intimate relationships.
♀	Venus	Leo	♌	9	Your Way of Relating manifests through your energetic and dramatic quest for and attraction to creative and romantic mastership of a body of knowledge.
♀	Venus	Leo	♌	10	Your Way of Relating manifests through your energetic and dramatic quest for and attraction to creative and romantic accomplishments.
♀	Venus	Leo	♌	11	Your Way of Relating manifests through your energetic and dramatic quest for and attraction to creative and romantic community.
♀	Venus	Leo	♌	12	Your Way of Relating manifests through your energetic and dramatic quest for and attraction to creative and romantic spirituality.

♀	Venus	Virgo	♍	1	Your Way of Relating manifests through your critically-minded and methodical quest for and attraction to meticulous and practical identity development.
♀	Venus	Virgo	♍	2	Your Way of Relating manifests through your critically-minded and methodical quest for and attraction to meticulous and practical values and ways to meet your needs.
♀	Venus	Virgo	♍	3	Your Way of Relating manifests through your critically-minded and methodical quest for and attraction to meticulous and practical understanding of the world around you.
♀	Venus	Virgo	♍	4	Your Way of Relating manifests through your critically-minded and methodical quest for and attraction to meticulous and practical emotional caretaking and traditions.
♀	Venus	Virgo	♍	5	Your Way of Relating manifests through your critically-minded and methodical quest for and attraction to meticulous and practical creative expression.
♀	Venus	Virgo	♍	6	Your Way of Relating manifests through your critically-minded and methodical quest for and attraction to meticulous and practical service for others.
♀	Venus	Virgo	♍	7	Your Way of Relating manifests through your critically-minded and methodical quest for and attraction to meticulous and practical life teachers.
♀	Venus	Virgo	♍	8	Your Way of Relating manifests through your critically-minded and methodical quest for and attraction to meticulous and practical intimate relationships.
♀	Venus	Virgo	♍	9	Your Way of Relating manifests through your critically-minded and methodical quest for and attraction to meticulous and practical mastership of a body of knowledge.
♀	Venus	Virgo	♍	10	Your Way of Relating manifests through your critically-minded and methodical quest for and attraction to meticulous and practical accomplishments.
♀	Venus	Virgo	♍	11	Your Way of Relating manifests through your critically-minded and methodical quest for and attraction to meticulous and practical community.
♀	Venus	Virgo	♍	12	Your Way of Relating manifests through your critically-minded and methodical quest for and attraction to meticulous and practical spirituality.

♀	Venus	Libra	♎	1	Your Way of Relating manifests through your analytical and balanced quest for and attraction to harmonious and logical identity development.
♀	Venus	Libra	♎	2	Your Way of Relating manifests through your analytical and balanced quest for and attraction to harmonious and logical values and ways to meet your needs.
♀	Venus	Libra	♎	3	Your Way of Relating manifests through your analytical and balanced quest for and attraction to harmonious and logical understanding of the world around you.
♀	Venus	Libra	♎	4	Your Way of Relating manifests through your analytical and balanced quest for and attraction to harmonious and logical emotional caretaking and traditions.
♀	Venus	Libra	♎	5	Your Way of Relating manifests through your analytical and balanced quest for and attraction to harmonious and logical creative expression.
♀	Venus	Libra	♎	6	Your Way of Relating manifests through your analytical and balanced quest for and attraction to harmonious and logical service for others.
♀	Venus	Libra	♎	7	Your Way of Relating manifests through your analytical and balanced quest for and attraction to harmonious and logical life teachers.
♀	Venus	Libra	♎	8	Your Way of Relating manifests through your analytical and balanced quest for and attraction to harmonious and logical intimate relationships.
♀	Venus	Libra	♎	9	Your Way of Relating manifests through your analytical and balanced quest for and attraction to harmonious and logical mastership of a body of knowledge.
♀	Venus	Libra	♎	10	Your Way of Relating manifests through your analytical and balanced quest for and attraction to harmonious and logical accomplishments.
♀	Venus	Libra	♎	11	Your Way of Relating manifests through your analytical and balanced quest for and attraction to harmonious and logical community.
♀	Venus	Libra	♎	12	Your Way of Relating manifests through your analytical and balanced quest for and attraction to harmonious and logical spirituality.

♀	Venus	Scorpio	♏	1	Your Way of Relating manifests through your intense and truth seeking quest for and attraction to penetrating and emotionally transformative identity development.
♀	Venus	Scorpio	♏	2	Your Way of Relating manifests through your intense and truth seeking quest for and attraction to penetrating and emotionally transformative values and ways to meet your needs.
♀	Venus	Scorpio	♏	3	Your Way of Relating manifests through your intense and truth seeking quest for and attraction to penetrating and emotionally transformative understanding of the world around you.
♀	Venus	Scorpio	♏	4	Your Way of Relating manifests through your intense and truth seeking quest for and attraction to penetrating and emotionally transformative emotional caretaking and traditions.
♀	Venus	Scorpio	♏	5	Your Way of Relating manifests through your intense and truth seeking quest for and attraction to penetrating and emotionally transformative creative expression.
♀	Venus	Scorpio	♏	6	Your Way of Relating manifests through your intense and truth seeking quest for and attraction to penetrating and emotionally transformative service for others.
♀	Venus	Scorpio	♏	7	Your Way of Relating manifests through your intense and truth seeking quest for and attraction to penetrating and emotionally transformative life teachers.
♀	Venus	Scorpio	♏	8	Your Way of Relating manifests through your intense and truth seeking quest for and attraction to penetrating and emotionally transformative intimate relationships.
♀	Venus	Scorpio	♏	9	Your Way of Relating manifests through your intense and truth seeking quest for and attraction to penetrating and emotionally transformative mastership of a body of knowledge.
♀	Venus	Scorpio	♏	10	Your Way of Relating manifests through your intense and truth seeking quest for and attraction to penetrating and emotionally transformative accomplishments.
♀	Venus	Scorpio	♏	11	Your Way of Relating manifests through your intense and truth seeking quest for and attraction to penetrating and emotionally transformative community.
♀	Venus	Scorpio	♏	12	Your Way of Relating manifests through your intense and truth seeking quest for and attraction to penetrating and emotionally transformative spirituality.

♀	Venus	Sagittarius	♐	1	Your Way of Relating manifests through your wide-ranging and open-minded quest for and attraction to experiential and risk-taking identity development.
♀	Venus	Sagittarius	♐	2	Your Way of Relating manifests through your wide-ranging and open-minded quest for and attraction to experiential and risk-taking values and ways to meet your needs.
♀	Venus	Sagittarius	♐	3	Your Way of Relating manifests through your wide-ranging and open-minded quest for and attraction to experiential and risk-taking understanding of the world around you.
♀	Venus	Sagittarius	♐	4	Your Way of Relating manifests through your wide-ranging and open-minded quest for and attraction to experiential and risk-taking emotional caretaking and traditions.
♀	Venus	Sagittarius	♐	5	Your Way of Relating manifests through your wide-ranging and open-minded quest for and attraction to experiential and risk-taking creative expression.
♀	Venus	Sagittarius	♐	6	Your Way of Relating manifests through your wide-ranging and open-minded quest for and attraction to experiential and risk-taking service for others.
♀	Venus	Sagittarius	♐	7	Your Way of Relating manifests through your wide-ranging and open-minded quest for and attraction to experiential and risk-taking life teachers.
♀	Venus	Sagittarius	♐	8	Your Way of Relating manifests through your wide-ranging and open-minded quest for and attraction to experiential and risk-taking intimate relationships.
♀	Venus	Sagittarius	♐	9	Your Way of Relating manifests through your wide-ranging and open-minded quest for and attraction to experiential and risk-taking mastership of a body of knowledge.
♀	Venus	Sagittarius	♐	10	Your Way of Relating manifests through your wide-ranging and open-minded quest for and attraction to experiential and risk-taking accomplishments.
♀	Venus	Sagittarius	♐	11	Your Way of Relating manifests through your wide-ranging and open-minded quest for and attraction to experiential and risk-taking community.
♀	Venus	Sagittarius	♐	12	Your Way of Relating manifests through your wide-ranging and open-minded quest for and attraction to experiential and risk-taking spirituality.

	Venus	Capricorn	♑	1	Your Way of Relating manifests through your goal-driven and focused quest for and attraction to results-oriented and successful identity development.
♀	Venus	Capricorn	♑	2	Your Way of Relating manifests through your goal-driven and focused quest for and attraction to results-oriented and successful values and ways to meet your needs.
♀	Venus	Capricorn	♑	3	Your Way of Relating manifests through your goal-driven and focused quest for and attraction to results-oriented and successful understanding of the world around you.
♀	Venus	Capricorn	♑	4	Your Way of Relating manifests through your goal-driven and focused quest for and attraction to results-oriented and successful emotional caretaking and traditions.
♀	Venus	Capricorn	♑	5	Your Way of Relating manifests through your goal-driven and focused quest for and attraction to results-oriented and successful creative expression.
♀	Venus	Capricorn	♑	6	Your Way of Relating manifests through your goal-driven and focused quest for and attraction to results-oriented and successful service for others.
♀	Venus	Capricorn	♑	7	Your Way of Relating manifests through your goal-driven and focused quest for and attraction to results-oriented and successful life teachers.
♀	Venus	Capricorn	♑	8	Your Way of Relating manifests through your goal-driven and focused quest for and attraction to results-oriented and successful intimate relationships.
♀	Venus	Capricorn	♑	9	Your Way of Relating manifests through your goal-driven and focused quest for and attraction to results-oriented and successful mastership of a body of knowledge.
♀	Venus	Capricorn	♑	10	Your Way of Relating manifests through your goal-driven and focused quest for and attraction to results-oriented and successful accomplishments.
♀	Venus	Capricorn	♑	11	Your Way of Relating manifests through your goal-driven and focused quest for and attraction to results-oriented and successful community.
♀	Venus	Capricorn	♑	12	Your Way of Relating manifests through your goal-driven and focused quest for and attraction to results-oriented and successful spirituality.

Astrology Unlocked by Philip Young, PhD

♀	Venus	Aquarius	♒	1	Your Way of Relating manifests through your unconventional and idealistic quest for and attraction to authentic and non-traditional identity development.
♀	Venus	Aquarius	♒	2	Your Way of Relating manifests through your unconventional and idealistic quest for and attraction to authentic and non-traditional values and ways to meet your needs.
♀	Venus	Aquarius	♒	3	Your Way of Relating manifests through your unconventional and idealistic quest for and attraction to authentic and non-traditional understanding of the world around you.
♀	Venus	Aquarius	♒	4	Your Way of Relating manifests through your unconventional and idealistic quest for and attraction to authentic and non-traditional emotional caretaking and traditions.
♀	Venus	Aquarius	♒	5	Your Way of Relating manifests through your unconventional and idealistic quest for and attraction to authentic and non-traditional creative expression.
♀	Venus	Aquarius	♒	6	Your Way of Relating manifests through your unconventional and idealistic quest for and attraction to authentic and non-traditional service for others.
♀	Venus	Aquarius	♒	7	Your Way of Relating manifests through your unconventional and idealistic quest for and attraction to authentic and non-traditional life teachers.
♀	Venus	Aquarius	♒	8	Your Way of Relating manifests through your unconventional and idealistic quest for and attraction to authentic and non-traditional intimate relationships.
♀	Venus	Aquarius	♒	9	Your Way of Relating manifests through your unconventional and idealistic quest for and attraction to authentic and non-traditional mastership of a body of knowledge.
♀	Venus	Aquarius	♒	10	Your Way of Relating manifests through your unconventional and idealistic quest for and attraction to authentic and non-traditional accomplishments.
♀	Venus	Aquarius	♒	11	Your Way of Relating manifests through your unconventional and idealistic quest for and attraction to authentic and non-traditional community.
♀	Venus	Aquarius	♒	12	Your Way of Relating manifests through your unconventional and idealistic quest for and attraction to authentic and non-traditional spirituality.

♀	Venus	Pisces	♓	1	Your Way of Relating manifests through your imaginative and faithful quest for and attraction to consciousness-raising and soulful identity development.
♀	Venus	Pisces	♓	2	Your Way of Relating manifests through your imaginative and faithful quest for and attraction to consciousness-raising and soulful values and ways to meet your needs.
♀	Venus	Pisces	♓	3	Your Way of Relating manifests through your imaginative and faithful quest for and attraction to consciousness-raising and soulful understanding of the world around you.
♀	Venus	Pisces	♓	4	Your Way of Relating manifests through your imaginative and faithful quest for and attraction to consciousness-raising and soulful emotional caretaking and traditions.
♀	Venus	Pisces	♓	5	Your Way of Relating manifests through your imaginative and faithful quest for and attraction to consciousness-raising and soulful creative expression.
♀	Venus	Pisces	♓	6	Your Way of Relating manifests through your imaginative and faithful quest for and attraction to consciousness-raising and soulful service for others.
♀	Venus	Pisces	♓	7	Your Way of Relating manifests through your imaginative and faithful quest for and attraction to consciousness-raising and soulful life teachers.
♀	Venus	Pisces	♓	8	Your Way of Relating manifests through your imaginative and faithful quest for and attraction to consciousness-raising and soulful intimate relationships.
♀	Venus	Pisces	♓	9	Your Way of Relating manifests through your imaginative and faithful quest for and attraction to consciousness-raising and soulful mastership of a body of knowledge.
♀	Venus	Pisces	♓	10	Your Way of Relating manifests through your imaginative and faithful quest for and attraction to consciousness-raising and soulful accomplishments.
♀	Venus	Pisces	♓	11	Your Way of Relating manifests through your imaginative and faithful quest for and attraction to consciousness-raising and soulful community.
♀	Venus	Pisces	♓	12	Your Way of Relating manifests through your imaginative and faithful quest for and attraction to consciousness-raising and soulful spirituality.

Mars | ♂

Energy Point Type: **Planet**
Co-Rules Sign: **Aries**
Co-Rules House: **1st**
Element: **Fire**
Key Phrase: **Way of Desire**

Mars represents your Way of Desire. Its placement in Sign and House reveals how we assert ourselves, where our aggression comes out, and where we are willing to fight for what we want. In my case my Way of Desire is expressed through Earth (Taurus) in my quest for knowledge from others (7th House). Earth's expression is accomplished, persistent, and practical. In Taurus the Element acts protectively, conservatively, and reliably. So, my key phrase is *"Your Way of Desire manifests through your steadfast and persistent quest for and attraction to enduring and secure life teachers."* In short, I desire to learn and have material security from and with my partners, business or intimate; and I am willing to go to great lengths to have that desire satisfied.

When you look up your own Mars in the Sign and House formula, think about the people, causes, and beliefs you would be willing to fight for, in battle or in personal defense, with your last breath. Now consider Mars in Cancer in the 8th House, *"Your Way of Desire manifests through your emotional and caring quest for and attraction to nurturing and supportive intimate relationships."* First and foremost, this individual will feel compelled to defend and protect his or her lover. The spiritual goal is to find a lover worthy of his or her desire and who will properly respect his or her willingness to fight, kill, or die to protect the lover. This person may be quite calm and even-tempered in every other area of his/her life, but not when it comes to how he/she feels about his/her intimate partner.

For more in depth reading about Mars, I recommend purchasing and reading:

- *Alan Oken's Complete Astrology* by Alan Oken (ISBN: 9780892541256)
- *Astrology for Beginners* by Joann Hampar (ISBN: 9780738711065)

- *Horoscope Symbols* by Robert Hand (ISBN: 0914918168)

- *The Inner Planets* by Liz Green & Howard Sasportas (ISBN: 0877287414)

- *The Inner Sky* by Steven Forrest (ISBN: 9780979067716)

- *Mythic Astrology Applied* by Ariel Guttman & Kenneth Johnson (ISBN: 0738704253)

- *Planets in Play* by Laurence Hillman (ISBN: 9781585425877)

- *Take Control with Astrology* by Lisa Tenzin-Dolma (ISBN: 9780071665049)

♂	Mars	Aries	♈	1	Your Way of Desire manifests through your independent and heroic quest for and attraction to maverick and individualistic identity development.
♂	Mars	Aries	♈	2	Your Way of Desire manifests through your independent and heroic quest for and attraction to maverick and individualistic values and ways to meet your needs.
♂	Mars	Aries	♈	3	Your Way of Desire manifests through your independent and heroic quest for and attraction to maverick and individualistic understanding of the world around you.
♂	Mars	Aries	♈	4	Your Way of Desire manifests through your independent and heroic quest for and attraction to maverick and individualistic emotional caretaking and traditions.
♂	Mars	Aries	♈	5	Your Way of Desire manifests through your independent and heroic quest for and attraction to maverick and individualistic creative expression.
♂	Mars	Aries	♈	6	Your Way of Desire manifests through your independent and heroic quest for and attraction to maverick and individualistic service for others.
♂	Mars	Aries	♈	7	Your Way of Desire manifests through your independent and heroic quest for and attraction to maverick and individualistic life teachers.
♂	Mars	Aries	♈	8	Your Way of Desire manifests through your independent and heroic quest for and attraction to maverick and individualistic intimate relationships.
♂	Mars	Aries	♈	9	Your Way of Desire manifests through your independent and heroic quest for and attraction to maverick and individualistic mastership of a body of knowledge
♂	Mars	Aries	♈	10	Your Way of Desire manifests through your independent and heroic quest for and attraction to maverick and individualistic accomplishments.
♂	Mars	Aries	♈	11	Your Way of Desire manifests through your independent and heroic quest for and attraction to maverick and individualistic community.
♂	Mars	Aries	♈	12	Your Way of Desire manifests through your independent and heroic quest for and attraction to maverick and individualistic spirituality.

	Mars	Taurus	♉	1	Your Way of Desire manifests through your steadfast and persistent quest for and attraction to enduring and secure identity development.
	Mars	Taurus	♉	2	Your Way of Desire manifests through your steadfast and persistent quest for and attraction to enduring and secure values and ways to meet your needs.
	Mars	Taurus	♉	3	Your Way of Desire manifests through your steadfast and persistent quest for and attraction to enduring and secure understanding of the world around you.
	Mars	Taurus	♉	4	Your Way of Desire manifests through your steadfast and persistent quest for and attraction to enduring and secure emotional caretaking and traditions.
	Mars	Taurus	♉	5	Your Way of Desire manifests through your steadfast and persistent quest for and attraction to enduring and secure creative expression.
	Mars	Taurus	♉	6	Your Way of Desire manifests through your steadfast and persistent quest for and attraction to enduring and secure service for others.
	Mars	Taurus	♉	7	Your Way of Desire manifests through your steadfast and persistent quest for and attraction to enduring and secure life teachers.
	Mars	Taurus	♉	8	Your Way of Desire manifests through your steadfast and persistent quest for and attraction to enduring and secure intimate relationships.
	Mars	Taurus	♉	9	Your Way of Desire manifests through your steadfast and persistent quest for and attraction to enduring and secure mastership of a body of knowledge
	Mars	Taurus	♉	10	Your Way of Desire manifests through your steadfast and persistent quest for and attraction to enduring and secure accomplishments.
	Mars	Taurus	♉	11	Your Way of Desire manifests through your steadfast and persistent quest for and attraction to enduring and secure community.
	Mars	Taurus	♉	12	Your Way of Desire manifests through your steadfast and persistent quest for and attraction to enduring and secure spirituality.

♂	Mars	Gemini	♊	1	Your Way of Desire manifests through your inquisitive and mentally agile quest for and attraction to ever changing and adaptable identity development.
♂	Mars	Gemini	♊	2	Your Way of Desire manifests through your inquisitive and mentally agile quest for and attraction to ever changing and adaptable values and ways to meet your needs.
♂	Mars	Gemini	♊	3	Your Way of Desire manifests through your inquisitive and mentally agile quest for and attraction to ever changing and adaptable understanding of the world around you.
♂	Mars	Gemini	♊	4	Your Way of Desire manifests through your inquisitive and mentally agile quest for and attraction to ever changing and adaptable emotional caretaking and traditions.
♂	Mars	Gemini	♊	5	Your Way of Desire manifests through your inquisitive and mentally agile quest for and attraction to ever changing and adaptable creative expression.
♂	Mars	Gemini	♊	6	Your Way of Desire manifests through your inquisitive and mentally agile quest for and attraction to ever changing and adaptable service for others.
♂	Mars	Gemini	♊	7	Your Way of Desire manifests through your inquisitive and mentally agile quest for and attraction to ever changing and adaptable life teachers.
♂	Mars	Gemini	♊	8	Your Way of Desire manifests through your inquisitive and mentally agile quest for and attraction to ever changing and adaptable intimate relationships.
♂	Mars	Gemini	♊	9	Your Way of Desire manifests through your inquisitive and mentally agile quest for and attraction to ever changing and adaptable mastership of a body of knowledge
♂	Mars	Gemini	♊	10	Your Way of Desire manifests through your inquisitive and mentally agile quest for and attraction to ever changing and adaptable accomplishments.
♂	Mars	Gemini	♊	11	Your Way of Desire manifests through your inquisitive and mentally agile quest for and attraction to ever changing and adaptable community.
♂	Mars	Gemini	♊	12	Your Way of Desire manifests through your inquisitive and mentally agile quest for and attraction to ever changing and adaptable spirituality.

Astrology Unlocked by Philip Young, PhD

♂	Mars	Cancer	♋	1	Your Way of Desire manifests through your emotional and caring quest for and attraction to nurturing and supportive identity development.
♂	Mars	Cancer	♋	2	Your Way of Desire manifests through your emotional and caring quest for and attraction to nurturing and supportive values and ways to meet your needs.
♂	Mars	Cancer	♋	3	Your Way of Desire manifests through your emotional and caring quest for and attraction to nurturing and supportive understanding of the world around you.
♂	Mars	Cancer	♋	4	Your Way of Desire manifests through your emotional and caring quest for and attraction to nurturing and supportive emotional caretaking and traditions.
♂	Mars	Cancer	♋	5	Your Way of Desire manifests through your emotional and caring quest for and attraction to nurturing and supportive creative expression.
♂	Mars	Cancer	♋	6	Your Way of Desire manifests through your emotional and caring quest for and attraction to nurturing and supportive service for others.
♂	Mars	Cancer	♋	7	Your Way of Desire manifests through your emotional and caring quest for and attraction to nurturing and supportive life teachers.
♂	Mars	Cancer	♋	8	Your Way of Desire manifests through your emotional and caring quest for and attraction to nurturing and supportive intimate relationships.
♂	Mars	Cancer	♋	9	Your Way of Desire manifests through your emotional and caring quest for and attraction to nurturing and supportive mastership of a body of knowledge
♂	Mars	Cancer	♋	10	Your Way of Desire manifests through your emotional and caring quest for and attraction to nurturing and supportive accomplishments.
♂	Mars	Cancer	♋	11	Your Way of Desire manifests through your emotional and caring quest for and attraction to nurturing and supportive community.
♂	Mars	Cancer	♋	12	Your Way of Desire manifests through your emotional and caring quest for and attraction to nurturing and supportive spirituality.

♂	Mars	Leo	♌	1	Your Way of Desire manifests through your energetic and dramatic quest for and attraction to creative and romantic identity development.
♂	Mars	Leo	♌	2	Your Way of Desire manifests through your energetic and dramatic quest for and attraction to creative and romantic values and ways to meet your needs.
♂	Mars	Leo	♌	3	Your Way of Desire manifests through your energetic and dramatic quest for and attraction to creative and romantic understanding of the world around you.
♂	Mars	Leo	♌	4	Your Way of Desire manifests through your energetic and dramatic quest for and attraction to creative and romantic emotional caretaking and traditions.
♂	Mars	Leo	♌	5	Your Way of Desire manifests through your energetic and dramatic quest for and attraction to creative and romantic creative expression.
♂	Mars	Leo	♌	6	Your Way of Desire manifests through your energetic and dramatic quest for and attraction to creative and romantic service for others.
♂	Mars	Leo	♌	7	Your Way of Desire manifests through your energetic and dramatic quest for and attraction to creative and romantic life teachers.
♂	Mars	Leo	♌	8	Your Way of Desire manifests through your energetic and dramatic quest for and attraction to creative and romantic intimate relationships.
♂	Mars	Leo	♌	9	Your Way of Desire manifests through your energetic and dramatic quest for and attraction to creative and romantic mastership of a body of knowledge
♂	Mars	Leo	♌	10	Your Way of Desire manifests through your energetic and dramatic quest for and attraction to creative and romantic accomplishments.
♂	Mars	Leo	♌	11	Your Way of Desire manifests through your energetic and dramatic quest for and attraction to creative and romantic community.
♂	Mars	Leo	♌	12	Your Way of Desire manifests through your energetic and dramatic quest for and attraction to creative and romantic spirituality.

♂	Mars	Virgo	♍	1	Your Way of Desire manifests through your critically-minded and methodical quest for and attraction to meticulous and practical identity development.
♂	Mars	Virgo	♍	2	Your Way of Desire manifests through your critically-minded and methodical quest for and attraction to meticulous and practical values and ways to meet your needs.
♂	Mars	Virgo	♍	3	Your Way of Desire manifests through your critically-minded and methodical quest for and attraction to meticulous and practical understanding of the world around you.
♂	Mars	Virgo	♍	4	Your Way of Desire manifests through your critically-minded and methodical quest for and attraction to meticulous and practical emotional caretaking and traditions.
♂	Mars	Virgo	♍	5	Your Way of Desire manifests through your critically-minded and methodical quest for and attraction to meticulous and practical creative expression.
♂	Mars	Virgo	♍	6	Your Way of Desire manifests through your critically-minded and methodical quest for and attraction to meticulous and practical service for others.
♂	Mars	Virgo	♍	7	Your Way of Desire manifests through your critically-minded and methodical quest for and attraction to meticulous and practical life teachers.
♂	Mars	Virgo	♍	8	Your Way of Desire manifests through your critically-minded and methodical quest for and attraction to meticulous and practical intimate relationships.
♂	Mars	Virgo	♍	9	Your Way of Desire manifests through your critically-minded and methodical quest for and attraction to meticulous and practical mastership of a body of knowledge
♂	Mars	Virgo	♍	10	Your Way of Desire manifests through your critically-minded and methodical quest for and attraction to meticulous and practical accomplishments.
♂	Mars	Virgo	♍	11	Your Way of Desire manifests through your critically-minded and methodical quest for and attraction to meticulous and practical community.
♂	Mars	Virgo	♍	12	Your Way of Desire manifests through your critically-minded and methodical quest for and attraction to meticulous and practical spirituality.

♂	Mars	Libra	♎	1	Your Way of Desire manifests through your analytical and balanced quest for and attraction to harmonious and logical identity development.
♂	Mars	Libra	♎	2	Your Way of Desire manifests through your analytical and balanced quest for and attraction to harmonious and logical values and ways to meet your needs.
♂	Mars	Libra	♎	3	Your Way of Desire manifests through your analytical and balanced quest for and attraction to harmonious and logical understanding of the world around you.
♂	Mars	Libra	♎	4	Your Way of Desire manifests through your analytical and balanced quest for and attraction to harmonious and logical emotional caretaking and traditions.
♂	Mars	Libra	♎	5	Your Way of Desire manifests through your analytical and balanced quest for and attraction to harmonious and logical creative expression.
♂	Mars	Libra	♎	6	Your Way of Desire manifests through your analytical and balanced quest for and attraction to harmonious and logical service for others.
♂	Mars	Libra	♎	7	Your Way of Desire manifests through your analytical and balanced quest for and attraction to harmonious and logical life teachers.
♂	Mars	Libra	♎	8	Your Way of Desire manifests through your analytical and balanced quest for and attraction to harmonious and logical intimate relationships.
♂	Mars	Libra	♎	9	Your Way of Desire manifests through your analytical and balanced quest for and attraction to harmonious and logical mastership of a body of knowledge
♂	Mars	Libra	♎	10	Your Way of Desire manifests through your analytical and balanced quest for and attraction to harmonious and logical accomplishments.
♂	Mars	Libra	♎	11	Your Way of Desire manifests through your analytical and balanced quest for and attraction to harmonious and logical community.
♂	Mars	Libra	♎	12	Your Way of Desire manifests through your analytical and balanced quest for and attraction to harmonious and logical spirituality.

	Mars	Scorpio	♏	1	Your Way of Desire manifests through your intense and truth seeking quest for and attraction to penetrating and emotionally transformative identity development.
♂	Mars	Scorpio	♏	2	Your Way of Desire manifests through your intense and truth seeking quest for and attraction to penetrating and emotionally transformative values and ways to meet your needs.
♂	Mars	Scorpio	♏	3	Your Way of Desire manifests through your intense and truth seeking quest for and attraction to penetrating and emotionally transformative understanding of the world around you.
♂	Mars	Scorpio	♏	4	Your Way of Desire manifests through your intense and truth seeking quest for and attraction to penetrating and emotionally transformative emotional caretaking and traditions.
♂	Mars	Scorpio	♏	5	Your Way of Desire manifests through your intense and truth seeking quest for and attraction to penetrating and emotionally transformative creative expression.
♂	Mars	Scorpio	♏	6	Your Way of Desire manifests through your intense and truth seeking quest for and attraction to penetrating and emotionally transformative service for others.
♂	Mars	Scorpio	♏	7	Your Way of Desire manifests through your intense and truth seeking quest for and attraction to penetrating and emotionally transformative life teachers.
♂	Mars	Scorpio	♏	8	Your Way of Desire manifests through your intense and truth seeking quest for and attraction to penetrating and emotionally transformative intimate relationships.
♂	Mars	Scorpio	♏	9	Your Way of Desire manifests through your intense and truth seeking quest for and attraction to penetrating and emotionally transformative mastership of a body of knowledge
♂	Mars	Scorpio	♏	10	Your Way of Desire manifests through your intense and truth seeking quest for and attraction to penetrating and emotionally transformative accomplishments.
♂	Mars	Scorpio	♏	11	Your Way of Desire manifests through your intense and truth seeking quest for and attraction to penetrating and emotionally transformative community.
♂	Mars	Scorpio	♏	12	Your Way of Desire manifests through your intense and truth seeking quest for and attraction to penetrating and emotionally transformative spirituality.

♂	Mars	Sagittarius	♐	1	Your Way of Desire manifests through your wide-ranging and open-minded quest for and attraction to experiential and risk-taking identity development.
♂	Mars	Sagittarius	♐	2	Your Way of Desire manifests through your wide-ranging and open-minded quest for and attraction to experiential and risk-taking values and ways to meet your needs.
♂	Mars	Sagittarius	♐	3	Your Way of Desire manifests through your wide-ranging and open-minded quest for and attraction to experiential and risk-taking understanding of the world around you.
♂	Mars	Sagittarius	♐	4	Your Way of Desire manifests through your wide-ranging and open-minded quest for and attraction to experiential and risk-taking emotional caretaking and traditions.
♂	Mars	Sagittarius	♐	5	Your Way of Desire manifests through your wide-ranging and open-minded quest for and attraction to experiential and risk-taking creative expression.
♂	Mars	Sagittarius	♐	6	Your Way of Desire manifests through your wide-ranging and open-minded quest for and attraction to experiential and risk-taking service for others.
♂	Mars	Sagittarius	♐	7	Your Way of Desire manifests through your wide-ranging and open-minded quest for and attraction to experiential and risk-taking life teachers.
♂	Mars	Sagittarius	♐	8	Your Way of Desire manifests through your wide-ranging and open-minded quest for and attraction to experiential and risk-taking intimate relationships.
♂	Mars	Sagittarius	♐	9	Your Way of Desire manifests through your wide-ranging and open-minded quest for and attraction to experiential and risk-taking mastership of a body of knowledge
♂	Mars	Sagittarius	♐	10	Your Way of Desire manifests through your wide-ranging and open-minded quest for and attraction to experiential and risk-taking accomplishments.
♂	Mars	Sagittarius	♐	11	Your Way of Desire manifests through your wide-ranging and open-minded quest for and attraction to experiential and risk-taking community.
♂	Mars	Sagittarius	♐	12	Your Way of Desire manifests through your wide-ranging and open-minded quest for and attraction to experiential and risk-taking spirituality.

♂	Mars	Capricorn	♑	1	Your Way of Desire manifests through your goal-driven and focused quest for and attraction to results-oriented and successful identity development.
♂	Mars	Capricorn	♑	2	Your Way of Desire manifests through your goal-driven and focused quest for and attraction to results-oriented and successful values and ways to meet your needs.
♂	Mars	Capricorn	♑	3	Your Way of Desire manifests through your goal-driven and focused quest for and attraction to results-oriented and successful understanding of the world around you.
♂	Mars	Capricorn	♑	4	Your Way of Desire manifests through your goal-driven and focused quest for and attraction to results-oriented and successful emotional caretaking and traditions.
♂	Mars	Capricorn	♑	5	Your Way of Desire manifests through your goal-driven and focused quest for and attraction to results-oriented and successful creative expression.
♂	Mars	Capricorn	♑	6	Your Way of Desire manifests through your goal-driven and focused quest for and attraction to results-oriented and successful service for others.
♂	Mars	Capricorn	♑	7	Your Way of Desire manifests through your goal-driven and focused quest for and attraction to results-oriented and successful life teachers.
♂	Mars	Capricorn	♑	8	Your Way of Desire manifests through your goal-driven and focused quest for and attraction to results-oriented and successful intimate relationships.
♂	Mars	Capricorn	♑	9	Your Way of Desire manifests through your goal-driven and focused quest for and attraction to results-oriented and successful mastership of a body of knowledge
♂	Mars	Capricorn	♑	10	Your Way of Desire manifests through your goal-driven and focused quest for and attraction to results-oriented and successful accomplishments.
♂	Mars	Capricorn	♑	11	Your Way of Desire manifests through your goal-driven and focused quest for and attraction to results-oriented and successful community.
♂	Mars	Capricorn	♑	12	Your Way of Desire manifests through your goal-driven and focused quest for and attraction to results-oriented and successful spirituality.

	Mars	Aquarius	♒	1	Your Way of Desire manifests through your unconventional and idealistic quest for and attraction to authentic and non-traditional identity development.
♂	Mars	Aquarius	♒	2	Your Way of Desire manifests through your unconventional and idealistic quest for and attraction to authentic and non-traditional values and ways to meet your needs.
♂	Mars	Aquarius	♒	3	Your Way of Desire manifests through your unconventional and idealistic quest for and attraction to authentic and non-traditional understanding of the world around you.
♂	Mars	Aquarius	♒	4	Your Way of Desire manifests through your unconventional and idealistic quest for and attraction to authentic and non-traditional emotional caretaking and traditions.
♂	Mars	Aquarius	♒	5	Your Way of Desire manifests through your unconventional and idealistic quest for and attraction to authentic and non-traditional creative expression.
♂	Mars	Aquarius	♒	6	Your Way of Desire manifests through your unconventional and idealistic quest for and attraction to authentic and non-traditional service for others.
♂	Mars	Aquarius	♒	7	Your Way of Desire manifests through your unconventional and idealistic quest for and attraction to authentic and non-traditional life teachers.
♂	Mars	Aquarius	♒	8	Your Way of Desire manifests through your unconventional and idealistic quest for and attraction to authentic and non-traditional intimate relationships.
♂	Mars	Aquarius	♒	9	Your Way of Desire manifests through your unconventional and idealistic quest for and attraction to authentic and non-traditional mastership of a body of knowledge
♂	Mars	Aquarius	♒	10	Your Way of Desire manifests through your unconventional and idealistic quest for and attraction to authentic and non-traditional accomplishments.
♂	Mars	Aquarius	♒	11	Your Way of Desire manifests through your unconventional and idealistic quest for and attraction to authentic and non-traditional community.
♂	Mars	Aquarius	♒	12	Your Way of Desire manifests through your unconventional and idealistic quest for and attraction to authentic and non-traditional spirituality.

Astrology Unlocked by Philip Young, PhD

♂	Mars	Pisces	♓	1	Your Way of Desire manifests through your imaginative and faithful quest for and attraction to consciousness-raising and soulful identity development.
♂	Mars	Pisces	♓	2	Your Way of Desire manifests through your imaginative and faithful quest for and attraction to consciousness-raising and soulful values and ways to meet your needs.
♂	Mars	Pisces	♓	3	Your Way of Desire manifests through your imaginative and faithful quest for and attraction to consciousness-raising and soulful understanding of the world around you.
♂	Mars	Pisces	♓	4	Your Way of Desire manifests through your imaginative and faithful quest for and attraction to consciousness-raising and soulful emotional caretaking and traditions.
♂	Mars	Pisces	♓	5	Your Way of Desire manifests through your imaginative and faithful quest for and attraction to consciousness-raising and soulful creative expression.
♂	Mars	Pisces	♓	6	Your Way of Desire manifests through your imaginative and faithful quest for and attraction to consciousness-raising and soulful service for others.
♂	Mars	Pisces	♓	7	Your Way of Desire manifests through your imaginative and faithful quest for and attraction to consciousness-raising and soulful life teachers.
♂	Mars	Pisces	♓	8	Your Way of Desire manifests through your imaginative and faithful quest for and attraction to consciousness-raising and soulful intimate relationships.
♂	Mars	Pisces	♓	9	Your Way of Desire manifests through your imaginative and faithful quest for and attraction to consciousness-raising and soulful mastership of a body of knowledge
♂	Mars	Pisces	♓	10	Your Way of Desire manifests through your imaginative and faithful quest for and attraction to consciousness-raising and soulful accomplishments.
♂	Mars	Pisces	♓	11	Your Way of Desire manifests through your imaginative and faithful quest for and attraction to consciousness-raising and soulful community.
♂	Mars	Pisces	♓	12	Your Way of Desire manifests through your imaginative and faithful quest for and attraction to consciousness-raising and soulful spirituality.

Jupiter | ♃

Energy Point Type: **Planet**

Co-Rules Sign: **Sagittarius**

Co-Rules House: **9th**

Element: **Fire**

Key Phrase: **Way of Exploring**

Jupiter represents your Way of Exploring. Its placement in Sign and House reveals how we expand and go out into the world to learn from experience. In my case my Way of Exploring is expressed through Fire (Leo) in my quest for public responsibility (10th House). Fire's expression is pioneering, creative, and exploratory. In Leo the Element acts dramatically, playfully, and romantically. So, my key phrase is *"Your Way of Exploring manifests through your energetic and dramatic quest for and attraction to creative and romantic career accomplishments."* In my career I can be very successful when I am able to perform for others and accomplish far-ranging goals.

When you look up your own Jupiter in the Sign and House formula, think about the how and where you like to explore, where you crave new experiences, and what subjects you want to learn at a very high level. Consider Jupiter in Pisces in the 2th House, *"Your Way of Exploring manifests through your imaginative and faithful quest for and attraction to consciousness-raising and soulful values and ways to meet your needs."* This individual might be perfectly suited to run a bed and breakfast (2nd House), especially one with a spiritual theme (Pisces), that would allow him or her to meet all kinds of new people each and every year (Jupiter). Before the discovery of Neptune, Jupiter Ruled Pisces and Sagittarius, so it gets a boost being in Pisces, giving the individual a naturally powerful and expansive spirituality that expresses itself in a constant pursuit of and expansion of values (2nd House) and may even be the way he or she brings resources into his or her home (2nd House), perhaps as a minister, life coach, or artist.

For more in depth reading about Jupiter, I recommend purchasing and reading:

- *Alan Oken's Complete Astrology* by Alan Oken (ISBN: 9780892541256)

- *Astrology for Beginners* by Joann Hampar (ISBN: 9780738711065)

- *Horoscope Symbols* by Robert Hand (ISBN: 0914918168)

- *The Inner Planets* by Liz Green & Howard Sasportas (ISBN: 0877287414)

- *The Inner Sky* by Steven Forrest (ISBN: 9780979067716)

- *Mythic Astrology Applied* by Ariel Guttman & Kenneth Johnson (ISBN: 0738704253)

- *Planets in Play* by Laurence Hillman (ISBN: 9781585425877)

- *Take Control with Astrology* by Lisa Tenzin-Dolma (ISBN: 9780071665049)

♃	Jupiter	Aries	♈	1	Your Way of Exploring manifests through your independent and heroic quest for and attraction to maverick and individualistic identity development.
♃	Jupiter	Aries	♈	2	Your Way of Exploring manifests through your independent and heroic quest for and attraction to maverick and individualistic values and ways to meet your needs.
♃	Jupiter	Aries	♈	3	Your Way of Exploring manifests through your independent and heroic quest for and attraction to maverick and individualistic understanding of the world around you.
♃	Jupiter	Aries	♈	4	Your Way of Exploring manifests through your independent and heroic quest for and attraction to maverick and individualistic emotional caretaking and traditions.
♃	Jupiter	Aries	♈	5	Your Way of Exploring manifests through your independent and heroic quest for and attraction to maverick and individualistic creative expression.
♃	Jupiter	Aries	♈	6	Your Way of Exploring manifests through your independent and heroic quest for and attraction to maverick and individualistic service for others.
♃	Jupiter	Aries	♈	7	Your Way of Exploring manifests through your independent and heroic quest for and attraction to maverick and individualistic life teachers.
♃	Jupiter	Aries	♈	8	Your Way of Exploring manifests through your independent and heroic quest for and attraction to maverick and individualistic intimate relationships.
♃	Jupiter	Aries	♈	9	Your Way of Exploring manifests through your independent and heroic quest for and attraction to maverick and individualistic mastership of a body of knowledge or life experience.
♃	Jupiter	Aries	♈	10	Your Way of Exploring manifests through your independent and heroic quest for and attraction to maverick and individualistic accomplishments.
♃	Jupiter	Aries	♈	11	Your Way of Exploring manifests through your independent and heroic quest for and attraction to maverick and individualistic community.
♃	Jupiter	Aries	♈	12	Your Way of Exploring manifests through your independent and heroic quest for and attraction to maverick and individualistic spirituality.

♃	Jupiter	Taurus	♉	1	Your Way of Exploring manifests through your steadfast and persistent quest for and attraction to enduring and secure identity development.
♃	Jupiter	Taurus	♉	2	Your Way of Exploring manifests through your steadfast and persistent quest for and attraction to enduring and secure values and ways to meet your needs.
♃	Jupiter	Taurus	♉	3	Your Way of Exploring manifests through your steadfast and persistent quest for and attraction to enduring and secure understanding of the world around you.
♃	Jupiter	Taurus	♉	4	Your Way of Exploring manifests through your steadfast and persistent quest for and attraction to enduring and secure emotional caretaking and traditions.
♃	Jupiter	Taurus	♉	5	Your Way of Exploring manifests through your steadfast and persistent quest for and attraction to enduring and secure creative expression.
♃	Jupiter	Taurus	♉	6	Your Way of Exploring manifests through your steadfast and persistent quest for and attraction to enduring and secure service for others.
♃	Jupiter	Taurus	♉	7	Your Way of Exploring manifests through your steadfast and persistent quest for and attraction to enduring and secure life teachers.
♃	Jupiter	Taurus	♉	8	Your Way of Exploring manifests through your steadfast and persistent quest for and attraction to enduring and secure intimate relationships.
♃	Jupiter	Taurus	♉	9	Your Way of Exploring manifests through your steadfast and persistent quest for and attraction to enduring and secure mastership of a body of knowledge or life experience.
♃	Jupiter	Taurus	♉	10	Your Way of Exploring manifests through your steadfast and persistent quest for and attraction to enduring and secure accomplishments.
♃	Jupiter	Taurus	♉	11	Your Way of Exploring manifests through your steadfast and persistent quest for and attraction to enduring and secure community.
♃	Jupiter	Taurus	♉	12	Your Way of Exploring manifests through your steadfast and persistent quest for and attraction to enduring and secure spirituality.

♃	Jupiter	Gemini	♊	1	Your Way of Exploring manifests through your inquisitive and mentally agile quest for and attraction to ever changing and adaptable identity development.
♃	Jupiter	Gemini	♊	2	Your Way of Exploring manifests through your inquisitive and mentally agile quest for and attraction to ever changing and adaptable values and ways to meet your needs.
♃	Jupiter	Gemini	♊	3	Your Way of Exploring manifests through your inquisitive and mentally agile quest for and attraction to ever changing and adaptable understanding of the world around you.
♃	Jupiter	Gemini	♊	4	Your Way of Exploring manifests through your inquisitive and mentally agile quest for and attraction to ever changing and adaptable emotional caretaking and traditions.
♃	Jupiter	Gemini	♊	5	Your Way of Exploring manifests through your inquisitive and mentally agile quest for and attraction to ever changing and adaptable creative expression.
♃	Jupiter	Gemini	♊	6	Your Way of Exploring manifests through your inquisitive and mentally agile quest for and attraction to ever changing and adaptable service for others.
♃	Jupiter	Gemini	♊	7	Your Way of Exploring manifests through your inquisitive and mentally agile quest for and attraction to ever changing and adaptable life teachers.
♃	Jupiter	Gemini	♊	8	Your Way of Exploring manifests through your inquisitive and mentally agile quest for and attraction to ever changing and adaptable intimate relationships.
♃	Jupiter	Gemini	♊	9	Your Way of Exploring manifests through your inquisitive and mentally agile quest for and attraction to ever changing and adaptable mastership of a body of knowledge or life experience.
♃	Jupiter	Gemini	♊	10	Your Way of Exploring manifests through your inquisitive and mentally agile quest for and attraction to ever changing and adaptable accomplishments.
♃	Jupiter	Gemini	♊	11	Your Way of Exploring manifests through your inquisitive and mentally agile quest for and attraction to ever changing and adaptable community.
♃	Jupiter	Gemini	♊	12	Your Way of Exploring manifests through your inquisitive and mentally agile quest for and attraction to ever changing and adaptable spirituality.

♃	Jupiter	Cancer	♋	1	Your Way of Exploring manifests through your emotional and caring quest for and attraction to nurturing and supportive identity development.
♃	Jupiter	Cancer	♋	2	Your Way of Exploring manifests through your emotional and caring quest for and attraction to nurturing and supportive values and ways to meet your needs.
♃	Jupiter	Cancer	♋	3	Your Way of Exploring manifests through your emotional and caring quest for and attraction to nurturing and supportive understanding of the world around you.
♃	Jupiter	Cancer	♋	4	Your Way of Exploring manifests through your emotional and caring quest for and attraction to nurturing and supportive emotional caretaking and traditions.
♃	Jupiter	Cancer	♋	5	Your Way of Exploring manifests through your emotional and caring quest for and attraction to nurturing and supportive creative expression.
♃	Jupiter	Cancer	♋	6	Your Way of Exploring manifests through your emotional and caring quest for and attraction to nurturing and supportive service for others.
♃	Jupiter	Cancer	♋	7	Your Way of Exploring manifests through your emotional and caring quest for and attraction to nurturing and supportive life teachers.
♃	Jupiter	Cancer	♋	8	Your Way of Exploring manifests through your emotional and caring quest for and attraction to nurturing and supportive intimate relationships.
♃	Jupiter	Cancer	♋	9	Your Way of Exploring manifests through your emotional and caring quest for and attraction to nurturing and supportive mastership of a body of knowledge or life experience.
♃	Jupiter	Cancer	♋	10	Your Way of Exploring manifests through your emotional and caring quest for and attraction to nurturing and supportive accomplishments.
♃	Jupiter	Cancer	♋	11	Your Way of Exploring manifests through your emotional and caring quest for and attraction to nurturing and supportive community.
♃	Jupiter	Cancer	♋	12	Your Way of Exploring manifests through your emotional and caring quest for and attraction to nurturing and supportive spirituality.

♃	Jupiter	Leo	♌	1	Your Way of Exploring manifests through your energetic and dramatic quest for and attraction to creative and romantic identity development.
♃	Jupiter	Leo	♌	2	Your Way of Exploring manifests through your energetic and dramatic quest for and attraction to creative and romantic values and ways to meet your needs.
♃	Jupiter	Leo	♌	3	Your Way of Exploring manifests through your energetic and dramatic quest for and attraction to creative and romantic understanding of the world around you.
♃	Jupiter	Leo	♌	4	Your Way of Exploring manifests through your energetic and dramatic quest for and attraction to creative and romantic emotional caretaking and traditions.
♃	Jupiter	Leo	♌	5	Your Way of Exploring manifests through your energetic and dramatic quest for and attraction to creative and romantic creative expression.
♃	Jupiter	Leo	♌	6	Your Way of Exploring manifests through your energetic and dramatic quest for and attraction to creative and romantic service for others.
♃	Jupiter	Leo	♌	7	Your Way of Exploring manifests through your energetic and dramatic quest for and attraction to creative and romantic life teachers.
♃	Jupiter	Leo	♌	8	Your Way of Exploring manifests through your energetic and dramatic quest for and attraction to creative and romantic intimate relationships.
♃	Jupiter	Leo	♌	9	Your Way of Exploring manifests through your energetic and dramatic quest for and attraction to creative and romantic mastership of a body of knowledge or life experience.
♃	Jupiter	Leo	♌	10	Your Way of Exploring manifests through your energetic and dramatic quest for and attraction to creative and romantic accomplishments.
♃	Jupiter	Leo	♌	11	Your Way of Exploring manifests through your energetic and dramatic quest for and attraction to creative and romantic community.
♃	Jupiter	Leo	♌	12	Your Way of Exploring manifests through your energetic and dramatic quest for and attraction to creative and romantic spirituality.

♃	Jupiter	Virgo	♍	1	Your Way of Exploring manifests through your critically-minded and methodical quest for and attraction to meticulous and practical identity development.
♃	Jupiter	Virgo	♍	2	Your Way of Exploring manifests through your critically-minded and methodical quest for and attraction to meticulous and practical values and ways to meet your needs.
♃	Jupiter	Virgo	♍	3	Your Way of Exploring manifests through your critically-minded and methodical quest for and attraction to meticulous and practical understanding of the world around you.
♃	Jupiter	Virgo	♍	4	Your Way of Exploring manifests through your critically-minded and methodical quest for and attraction to meticulous and practical emotional caretaking and traditions.
♃	Jupiter	Virgo	♍	5	Your Way of Exploring manifests through your critically-minded and methodical quest for and attraction to meticulous and practical creative expression.
♃	Jupiter	Virgo	♍	6	Your Way of Exploring manifests through your critically-minded and methodical quest for and attraction to meticulous and practical service for others.
♃	Jupiter	Virgo	♍	7	Your Way of Exploring manifests through your critically-minded and methodical quest for and attraction to meticulous and practical life teachers.
♃	Jupiter	Virgo	♍	8	Your Way of Exploring manifests through your critically-minded and methodical quest for and attraction to meticulous and practical intimate relationships.
♃	Jupiter	Virgo	♍	9	Your Way of Exploring manifests through your critically-minded and methodical quest for and attraction to meticulous and practical mastership of a body of knowledge or life experience.
♃	Jupiter	Virgo	♍	10	Your Way of Exploring manifests through your critically-minded and methodical quest for and attraction to meticulous and practical accomplishments.
♃	Jupiter	Virgo	♍	11	Your Way of Exploring manifests through your critically-minded and methodical quest for and attraction to meticulous and practical community.
♃	Jupiter	Virgo	♍	12	Your Way of Exploring manifests through your critically-minded and methodical quest for and attraction to meticulous and practical spirituality.

♃	Jupiter	Libra	♎	1	Your Way of Exploring manifests through your analytical and balanced quest for and attraction to harmonious and logical identity development.
♃	Jupiter	Libra	♎	2	Your Way of Exploring manifests through your analytical and balanced quest for and attraction to harmonious and logical values and ways to meet your needs.
♃	Jupiter	Libra	♎	3	Your Way of Exploring manifests through your analytical and balanced quest for and attraction to harmonious and logical understanding of the world around you.
♃	Jupiter	Libra	♎	4	Your Way of Exploring manifests through your analytical and balanced quest for and attraction to harmonious and logical emotional caretaking and traditions.
♃	Jupiter	Libra	♎	5	Your Way of Exploring manifests through your analytical and balanced quest for and attraction to harmonious and logical creative expression.
♃	Jupiter	Libra	♎	6	Your Way of Exploring manifests through your analytical and balanced quest for and attraction to harmonious and logical service for others.
♃	Jupiter	Libra	♎	7	Your Way of Exploring manifests through your analytical and balanced quest for and attraction to harmonious and logical life teachers.
♃	Jupiter	Libra	♎	8	Your Way of Exploring manifests through your analytical and balanced quest for and attraction to harmonious and logical intimate relationships.
♃	Jupiter	Libra	♎	9	Your Way of Exploring manifests through your analytical and balanced quest for and attraction to harmonious and logical mastership of a body of knowledge or life experience.
♃	Jupiter	Libra	♎	10	Your Way of Exploring manifests through your analytical and balanced quest for and attraction to harmonious and logical accomplishments.
♃	Jupiter	Libra	♎	11	Your Way of Exploring manifests through your analytical and balanced quest for and attraction to harmonious and logical community.
♃	Jupiter	Libra	♎	12	Your Way of Exploring manifests through your analytical and balanced quest for and attraction to harmonious and logical spirituality.

♃	Jupiter	Scorpio	♏	1	Your Way of Exploring manifests through your intense and truth seeking quest for and attraction to penetrating and emotionally transformative identity development.
♃	Jupiter	Scorpio	♏	2	Your Way of Exploring manifests through your intense and truth seeking quest for and attraction to penetrating and emotionally transformative values and ways to meet your needs.
♃	Jupiter	Scorpio	♏	3	Your Way of Exploring manifests through your intense and truth seeking quest for and attraction to penetrating and emotionally transformative understanding of the world around you.
♃	Jupiter	Scorpio	♏	4	Your Way of Exploring manifests through your intense and truth seeking quest for and attraction to penetrating and emotionally transformative emotional caretaking and traditions.
♃	Jupiter	Scorpio	♏	5	Your Way of Exploring manifests through your intense and truth seeking quest for and attraction to penetrating and emotionally transformative creative expression.
♃	Jupiter	Scorpio	♏	6	Your Way of Exploring manifests through your intense and truth seeking quest for and attraction to penetrating and emotionally transformative service for others.
♃	Jupiter	Scorpio	♏	7	Your Way of Exploring manifests through your intense and truth seeking quest for and attraction to penetrating and emotionally transformative life teachers.
♃	Jupiter	Scorpio	♏	8	Your Way of Exploring manifests through your intense and truth seeking quest for and attraction to penetrating and emotionally transformative intimate relationships.
♃	Jupiter	Scorpio	♏	9	Your Way of Exploring manifests through your intense and truth seeking quest for and attraction to penetrating and emotionally transformative mastership of a body of knowledge or life experience.
♃	Jupiter	Scorpio	♏	10	Your Way of Exploring manifests through your intense and truth seeking quest for and attraction to penetrating and emotionally transformative accomplishments.
♃	Jupiter	Scorpio	♏	11	Your Way of Exploring manifests through your intense and truth seeking quest for and attraction to penetrating and emotionally transformative community.
♃	Jupiter	Scorpio	♏	12	Your Way of Exploring manifests through your intense and truth seeking quest for and attraction to penetrating and emotionally transformative spirituality.

♃	Jupiter	Sagittarius	♐	1	Your Way of Exploring manifests through your wide-ranging and open-minded quest for and attraction to experiential and risk-taking identity development.
♃	Jupiter	Sagittarius	♐	2	Your Way of Exploring manifests through your wide-ranging and open-minded quest for and attraction to experiential and risk-taking values and ways to meet your needs.
♃	Jupiter	Sagittarius	♐	3	Your Way of Exploring manifests through your wide-ranging and open-minded quest for and attraction to experiential and risk-taking understanding of the world around you.
♃	Jupiter	Sagittarius	♐	4	Your Way of Exploring manifests through your wide-ranging and open-minded quest for and attraction to experiential and risk-taking emotional caretaking and traditions.
♃	Jupiter	Sagittarius	♐	5	Your Way of Exploring manifests through your wide-ranging and open-minded quest for and attraction to experiential and risk-taking creative expression.
♃	Jupiter	Sagittarius	♐	6	Your Way of Exploring manifests through your wide-ranging and open-minded quest for and attraction to experiential and risk-taking service for others.
♃	Jupiter	Sagittarius	♐	7	Your Way of Exploring manifests through your wide-ranging and open-minded quest for and attraction to experiential and risk-taking life teachers.
♃	Jupiter	Sagittarius	♐	8	Your Way of Exploring manifests through your wide-ranging and open-minded quest for and attraction to experiential and risk-taking intimate relationships.
♃	Jupiter	Sagittarius	♐	9	Your Way of Exploring manifests through your wide-ranging and open-minded quest for and attraction to experiential and risk-taking mastership of a body of knowledge or life experience.
♃	Jupiter	Sagittarius	♐	10	Your Way of Exploring manifests through your wide-ranging and open-minded quest for and attraction to experiential and risk-taking accomplishments.
♃	Jupiter	Sagittarius	♐	11	Your Way of Exploring manifests through your wide-ranging and open-minded quest for and attraction to experiential and risk-taking community.
♃	Jupiter	Sagittarius	♐	12	Your Way of Exploring manifests through your wide-ranging and open-minded quest for and attraction to experiential and risk-taking spirituality.

♃	Jupiter	Capricorn	♑	1	Your Way of Exploring manifests through your goal-driven and focused quest for and attraction to results-oriented and successful identity development.
♃	Jupiter	Capricorn	♑	2	Your Way of Exploring manifests through your goal-driven and focused quest for and attraction to results-oriented and successful values and ways to meet your needs.
♃	Jupiter	Capricorn	♑	3	Your Way of Exploring manifests through your goal-driven and focused quest for and attraction to results-oriented and successful understanding of the world around you.
♃	Jupiter	Capricorn	♑	4	Your Way of Exploring manifests through your goal-driven and focused quest for and attraction to results-oriented and successful emotional caretaking and traditions.
♃	Jupiter	Capricorn	♑	5	Your Way of Exploring manifests through your goal-driven and focused quest for and attraction to results-oriented and successful creative expression.
♃	Jupiter	Capricorn	♑	6	Your Way of Exploring manifests through your goal-driven and focused quest for and attraction to results-oriented and successful service for others.
♃	Jupiter	Capricorn	♑	7	Your Way of Exploring manifests through your goal-driven and focused quest for and attraction to results-oriented and successful life teachers.
♃	Jupiter	Capricorn	♑	8	Your Way of Exploring manifests through your goal-driven and focused quest for and attraction to results-oriented and successful intimate relationships.
♃	Jupiter	Capricorn	♑	9	Your Way of Exploring manifests through your goal-driven and focused quest for and attraction to results-oriented and successful mastership of a body of knowledge or life experience.
♃	Jupiter	Capricorn	♑	10	Your Way of Exploring manifests through your goal-driven and focused quest for and attraction to results-oriented and successful accomplishments.
♃	Jupiter	Capricorn	♑	11	Your Way of Exploring manifests through your goal-driven and focused quest for and attraction to results-oriented and successful community.
♃	Jupiter	Capricorn	♑	12	Your Way of Exploring manifests through your goal-driven and focused quest for and attraction to results-oriented and successful spirituality.

♃	Jupiter	Aquarius	♒	1	Your Way of Exploring manifests through your unconventional and idealistic quest for and attraction to authentic and non-traditional identity development.
♃	Jupiter	Aquarius	♒	2	Your Way of Exploring manifests through your unconventional and idealistic quest for and attraction to authentic and non-traditional values and ways to meet your needs.
♃	Jupiter	Aquarius	♒	3	Your Way of Exploring manifests through your unconventional and idealistic quest for and attraction to authentic and non-traditional understanding of the world around you.
♃	Jupiter	Aquarius	♒	4	Your Way of Exploring manifests through your unconventional and idealistic quest for and attraction to authentic and non-traditional emotional caretaking and traditions.
♃	Jupiter	Aquarius	♒	5	Your Way of Exploring manifests through your unconventional and idealistic quest for and attraction to authentic and non-traditional creative expression.
♃	Jupiter	Aquarius	♒	6	Your Way of Exploring manifests through your unconventional and idealistic quest for and attraction to authentic and non-traditional service for others.
♃	Jupiter	Aquarius	♒	7	Your Way of Exploring manifests through your unconventional and idealistic quest for and attraction to authentic and non-traditional life teachers.
♃	Jupiter	Aquarius	♒	8	Your Way of Exploring manifests through your unconventional and idealistic quest for and attraction to authentic and non-traditional intimate relationships.
♃	Jupiter	Aquarius	♒	9	Your Way of Exploring manifests through your unconventional and idealistic quest for and attraction to authentic and non-traditional mastership of a body of knowledge or life experience.
♃	Jupiter	Aquarius	♒	10	Your Way of Exploring manifests through your unconventional and idealistic quest for and attraction to authentic and non-traditional accomplishments.
♃	Jupiter	Aquarius	♒	11	Your Way of Exploring manifests through your unconventional and idealistic quest for and attraction to authentic and non-traditional community.
♃	Jupiter	Aquarius	♒	12	Your Way of Exploring manifests through your unconventional and idealistic quest for and attraction to authentic and non-traditional spirituality.

♃	Jupiter	Pisces	♓	1	Your Way of Exploring manifests through your imaginative and faithful quest for and attraction to consciousness-raising and soulful identity development.
♃	Jupiter	Pisces	♓	2	Your Way of Exploring manifests through your imaginative and faithful quest for and attraction to consciousness-raising and soulful values and ways to meet your needs.
♃	Jupiter	Pisces	♓	3	Your Way of Exploring manifests through your imaginative and faithful quest for and attraction to consciousness-raising and soulful understanding of the world around you.
♃	Jupiter	Pisces	♓	4	Your Way of Exploring manifests through your imaginative and faithful quest for and attraction to consciousness-raising and soulful emotional caretaking and traditions.
♃	Jupiter	Pisces	♓	5	Your Way of Exploring manifests through your imaginative and faithful quest for and attraction to consciousness-raising and soulful creative expression.
♃	Jupiter	Pisces	♓	6	Your Way of Exploring manifests through your imaginative and faithful quest for and attraction to consciousness-raising and soulful service for others.
♃	Jupiter	Pisces	♓	7	Your Way of Exploring manifests through your imaginative and faithful quest for and attraction to consciousness-raising and soulful life teachers.
♃	Jupiter	Pisces	♓	8	Your Way of Exploring manifests through your imaginative and faithful quest for and attraction to consciousness-raising and soulful intimate relationships.
♃	Jupiter	Pisces	♓	9	Your Way of Exploring manifests through your imaginative and faithful quest for and attraction to consciousness-raising and soulful mastership of a body of knowledge or life experience.
♃	Jupiter	Pisces	♓	10	Your Way of Exploring manifests through your imaginative and faithful quest for and attraction to consciousness-raising and soulful accomplishments.
♃	Jupiter	Pisces	♓	11	Your Way of Exploring manifests through your imaginative and faithful quest for and attraction to consciousness-raising and soulful community.
♃	Jupiter	Pisces	♓	12	Your Way of Exploring manifests through your imaginative and faithful quest for and attraction to consciousness-raising and soulful spirituality.

Saturn | ♄

Energy Point Type: **Planet**
Co-Rules Sign: **Capricorn**
Co-House: **10ᵗʰ**
Element: **Earth**
Key Phrase: **Way of Structure**

Saturn represents your Way of Structure. Its placement in Sign and House reveals how we want to structure our lives and where we face particular restrictions that we must overcome or accept. In my case my Way of Structure is expressed through Fire (Aries) in my quest for service (6ᵗʰ House). Fire's expression is pioneering, creative, and exploratory. In Aries the Element acts independently, heroically, and aggressively. So, my key phrase is *"Your Way of Structure manifests through your independent and heroic quest for and attraction to maverick and individualistic service for others."* In short, I complete tasks and meet deadlines best when I am left alone to structure my own process and timetable. Micro-managing me is a very bad idea.

When you look up your own Saturn in the Sign and House formula, think about how you structure your life (Sign) and where you face and must overcome/accept your limitations (House). Saturn restricts us to test us; and when we follow its structured energy, we often find its grace. Consider Saturn in Cancer in the 9ᵗʰ House, *"Your Way of Structure manifests through your emotional and caring quest for and attraction to nurturing and supportive mastership of a body of knowledge."* This placement is great for a person interested in the medical or psychological fields, especially if their goal is to advance knowledge and then one day teach that knowledge. The 9ᵗʰ House is about authority, which comes through mastership, either by practice, research, or study (or, more likely, all three). Since the 9ᵗʰ House also Rules authoritative institutions (like the church, higher education, and specialized fields), Saturn is particularly well-suited to help the individual develop at a high level and "go the distance" in his or her chosen field of study and practice.

Astrology Unlocked by Philip Young, PhD

For more in depth reading about Saturn, I recommend purchasing and reading:

- *Alan Oken's Complete Astrology* by Alan Oken (ISBN: 9780892541256)
- *Astrology for Beginners* by Joann Hampar (ISBN: 9780738711065)
- *Horoscope Symbols* by Robert Hand (ISBN: 0914918168)
- *The Inner Sky* by Steven Forrest (ISBN: 9780979067716)
- *Mythic Astrology Applied* by Ariel Guttman & Kenneth Johnson (ISBN: 0738704253)
- *Planets in Play* by Laurence Hillman (ISBN: 9781585425877)
- *Saturn: A New Look at an Old Devil* by Liz Greene (ISBN: 0877283060)
- *Take Control with Astrology* by Lisa Tenzin-Dolma (ISBN: 9780071665049)

♄	Saturn	Aries	♈	1	Your Way of Structure manifests through your independent and heroic quest for and attraction to maverick and individualistic identity development.
♄	Saturn	Aries	♈	2	Your Way of Structure manifests through your independent and heroic quest for and attraction to maverick and individualistic values and ways to meet your needs.
♄	Saturn	Aries	♈	3	Your Way of Structure manifests through your independent and heroic quest for and attraction to maverick and individualistic understanding of the world around you.
♄	Saturn	Aries	♈	4	Your Way of Structure manifests through your independent and heroic quest for and attraction to maverick and individualistic emotional caretaking and traditions.
♄	Saturn	Aries	♈	5	Your Way of Structure manifests through your independent and heroic quest for and attraction to maverick and individualistic creative expression.
♄	Saturn	Aries	♈	6	Your Way of Structure manifests through your independent and heroic quest for and attraction to maverick and individualistic service for others.
♄	Saturn	Aries	♈	7	Your Way of Structure manifests through your independent and heroic quest for and attraction to maverick and individualistic life teachers.
♄	Saturn	Aries	♈	8	Your Way of Structure manifests through your independent and heroic quest for and attraction to maverick and individualistic intimate relationships.
♄	Saturn	Aries	♈	9	Your Way of Structure manifests through your independent and heroic quest for and attraction to maverick and individualistic mastership of a body of knowledge.
♄	Saturn	Aries	♈	10	Your Way of Structure manifests through your independent and heroic quest for and attraction to maverick and individualistic accomplishments.
♄	Saturn	Aries	♈	11	Your Way of Structure manifests through your independent and heroic quest for and attraction to maverick and individualistic community.
♄	Saturn	Aries	♈	12	Your Way of Structure manifests through your independent and heroic quest for and attraction to maverick and individualistic spirituality.

♄	Saturn	Taurus	♉	1	Your Way of Structure manifests through your steadfast and persistent quest for and attraction to enduring and secure identity development.
♄	Saturn	Taurus	♉	2	Your Way of Structure manifests through your steadfast and persistent quest for and attraction to enduring and secure values and ways to meet your needs.
♄	Saturn	Taurus	♉	3	Your Way of Structure manifests through your steadfast and persistent quest for and attraction to enduring and secure understanding of the world around you.
♄	Saturn	Taurus	♉	4	Your Way of Structure manifests through your steadfast and persistent quest for and attraction to enduring and secure emotional caretaking and traditions.
♄	Saturn	Taurus	♉	5	Your Way of Structure manifests through your steadfast and persistent quest for and attraction to enduring and secure creative expression.
♄	Saturn	Taurus	♉	6	Your Way of Structure manifests through your steadfast and persistent quest for and attraction to enduring and secure service for others.
♄	Saturn	Taurus	♉	7	Your Way of Structure manifests through your steadfast and persistent quest for and attraction to enduring and secure life teachers.
♄	Saturn	Taurus	♉	8	Your Way of Structure manifests through your steadfast and persistent quest for and attraction to enduring and secure intimate relationships.
♄	Saturn	Taurus	♉	9	Your Way of Structure manifests through your steadfast and persistent quest for and attraction to enduring and secure mastership of a body of knowledge.
♄	Saturn	Taurus	♉	10	Your Way of Structure manifests through your steadfast and persistent quest for and attraction to enduring and secure accomplishments.
♄	Saturn	Taurus	♉	11	Your Way of Structure manifests through your steadfast and persistent quest for and attraction to enduring and secure community.
♄	Saturn	Taurus	♉	12	Your Way of Structure manifests through your steadfast and persistent quest for and attraction to enduring and secure spirituality.

♄	Saturn	Gemini	♊	1	Your Way of Structure manifests through your inquisitive and mentally agile quest for and attraction to ever changing and adaptable identity development.
♄	Saturn	Gemini	♊	2	Your Way of Structure manifests through your inquisitive and mentally agile quest for and attraction to ever changing and adaptable values and ways to meet your needs.
♄	Saturn	Gemini	♊	3	Your Way of Structure manifests through your inquisitive and mentally agile quest for and attraction to ever changing and adaptable understanding of the world around you.
♄	Saturn	Gemini	♊	4	Your Way of Structure manifests through your inquisitive and mentally agile quest for and attraction to ever changing and adaptable emotional caretaking and traditions.
♄	Saturn	Gemini	♊	5	Your Way of Structure manifests through your inquisitive and mentally agile quest for and attraction to ever changing and adaptable creative expression.
♄	Saturn	Gemini	♊	6	Your Way of Structure manifests through your inquisitive and mentally agile quest for and attraction to ever changing and adaptable service for others.
♄	Saturn	Gemini	♊	7	Your Way of Structure manifests through your inquisitive and mentally agile quest for and attraction to ever changing and adaptable life teachers.
♄	Saturn	Gemini	♊	8	Your Way of Structure manifests through your inquisitive and mentally agile quest for and attraction to ever changing and adaptable intimate relationships.
♄	Saturn	Gemini	♊	9	Your Way of Structure manifests through your inquisitive and mentally agile quest for and attraction to ever changing and adaptable mastership of a body of knowledge.
♄	Saturn	Gemini	♊	10	Your Way of Structure manifests through your inquisitive and mentally agile quest for and attraction to ever changing and adaptable accomplishments.
♄	Saturn	Gemini	♊	11	Your Way of Structure manifests through your inquisitive and mentally agile quest for and attraction to ever changing and adaptable community.
♄	Saturn	Gemini	♊	12	Your Way of Structure manifests through your inquisitive and mentally agile quest for and attraction to ever changing and adaptable spirituality.

	Saturn	Cancer	♋	1	Your Way of Structure manifests through your emotional and caring quest for and attraction to nurturing and supportive identity development.
♄	Saturn	Cancer	♋	2	Your Way of Structure manifests through your emotional and caring quest for and attraction to nurturing and supportive values and ways to meet your needs.
♄	Saturn	Cancer	♋	3	Your Way of Structure manifests through your emotional and caring quest for and attraction to nurturing and supportive understanding of the world around you.
♄	Saturn	Cancer	♋	4	Your Way of Structure manifests through your emotional and caring quest for and attraction to nurturing and supportive emotional caretaking and traditions.
♄	Saturn	Cancer	♋	5	Your Way of Structure manifests through your emotional and caring quest for and attraction to nurturing and supportive creative expression.
♄	Saturn	Cancer	♋	6	Your Way of Structure manifests through your emotional and caring quest for and attraction to nurturing and supportive service for others.
♄	Saturn	Cancer	♋	7	Your Way of Structure manifests through your emotional and caring quest for and attraction to nurturing and supportive life teachers.
♄	Saturn	Cancer	♋	8	Your Way of Structure manifests through your emotional and caring quest for and attraction to nurturing and supportive intimate relationships.
♄	Saturn	Cancer	♋	9	Your Way of Structure manifests through your emotional and caring quest for and attraction to nurturing and supportive mastership of a body of knowledge.
♄	Saturn	Cancer	♋	10	Your Way of Structure manifests through your emotional and caring quest for and attraction to nurturing and supportive accomplishments.
♄	Saturn	Cancer	♋	11	Your Way of Structure manifests through your emotional and caring quest for and attraction to nurturing and supportive community.
♄	Saturn	Cancer	♋	12	Your Way of Structure manifests through your emotional and caring quest for and attraction to nurturing and supportive spirituality.

♄	Saturn	Leo	♌	1	Your Way of Structure manifests through your energetic and dramatic quest for and attraction to creative and romantic identity development.
♄	Saturn	Leo	♌	2	Your Way of Structure manifests through your energetic and dramatic quest for and attraction to creative and romantic values and ways to meet your needs.
♄	Saturn	Leo	♌	3	Your Way of Structure manifests through your energetic and dramatic quest for and attraction to creative and romantic understanding of the world around you.
♄	Saturn	Leo	♌	4	Your Way of Structure manifests through your energetic and dramatic quest for and attraction to creative and romantic emotional caretaking and traditions.
♄	Saturn	Leo	♌	5	Your Way of Structure manifests through your energetic and dramatic quest for and attraction to creative and romantic creative expression.
♄	Saturn	Leo	♌	6	Your Way of Structure manifests through your energetic and dramatic quest for and attraction to creative and romantic service for others.
♄	Saturn	Leo	♌	7	Your Way of Structure manifests through your energetic and dramatic quest for and attraction to creative and romantic life teachers.
♄	Saturn	Leo	♌	8	Your Way of Structure manifests through your energetic and dramatic quest for and attraction to creative and romantic intimate relationships.
♄	Saturn	Leo	♌	9	Your Way of Structure manifests through your energetic and dramatic quest for and attraction to creative and romantic mastership of a body of knowledge.
♄	Saturn	Leo	♌	10	Your Way of Structure manifests through your energetic and dramatic quest for and attraction to creative and romantic accomplishments.
♄	Saturn	Leo	♌	11	Your Way of Structure manifests through your energetic and dramatic quest for and attraction to creative and romantic community.
♄	Saturn	Leo	♌	12	Your Way of Structure manifests through your energetic and dramatic quest for and attraction to creative and romantic spirituality.

♄	Saturn	Virgo	♍	1	Your Way of Structure manifests through your critically-minded and methodical quest for and attraction to meticulous and practical identity development.
♄	Saturn	Virgo	♍	2	Your Way of Structure manifests through your critically-minded and methodical quest for and attraction to meticulous and practical values and ways to meet your needs.
♄	Saturn	Virgo	♍	3	Your Way of Structure manifests through your critically-minded and methodical quest for and attraction to meticulous and practical understanding of the world around you.
♄	Saturn	Virgo	♍	4	Your Way of Structure manifests through your critically-minded and methodical quest for and attraction to meticulous and practical emotional caretaking and traditions.
♄	Saturn	Virgo	♍	5	Your Way of Structure manifests through your critically-minded and methodical quest for and attraction to meticulous and practical creative expression.
♄	Saturn	Virgo	♍	6	Your Way of Structure manifests through your critically-minded and methodical quest for and attraction to meticulous and practical service for others.
♄	Saturn	Virgo	♍	7	Your Way of Structure manifests through your critically-minded and methodical quest for and attraction to meticulous and practical life teachers.
♄	Saturn	Virgo	♍	8	Your Way of Structure manifests through your critically-minded and methodical quest for and attraction to meticulous and practical intimate relationships.
♄	Saturn	Virgo	♍	9	Your Way of Structure manifests through your critically-minded and methodical quest for and attraction to meticulous and practical mastership of a body of knowledge.
♄	Saturn	Virgo	♍	10	Your Way of Structure manifests through your critically-minded and methodical quest for and attraction to meticulous and practical accomplishments.
♄	Saturn	Virgo	♍	11	Your Way of Structure manifests through your critically-minded and methodical quest for and attraction to meticulous and practical community.
♄	Saturn	Virgo	♍	12	Your Way of Structure manifests through your critically-minded and methodical quest for and attraction to meticulous and practical spirituality.

Astrology Unlocked by Philip Young, PhD

♄	Saturn	Libra	♎	1	Your Way of Structure manifests through your analytical and balanced quest for and attraction to harmonious and logical identity development.
♄	Saturn	Libra	♎	2	Your Way of Structure manifests through your analytical and balanced quest for and attraction to harmonious and logical values and ways to meet your needs.
♄	Saturn	Libra	♎	3	Your Way of Structure manifests through your analytical and balanced quest for and attraction to harmonious and logical understanding of the world around you.
♄	Saturn	Libra	♎	4	Your Way of Structure manifests through your analytical and balanced quest for and attraction to harmonious and logical emotional caretaking and traditions.
♄	Saturn	Libra	♎	5	Your Way of Structure manifests through your analytical and balanced quest for and attraction to harmonious and logical creative expression.
♄	Saturn	Libra	♎	6	Your Way of Structure manifests through your analytical and balanced quest for and attraction to harmonious and logical service for others.
♄	Saturn	Libra	♎	7	Your Way of Structure manifests through your analytical and balanced quest for and attraction to harmonious and logical life teachers.
♄	Saturn	Libra	♎	8	Your Way of Structure manifests through your analytical and balanced quest for and attraction to harmonious and logical intimate relationships.
♄	Saturn	Libra	♎	9	Your Way of Structure manifests through your analytical and balanced quest for and attraction to harmonious and logical mastership of a body of knowledge.
♄	Saturn	Libra	♎	10	Your Way of Structure manifests through your analytical and balanced quest for and attraction to harmonious and logical accomplishments.
♄	Saturn	Libra	♎	11	Your Way of Structure manifests through your analytical and balanced quest for and attraction to harmonious and logical community.
♄	Saturn	Libra	♎	12	Your Way of Structure manifests through your analytical and balanced quest for and attraction to harmonious and logical spirituality.

♄	Saturn	Scorpio	♏	1	Your Way of Structure manifests through your intense and truth seeking quest for and attraction to penetrating and emotionally transformative identity development.
♄	Saturn	Scorpio	♏	2	Your Way of Structure manifests through your intense and truth seeking quest for and attraction to penetrating and emotionally transformative values and ways to meet your needs.
♄	Saturn	Scorpio	♏	3	Your Way of Structure manifests through your intense and truth seeking quest for and attraction to penetrating and emotionally transformative understanding of the world around you.
♄	Saturn	Scorpio	♏	4	Your Way of Structure manifests through your intense and truth seeking quest for and attraction to penetrating and emotionally transformative emotional caretaking and traditions.
♄	Saturn	Scorpio	♏	5	Your Way of Structure manifests through your intense and truth seeking quest for and attraction to penetrating and emotionally transformative creative expression.
♄	Saturn	Scorpio	♏	6	Your Way of Structure manifests through your intense and truth seeking quest for and attraction to penetrating and emotionally transformative service for others.
♄	Saturn	Scorpio	♏	7	Your Way of Structure manifests through your intense and truth seeking quest for and attraction to penetrating and emotionally transformative life teachers.
♄	Saturn	Scorpio	♏	8	Your Way of Structure manifests through your intense and truth seeking quest for and attraction to penetrating and emotionally transformative intimate relationships.
♄	Saturn	Scorpio	♏	9	Your Way of Structure manifests through your intense and truth seeking quest for and attraction to penetrating and emotionally transformative mastership of a body of knowledge.
♄	Saturn	Scorpio	♏	10	Your Way of Structure manifests through your intense and truth seeking quest for and attraction to penetrating and emotionally transformative accomplishments.
♄	Saturn	Scorpio	♏	11	Your Way of Structure manifests through your intense and truth seeking quest for and attraction to penetrating and emotionally transformative community.
♄	Saturn	Scorpio	♏	12	Your Way of Structure manifests through your intense and truth seeking quest for and attraction to penetrating and emotionally transformative spirituality.

♄	Saturn	Sagittarius	↗	1	Your Way of Structure manifests through your wide-ranging and open-minded quest for and attraction to experiential and risk-taking identity development.
♄	Saturn	Sagittarius	↗	2	Your Way of Structure manifests through your wide-ranging and open-minded quest for and attraction to experiential and risk-taking values and ways to meet your needs.
♄	Saturn	Sagittarius	↗	3	Your Way of Structure manifests through your wide-ranging and open-minded quest for and attraction to experiential and risk-taking understanding of the world around you.
♄	Saturn	Sagittarius	↗	4	Your Way of Structure manifests through your wide-ranging and open-minded quest for and attraction to experiential and risk-taking emotional caretaking and traditions.
♄	Saturn	Sagittarius	↗	5	Your Way of Structure manifests through your wide-ranging and open-minded quest for and attraction to experiential and risk-taking creative expression.
♄	Saturn	Sagittarius	↗	6	Your Way of Structure manifests through your wide-ranging and open-minded quest for and attraction to experiential and risk-taking service for others.
♄	Saturn	Sagittarius	↗	7	Your Way of Structure manifests through your wide-ranging and open-minded quest for and attraction to experiential and risk-taking life teachers.
♄	Saturn	Sagittarius	↗	8	Your Way of Structure manifests through your wide-ranging and open-minded quest for and attraction to experiential and risk-taking intimate relationships.
♄	Saturn	Sagittarius	↗	9	Your Way of Structure manifests through your wide-ranging and open-minded quest for and attraction to experiential and risk-taking mastership of a body of knowledge.
♄	Saturn	Sagittarius	↗	10	Your Way of Structure manifests through your wide-ranging and open-minded quest for and attraction to experiential and risk-taking accomplishments.
♄	Saturn	Sagittarius	↗	11	Your Way of Structure manifests through your wide-ranging and open-minded quest for and attraction to experiential and risk-taking community.
♄	Saturn	Sagittarius	↗	12	Your Way of Structure manifests through your wide-ranging and open-minded quest for and attraction to experiential and risk-taking spirituality.

♄	Saturn	Capricorn	♑	1	Your Way of Structure manifests through your goal-driven and focused quest for and attraction to results-oriented and successful identity development.
♄	Saturn	Capricorn	♑	2	Your Way of Structure manifests through your goal-driven and focused quest for and attraction to results-oriented and successful values and ways to meet your needs.
♄	Saturn	Capricorn	♑	3	Your Way of Structure manifests through your goal-driven and focused quest for and attraction to results-oriented and successful understanding of the world around you.
♄	Saturn	Capricorn	♑	4	Your Way of Structure manifests through your goal-driven and focused quest for and attraction to results-oriented and successful emotional caretaking and traditions.
♄	Saturn	Capricorn	♑	5	Your Way of Structure manifests through your goal-driven and focused quest for and attraction to results-oriented and successful creative expression.
♄	Saturn	Capricorn	♑	6	Your Way of Structure manifests through your goal-driven and focused quest for and attraction to results-oriented and successful service for others.
♄	Saturn	Capricorn	♑	7	Your Way of Structure manifests through your goal-driven and focused quest for and attraction to results-oriented and successful life teachers.
♄	Saturn	Capricorn	♑	8	Your Way of Structure manifests through your goal-driven and focused quest for and attraction to results-oriented and successful intimate relationships.
♄	Saturn	Capricorn	♑	9	Your Way of Structure manifests through your goal-driven and focused quest for and attraction to results-oriented and successful mastership of a body of knowledge.
♄	Saturn	Capricorn	♑	10	Your Way of Structure manifests through your goal-driven and focused quest for and attraction to results-oriented and successful accomplishments.
♄	Saturn	Capricorn	♑	11	Your Way of Structure manifests through your goal-driven and focused quest for and attraction to results-oriented and successful community.
♄	Saturn	Capricorn	♑	12	Your Way of Structure manifests through your goal-driven and focused quest for and attraction to results-oriented and successful spirituality.

Astrology Unlocked by Philip Young, PhD

♄	Saturn	Aquarius	♒	1	Your Way of Structure manifests through your unconventional and idealistic quest for and attraction to authentic and non-traditional identity development.
♄	Saturn	Aquarius	♒	2	Your Way of Structure manifests through your unconventional and idealistic quest for and attraction to authentic and non-traditional values and ways to meet your needs.
♄	Saturn	Aquarius	♒	3	Your Way of Structure manifests through your unconventional and idealistic quest for and attraction to authentic and non-traditional understanding of the world around you.
♄	Saturn	Aquarius	♒	4	Your Way of Structure manifests through your unconventional and idealistic quest for and attraction to authentic and non-traditional emotional caretaking and traditions.
♄	Saturn	Aquarius	♒	5	Your Way of Structure manifests through your unconventional and idealistic quest for and attraction to authentic and non-traditional creative expression.
♄	Saturn	Aquarius	♒	6	Your Way of Structure manifests through your unconventional and idealistic quest for and attraction to authentic and non-traditional service for others.
♄	Saturn	Aquarius	♒	7	Your Way of Structure manifests through your unconventional and idealistic quest for and attraction to authentic and non-traditional life teachers.
♄	Saturn	Aquarius	♒	8	Your Way of Structure manifests through your unconventional and idealistic quest for and attraction to authentic and non-traditional intimate relationships.
♄	Saturn	Aquarius	♒	9	Your Way of Structure manifests through your unconventional and idealistic quest for and attraction to authentic and non-traditional mastership of a body of knowledge.
♄	Saturn	Aquarius	♒	10	Your Way of Structure manifests through your unconventional and idealistic quest for and attraction to authentic and non-traditional accomplishments.
♄	Saturn	Aquarius	♒	11	Your Way of Structure manifests through your unconventional and idealistic quest for and attraction to authentic and non-traditional community.
♄	Saturn	Aquarius	♒	12	Your Way of Structure manifests through your unconventional and idealistic quest for and attraction to authentic and non-traditional spirituality.

	Saturn	Pisces	♓	1	Your Way of Structure manifests through your imaginative and faithful quest for and attraction to consciousness-raising and soulful identity development.
♄	Saturn	Pisces	♓	2	Your Way of Structure manifests through your imaginative and faithful quest for and attraction to consciousness-raising and soulful values and ways to meet your needs.
♄	Saturn	Pisces	♓	3	Your Way of Structure manifests through your imaginative and faithful quest for and attraction to consciousness-raising and soulful understanding of the world around you.
♄	Saturn	Pisces	♓	4	Your Way of Structure manifests through your imaginative and faithful quest for and attraction to consciousness-raising and soulful emotional caretaking and traditions.
♄	Saturn	Pisces	♓	5	Your Way of Structure manifests through your imaginative and faithful quest for and attraction to consciousness-raising and soulful creative expression.
♄	Saturn	Pisces	♓	6	Your Way of Structure manifests through your imaginative and faithful quest for and attraction to consciousness-raising and soulful service for others.
♄	Saturn	Pisces	♓	7	Your Way of Structure manifests through your imaginative and faithful quest for and attraction to consciousness-raising and soulful life teachers.
♄	Saturn	Pisces	♓	8	Your Way of Structure manifests through your imaginative and faithful quest for and attraction to consciousness-raising and soulful intimate relationships.
♄	Saturn	Pisces	♓	9	Your Way of Structure manifests through your imaginative and faithful quest for and attraction to consciousness-raising and soulful mastership of a body of knowledge.
♄	Saturn	Pisces	♓	10	Your Way of Structure manifests through your imaginative and faithful quest for and attraction to consciousness-raising and soulful accomplishments.
♄	Saturn	Pisces	♓	11	Your Way of Structure manifests through your imaginative and faithful quest for and attraction to consciousness-raising and soulful community.
♄	Saturn	Pisces	♓	12	Your Way of Structure manifests through your imaginative and faithful quest for and attraction to consciousness-raising and soulful spirituality.

Astrology Unlocked by Philip Young, PhD

Uranus | ⛢

Energy Point Type: **Planet**
Co-Rules Sign: **Aquarius**
Co-Rules House: **11**th
Element: **Air**
Key Phrase: **Way of Awakening**

Uranus represents your Way of Awakening. Its placement in Sign and House reveals where we must be unconventional and challenge norms, where we need to do or encounter the unexpected, and how we need to express our authenticity. In my case my Way of Awakening is expressed through Earth (Virgo) in my quest for community (11th House). Earth's expression is accomplished, persistent, and practical. In Virgo the Element acts critically, meticulously, and pragmatically. So, my key phrase is *"Your Way of Awakening manifests through your critically-minded and methodical quest for and attraction to meticulous and practical community."* In short, I am looking for a practically unusual tribe or an unusually pragmatic community. Jest aside, I seek to join with others who have been awakened by the need to build and join in the practical steps to make and sustain a community.

When you look up your Uranus in the Sign and House formula, consider what you have been awakened to, need to be fully authentic about, and which area of your life needs to be unconventional and challenging to the norms of society (in order to improve and help it evolve). Consider Uranus in Libra in the 12th House, *"Your Way of Awakening manifests through your analytical and balanced quest for and attraction to harmonious and logical spirituality."* This individual will discover epiphanies through logical thinking and deductive reasoning, reaching "aha!" moments intellectually (Libra). The reasoned process they use is the one they need to awaken and understand their authentic spiritual path (12th House). When they find harmony and are in balance, they will be open to the shocking Uranus energy and the insights they need to evolve in sudden leaps.

Astrology Unlocked by Philip Young, PhD

For more in depth reading about Uranus, I recommend purchasing and reading:

- *Alan Oken's Complete Astrology* by Alan Oken (ISBN: 9780892541256)
- *Astrology for Beginners* by Joann Hampar (ISBN: 9780738711065)
- *The Astrology of Midlife and Aging* by Erin Sullivan (ISBN: 1585424080)
- *Horoscope Symbols* by Robert Hand (ISBN: 0914918168)
- *The Inner Sky* by Steven Forrest (ISBN: 9780979067716)
- *Liquid Light of Sex* by Barbara Hand Clow (ISBN: 0939680963)
- *Mythic Astrology Applied* by Ariel Guttman & Kenneth Johnson (ISBN: 0738704253)
- *Planets in Play* by Laurence Hillman (ISBN: 9781585425877)
- *Take Control with Astrology* by Lisa Tenzin-Dolma (ISBN: 9780071665049)
- *Uranus: Freedom from the Known* by Jeff Green (ISBN: 0875422977)

♅	Uranus	Aries	♈	1	Your Way of Awakening manifests through your independent and heroic quest for and attraction to maverick and individualistic identity development.
♅	Uranus	Aries	♈	2	Your Way of Awakening manifests through your independent and heroic quest for and attraction to maverick and individualistic values and ways to meet your needs.
♅	Uranus	Aries	♈	3	Your Way of Awakening manifests through your independent and heroic quest for and attraction to maverick and individualistic understanding of the world around you.
♅	Uranus	Aries	♈	4	Your Way of Awakening manifests through your independent and heroic quest for and attraction to maverick and individualistic emotional caretaking and traditions.
♅	Uranus	Aries	♈	5	Your Way of Awakening manifests through your independent and heroic quest for and attraction to maverick and individualistic creative expression.
♅	Uranus	Aries	♈	6	Your Way of Awakening manifests through your independent and heroic quest for and attraction to maverick and individualistic service for others.
♅	Uranus	Aries	♈	7	Your Way of Awakening manifests through your independent and heroic quest for and attraction to maverick and individualistic life teachers.
♅	Uranus	Aries	♈	8	Your Way of Awakening manifests through your independent and heroic quest for and attraction to maverick and individualistic intimate relationships.
♅	Uranus	Aries	♈	9	Your Way of Awakening manifests through your independent and heroic quest for and attraction to maverick and individualistic mastership of a body of knowledge.
♅	Uranus	Aries	♈	10	Your Way of Awakening manifests through your independent and heroic quest for and attraction to maverick and individualistic accomplishments.
♅	Uranus	Aries	♈	11	Your Way of Awakening manifests through your independent and heroic quest for and attraction to maverick and individualistic community.
♅	Uranus	Aries	♈	12	Your Way of Awakening manifests through your independent and heroic quest for and attraction to maverick and individualistic spirituality.

♅	Uranus	Taurus	♉	1	Your Way of Awakening manifests through your steadfast and persistent quest for and attraction to enduring and secure identity development.
♅	Uranus	Taurus	♉	2	Your Way of Awakening manifests through your steadfast and persistent quest for and attraction to enduring and secure values and ways to meet your needs.
♅	Uranus	Taurus	♉	3	Your Way of Awakening manifests through your steadfast and persistent quest for and attraction to enduring and secure understanding of the world around you.
♅	Uranus	Taurus	♉	4	Your Way of Awakening manifests through your steadfast and persistent quest for and attraction to enduring and secure emotional caretaking and traditions.
♅	Uranus	Taurus	♉	5	Your Way of Awakening manifests through your steadfast and persistent quest for and attraction to enduring and secure creative expression.
♅	Uranus	Taurus	♉	6	Your Way of Awakening manifests through your steadfast and persistent quest for and attraction to enduring and secure service for others.
♅	Uranus	Taurus	♉	7	Your Way of Awakening manifests through your steadfast and persistent quest for and attraction to enduring and secure life teachers.
♅	Uranus	Taurus	♉	8	Your Way of Awakening manifests through your steadfast and persistent quest for and attraction to enduring and secure intimate relationships.
♅	Uranus	Taurus	♉	9	Your Way of Awakening manifests through your steadfast and persistent quest for and attraction to enduring and secure mastership of a body of knowledge.
♅	Uranus	Taurus	♉	10	Your Way of Awakening manifests through your steadfast and persistent quest for and attraction to enduring and secure accomplishments.
♅	Uranus	Taurus	♉	11	Your Way of Awakening manifests through your steadfast and persistent quest for and attraction to enduring and secure community.
♅	Uranus	Taurus	♉	12	Your Way of Awakening manifests through your steadfast and persistent quest for and attraction to enduring and secure spirituality.

	Uranus	Gemini	♊	1	Your Way of Awakening manifests through your inquisitive and mentally agile quest for and attraction to ever changing and adaptable identity development.
	Uranus	Gemini	♊	2	Your Way of Awakening manifests through your inquisitive and mentally agile quest for and attraction to ever changing and adaptable values and ways to meet your needs.
	Uranus	Gemini	♊	3	Your Way of Awakening manifests through your inquisitive and mentally agile quest for and attraction to ever changing and adaptable understanding of the world around you.
	Uranus	Gemini	♊	4	Your Way of Awakening manifests through your inquisitive and mentally agile quest for and attraction to ever changing and adaptable emotional caretaking and traditions.
	Uranus	Gemini	♊	5	Your Way of Awakening manifests through your inquisitive and mentally agile quest for and attraction to ever changing and adaptable creative expression.
	Uranus	Gemini	♊	6	Your Way of Awakening manifests through your inquisitive and mentally agile quest for and attraction to ever changing and adaptable service for others.
	Uranus	Gemini	♊	7	Your Way of Awakening manifests through your inquisitive and mentally agile quest for and attraction to ever changing and adaptable life teachers.
	Uranus	Gemini	♊	8	Your Way of Awakening manifests through your inquisitive and mentally agile quest for and attraction to ever changing and adaptable intimate relationships.
	Uranus	Gemini	♊	9	Your Way of Awakening manifests through your inquisitive and mentally agile quest for and attraction to ever changing and adaptable mastership of a body of knowledge.
	Uranus	Gemini	♊	10	Your Way of Awakening manifests through your inquisitive and mentally agile quest for and attraction to ever changing and adaptable accomplishments.
	Uranus	Gemini	♊	11	Your Way of Awakening manifests through your inquisitive and mentally agile quest for and attraction to ever changing and adaptable community.
	Uranus	Gemini	♊	12	Your Way of Awakening manifests through your inquisitive and mentally agile quest for and attraction to ever changing and adaptable spirituality.

	Uranus	Cancer	♋	1	Your Way of Awakening manifests through your emotional and caring quest for and attraction to nurturing and supportive identity development.
	Uranus	Cancer	♋	2	Your Way of Awakening manifests through your emotional and caring quest for and attraction to nurturing and supportive values and ways to meet your needs.
	Uranus	Cancer	♋	3	Your Way of Awakening manifests through your emotional and caring quest for and attraction to nurturing and supportive understanding of the world around you.
	Uranus	Cancer	♋	4	Your Way of Awakening manifests through your emotional and caring quest for and attraction to nurturing and supportive emotional caretaking and traditions.
	Uranus	Cancer	♋	5	Your Way of Awakening manifests through your emotional and caring quest for and attraction to nurturing and supportive creative expression.
	Uranus	Cancer	♋	6	Your Way of Awakening manifests through your emotional and caring quest for and attraction to nurturing and supportive service for others.
	Uranus	Cancer	♋	7	Your Way of Awakening manifests through your emotional and caring quest for and attraction to nurturing and supportive life teachers.
	Uranus	Cancer	♋	8	Your Way of Awakening manifests through your emotional and caring quest for and attraction to nurturing and supportive intimate relationships.
	Uranus	Cancer	♋	9	Your Way of Awakening manifests through your emotional and caring quest for and attraction to nurturing and supportive mastership of a body of knowledge.
	Uranus	Cancer	♋	10	Your Way of Awakening manifests through your emotional and caring quest for and attraction to nurturing and supportive accomplishments.
	Uranus	Cancer	♋	11	Your Way of Awakening manifests through your emotional and caring quest for and attraction to nurturing and supportive community.
	Uranus	Cancer	♋	12	Your Way of Awakening manifests through your emotional and caring quest for and attraction to nurturing and supportive spirituality.

Astrology Unlocked by Philip Young, PhD

♅	Uranus	Leo	♌	1	Your Way of Awakening manifests through your energetic and dramatic quest for and attraction to creative and romantic identity development.
♅	Uranus	Leo	♌	2	Your Way of Awakening manifests through your energetic and dramatic quest for and attraction to creative and romantic values and ways to meet your needs.
♅	Uranus	Leo	♌	3	Your Way of Awakening manifests through your energetic and dramatic quest for and attraction to creative and romantic understanding of the world around you.
♅	Uranus	Leo	♌	4	Your Way of Awakening manifests through your energetic and dramatic quest for and attraction to creative and romantic emotional caretaking and traditions.
♅	Uranus	Leo	♌	5	Your Way of Awakening manifests through your energetic and dramatic quest for and attraction to creative and romantic creative expression.
♅	Uranus	Leo	♌	6	Your Way of Awakening manifests through your energetic and dramatic quest for and attraction to creative and romantic service for others.
♅	Uranus	Leo	♌	7	Your Way of Awakening manifests through your energetic and dramatic quest for and attraction to creative and romantic life teachers.
♅	Uranus	Leo	♌	8	Your Way of Awakening manifests through your energetic and dramatic quest for and attraction to creative and romantic intimate relationships.
♅	Uranus	Leo	♌	9	Your Way of Awakening manifests through your energetic and dramatic quest for and attraction to creative and romantic mastership of a body of knowledge.
♅	Uranus	Leo	♌	10	Your Way of Awakening manifests through your energetic and dramatic quest for and attraction to creative and romantic accomplishments.
♅	Uranus	Leo	♌	11	Your Way of Awakening manifests through your energetic and dramatic quest for and attraction to creative and romantic community.
♅	Uranus	Leo	♌	12	Your Way of Awakening manifests through your energetic and dramatic quest for and attraction to creative and romantic spirituality.

	Uranus	Virgo	♍	1	Your Way of Awakening manifests through your critically-minded and methodical quest for and attraction to meticulous and practical identity development.
	Uranus	Virgo	♍	2	Your Way of Awakening manifests through your critically-minded and methodical quest for and attraction to meticulous and practical values and ways to meet your needs.
	Uranus	Virgo	♍	3	Your Way of Awakening manifests through your critically-minded and methodical quest for and attraction to meticulous and practical understanding of the world around you.
	Uranus	Virgo	♍	4	Your Way of Awakening manifests through your critically-minded and methodical quest for and attraction to meticulous and practical emotional caretaking and traditions.
	Uranus	Virgo	♍	5	Your Way of Awakening manifests through your critically-minded and methodical quest for and attraction to meticulous and practical creative expression.
	Uranus	Virgo	♍	6	Your Way of Awakening manifests through your critically-minded and methodical quest for and attraction to meticulous and practical service for others.
	Uranus	Virgo	♍	7	Your Way of Awakening manifests through your critically-minded and methodical quest for and attraction to meticulous and practical life teachers.
	Uranus	Virgo	♍	8	Your Way of Awakening manifests through your critically-minded and methodical quest for and attraction to meticulous and practical intimate relationships.
	Uranus	Virgo	♍	9	Your Way of Awakening manifests through your critically-minded and methodical quest for and attraction to meticulous and practical mastership of a body of knowledge.
	Uranus	Virgo	♍	10	Your Way of Awakening manifests through your critically-minded and methodical quest for and attraction to meticulous and practical accomplishments.
	Uranus	Virgo	♍	11	Your Way of Awakening manifests through your critically-minded and methodical quest for and attraction to meticulous and practical community.
	Uranus	Virgo	♍	12	Your Way of Awakening manifests through your critically-minded and methodical quest for and attraction to meticulous and practical spirituality.

Astrology Unlocked by Philip Young, PhD

♅	Uranus	Libra	♎	1	Your Way of Awakening manifests through your analytical and balanced quest for and attraction to harmonious and logical identity development.
♅	Uranus	Libra	♎	2	Your Way of Awakening manifests through your analytical and balanced quest for and attraction to harmonious and logical values and ways to meet your needs.
♅	Uranus	Libra	♎	3	Your Way of Awakening manifests through your analytical and balanced quest for and attraction to harmonious and logical understanding of the world around you.
♅	Uranus	Libra	♎	4	Your Way of Awakening manifests through your analytical and balanced quest for and attraction to harmonious and logical emotional caretaking and traditions.
♅	Uranus	Libra	♎	5	Your Way of Awakening manifests through your analytical and balanced quest for and attraction to harmonious and logical creative expression.
♅	Uranus	Libra	♎	6	Your Way of Awakening manifests through your analytical and balanced quest for and attraction to harmonious and logical service for others.
♅	Uranus	Libra	♎	7	Your Way of Awakening manifests through your analytical and balanced quest for and attraction to harmonious and logical life teachers.
♅	Uranus	Libra	♎	8	Your Way of Awakening manifests through your analytical and balanced quest for and attraction to harmonious and logical intimate relationships.
♅	Uranus	Libra	♎	9	Your Way of Awakening manifests through your analytical and balanced quest for and attraction to harmonious and logical mastership of a body of knowledge.
♅	Uranus	Libra	♎	10	Your Way of Awakening manifests through your analytical and balanced quest for and attraction to harmonious and logical accomplishments.
♅	Uranus	Libra	♎	11	Your Way of Awakening manifests through your analytical and balanced quest for and attraction to harmonious and logical community.
♅	Uranus	Libra	♎	12	Your Way of Awakening manifests through your analytical and balanced quest for and attraction to harmonious and logical spirituality.

	Uranus	Scorpio	♏	1	Your Way of Awakening manifests through your intense and truth seeking quest for and attraction to penetrating and emotionally transformative identity development.
	Uranus	Scorpio	♏	2	Your Way of Awakening manifests through your intense and truth seeking quest for and attraction to penetrating and emotionally transformative values and ways to meet your needs.
	Uranus	Scorpio	♏	3	Your Way of Awakening manifests through your intense and truth seeking quest for and attraction to penetrating and emotionally transformative understanding of the world around you.
	Uranus	Scorpio	♏	4	Your Way of Awakening manifests through your intense and truth seeking quest for and attraction to penetrating and emotionally transformative emotional caretaking and traditions.
	Uranus	Scorpio	♏	5	Your Way of Awakening manifests through your intense and truth seeking quest for and attraction to penetrating and emotionally transformative creative expression.
	Uranus	Scorpio	♏	6	Your Way of Awakening manifests through your intense and truth seeking quest for and attraction to penetrating and emotionally transformative service for others.
	Uranus	Scorpio	♏	7	Your Way of Awakening manifests through your intense and truth seeking quest for and attraction to penetrating and emotionally transformative life teachers.
	Uranus	Scorpio	♏	8	Your Way of Awakening manifests through your intense and truth seeking quest for and attraction to penetrating and emotionally transformative intimate relationships.
	Uranus	Scorpio	♏	9	Your Way of Awakening manifests through your intense and truth seeking quest for and attraction to penetrating and emotionally transformative mastership of a body of knowledge.
	Uranus	Scorpio	♏	10	Your Way of Awakening manifests through your intense and truth seeking quest for and attraction to penetrating and emotionally transformative accomplishments.
	Uranus	Scorpio	♏	11	Your Way of Awakening manifests through your intense and truth seeking quest for and attraction to penetrating and emotionally transformative community.
	Uranus	Scorpio	♏	12	Your Way of Awakening manifests through your intense and truth seeking quest for and attraction to penetrating and emotionally transformative spirituality.

♅	Uranus	Sagittarius	♐	1	Your Way of Awakening manifests through your wide-ranging and open-minded quest for and attraction to experiential and risk-taking identity development.
♅	Uranus	Sagittarius	♐	2	Your Way of Awakening manifests through your wide-ranging and open-minded quest for and attraction to experiential and risk-taking values and ways to meet your needs.
♅	Uranus	Sagittarius	♐	3	Your Way of Awakening manifests through your wide-ranging and open-minded quest for and attraction to experiential and risk-taking understanding of the world around you.
♅	Uranus	Sagittarius	♐	4	Your Way of Awakening manifests through your wide-ranging and open-minded quest for and attraction to experiential and risk-taking emotional caretaking and traditions.
♅	Uranus	Sagittarius	♐	5	Your Way of Awakening manifests through your wide-ranging and open-minded quest for and attraction to experiential and risk-taking creative expression.
♅	Uranus	Sagittarius	♐	6	Your Way of Awakening manifests through your wide-ranging and open-minded quest for and attraction to experiential and risk-taking service for others.
♅	Uranus	Sagittarius	♐	7	Your Way of Awakening manifests through your wide-ranging and open-minded quest for and attraction to experiential and risk-taking life teachers.
♅	Uranus	Sagittarius	♐	8	Your Way of Awakening manifests through your wide-ranging and open-minded quest for and attraction to experiential and risk-taking intimate relationships.
♅	Uranus	Sagittarius	♐	9	Your Way of Awakening manifests through your wide-ranging and open-minded quest for and attraction to experiential and risk-taking mastership of a body of knowledge.
♅	Uranus	Sagittarius	♐	10	Your Way of Awakening manifests through your wide-ranging and open-minded quest for and attraction to experiential and risk-taking accomplishments.
♅	Uranus	Sagittarius	♐	11	Your Way of Awakening manifests through your wide-ranging and open-minded quest for and attraction to experiential and risk-taking community.
♅	Uranus	Sagittarius	♐	12	Your Way of Awakening manifests through your wide-ranging and open-minded quest for and attraction to experiential and risk-taking spirituality.

♅	Uranus	Capricorn	♑	1	Your Way of Awakening manifests through your goal-driven and focused quest for and attraction to results-oriented and successful identity development.
♅	Uranus	Capricorn	♑	2	Your Way of Awakening manifests through your goal-driven and focused quest for and attraction to results-oriented and successful values and ways to meet your needs.
♅	Uranus	Capricorn	♑	3	Your Way of Awakening manifests through your goal-driven and focused quest for and attraction to results-oriented and successful understanding of the world around you.
♅	Uranus	Capricorn	♑	4	Your Way of Awakening manifests through your goal-driven and focused quest for and attraction to results-oriented and successful emotional caretaking and traditions.
♅	Uranus	Capricorn	♑	5	Your Way of Awakening manifests through your goal-driven and focused quest for and attraction to results-oriented and successful creative expression.
♅	Uranus	Capricorn	♑	6	Your Way of Awakening manifests through your goal-driven and focused quest for and attraction to results-oriented and successful service for others.
♅	Uranus	Capricorn	♑	7	Your Way of Awakening manifests through your goal-driven and focused quest for and attraction to results-oriented and successful life teachers.
♅	Uranus	Capricorn	♑	8	Your Way of Awakening manifests through your goal-driven and focused quest for and attraction to results-oriented and successful intimate relationships.
♅	Uranus	Capricorn	♑	9	Your Way of Awakening manifests through your goal-driven and focused quest for and attraction to results-oriented and successful mastership of a body of knowledge.
♅	Uranus	Capricorn	♑	10	Your Way of Awakening manifests through your goal-driven and focused quest for and attraction to results-oriented and successful accomplishments.
♅	Uranus	Capricorn	♑	11	Your Way of Awakening manifests through your goal-driven and focused quest for and attraction to results-oriented and successful community.
♅	Uranus	Capricorn	♑	12	Your Way of Awakening manifests through your goal-driven and focused quest for and attraction to results-oriented and successful spirituality.

♅	Uranus	Aquarius	♒	1	Your Way of Awakening manifests through your unconventional and idealistic quest for and attraction to authentic and non-traditional identity development.
♅	Uranus	Aquarius	♒	2	Your Way of Awakening manifests through your unconventional and idealistic quest for and attraction to authentic and non-traditional values and ways to meet your needs.
♅	Uranus	Aquarius	♒	3	Your Way of Awakening manifests through your unconventional and idealistic quest for and attraction to authentic and non-traditional understanding of the world around you.
♅	Uranus	Aquarius	♒	4	Your Way of Awakening manifests through your unconventional and idealistic quest for and attraction to authentic and non-traditional emotional caretaking and traditions.
♅	Uranus	Aquarius	♒	5	Your Way of Awakening manifests through your unconventional and idealistic quest for and attraction to authentic and non-traditional creative expression.
♅	Uranus	Aquarius	♒	6	Your Way of Awakening manifests through your unconventional and idealistic quest for and attraction to authentic and non-traditional service for others.
♅	Uranus	Aquarius	♒	7	Your Way of Awakening manifests through your unconventional and idealistic quest for and attraction to authentic and non-traditional life teachers.
♅	Uranus	Aquarius	♒	8	Your Way of Awakening manifests through your unconventional and idealistic quest for and attraction to authentic and non-traditional intimate relationships.
♅	Uranus	Aquarius	♒	9	Your Way of Awakening manifests through your unconventional and idealistic quest for and attraction to authentic and non-traditional mastership of a body of knowledge.
♅	Uranus	Aquarius	♒	10	Your Way of Awakening manifests through your unconventional and idealistic quest for and attraction to authentic and non-traditional accomplishments.
♅	Uranus	Aquarius	♒	11	Your Way of Awakening manifests through your unconventional and idealistic quest for and attraction to authentic and non-traditional community.
♅	Uranus	Aquarius	♒	12	Your Way of Awakening manifests through your unconventional and idealistic quest for and attraction to authentic and non-traditional spirituality.

Astrology Unlocked by Philip Young, PhD

	Uranus	Pisces	♓	1	Your Way of Awakening manifests through your imaginative and faithful quest for and attraction to consciousness-raising and soulful identity development.
	Uranus	Pisces	♓	2	Your Way of Awakening manifests through your imaginative and faithful quest for and attraction to consciousness-raising and soulful values and ways to meet your needs.
	Uranus	Pisces	♓	3	Your Way of Awakening manifests through your imaginative and faithful quest for and attraction to consciousness-raising and soulful understanding of the world around you.
	Uranus	Pisces	♓	4	Your Way of Awakening manifests through your imaginative and faithful quest for and attraction to consciousness-raising and soulful emotional caretaking and traditions.
	Uranus	Pisces	♓	5	Your Way of Awakening manifests through your imaginative and faithful quest for and attraction to consciousness-raising and soulful creative expression.
	Uranus	Pisces	♓	6	Your Way of Awakening manifests through your imaginative and faithful quest for and attraction to consciousness-raising and soulful service for others.
	Uranus	Pisces	♓	7	Your Way of Awakening manifests through your imaginative and faithful quest for and attraction to consciousness-raising and soulful life teachers.
	Uranus	Pisces	♓	8	Your Way of Awakening manifests through your imaginative and faithful quest for and attraction to consciousness-raising and soulful intimate relationships.
	Uranus	Pisces	♓	9	Your Way of Awakening manifests through your imaginative and faithful quest for and attraction to consciousness-raising and soulful mastership of a body of knowledge.
	Uranus	Pisces	♓	10	Your Way of Awakening manifests through your imaginative and faithful quest for and attraction to consciousness-raising and soulful accomplishments.
	Uranus	Pisces	♓	11	Your Way of Awakening manifests through your imaginative and faithful quest for and attraction to consciousness-raising and soulful community.
	Uranus	Pisces	♓	12	Your Way of Awakening manifests through your imaginative and faithful quest for and attraction to consciousness-raising and soulful spirituality.

Neptune | ♆

Energy Point Type: **Planet**

Co-Rules Sign: **Pisces**

Co-Rules House: **12**th

Element: **Water**

Key Phrase: **Way of Mystery**

Neptune represents your Way of Mystery. Its placement in Sign and House reveals how we are connected to the mass consciousness and the spiritual energy of the universe. In my case my Way of Mystery is expressed through Water (Scorpio) in my quest for identity (1st House. Water's expression is emotional, intense, and imaginative. In Scorpio the Element acts intensely, transformatively, and unrelentingly. So, my key phrase is *"Your Way of Mystery manifests through your intense and truth seeking quest for and attraction to penetrating and emotionally transformative identity development."* In short, I see my search for identity as a mystery to be solved.

When you look up your own Neptune in the Sign and House formula, think about where you need to dream, imagine, and surrender. Now consider Neptune in Capricorn in the 10th House, *"Your Way of Mystery manifests through your goal-driven and focused quest for and attraction to results-oriented and successful career accomplishments."* Think of every major dream to become part of reality: proving the world was round by sailing around it (not just mathematical computations), human flight in airplanes, a space ship, and so on. People with Neptune in Capricorn will be driven to make dreams manifest in reality. Those with a 10th House placement will focus on making their dreams their careers and achieving material success in the world with and through their dreams.

For more in depth reading about Neptune, I recommend purchasing and reading:

- *Alan Oken's Complete Astrology* by Alan Oken (ISBN: 9780892541256)
- *Astrology for Beginners* by Joann Hampar (ISBN: 9780738711065)
- *Horoscope Symbols* by Robert Hand (ISBN: 0914918168)

- *The Inner Sky* by Steven Forrest (ISBN: 9780979067716)

- *Mythic Astrology Applied* by Ariel Guttman & Kenneth Johnson (ISBN: 0738704253)

- *Planets in Play* by Laurence Hillman (ISBN: 9781585425877)

- *Take Control with Astrology* by Lisa Tenzin-Dolma (ISBN: 9780071665049)

♆	Neptune	Aries	♈	1	Your Way of Mystery manifests through your independent and heroic quest for and attraction to maverick and individualistic identity development.
♆	Neptune	Aries	♈	2	Your Way of Mystery manifests through your independent and heroic quest for and attraction to maverick and individualistic values and ways to meet your needs.
♆	Neptune	Aries	♈	3	Your Way of Mystery manifests through your independent and heroic quest for and attraction to maverick and individualistic understanding of the world around you.
♆	Neptune	Aries	♈	4	Your Way of Mystery manifests through your independent and heroic quest for and attraction to maverick and individualistic emotional caretaking and traditions.
♆	Neptune	Aries	♈	5	Your Way of Mystery manifests through your independent and heroic quest for and attraction to maverick and individualistic creative expression.
♆	Neptune	Aries	♈	6	Your Way of Mystery manifests through your independent and heroic quest for and attraction to maverick and individualistic service for others.
♆	Neptune	Aries	♈	7	Your Way of Mystery manifests through your independent and heroic quest for and attraction to maverick and individualistic life teachers.
♆	Neptune	Aries	♈	8	Your Way of Mystery manifests through your independent and heroic quest for and attraction to maverick and individualistic intimate relationships.
♆	Neptune	Aries	♈	9	Your Way of Mystery manifests through your independent and heroic quest for and attraction to maverick and individualistic mastership of a body of knowledge.
♆	Neptune	Aries	♈	10	Your Way of Mystery manifests through your independent and heroic quest for and attraction to maverick and individualistic accomplishments.
♆	Neptune	Aries	♈	11	Your Way of Mystery manifests through your independent and heroic quest for and attraction to maverick and individualistic community.
♆	Neptune	Aries	♈	12	Your Way of Mystery manifests through your independent and heroic quest for and attraction to maverick and individualistic spirituality.

♆	Neptune	Taurus	♉	1	Your Way of Mystery manifests through your steadfast and persistent quest for and attraction to enduring and secure identity development.
♆	Neptune	Taurus	♉	2	Your Way of Mystery manifests through your steadfast and persistent quest for and attraction to enduring and secure values and ways to meet your needs.
♆	Neptune	Taurus	♉	3	Your Way of Mystery manifests through your steadfast and persistent quest for and attraction to enduring and secure understanding of the world around you.
♆	Neptune	Taurus	♉	4	Your Way of Mystery manifests through your steadfast and persistent quest for and attraction to enduring and secure emotional caretaking and traditions.
♆	Neptune	Taurus	♉	5	Your Way of Mystery manifests through your steadfast and persistent quest for and attraction to enduring and secure creative expression.
♆	Neptune	Taurus	♉	6	Your Way of Mystery manifests through your steadfast and persistent quest for and attraction to enduring and secure service for others.
♆	Neptune	Taurus	♉	7	Your Way of Mystery manifests through your steadfast and persistent quest for and attraction to enduring and secure life teachers.
♆	Neptune	Taurus	♉	8	Your Way of Mystery manifests through your steadfast and persistent quest for and attraction to enduring and secure intimate relationships.
♆	Neptune	Taurus	♉	9	Your Way of Mystery manifests through your steadfast and persistent quest for and attraction to enduring and secure mastership of a body of knowledge.
♆	Neptune	Taurus	♉	10	Your Way of Mystery manifests through your steadfast and persistent quest for and attraction to enduring and secure accomplishments.
♆	Neptune	Taurus	♉	11	Your Way of Mystery manifests through your steadfast and persistent quest for and attraction to enduring and secure community.
♆	Neptune	Taurus	♉	12	Your Way of Mystery manifests through your steadfast and persistent quest for and attraction to enduring and secure spirituality.

Ψ	Neptune	Gemini	♊	1	Your Way of Mystery manifests through your inquisitive and mentally agile quest for and attraction to ever changing and adaptable identity development.
Ψ	Neptune	Gemini	♊	2	Your Way of Mystery manifests through your inquisitive and mentally agile quest for and attraction to ever changing and adaptable values and ways to meet your needs.
Ψ	Neptune	Gemini	♊	3	Your Way of Mystery manifests through your inquisitive and mentally agile quest for and attraction to ever changing and adaptable understanding of the world around you.
Ψ	Neptune	Gemini	♊	4	Your Way of Mystery manifests through your inquisitive and mentally agile quest for and attraction to ever changing and adaptable emotional caretaking and traditions.
Ψ	Neptune	Gemini	♊	5	Your Way of Mystery manifests through your inquisitive and mentally agile quest for and attraction to ever changing and adaptable creative expression.
Ψ	Neptune	Gemini	♊	6	Your Way of Mystery manifests through your inquisitive and mentally agile quest for and attraction to ever changing and adaptable service for others.
Ψ	Neptune	Gemini	♊	7	Your Way of Mystery manifests through your inquisitive and mentally agile quest for and attraction to ever changing and adaptable life teachers.
Ψ	Neptune	Gemini	♊	8	Your Way of Mystery manifests through your inquisitive and mentally agile quest for and attraction to ever changing and adaptable intimate relationships.
Ψ	Neptune	Gemini	♊	9	Your Way of Mystery manifests through your inquisitive and mentally agile quest for and attraction to ever changing and adaptable mastership of a body of knowledge.
Ψ	Neptune	Gemini	♊	10	Your Way of Mystery manifests through your inquisitive and mentally agile quest for and attraction to ever changing and adaptable accomplishments.
Ψ	Neptune	Gemini	♊	11	Your Way of Mystery manifests through your inquisitive and mentally agile quest for and attraction to ever changing and adaptable community.
Ψ	Neptune	Gemini	♊	12	Your Way of Mystery manifests through your inquisitive and mentally agile quest for and attraction to ever changing and adaptable spirituality.

♆	Neptune	Leo	♋	1	Your Way of Mystery manifests through your emotional and caring quest for and attraction to nurturing and supportive identity development.
♆	Neptune	Leo	♋	2	Your Way of Mystery manifests through your emotional and caring quest for and attraction to nurturing and supportive values and ways to meet your needs.
♆	Neptune	Leo	♋	3	Your Way of Mystery manifests through your emotional and caring quest for and attraction to nurturing and supportive understanding of the world around you.
♆	Neptune	Leo	♋	4	Your Way of Mystery manifests through your emotional and caring quest for and attraction to nurturing and supportive emotional caretaking and traditions.
♆	Neptune	Leo	♋	5	Your Way of Mystery manifests through your emotional and caring quest for and attraction to nurturing and supportive creative expression.
♆	Neptune	Leo	♋	6	Your Way of Mystery manifests through your emotional and caring quest for and attraction to nurturing and supportive service for others.
♆	Neptune	Leo	♋	7	Your Way of Mystery manifests through your emotional and caring quest for and attraction to nurturing and supportive life teachers.
♆	Neptune	Leo	♋	8	Your Way of Mystery manifests through your emotional and caring quest for and attraction to nurturing and supportive intimate relationships.
♆	Neptune	Leo	♋	9	Your Way of Mystery manifests through your emotional and caring quest for and attraction to nurturing and supportive mastership of a body of knowledge.
♆	Neptune	Leo	♋	10	Your Way of Mystery manifests through your emotional and caring quest for and attraction to nurturing and supportive accomplishments.
♆	Neptune	Leo	♋	11	Your Way of Mystery manifests through your emotional and caring quest for and attraction to nurturing and supportive community.
♆	Neptune	Leo	♋	12	Your Way of Mystery manifests through your emotional and caring quest for and attraction to nurturing and supportive spirituality.

♆	Neptune	Leo	♌	1	Your Way of Mystery manifests through your energetic and dramatic quest for and attraction to creative and romantic identity development.
♆	Neptune	Leo	♌	2	Your Way of Mystery manifests through your energetic and dramatic quest for and attraction to creative and romantic values and ways to meet your needs.
♆	Neptune	Leo	♌	3	Your Way of Mystery manifests through your energetic and dramatic quest for and attraction to creative and romantic understanding of the world around you.
♆	Neptune	Leo	♌	4	Your Way of Mystery manifests through your energetic and dramatic quest for and attraction to creative and romantic emotional caretaking and traditions.
♆	Neptune	Leo	♌	5	Your Way of Mystery manifests through your energetic and dramatic quest for and attraction to creative and romantic creative expression.
♆	Neptune	Leo	♌	6	Your Way of Mystery manifests through your energetic and dramatic quest for and attraction to creative and romantic service for others.
♆	Neptune	Leo	♌	7	Your Way of Mystery manifests through your energetic and dramatic quest for and attraction to creative and romantic life teachers.
♆	Neptune	Leo	♌	8	Your Way of Mystery manifests through your energetic and dramatic quest for and attraction to creative and romantic intimate relationships.
♆	Neptune	Leo	♌	9	Your Way of Mystery manifests through your energetic and dramatic quest for and attraction to creative and romantic mastership of a body of knowledge.
♆	Neptune	Leo	♌	10	Your Way of Mystery manifests through your energetic and dramatic quest for and attraction to creative and romantic accomplishments.
♆	Neptune	Leo	♌	11	Your Way of Mystery manifests through your energetic and dramatic quest for and attraction to creative and romantic community.
♆	Neptune	Leo	♌	12	Your Way of Mystery manifests through your energetic and dramatic quest for and attraction to creative and romantic spirituality.

	Neptune	Virgo	♍	1	Your Way of Mystery manifests through your critically-minded and methodical quest for and attraction to meticulous and practical identity development.
♆	Neptune	Virgo	♍	2	Your Way of Mystery manifests through your critically-minded and methodical quest for and attraction to meticulous and practical values and ways to meet your needs.
♆	Neptune	Virgo	♍	3	Your Way of Mystery manifests through your critically-minded and methodical quest for and attraction to meticulous and practical understanding of the world around you.
♆	Neptune	Virgo	♍	4	Your Way of Mystery manifests through your critically-minded and methodical quest for and attraction to meticulous and practical emotional caretaking and traditions.
♆	Neptune	Virgo	♍	5	Your Way of Mystery manifests through your critically-minded and methodical quest for and attraction to meticulous and practical creative expression.
♆	Neptune	Virgo	♍	6	Your Way of Mystery manifests through your critically-minded and methodical quest for and attraction to meticulous and practical service for others.
♆	Neptune	Virgo	♍	7	Your Way of Mystery manifests through your critically-minded and methodical quest for and attraction to meticulous and practical life teachers.
♆	Neptune	Virgo	♍	8	Your Way of Mystery manifests through your critically-minded and methodical quest for and attraction to meticulous and practical intimate relationships.
♆	Neptune	Virgo	♍	9	Your Way of Mystery manifests through your critically-minded and methodical quest for and attraction to meticulous and practical mastership of a body of knowledge.
♆	Neptune	Virgo	♍	10	Your Way of Mystery manifests through your critically-minded and methodical quest for and attraction to meticulous and practical accomplishments.
♆	Neptune	Virgo	♍	11	Your Way of Mystery manifests through your critically-minded and methodical quest for and attraction to meticulous and practical community.
♆	Neptune	Virgo	♍	12	Your Way of Mystery manifests through your critically-minded and methodical quest for and attraction to meticulous and practical spirituality.

	Neptune	Libra	♎	1	Your Way of Mystery manifests through your analytical and balanced quest for and attraction to harmonious and logical identity development.
	Neptune	Libra	♎	2	Your Way of Mystery manifests through your analytical and balanced quest for and attraction to harmonious and logical values and ways to meet your needs.
	Neptune	Libra	♎	3	Your Way of Mystery manifests through your analytical and balanced quest for and attraction to harmonious and logical understanding of the world around you.
	Neptune	Libra	♎	4	Your Way of Mystery manifests through your analytical and balanced quest for and attraction to harmonious and logical emotional caretaking and traditions.
	Neptune	Libra	♎	5	Your Way of Mystery manifests through your analytical and balanced quest for and attraction to harmonious and logical creative expression.
	Neptune	Libra	♎	6	Your Way of Mystery manifests through your analytical and balanced quest for and attraction to harmonious and logical service for others.
	Neptune	Libra	♎	7	Your Way of Mystery manifests through your analytical and balanced quest for and attraction to harmonious and logical life teachers.
	Neptune	Libra	♎	8	Your Way of Mystery manifests through your analytical and balanced quest for and attraction to harmonious and logical intimate relationships.
	Neptune	Libra	♎	9	Your Way of Mystery manifests through your analytical and balanced quest for and attraction to harmonious and logical mastership of a body of knowledge.
	Neptune	Libra	♎	10	Your Way of Mystery manifests through your analytical and balanced quest for and attraction to harmonious and logical accomplishments.
	Neptune	Libra	♎	11	Your Way of Mystery manifests through your analytical and balanced quest for and attraction to harmonious and logical community.
	Neptune	Libra	♎	12	Your Way of Mystery manifests through your analytical and balanced quest for and attraction to harmonious and logical spirituality.

Ψ	Neptune	Scorpio	♏	1	Your Way of Mystery manifests through your intense and truth seeking quest for and attraction to penetrating and emotionally transformative identity development.
Ψ	Neptune	Scorpio	♏	2	Your Way of Mystery manifests through your intense and truth seeking quest for and attraction to penetrating and emotionally transformative values and ways to meet your needs.
Ψ	Neptune	Scorpio	♏	3	Your Way of Mystery manifests through your intense and truth seeking quest for and attraction to penetrating and emotionally transformative understanding of the world around you.
Ψ	Neptune	Scorpio	♏	4	Your Way of Mystery manifests through your intense and truth seeking quest for and attraction to penetrating and emotionally transformative emotional caretaking and traditions.
Ψ	Neptune	Scorpio	♏	5	Your Way of Mystery manifests through your intense and truth seeking quest for and attraction to penetrating and emotionally transformative creative expression.
Ψ	Neptune	Scorpio	♏	6	Your Way of Mystery manifests through your intense and truth seeking quest for and attraction to penetrating and emotionally transformative service for others.
Ψ	Neptune	Scorpio	♏	7	Your Way of Mystery manifests through your intense and truth seeking quest for and attraction to penetrating and emotionally transformative life teachers.
Ψ	Neptune	Scorpio	♏	8	Your Way of Mystery manifests through your intense and truth seeking quest for and attraction to penetrating and emotionally transformative intimate relationships.
Ψ	Neptune	Scorpio	♏	9	Your Way of Mystery manifests through your intense and truth seeking quest for and attraction to penetrating and emotionally transformative mastership of a body of knowledge.
Ψ	Neptune	Scorpio	♏	10	Your Way of Mystery manifests through your intense and truth seeking quest for and attraction to penetrating and emotionally transformative accomplishments.
Ψ	Neptune	Scorpio	♏	11	Your Way of Mystery manifests through your intense and truth seeking quest for and attraction to penetrating and emotionally transformative community.
Ψ	Neptune	Scorpio	♏	12	Your Way of Mystery manifests through your intense and truth seeking quest for and attraction to penetrating and emotionally transformative spirituality.

♆	Neptune	Sagittarius	♐	1	Your Way of Mystery manifests through your wide-ranging and open-minded quest for and attraction to experiential and risk-taking identity development.
♆	Neptune	Sagittarius	♐	2	Your Way of Mystery manifests through your wide-ranging and open-minded quest for and attraction to experiential and risk-taking values and ways to meet your needs.
♆	Neptune	Sagittarius	♐	3	Your Way of Mystery manifests through your wide-ranging and open-minded quest for and attraction to experiential and risk-taking understanding of the world around you.
♆	Neptune	Sagittarius	♐	4	Your Way of Mystery manifests through your wide-ranging and open-minded quest for and attraction to experiential and risk-taking emotional caretaking and traditions.
♆	Neptune	Sagittarius	♐	5	Your Way of Mystery manifests through your wide-ranging and open-minded quest for and attraction to experiential and risk-taking creative expression.
♆	Neptune	Sagittarius	♐	6	Your Way of Mystery manifests through your wide-ranging and open-minded quest for and attraction to experiential and risk-taking service for others.
♆	Neptune	Sagittarius	♐	7	Your Way of Mystery manifests through your wide-ranging and open-minded quest for and attraction to experiential and risk-taking life teachers.
♆	Neptune	Sagittarius	♐	8	Your Way of Mystery manifests through your wide-ranging and open-minded quest for and attraction to experiential and risk-taking intimate relationships.
♆	Neptune	Sagittarius	♐	9	Your Way of Mystery manifests through your wide-ranging and open-minded quest for and attraction to experiential and risk-taking mastership of a body of knowledge.
♆	Neptune	Sagittarius	♐	10	Your Way of Mystery manifests through your wide-ranging and open-minded quest for and attraction to experiential and risk-taking accomplishments.
♆	Neptune	Sagittarius	♐	11	Your Way of Mystery manifests through your wide-ranging and open-minded quest for and attraction to experiential and risk-taking community.
♆	Neptune	Sagittarius	♐	12	Your Way of Mystery manifests through your wide-ranging and open-minded quest for and attraction to experiential and risk-taking spirituality.

183

♆	Neptune	Capricorn	♑	1	Your Way of Mystery manifests through your goal-driven and focused quest for and attraction to results-oriented and successful identity development.
♆	Neptune	Capricorn	♑	2	Your Way of Mystery manifests through your goal-driven and focused quest for and attraction to results-oriented and successful values and ways to meet your needs.
♆	Neptune	Capricorn	♑	3	Your Way of Mystery manifests through your goal-driven and focused quest for and attraction to results-oriented and successful understanding of the world around you.
♆	Neptune	Capricorn	♑	4	Your Way of Mystery manifests through your goal-driven and focused quest for and attraction to results-oriented and successful emotional caretaking and traditions.
♆	Neptune	Capricorn	♑	5	Your Way of Mystery manifests through your goal-driven and focused quest for and attraction to results-oriented and successful creative expression.
♆	Neptune	Capricorn	♑	6	Your Way of Mystery manifests through your goal-driven and focused quest for and attraction to results-oriented and successful service for others.
♆	Neptune	Capricorn	♑	7	Your Way of Mystery manifests through your goal-driven and focused quest for and attraction to results-oriented and successful life teachers.
♆	Neptune	Capricorn	♑	8	Your Way of Mystery manifests through your goal-driven and focused quest for and attraction to results-oriented and successful intimate relationships.
♆	Neptune	Capricorn	♑	9	Your Way of Mystery manifests through your goal-driven and focused quest for and attraction to results-oriented and successful mastership of a body of knowledge.
♆	Neptune	Capricorn	♑	10	Your Way of Mystery manifests through your goal-driven and focused quest for and attraction to results-oriented and successful accomplishments.
♆	Neptune	Capricorn	♑	11	Your Way of Mystery manifests through your goal-driven and focused quest for and attraction to results-oriented and successful community.
♆	Neptune	Capricorn	♑	12	Your Way of Mystery manifests through your goal-driven and focused quest for and attraction to results-oriented and successful spirituality.

	Neptune	Aquarius	♒	1	Your Way of Mystery manifests through your unconventional and idealistic quest for and attraction to authentic and non-traditional identity development.
♆	Neptune	Aquarius	♒	2	Your Way of Mystery manifests through your unconventional and idealistic quest for and attraction to authentic and non-traditional values and ways to meet your needs.
♆	Neptune	Aquarius	♒	3	Your Way of Mystery manifests through your unconventional and idealistic quest for and attraction to authentic and non-traditional understanding of the world around you.
♆	Neptune	Aquarius	♒	4	Your Way of Mystery manifests through your unconventional and idealistic quest for and attraction to authentic and non-traditional emotional caretaking and traditions.
♆	Neptune	Aquarius	♒	5	Your Way of Mystery manifests through your unconventional and idealistic quest for and attraction to authentic and non-traditional creative expression.
♆	Neptune	Aquarius	♒	6	Your Way of Mystery manifests through your unconventional and idealistic quest for and attraction to authentic and non-traditional service for others.
♆	Neptune	Aquarius	♒	7	Your Way of Mystery manifests through your unconventional and idealistic quest for and attraction to authentic and non-traditional life teachers.
♆	Neptune	Aquarius	♒	8	Your Way of Mystery manifests through your unconventional and idealistic quest for and attraction to authentic and non-traditional intimate relationships.
♆	Neptune	Aquarius	♒	9	Your Way of Mystery manifests through your unconventional and idealistic quest for and attraction to authentic and non-traditional mastership of a body of knowledge.
♆	Neptune	Aquarius	♒	10	Your Way of Mystery manifests through your unconventional and idealistic quest for and attraction to authentic and non-traditional accomplishments.
♆	Neptune	Aquarius	♒	11	Your Way of Mystery manifests through your unconventional and idealistic quest for and attraction to authentic and non-traditional community.
♆	Neptune	Aquarius	♒	12	Your Way of Mystery manifests through your unconventional and idealistic quest for and attraction to authentic and non-traditional spirituality.

	Neptune	Pisces	♓	1	Your Way of Mystery manifests through your imaginative and faithful quest for and attraction to consciousness-raising and soulful identity development.
	Neptune	Pisces	♓	2	Your Way of Mystery manifests through your imaginative and faithful quest for and attraction to consciousness-raising and soulful values and ways to meet your needs.
	Neptune	Pisces	♓	3	Your Way of Mystery manifests through your imaginative and faithful quest for and attraction to consciousness-raising and soulful understanding of the world around you.
	Neptune	Pisces	♓	4	Your Way of Mystery manifests through your imaginative and faithful quest for and attraction to consciousness-raising and soulful emotional caretaking and traditions.
	Neptune	Pisces	♓	5	Your Way of Mystery manifests through your imaginative and faithful quest for and attraction to consciousness-raising and soulful creative expression.
	Neptune	Pisces	♓	6	Your Way of Mystery manifests through your imaginative and faithful quest for and attraction to consciousness-raising and soulful service for others.
	Neptune	Pisces	♓	7	Your Way of Mystery manifests through your imaginative and faithful quest for and attraction to consciousness-raising and soulful life teachers.
	Neptune	Pisces	♓	8	Your Way of Mystery manifests through your imaginative and faithful quest for and attraction to consciousness-raising and soulful intimate relationships.
	Neptune	Pisces	♓	9	Your Way of Mystery manifests through your imaginative and faithful quest for and attraction to consciousness-raising and soulful mastership of a body of knowledge.
	Neptune	Pisces	♓	10	Your Way of Mystery manifests through your imaginative and faithful quest for and attraction to consciousness-raising and soulful accomplishments.
	Neptune	Pisces	♓	11	Your Way of Mystery manifests through your imaginative and faithful quest for and attraction to consciousness-raising and soulful community.
	Neptune	Pisces	♓	12	Your Way of Mystery manifests through your imaginative and faithful quest for and attraction to consciousness-raising and soulful spirituality.

Astrology Unlocked by Philip Young, PhD

Pluto | ♇

Energy Point Type: **Dwarf Planet**
Co-Rules Sign: **Scorpio**
Co-Rules House: **8**th
Element: **Water**
Key Phrase: **Way of Transforming**

Pluto represents your Way of Transforming. Its placement in Sign and House reveals how and where we bring about transformation and are transformed as well. In my case my Way of Transforming is expressed through Earth (Virgo) in my quest for community (11th House). Earth's expression is accomplished, persistent, and practical. In Virgo the Element acts critically, meticulously, and pragmatically. So, my key phrase is *"Your Way of Transforming manifests through your critically-minded and methodical quest for and attraction to meticulous and practical community."* In short, I seek to be a member of a community of people who want to make concrete and definable change in the world – building, repairing, growing, and doing in practical ways.

When considering Pluto's placement in your chart, think about how and where you experience and need to create transformation. Earth Signs transform and are transformed by the material world; Fire Signs, by creativity and spirituality; Air Signs, by communication and thought; and Water Signs, by emotions. Now consider Pluto in Libra in the 9th House, *"Your Way of Transforming manifests through your analytical and balanced quest for and attraction to harmonious and logical mastership of a body of knowledge."* Here is an individual who can really get all the transformative power out of education, especially higher education (9th House). This person will use his or her mind to pursue and initiate transformations while also being transformed through communication and intellectual input from the outside world (Libra). Words transform and words are used to transform.

For more in depth reading about Pluto, I recommend purchasing and reading:

- *Alan Oken's Complete Astrology* by Alan Oken (ISBN: 9780892541256)

- *Astrology for Beginners* by Joann Hampar (ISBN: 9780738711065)

- *Healing Pluto Problems* by Donna Cunningham (ISBN: 0877283982)

- *Horoscope Symbols* by Robert Hand (ISBN: 0914918168)

- *The Inner Sky* by Steven Forrest (ISBN: 9780979067716)

- *Mythic Astrology Applied* by Ariel Guttman & Kenneth Johnson (ISBN: 0738704253)

- *Planets in Play* by Laurence Hillman (ISBN: 9781585425877)

- *Pluto: The Evolutionary Journey of the Soul, Volume 1* by Jeff Green (ISBN: 0875422969)

- *Take Control with Astrology* by Lisa Tenzin-Dolma (ISBN: 9780071665049)

	Pluto	Aries	♈	1	Your Way of Transforming manifests through your independent and heroic quest for and attraction to maverick and individualistic identity development.
	Pluto	Aries	♈	2	Your Way of Transforming manifests through your independent and heroic quest for and attraction to maverick and individualistic values and ways to meet your needs.
	Pluto	Aries	♈	3	Your Way of Transforming manifests through your independent and heroic quest for and attraction to maverick and individualistic understanding of the world around you.
	Pluto	Aries	♈	4	Your Way of Transforming manifests through your independent and heroic quest for and attraction to maverick and individualistic emotional caretaking and traditions.
	Pluto	Aries	♈	5	Your Way of Transforming manifests through your independent and heroic quest for and attraction to maverick and individualistic creative expression.
	Pluto	Aries	♈	6	Your Way of Transforming manifests through your independent and heroic quest for and attraction to maverick and individualistic service for others.
	Pluto	Aries	♈	7	Your Way of Transforming manifests through your independent and heroic quest for and attraction to maverick and individualistic life teachers.
	Pluto	Aries	♈	8	Your Way of Transforming manifests through your independent and heroic quest for and attraction to maverick and individualistic intimate relationships.
	Pluto	Aries	♈	9	Your Way of Transforming manifests through your independent and heroic quest for and attraction to maverick and individualistic mastership of a body of knowledge.
	Pluto	Aries	♈	10	Your Way of Transforming manifests through your independent and heroic quest for and attraction to maverick and individualistic accomplishments.
	Pluto	Aries	♈	11	Your Way of Transforming manifests through your independent and heroic quest for and attraction to maverick and individualistic community.
	Pluto	Aries	♈	12	Your Way of Transforming manifests through your independent and heroic quest for and attraction to maverick and individualistic spirituality.

	Pluto	Taurus	♉	1	Your Way of Transforming manifests through your steadfast and persistent quest for and attraction to enduring and secure identity development.
♇	Pluto	Taurus	♉	2	Your Way of Transforming manifests through your steadfast and persistent quest for and attraction to enduring and secure values and ways to meet your needs.
♇	Pluto	Taurus	♉	3	Your Way of Transforming manifests through your steadfast and persistent quest for and attraction to enduring and secure understanding of the world around you.
♇	Pluto	Taurus	♉	4	Your Way of Transforming manifests through your steadfast and persistent quest for and attraction to enduring and secure emotional caretaking and traditions.
♇	Pluto	Taurus	♉	5	Your Way of Transforming manifests through your steadfast and persistent quest for and attraction to enduring and secure creative expression.
♇	Pluto	Taurus	♉	6	Your Way of Transforming manifests through your steadfast and persistent quest for and attraction to enduring and secure service for others.
♇	Pluto	Taurus	♉	7	Your Way of Transforming manifests through your steadfast and persistent quest for and attraction to enduring and secure life teachers.
♇	Pluto	Taurus	♉	8	Your Way of Transforming manifests through your steadfast and persistent quest for and attraction to enduring and secure intimate relationships.
♇	Pluto	Taurus	♉	9	Your Way of Transforming manifests through your steadfast and persistent quest for and attraction to enduring and secure mastership of a body of knowledge.
♇	Pluto	Taurus	♉	10	Your Way of Transforming manifests through your steadfast and persistent quest for and attraction to enduring and secure accomplishments.
♇	Pluto	Taurus	♉	11	Your Way of Transforming manifests through your steadfast and persistent quest for and attraction to enduring and secure community.
♇	Pluto	Taurus	♉	12	Your Way of Transforming manifests through your steadfast and persistent quest for and attraction to enduring and secure spirituality.

Astrology Unlocked by Philip Young, PhD

	Pluto	Gemini	♊	1	Your Way of Transforming manifests through your inquisitive and mentally agile quest for and attraction to ever changing and adaptable identity development.
♇	Pluto	Gemini	♊	2	Your Way of Transforming manifests through your inquisitive and mentally agile quest for and attraction to ever changing and adaptable values and ways to meet your needs.
♇	Pluto	Gemini	♊	3	Your Way of Transforming manifests through your inquisitive and mentally agile quest for and attraction to ever changing and adaptable understanding of the world around you.
♇	Pluto	Gemini	♊	4	Your Way of Transforming manifests through your inquisitive and mentally agile quest for and attraction to ever changing and adaptable emotional caretaking and traditions.
♇	Pluto	Gemini	♊	5	Your Way of Transforming manifests through your inquisitive and mentally agile quest for and attraction to ever changing and adaptable creative expression.
♇	Pluto	Gemini	♊	6	Your Way of Transforming manifests through your inquisitive and mentally agile quest for and attraction to ever changing and adaptable service for others.
♇	Pluto	Gemini	♊	7	Your Way of Transforming manifests through your inquisitive and mentally agile quest for and attraction to ever changing and adaptable life teachers.
♇	Pluto	Gemini	♊	8	Your Way of Transforming manifests through your inquisitive and mentally agile quest for and attraction to ever changing and adaptable intimate relationships.
♇	Pluto	Gemini	♊	9	Your Way of Transforming manifests through your inquisitive and mentally agile quest for and attraction to ever changing and adaptable mastership of a body of knowledge.
♇	Pluto	Gemini	♊	10	Your Way of Transforming manifests through your inquisitive and mentally agile quest for and attraction to ever changing and adaptable accomplishments.
♇	Pluto	Gemini	♊	11	Your Way of Transforming manifests through your inquisitive and mentally agile quest for and attraction to ever changing and adaptable community.
♇	Pluto	Gemini	♊	12	Your Way of Transforming manifests through your inquisitive and mentally agile quest for and attraction to ever changing and adaptable spirituality.

	Pluto	Cancer	♋	1	Your Way of Transforming manifests through your emotional and caring quest for and attraction to nurturing and supportive identity development.
	Pluto	Cancer	♋	2	Your Way of Transforming manifests through your emotional and caring quest for and attraction to nurturing and supportive values and ways to meet your needs.
	Pluto	Cancer	♋	3	Your Way of Transforming manifests through your emotional and caring quest for and attraction to nurturing and supportive understanding of the world around you.
	Pluto	Cancer	♋	4	Your Way of Transforming manifests through your emotional and caring quest for and attraction to nurturing and supportive emotional caretaking and traditions.
	Pluto	Cancer	♋	5	Your Way of Transforming manifests through your emotional and caring quest for and attraction to nurturing and supportive creative expression.
	Pluto	Cancer	♋	6	Your Way of Transforming manifests through your emotional and caring quest for and attraction to nurturing and supportive service for others.
	Pluto	Cancer	♋	7	Your Way of Transforming manifests through your emotional and caring quest for and attraction to nurturing and supportive life teachers.
	Pluto	Cancer	♋	8	Your Way of Transforming manifests through your emotional and caring quest for and attraction to nurturing and supportive intimate relationships.
	Pluto	Cancer	♋	9	Your Way of Transforming manifests through your emotional and caring quest for and attraction to nurturing and supportive mastership of a body of knowledge.
	Pluto	Cancer	♋	10	Your Way of Transforming manifests through your emotional and caring quest for and attraction to nurturing and supportive accomplishments.
	Pluto	Cancer	♋	11	Your Way of Transforming manifests through your emotional and caring quest for and attraction to nurturing and supportive community.
	Pluto	Cancer	♋	12	Your Way of Transforming manifests through your emotional and caring quest for and attraction to nurturing and supportive spirituality.

	Pluto	Leo	♌	1	Your Way of Transforming manifests through your energetic and dramatic quest for and attraction to creative and romantic identity development.
	Pluto	Leo	♌	2	Your Way of Transforming manifests through your energetic and dramatic quest for and attraction to creative and romantic values and ways to meet your needs.
	Pluto	Leo	♌	3	Your Way of Transforming manifests through your energetic and dramatic quest for and attraction to creative and romantic understanding of the world around you.
	Pluto	Leo	♌	4	Your Way of Transforming manifests through your energetic and dramatic quest for and attraction to creative and romantic emotional caretaking and traditions.
	Pluto	Leo	♌	5	Your Way of Transforming manifests through your energetic and dramatic quest for and attraction to creative and romantic creative expression.
	Pluto	Leo	♌	6	Your Way of Transforming manifests through your energetic and dramatic quest for and attraction to creative and romantic service for others.
	Pluto	Leo	♌	7	Your Way of Transforming manifests through your energetic and dramatic quest for and attraction to creative and romantic life teachers.
	Pluto	Leo	♌	8	Your Way of Transforming manifests through your energetic and dramatic quest for and attraction to creative and romantic intimate relationships.
	Pluto	Leo	♌	9	Your Way of Transforming manifests through your energetic and dramatic quest for and attraction to creative and romantic mastership of a body of knowledge.
	Pluto	Leo	♌	10	Your Way of Transforming manifests through your energetic and dramatic quest for and attraction to creative and romantic accomplishments.
	Pluto	Leo	♌	11	Your Way of Transforming manifests through your energetic and dramatic quest for and attraction to creative and romantic community.
	Pluto	Leo	♌	12	Your Way of Transforming manifests through your energetic and dramatic quest for and attraction to creative and romantic spirituality.

	Pluto	Virgo	♍	1	Your Way of Transforming manifests through your critically-minded and methodical quest for and attraction to meticulous and practical identity development.
	Pluto	Virgo	♍	2	Your Way of Transforming manifests through your critically-minded and methodical quest for and attraction to meticulous and practical values and ways to meet your needs.
	Pluto	Virgo	♍	3	Your Way of Transforming manifests through your critically-minded and methodical quest for and attraction to meticulous and practical understanding of the world around you.
	Pluto	Virgo	♍	4	Your Way of Transforming manifests through your critically-minded and methodical quest for and attraction to meticulous and practical emotional caretaking and traditions.
	Pluto	Virgo	♍	5	Your Way of Transforming manifests through your critically-minded and methodical quest for and attraction to meticulous and practical creative expression.
	Pluto	Virgo	♍	6	Your Way of Transforming manifests through your critically-minded and methodical quest for and attraction to meticulous and practical service for others.
	Pluto	Virgo	♍	7	Your Way of Transforming manifests through your critically-minded and methodical quest for and attraction to meticulous and practical life teachers.
	Pluto	Virgo	♍	8	Your Way of Transforming manifests through your critically-minded and methodical quest for and attraction to meticulous and practical intimate relationships.
	Pluto	Virgo	♍	9	Your Way of Transforming manifests through your critically-minded and methodical quest for and attraction to meticulous and practical mastership of a body of knowledge.
	Pluto	Virgo	♍	10	Your Way of Transforming manifests through your critically-minded and methodical quest for and attraction to meticulous and practical accomplishments.
	Pluto	Virgo	♍	11	Your Way of Transforming manifests through your critically-minded and methodical quest for and attraction to meticulous and practical community.
	Pluto	Virgo	♍	12	Your Way of Transforming manifests through your critically-minded and methodical quest for and attraction to meticulous and practical spirituality.

Astrology Unlocked by Philip Young, PhD

	Pluto	Libra	♎	1	Your Way of Transforming manifests through your analytical and balanced quest for and attraction to harmonious and logical identity development.
	Pluto	Libra	♎	2	Your Way of Transforming manifests through your analytical and balanced quest for and attraction to harmonious and logical values and ways to meet your needs.
	Pluto	Libra	♎	3	Your Way of Transforming manifests through your analytical and balanced quest for and attraction to harmonious and logical understanding of the world around you.
	Pluto	Libra	♎	4	Your Way of Transforming manifests through your analytical and balanced quest for and attraction to harmonious and logical emotional caretaking and traditions.
	Pluto	Libra	♎	5	Your Way of Transforming manifests through your analytical and balanced quest for and attraction to harmonious and logical creative expression.
	Pluto	Libra	♎	6	Your Way of Transforming manifests through your analytical and balanced quest for and attraction to harmonious and logical service for others.
	Pluto	Libra	♎	7	Your Way of Transforming manifests through your analytical and balanced quest for and attraction to harmonious and logical life teachers.
	Pluto	Libra	♎	8	Your Way of Transforming manifests through your analytical and balanced quest for and attraction to harmonious and logical intimate relationships.
	Pluto	Libra	♎	9	Your Way of Transforming manifests through your analytical and balanced quest for and attraction to harmonious and logical mastership of a body of knowledge.
	Pluto	Libra	♎	10	Your Way of Transforming manifests through your analytical and balanced quest for and attraction to harmonious and logical accomplishments.
	Pluto	Libra	♎	11	Your Way of Transforming manifests through your analytical and balanced quest for and attraction to harmonious and logical community.
	Pluto	Libra	♎	12	Your Way of Transforming manifests through your analytical and balanced quest for and attraction to harmonious and logical spirituality.

♇	Pluto	Scorpio	♏	1	Your Way of Transforming manifests through your intense and truth seeking quest for and attraction to penetrating and emotionally transformative identity development.
♇	Pluto	Scorpio	♏	2	Your Way of Transforming manifests through your intense and truth seeking quest for and attraction to penetrating and emotionally transformative values and ways to meet your needs.
♇	Pluto	Scorpio	♏	3	Your Way of Transforming manifests through your intense and truth seeking quest for and attraction to penetrating and emotionally transformative understanding of the world around you.
♇	Pluto	Scorpio	♏	4	Your Way of Transforming manifests through your intense and truth seeking quest for and attraction to penetrating and emotionally transformative emotional caretaking and traditions.
♇	Pluto	Scorpio	♏	5	Your Way of Transforming manifests through your intense and truth seeking quest for and attraction to penetrating and emotionally transformative creative expression.
♇	Pluto	Scorpio	♏	6	Your Way of Transforming manifests through your intense and truth seeking quest for and attraction to penetrating and emotionally transformative service for others.
♇	Pluto	Scorpio	♏	7	Your Way of Transforming manifests through your intense and truth seeking quest for and attraction to penetrating and emotionally transformative life teachers.
♇	Pluto	Scorpio	♏	8	Your Way of Transforming manifests through your intense and truth seeking quest for and attraction to penetrating and emotionally transformative intimate relationships.
♇	Pluto	Scorpio	♏	9	Your Way of Transforming manifests through your intense and truth seeking quest for and attraction to penetrating and emotionally transformative mastership of a body of knowledge.
♇	Pluto	Scorpio	♏	10	Your Way of Transforming manifests through your intense and truth seeking quest for and attraction to penetrating and emotionally transformative accomplishments.
♇	Pluto	Scorpio	♏	11	Your Way of Transforming manifests through your intense and truth seeking quest for and attraction to penetrating and emotionally transformative community.
♇	Pluto	Scorpio	♏	12	Your Way of Transforming manifests through your intense and truth seeking quest for and attraction to penetrating and emotionally transformative spirituality.

Astrology Unlocked by Philip Young, PhD

♇	Pluto	Sagittarius	⚐	1	Your Way of Transforming manifests through your wide-ranging and open-minded quest for and attraction to experiential and risk-taking identity development.
♇	Pluto	Sagittarius	⚐	2	Your Way of Transforming manifests through your wide-ranging and open-minded quest for and attraction to experiential and risk-taking values and ways to meet your needs.
♇	Pluto	Sagittarius	⚐	3	Your Way of Transforming manifests through your wide-ranging and open-minded quest for and attraction to experiential and risk-taking understanding of the world around you.
♇	Pluto	Sagittarius	⚐	4	Your Way of Transforming manifests through your wide-ranging and open-minded quest for and attraction to experiential and risk-taking emotional caretaking and traditions.
♇	Pluto	Sagittarius	⚐	5	Your Way of Transforming manifests through your wide-ranging and open-minded quest for and attraction to experiential and risk-taking creative expression.
♇	Pluto	Sagittarius	⚐	6	Your Way of Transforming manifests through your wide-ranging and open-minded quest for and attraction to experiential and risk-taking service for others.
♇	Pluto	Sagittarius	⚐	7	Your Way of Transforming manifests through your wide-ranging and open-minded quest for and attraction to experiential and risk-taking life teachers.
♇	Pluto	Sagittarius	⚐	8	Your Way of Transforming manifests through your wide-ranging and open-minded quest for and attraction to experiential and risk-taking intimate relationships.
♇	Pluto	Sagittarius	⚐	9	Your Way of Transforming manifests through your wide-ranging and open-minded quest for and attraction to experiential and risk-taking mastership of a body of knowledge.
♇	Pluto	Sagittarius	⚐	10	Your Way of Transforming manifests through your wide-ranging and open-minded quest for and attraction to experiential and risk-taking accomplishments.
♇	Pluto	Sagittarius	⚐	11	Your Way of Transforming manifests through your wide-ranging and open-minded quest for and attraction to experiential and risk-taking community.
♇	Pluto	Sagittarius	⚐	12	Your Way of Transforming manifests through your wide-ranging and open-minded quest for and attraction to experiential and risk-taking spirituality.

	Pluto	Capricorn	♑	1	Your Way of Transforming manifests through your goal-driven and focused quest for and attraction to results-oriented and successful identity development.
	Pluto	Capricorn	♑	2	Your Way of Transforming manifests through your goal-driven and focused quest for and attraction to results-oriented and successful values and ways to meet your needs.
	Pluto	Capricorn	♑	3	Your Way of Transforming manifests through your goal-driven and focused quest for and attraction to results-oriented and successful understanding of the world around you.
	Pluto	Capricorn	♑	4	Your Way of Transforming manifests through your goal-driven and focused quest for and attraction to results-oriented and successful emotional caretaking and traditions.
	Pluto	Capricorn	♑	5	Your Way of Transforming manifests through your goal-driven and focused quest for and attraction to results-oriented and successful creative expression.
	Pluto	Capricorn	♑	6	Your Way of Transforming manifests through your goal-driven and focused quest for and attraction to results-oriented and successful service for others.
	Pluto	Capricorn	♑	7	Your Way of Transforming manifests through your goal-driven and focused quest for and attraction to results-oriented and successful life teachers.
	Pluto	Capricorn	♑	8	Your Way of Transforming manifests through your goal-driven and focused quest for and attraction to results-oriented and successful intimate relationships.
	Pluto	Capricorn	♑	9	Your Way of Transforming manifests through your goal-driven and focused quest for and attraction to results-oriented and successful mastership of a body of knowledge.
	Pluto	Capricorn	♑	10	Your Way of Transforming manifests through your goal-driven and focused quest for and attraction to results-oriented and successful accomplishments.
	Pluto	Capricorn	♑	11	Your Way of Transforming manifests through your goal-driven and focused quest for and attraction to results-oriented and successful community.
	Pluto	Capricorn	♑	12	Your Way of Transforming manifests through your goal-driven and focused quest for and attraction to results-oriented and successful spirituality.

	Pluto	Aquarius	♒	1	Your Way of Transforming manifests through your unconventional and idealistic quest for and attraction to authentic and non-traditional identity development.
	Pluto	Aquarius	♒	2	Your Way of Transforming manifests through your unconventional and idealistic quest for and attraction to authentic and non-traditional values and ways to meet your needs.
	Pluto	Aquarius	♒	3	Your Way of Transforming manifests through your unconventional and idealistic quest for and attraction to authentic and non-traditional understanding of the world around you.
	Pluto	Aquarius	♒	4	Your Way of Transforming manifests through your unconventional and idealistic quest for and attraction to authentic and non-traditional emotional caretaking and traditions.
	Pluto	Aquarius	♒	5	Your Way of Transforming manifests through your unconventional and idealistic quest for and attraction to authentic and non-traditional creative expression.
	Pluto	Aquarius	♒	6	Your Way of Transforming manifests through your unconventional and idealistic quest for and attraction to authentic and non-traditional service for others.
	Pluto	Aquarius	♒	7	Your Way of Transforming manifests through your unconventional and idealistic quest for and attraction to authentic and non-traditional life teachers.
	Pluto	Aquarius	♒	8	Your Way of Transforming manifests through your unconventional and idealistic quest for and attraction to authentic and non-traditional intimate relationships.
	Pluto	Aquarius	♒	9	Your Way of Transforming manifests through your unconventional and idealistic quest for and attraction to authentic and non-traditional mastership of a body of knowledge.
	Pluto	Aquarius	♒	10	Your Way of Transforming manifests through your unconventional and idealistic quest for and attraction to authentic and non-traditional accomplishments.
	Pluto	Aquarius	♒	11	Your Way of Transforming manifests through your unconventional and idealistic quest for and attraction to authentic and non-traditional community.
	Pluto	Aquarius	♒	12	Your Way of Transforming manifests through your unconventional and idealistic quest for and attraction to authentic and non-traditional spirituality.

	Pluto	Pisces	♓	1	Your Way of Transforming manifests through your imaginative and faithful quest for and attraction to consciousness-raising and soulful identity development.
	Pluto	Pisces	♓	2	Your Way of Transforming manifests through your imaginative and faithful quest for and attraction to consciousness-raising and soulful values and ways to meet your needs.
	Pluto	Pisces	♓	3	Your Way of Transforming manifests through your imaginative and faithful quest for and attraction to consciousness-raising and soulful understanding of the world around you.
	Pluto	Pisces	♓	4	Your Way of Transforming manifests through your imaginative and faithful quest for and attraction to consciousness-raising and soulful emotional caretaking and traditions.
	Pluto	Pisces	♓	5	Your Way of Transforming manifests through your imaginative and faithful quest for and attraction to consciousness-raising and soulful creative expression.
	Pluto	Pisces	♓	6	Your Way of Transforming manifests through your imaginative and faithful quest for and attraction to consciousness-raising and soulful service for others.
	Pluto	Pisces	♓	7	Your Way of Transforming manifests through your imaginative and faithful quest for and attraction to consciousness-raising and soulful life teachers.
	Pluto	Pisces	♓	8	Your Way of Transforming manifests through your imaginative and faithful quest for and attraction to consciousness-raising and soulful intimate relationships.
	Pluto	Pisces	♓	9	Your Way of Transforming manifests through your imaginative and faithful quest for and attraction to consciousness-raising and soulful mastership of a body of knowledge.
	Pluto	Pisces	♓	10	Your Way of Transforming manifests through your imaginative and faithful quest for and attraction to consciousness-raising and soulful accomplishments.
	Pluto	Pisces	♓	11	Your Way of Transforming manifests through your imaginative and faithful quest for and attraction to consciousness-raising and soulful community.
	Pluto	Pisces	♓	12	Your Way of Transforming manifests through your imaginative and faithful quest for and attraction to consciousness-raising and soulful spirituality.

Chiron | ⚷

Energy Point Type: **Asteroid**

Co-Rules Sign: **Virgo**

Co-Rules House: **6**th

Element: **Earth**

Key Phrase: **Way of Wounding and Healing**

Chiron represents your Way of Wounding and Healing. Its placement in Sign and House reveals where we have our spiritual wound that we must work to heal in this lifetime. In my case my Way of Wounding and Healing is expressed through Fire (Aries) in my quest for service (6th House). Fire's expression is pioneering, creative, and exploratory. In Aries the Element acts independently, heroically, and aggressively. So my key phrase is *"Your Way of Wounding and Healing manifests through your independent and heroic quest for and attraction to maverick and individualistic service for others."* In short, I am wounded when I act independently in my day-to-day work if I work for someone or a company. My healing has come by starting and running my own business, independently.

When considering your Chiron placement, think about how and where you receive your wounding and need to do your healing work. Consider Chiron in Gemini in the 3rd House, *"Your Way of Wounding and Healing manifests through your inquisitive and mentally agile quest for and attraction to ever changing and adaptable understanding of the world around you."* In essence, here is a person who struggles to either understand others or be understood, or both. The wound can show up as any form of difficult communication, a hard time learning and comprehending new ideas, challenges making friendships (Gemini) and connecting with people in his or her day-to-day life (3rd House). To help heal the wound this person would need to do the extra work to study communication styles, learn social conventions, and understand his or her learning style. He or she would need to make sure new ideas and information can be accessed through his or her style of learning.

For more in depth reading about Chiron, I recommend purchasing and reading:

- *Chiron and the Healing Journey: An Astrological and Psychological Perspective* by Melanie Rienhart (ISBN: 0140192093)
- *Liquid Light of Sex* by Barbara Hand Clow (ISBN: 0939680963)
- *Mythic Astrology Applied* by Ariel Guttman & Kenneth Johnson (ISBN: 0738704253)

⚷	Chiron	Aries	♈	1	Your Way of Wounding and Healing manifests through your independent and heroic quest for and attraction to maverick and individualistic identity development.
⚷	Chiron	Aries	♈	2	Your Way of Wounding and Healing manifests through your independent and heroic quest for and attraction to maverick and individualistic values and ways to meet your needs.
⚷	Chiron	Aries	♈	3	Your Way of Wounding and Healing manifests through your independent and heroic quest for and attraction to maverick and individualistic understanding of the world around you.
⚷	Chiron	Aries	♈	4	Your Way of Wounding and Healing manifests through your independent and heroic quest for and attraction to maverick and individualistic emotional caretaking and traditions.
⚷	Chiron	Aries	♈	5	Your Way of Wounding and Healing manifests through your independent and heroic quest for and attraction to maverick and individualistic creative expression.
⚷	Chiron	Aries	♈	6	Your Way of Wounding and Healing manifests through your independent and heroic quest for and attraction to maverick and individualistic service for others.
⚷	Chiron	Aries	♈	7	Your Way of Wounding and Healing manifests through your independent and heroic quest for and attraction to maverick and individualistic partnerships and life teachers.
⚷	Chiron	Aries	♈	8	Your Way of Wounding and Healing manifests through your independent and heroic quest for and attraction to maverick and individualistic intimate relationships.
⚷	Chiron	Aries	♈	9	Your Way of Wounding and Healing manifests through your independent and heroic quest for and attraction to maverick and individualistic mastership of a body of knowledge.
⚷	Chiron	Aries	♈	10	Your Way of Wounding and Healing manifests through your independent and heroic quest for and attraction to maverick and individualistic accomplishments.
⚷	Chiron	Aries	♈	11	Your Way of Wounding and Healing manifests through your independent and heroic quest for and attraction to maverick and individualistic community.
⚷	Chiron	Aries	♈	12	Your Way of Wounding and Healing manifests through your independent and heroic quest for and attraction to maverick and individualistic spirituality.

203

	Chiron	Taurus	♉	1	Your Way of Wounding and Healing manifests through your steadfast and persistent quest for and attraction to enduring and secure identity development.
	Chiron	Taurus	♉	2	Your Way of Wounding and Healing manifests through your steadfast and persistent quest for and attraction to enduring and secure values and ways to meet your needs.
	Chiron	Taurus	♉	3	Your Way of Wounding and Healing manifests through your steadfast and persistent quest for and attraction to enduring and secure understanding of the world around you.
	Chiron	Taurus	♉	4	Your Way of Wounding and Healing manifests through your steadfast and persistent quest for and attraction to enduring and secure emotional caretaking and traditions.
	Chiron	Taurus	♉	5	Your Way of Wounding and Healing manifests through your steadfast and persistent quest for and attraction to enduring and secure creative expression.
	Chiron	Taurus	♉	6	Your Way of Wounding and Healing manifests through your steadfast and persistent quest for and attraction to enduring and secure service for others.
	Chiron	Taurus	♉	7	Your Way of Wounding and Healing manifests through your steadfast and persistent quest for and attraction to enduring and secure partnerships and life teachers.
	Chiron	Taurus	♉	8	Your Way of Wounding and Healing manifests through your steadfast and persistent quest for and attraction to enduring and secure intimate relationships.
	Chiron	Taurus	♉	9	Your Way of Wounding and Healing manifests through your steadfast and persistent quest for and attraction to enduring and secure mastership of a body of knowledge.
	Chiron	Taurus	♉	10	Your Way of Wounding and Healing manifests through your steadfast and persistent quest for and attraction to enduring and secure accomplishments.
	Chiron	Taurus	♉	11	Your Way of Wounding and Healing manifests through your steadfast and persistent quest for and attraction to enduring and secure community.
	Chiron	Taurus	♉	12	Your Way of Wounding and Healing manifests through your steadfast and persistent quest for and attraction to enduring and secure spirituality.

	Chiron	Gemini	♊	1	Your Way of Wounding and Healing manifests through your inquisitive and mentally agile quest for and attraction to ever changing and adaptable identity development.
	Chiron	Gemini	♊	2	Your Way of Wounding and Healing manifests through your inquisitive and mentally agile quest for and attraction to ever changing and adaptable values and ways to meet your needs.
	Chiron	Gemini	♊	3	Your Way of Wounding and Healing manifests through your inquisitive and mentally agile quest for and attraction to ever changing and adaptable understanding of the world around you.
	Chiron	Gemini	♊	4	Your Way of Wounding and Healing manifests through your inquisitive and mentally agile quest for and attraction to ever changing and adaptable emotional caretaking and traditions.
	Chiron	Gemini	♊	5	Your Way of Wounding and Healing manifests through your inquisitive and mentally agile quest for and attraction to ever changing and adaptable creative expression.
	Chiron	Gemini	♊	6	Your Way of Wounding and Healing manifests through your inquisitive and mentally agile quest for and attraction to ever changing and adaptable service for others.
	Chiron	Gemini	♊	7	Your Way of Wounding and Healing manifests through your inquisitive and mentally agile quest for and attraction to ever changing and adaptable partnerships.
	Chiron	Gemini	♊	8	Your Way of Wounding and Healing manifests through your inquisitive and mentally agile quest for and attraction to ever changing and adaptable intimate relationships.
	Chiron	Gemini	♊	9	Your Way of Wounding and Healing manifests through your inquisitive and mentally agile quest for and attraction to ever changing and adaptable mastership of a body of knowledge.
	Chiron	Gemini	♊	10	Your Way of Wounding and Healing manifests through your inquisitive and mentally agile quest for and attraction to ever changing and adaptable accomplishments.
	Chiron	Gemini	♊	11	Your Way of Wounding and Healing manifests through your inquisitive and mentally agile quest for and attraction to ever changing and adaptable community.
	Chiron	Gemini	♊	12	Your Way of Wounding and Healing manifests through your inquisitive and mentally agile quest for and attraction to ever changing and adaptable spirituality.

	Chiron	Cancer	♋	1	Your Way of Wounding and Healing manifests through your emotional and caring quest for and attraction to nurturing and supportive identity development.
	Chiron	Cancer	♋	2	Your Way of Wounding and Healing manifests through your emotional and caring quest for and attraction to nurturing and supportive values and ways to meet your needs.
	Chiron	Cancer	♋	3	Your Way of Wounding and Healing manifests through your emotional and caring quest for and attraction to nurturing and supportive understanding of the world around you.
	Chiron	Cancer	♋	4	Your Way of Wounding and Healing manifests through your emotional and caring quest for and attraction to nurturing and supportive emotional caretaking and traditions.
	Chiron	Cancer	♋	5	Your Way of Wounding and Healing manifests through your emotional and caring quest for and attraction to nurturing and supportive creative expression.
	Chiron	Cancer	♋	6	Your Way of Wounding and Healing manifests through your emotional and caring quest for and attraction to nurturing and supportive service for others.
	Chiron	Cancer	♋	7	Your Way of Wounding and Healing manifests through your emotional and caring quest for and attraction to nurturing and supportive partnerships and life teachers.
	Chiron	Cancer	♋	8	Your Way of Wounding and Healing manifests through your emotional and caring quest for and attraction to nurturing and supportive intimate relationships.
	Chiron	Cancer	♋	9	Your Way of Wounding and Healing manifests through your emotional and caring quest for and attraction to nurturing and supportive mastership of a body of knowledge.
	Chiron	Cancer	♋	10	Your Way of Wounding and Healing manifests through your emotional and caring quest for and attraction to nurturing and supportive accomplishments.
	Chiron	Cancer	♋	11	Your Way of Wounding and Healing manifests through your emotional and caring quest for and attraction to nurturing and supportive community.
	Chiron	Cancer	♋	12	Your Way of Wounding and Healing manifests through your emotional and caring quest for and attraction to nurturing and supportive spirituality.

⚷	Chiron	Leo	♌	1	Your Way of Wounding and Healing manifests through your energetic and dramatic quest for and attraction to creative and romantic identity development.
⚷	Chiron	Leo	♌	2	Your Way of Wounding and Healing manifests through your energetic and dramatic quest for and attraction to creative and romantic values and ways to meet your needs.
⚷	Chiron	Leo	♌	3	Your Way of Wounding and Healing manifests through your energetic and dramatic quest for and attraction to creative and romantic understanding of the world around you.
⚷	Chiron	Leo	♌	4	Your Way of Wounding and Healing manifests through your energetic and dramatic quest for and attraction to creative and romantic emotional caretaking and traditions.
⚷	Chiron	Leo	♌	5	Your Way of Wounding and Healing manifests through your energetic and dramatic quest for and attraction to creative and romantic creative expression.
⚷	Chiron	Leo	♌	6	Your Way of Wounding and Healing manifests through your energetic and dramatic quest for and attraction to creative and romantic service for others.
⚷	Chiron	Leo	♌	7	Your Way of Wounding and Healing manifests through your energetic and dramatic quest for and attraction to creative and romantic partnerships and life teachers.
⚷	Chiron	Leo	♌	8	Your Way of Wounding and Healing manifests through your energetic and dramatic quest for and attraction to creative and romantic intimate relationships.
⚷	Chiron	Leo	♌	9	Your Way of Wounding and Healing manifests through your energetic and dramatic quest for and attraction to creative and romantic mastership of a body of knowledge.
⚷	Chiron	Leo	♌	10	Your Way of Wounding and Healing manifests through your energetic and dramatic quest for and attraction to creative and romantic accomplishments.
⚷	Chiron	Leo	♌	11	Your Way of Wounding and Healing manifests through your energetic and dramatic quest for and attraction to creative and romantic community.
⚷	Chiron	Leo	♌	12	Your Way of Wounding and Healing manifests through your energetic and dramatic quest for and attraction to creative and romantic spirituality.

	Chiron	Virgo	♍	1	Your Way of Wounding and Healing manifests through your critically-minded and methodical quest for and attraction to meticulous and practical identity development.
⚷	Chiron	Virgo	♍	2	Your Way of Wounding and Healing manifests through your critically-minded and methodical quest for and attraction to meticulous and practical values and ways to meet your needs.
⚷	Chiron	Virgo	♍	3	Your Way of Wounding and Healing manifests through your critically-minded and methodical quest for and attraction to meticulous and practical understanding of the world around you.
⚷	Chiron	Virgo	♍	4	Your Way of Wounding and Healing manifests through your critically-minded and methodical quest for and attraction to meticulous and practical emotional caretaking and traditions.
⚷	Chiron	Virgo	♍	5	Your Way of Wounding and Healing manifests through your critically-minded and methodical quest for and attraction to meticulous and practical creative expression.
⚷	Chiron	Virgo	♍	6	Your Way of Wounding and Healing manifests through your critically-minded and methodical quest for and attraction to meticulous and practical service for others.
⚷	Chiron	Virgo	♍	7	Your Way of Wounding and Healing manifests through your critically-minded and methodical quest for and attraction to meticulous and practical partnerships and life teachers.
⚷	Chiron	Virgo	♍	8	Your Way of Wounding and Healing manifests through your critically-minded and methodical quest for and attraction to meticulous and practical intimate relationships.
⚷	Chiron	Virgo	♍	9	Your Way of Wounding and Healing manifests through your critically-minded and methodical quest for and attraction to meticulous and practical mastership of a body of knowledge.
⚷	Chiron	Virgo	♍	10	Your Way of Wounding and Healing manifests through your critically-minded and methodical quest for and attraction to meticulous and practical accomplishments.
⚷	Chiron	Virgo	♍	11	Your Way of Wounding and Healing manifests through your critically-minded and methodical quest for and attraction to meticulous and practical community.
⚷	Chiron	Virgo	♍	12	Your Way of Wounding and Healing manifests through your critically-minded and methodical quest for and attraction to meticulous and practical spirituality.

Astrology Unlocked by Philip Young, PhD

	Chiron	Libra	♎	1	Your Way of Wounding and Healing manifests through your analytical and balanced quest for and attraction to harmonious and logical identity development.
	Chiron	Libra	♎	2	Your Way of Wounding and Healing manifests through your analytical and balanced quest for and attraction to harmonious and logical values and ways to meet your needs.
	Chiron	Libra	♎	3	Your Way of Wounding and Healing manifests through your analytical and balanced quest for and attraction to harmonious and logical understanding of the world around you.
	Chiron	Libra	♎	4	Your Way of Wounding and Healing manifests through your analytical and balanced quest for and attraction to harmonious and logical emotional caretaking and traditions.
	Chiron	Libra	♎	5	Your Way of Wounding and Healing manifests through your analytical and balanced quest for and attraction to harmonious and logical creative expression.
	Chiron	Libra	♎	6	Your Way of Wounding and Healing manifests through your analytical and balanced quest for and attraction to harmonious and logical service for others.
	Chiron	Libra	♎	7	Your Way of Wounding and Healing manifests through your analytical and balanced quest for and attraction to harmonious and logical partnerships and life teachers.
	Chiron	Libra	♎	8	Your Way of Wounding and Healing manifests through your analytical and balanced quest for and attraction to harmonious and logical intimate relationships.
	Chiron	Libra	♎	9	Your Way of Wounding and Healing manifests through your analytical and balanced quest for and attraction to harmonious and logical mastership of a body of knowledge.
	Chiron	Libra	♎	10	Your Way of Wounding and Healing manifests through your analytical and balanced quest for and attraction to harmonious and logical accomplishments.
	Chiron	Libra	♎	11	Your Way of Wounding and Healing manifests through your analytical and balanced quest for and attraction to harmonious and logical community.
	Chiron	Libra	♎	12	Your Way of Wounding and Healing manifests through your analytical and balanced quest for and attraction to harmonious and logical spirituality.

209

	Chiron	Scorpio	♏	1	Your Way of Wounding and Healing manifests through your intense and truth seeking quest for and attraction to penetrating and emotionally transformative identity development.
⚷	Chiron	Scorpio	♏	2	Your Way of Wounding and Healing manifests through your intense and truth seeking quest for and attraction to penetrating and emotionally transformative values and ways to meet your needs.
⚷	Chiron	Scorpio	♏	3	Your Way of Wounding and Healing manifests through your intense and truth seeking quest for and attraction to penetrating and emotionally transformative understanding of the world around you.
⚷	Chiron	Scorpio	♏	4	Your Way of Wounding and Healing manifests through your intense and truth seeking quest for and attraction to penetrating and emotionally transformative emotional caretaking and traditions.
⚷	Chiron	Scorpio	♏	5	Your Way of Wounding and Healing manifests through your intense and truth seeking quest for and attraction to penetrating and emotionally transformative creative expression.
⚷	Chiron	Scorpio	♏	6	Your Way of Wounding and Healing manifests through your intense and truth seeking quest for and attraction to penetrating and emotionally transformative service for others.
⚷	Chiron	Scorpio	♏	7	Your Way of Wounding and Healing manifests through your intense and truth seeking quest for and attraction to penetrating and emotionally transformative partnerships.
⚷	Chiron	Scorpio	♏	8	Your Way of Wounding and Healing manifests through your intense and truth seeking quest for and attraction to penetrating and emotionally transformative intimate relationships.
⚷	Chiron	Scorpio	♏	9	Your Way of Wounding and Healing manifests through your intense and truth seeking quest for and attraction to penetrating and emotionally transformative mastership of a body of knowledge.
⚷	Chiron	Scorpio	♏	10	Your Way of Wounding and Healing manifests through your intense and truth seeking quest for and attraction to penetrating and emotionally transformative accomplishments.
⚷	Chiron	Scorpio	♏	11	Your Way of Wounding and Healing manifests through your intense and truth seeking quest for and attraction to penetrating and emotionally transformative community.
⚷	Chiron	Scorpio	♏	12	Your Way of Wounding and Healing manifests through your intense and truth seeking quest for and attraction to penetrating and emotionally transformative spirituality.

	Chiron	Sagittarius	↗	1	Your Way of Wounding and Healing manifests through your wide-ranging and open-minded quest for and attraction to experiential and risk-taking identity development.
	Chiron	Sagittarius	↗	2	Your Way of Wounding and Healing manifests through your wide-ranging and open-minded quest for and attraction to experiential and risk-taking values and ways to meet your needs.
	Chiron	Sagittarius	↗	3	Your Way of Wounding and Healing manifests through your wide-ranging and open-minded quest for and attraction to experiential and risk-taking understanding of the world around you.
	Chiron	Sagittarius	↗	4	Your Way of Wounding and Healing manifests through your wide-ranging and open-minded quest for and attraction to experiential and risk-taking emotional caretaking and traditions.
	Chiron	Sagittarius	↗	5	Your Way of Wounding and Healing manifests through your wide-ranging and open-minded quest for and attraction to experiential and risk-taking creative expression.
	Chiron	Sagittarius	↗	6	Your Way of Wounding and Healing manifests through your wide-ranging and open-minded quest for and attraction to experiential and risk-taking service for others.
	Chiron	Sagittarius	↗	7	Your Way of Wounding and Healing manifests through your wide-ranging and open-minded quest for and attraction to experiential and risk-taking partnerships.
	Chiron	Sagittarius	↗	8	Your Way of Wounding and Healing manifests through your wide-ranging and open-minded quest for and attraction to experiential and risk-taking intimate relationships.
	Chiron	Sagittarius	↗	9	Your Way of Wounding and Healing manifests through your wide-ranging and open-minded quest for and attraction to experiential and risk-taking mastership of a body of knowledge.
	Chiron	Sagittarius	↗	10	Your Way of Wounding and Healing manifests through your wide-ranging and open-minded quest for and attraction to experiential and risk-taking accomplishments.
	Chiron	Sagittarius	↗	11	Your Way of Wounding and Healing manifests through your wide-ranging and open-minded quest for and attraction to experiential and risk-taking community.
	Chiron	Sagittarius	↗	12	Your Way of Wounding and Healing manifests through your wide-ranging and open-minded quest for and attraction to experiential and risk-taking spirituality.

	Chiron	Capricorn		1	Your Way of Wounding and Healing manifests through your goal-driven and focused quest for and attraction to results-oriented and successful identity development.
	Chiron	Capricorn		2	Your Way of Wounding and Healing manifests through your goal-driven and focused quest for and attraction to results-oriented and successful values and ways to meet your needs.
	Chiron	Capricorn		3	Your Way of Wounding and Healing manifests through your goal-driven and focused quest for and attraction to results-oriented and successful understanding of the world around you.
	Chiron	Capricorn		4	Your Way of Wounding and Healing manifests through your goal-driven and focused quest for and attraction to results-oriented and successful emotional caretaking and traditions.
	Chiron	Capricorn		5	Your Way of Wounding and Healing manifests through your goal-driven and focused quest for and attraction to results-oriented and successful creative expression.
	Chiron	Capricorn		6	Your Way of Wounding and Healing manifests through your goal-driven and focused quest for and attraction to results-oriented and successful service for others.
	Chiron	Capricorn		7	Your Way of Wounding and Healing manifests through your goal-driven and focused quest for and attraction to results-oriented and successful partnerships and life teachers.
	Chiron	Capricorn		8	Your Way of Wounding and Healing manifests through your goal-driven and focused quest for and attraction to results-oriented and successful intimate relationships.
	Chiron	Capricorn		9	Your Way of Wounding and Healing manifests through your goal-driven and focused quest for and attraction to results-oriented and successful mastership of a body of knowledge.
	Chiron	Capricorn		10	Your Way of Wounding and Healing manifests through your goal-driven and focused quest for and attraction to results-oriented and successful accomplishments.
	Chiron	Capricorn		11	Your Way of Wounding and Healing manifests through your goal-driven and focused quest for and attraction to results-oriented and successful community.
	Chiron	Capricorn		12	Your Way of Wounding and Healing manifests through your goal-driven and focused quest for and attraction to results-oriented and successful spirituality.

	Chiron	Aquarius	♒	1	Your Way of Wounding and Healing manifests through your unconventional and idealistic quest for and attraction to authentic and non-traditional identity development.
	Chiron	Aquarius	♒	2	Your Way of Wounding and Healing manifests through your unconventional and idealistic quest for and attraction to authentic and non-traditional values and ways to meet your needs.
	Chiron	Aquarius	♒	3	Your Way of Wounding and Healing manifests through your unconventional and idealistic quest for and attraction to authentic and non-traditional understanding of the world around you.
	Chiron	Aquarius	♒	4	Your Way of Wounding and Healing manifests through your unconventional and idealistic quest for and attraction to authentic and non-traditional emotional caretaking and traditions.
	Chiron	Aquarius	♒	5	Your Way of Wounding and Healing manifests through your unconventional and idealistic quest for and attraction to authentic and non-traditional creative expression.
	Chiron	Aquarius	♒	6	Your Way of Wounding and Healing manifests through your unconventional and idealistic quest for and attraction to authentic and non-traditional service for others.
	Chiron	Aquarius	♒	7	Your Way of Wounding and Healing manifests through your unconventional and idealistic quest for and attraction to authentic and non-traditional partnerships.
	Chiron	Aquarius	♒	8	Your Way of Wounding and Healing manifests through your unconventional and idealistic quest for and attraction to authentic and non-traditional intimate relationships.
	Chiron	Aquarius	♒	9	Your Way of Wounding and Healing manifests through your unconventional and idealistic quest for and attraction to authentic and non-traditional mastership of a body of knowledge.
	Chiron	Aquarius	♒	10	Your Way of Wounding and Healing manifests through your unconventional and idealistic quest for and attraction to authentic and non-traditional accomplishments.
	Chiron	Aquarius	♒	11	Your Way of Wounding and Healing manifests through your unconventional and idealistic quest for and attraction to authentic and non-traditional community.
	Chiron	Aquarius	♒	12	Your Way of Wounding and Healing manifests through your unconventional and idealistic quest for and attraction to authentic and non-traditional spirituality.

	Chiron	Pisces	♓	1	Your Way of Wounding and Healing manifests through your imaginative and faithful quest for and attraction to consciousness-raising and soulful identity development.
	Chiron	Pisces	♓	2	Your Way of Wounding and Healing manifests through your imaginative and faithful quest for and attraction to consciousness-raising and soulful values and ways to meet your needs.
	Chiron	Pisces	♓	3	Your Way of Wounding and Healing manifests through your imaginative and faithful quest for and attraction to consciousness-raising and soulful understanding of the world around you.
	Chiron	Pisces	♓	4	Your Way of Wounding and Healing manifests through your imaginative and faithful quest for and attraction to consciousness-raising and soulful emotional caretaking and traditions.
	Chiron	Pisces	♓	5	Your Way of Wounding and Healing manifests through your imaginative and faithful quest for and attraction to consciousness-raising and soulful creative expression.
	Chiron	Pisces	♓	6	Your Way of Wounding and Healing manifests through your imaginative and faithful quest for and attraction to consciousness-raising and soulful service for others.
	Chiron	Pisces	♓	7	Your Way of Wounding and Healing manifests through your imaginative and faithful quest for and attraction to consciousness-raising and soulful partnerships and life teachers.
	Chiron	Pisces	♓	8	Your Way of Wounding and Healing manifests through your imaginative and faithful quest for and attraction to consciousness-raising and soulful intimate relationships.
	Chiron	Pisces	♓	9	Your Way of Wounding and Healing manifests through your imaginative and faithful quest for and attraction to consciousness-raising and soulful mastership of a body of knowledge.
	Chiron	Pisces	♓	10	Your Way of Wounding and Healing manifests through your imaginative and faithful quest for and attraction to consciousness-raising and soulful accomplishments.
	Chiron	Pisces	♓	11	Your Way of Wounding and Healing manifests through your imaginative and faithful quest for and attraction to consciousness-raising and soulful community.
	Chiron	Pisces	♓	12	Your Way of Wounding and Healing manifests through your imaginative and faithful quest for and attraction to consciousness-raising and soulful spirituality.

Ceres | ♀

Energy Point Type: **Asteroid**

Co-Rules Sign: **Capricorn**

Co-Rules House: **10ᵗʰ**

Element: **Earth**

Key Phrase: **Way of Meeting Your Needs**

Ceres represents your Way of Meeting Your Needs (reaping what you sow, your harvest). Its placement in Sign and House reveals where we must put forth our energy into the world in order to get back the resources we need to survive and thrive. In my case my Way of Meeting Your Needs is expressed through Water (Scorpio) in my quest for identity (1ˢᵗ House). Water's expression is emotional, intense, and imaginative. In Scorpio the Element acts intensely, transformatively, and unrelentingly. So, my key phrase is *"Your Way of Meeting Your Needs manifests through your intense and truth seeking quest for and attraction to penetrating and emotionally transformative identity development."* In short, I make my harvest through the exploration of identity, starting with my own. A career as a therapist, life coach, counselor, or astrologer would all be good ways to get my material needs met.

When considering your Ceres placement, think about what you have as the seeds you need to sow in order to have your material (income and resources) needs met. Air Signs will harvest with communication and analysis; Earth Signs with … well, actual seeds possibly; Fire Signs with creativity and energy, and Water Signs with emotions and connections to others. Consider Ceres in Taurus in the 8ᵗʰ House, *"Your Way of Meeting Your Needs manifests through your steadfast and persistent quest for and attraction to enduring and secure intimate relationships."* This individual will find resource through his or her intimate relationships (8ᵗʰ House), with a lover perhaps, by helping that person succeed or having that person help him or her establish himself or herself in the world (Taurus). The 8ᵗʰ House is the House, professionally, where the individual might find some kind of counseling, psychological, psychiatric, or trauma work (EMT, nurse, or doctor) suits the combination of emotion (8ᵗʰ House) and practical results (Taurus) as the way to make a living.

For more in depth reading about Ceres, I recommend purchasing and reading:

- *Asteroid Goddesses: The Mythology, Psychology and Astrology of the Reemerging Feminine* by Demetra George, with Douglas Bloch (ISBN: 00935127151)
- *The Ultimate Asteroid Book* by J. Lee Lehman, PhD (ISBN: 0914918788)

♀	Ceres	Aries	♈	1	Your Way of Meeting Your Needs manifests through your independent and heroic quest for and attraction to maverick and individualistic identity development.
♀	Ceres	Aries	♈	2	Your Way of Meeting Your Needs manifests through your independent and heroic quest for and attraction to maverick and individualistic values and ways to meet your needs.
♀	Ceres	Aries	♈	3	Your Way of Meeting Your Needs manifests through your independent and heroic quest for and attraction to maverick and individualistic understanding of the world around you.
♀	Ceres	Aries	♈	4	Your Way of Meeting Your Needs manifests through your independent and heroic quest for and attraction to maverick and individualistic emotional caretaking and traditions.
♀	Ceres	Aries	♈	5	Your Way of Meeting Your Needs manifests through your independent and heroic quest for and attraction to maverick and individualistic creative expression.
♀	Ceres	Aries	♈	6	Your Way of Meeting Your Needs manifests through your independent and heroic quest for and attraction to maverick and individualistic service for others.
♀	Ceres	Aries	♈	7	Your Way of Meeting Your Needs manifests through your independent and heroic quest for and attraction to maverick and individualistic life teachers.
♀	Ceres	Aries	♈	8	Your Way of Meeting Your Needs manifests through your independent and heroic quest for and attraction to maverick and individualistic intimate relationships.
♀	Ceres	Aries	♈	9	Your Way of Meeting Your Needs manifests through your independent and heroic quest for and attraction to maverick and individualistic mastership of a body of knowledge.
♀	Ceres	Aries	♈	10	Your Way of Meeting Your Needs manifests through your independent and heroic quest for and attraction to maverick and individualistic accomplishments.
♀	Ceres	Aries	♈	11	Your Way of Meeting Your Needs manifests through your independent and heroic quest for and attraction to maverick and individualistic community.
♀	Ceres	Aries	♈	12	Your Way of Meeting Your Needs manifests through your independent and heroic quest for and attraction to maverick and individualistic spirituality.

♀	Ceres	Taurus	♉	1	Your Way of Meeting Your Needs manifests through your steadfast and persistent quest for and attraction to enduring and secure identity development.
♀	Ceres	Taurus	♉	2	Your Way of Meeting Your Needs manifests through your steadfast and persistent quest for and attraction to enduring and secure values and ways to meet your needs.
♀	Ceres	Taurus	♉	3	Your Way of Meeting Your Needs manifests through your steadfast and persistent quest for and attraction to enduring and secure understanding of the world around you.
♀	Ceres	Taurus	♉	4	Your Way of Meeting Your Needs manifests through your steadfast and persistent quest for and attraction to enduring and secure emotional caretaking and traditions.
♀	Ceres	Taurus	♉	5	Your Way of Meeting Your Needs manifests through your steadfast and persistent quest for and attraction to enduring and secure creative expression.
♀	Ceres	Taurus	♉	6	Your Way of Meeting Your Needs manifests through your steadfast and persistent quest for and attraction to enduring and secure service for others.
♀	Ceres	Taurus	♉	7	Your Way of Meeting Your Needs manifests through your steadfast and persistent quest for and attraction to enduring and secure life teachers.
♀	Ceres	Taurus	♉	8	Your Way of Meeting Your Needs manifests through your steadfast and persistent quest for and attraction to enduring and secure intimate relationships.
♀	Ceres	Taurus	♉	9	Your Way of Meeting Your Needs manifests through your steadfast and persistent quest for and attraction to enduring and secure mastership of a body of knowledge.
♀	Ceres	Taurus	♉	10	Your Way of Meeting Your Needs manifests through your steadfast and persistent quest for and attraction to enduring and secure accomplishments.
♀	Ceres	Taurus	♉	11	Your Way of Meeting Your Needs manifests through your steadfast and persistent quest for and attraction to enduring and secure community.
♀	Ceres	Taurus	♉	12	Your Way of Meeting Your Needs manifests through your steadfast and persistent quest for and attraction to enduring and secure spirituality.

♀	Ceres	Gemini	♊	1	Your Way of Meeting Your Needs manifests through your inquisitive and mentally agile quest for and attraction to ever changing and adaptable identity development.
♀	Ceres	Gemini	♊	2	Your Way of Meeting Your Needs manifests through your inquisitive and mentally agile quest for and attraction to ever changing and adaptable values and ways to meet your needs.
♀	Ceres	Gemini	♊	3	Your Way of Meeting Your Needs manifests through your inquisitive and mentally agile quest for and attraction to ever changing and adaptable understanding of the world around you.
♀	Ceres	Gemini	♊	4	Your Way of Meeting Your Needs manifests through your inquisitive and mentally agile quest for and attraction to ever changing and adaptable emotional caretaking and traditions.
♀	Ceres	Gemini	♊	5	Your Way of Meeting Your Needs manifests through your inquisitive and mentally agile quest for and attraction to ever changing and adaptable creative expression.
♀	Ceres	Gemini	♊	6	Your Way of Meeting Your Needs manifests through your inquisitive and mentally agile quest for and attraction to ever changing and adaptable service for others.
♀	Ceres	Gemini	♊	7	Your Way of Meeting Your Needs manifests through your inquisitive and mentally agile quest for and attraction to ever changing and adaptable life teachers.
♀	Ceres	Gemini	♊	8	Your Way of Meeting Your Needs manifests through your inquisitive and mentally agile quest for and attraction to ever changing and adaptable intimate relationships.
♀	Ceres	Gemini	♊	9	Your Way of Meeting Your Needs manifests through your inquisitive and mentally agile quest for and attraction to ever changing and adaptable mastership of a body of knowledge.
♀	Ceres	Gemini	♊	10	Your Way of Meeting Your Needs manifests through your inquisitive and mentally agile quest for and attraction to ever changing and adaptable accomplishments.
♀	Ceres	Gemini	♊	11	Your Way of Meeting Your Needs manifests through your inquisitive and mentally agile quest for and attraction to ever changing and adaptable community.
♀	Ceres	Gemini	♊	12	Your Way of Meeting Your Needs manifests through your inquisitive and mentally agile quest for and attraction to ever changing and adaptable spirituality.

	Ceres	Cancer	♋	1	Your Way of Meeting Your Needs manifests through your emotional and caring quest for and attraction to nurturing and supportive identity development.
	Ceres	Cancer	♋	2	Your Way of Meeting Your Needs manifests through your emotional and caring quest for and attraction to nurturing and supportive values and ways to meet your needs.
	Ceres	Cancer	♋	3	Your Way of Meeting Your Needs manifests through your emotional and caring quest for and attraction to nurturing and supportive understanding of the world around you.
	Ceres	Cancer	♋	4	Your Way of Meeting Your Needs manifests through your emotional and caring quest for and attraction to nurturing and supportive emotional caretaking and traditions.
	Ceres	Cancer	♋	5	Your Way of Meeting Your Needs manifests through your emotional and caring quest for and attraction to nurturing and supportive creative expression.
	Ceres	Cancer	♋	6	Your Way of Meeting Your Needs manifests through your emotional and caring quest for and attraction to nurturing and supportive service for others.
	Ceres	Cancer	♋	7	Your Way of Meeting Your Needs manifests through your emotional and caring quest for and attraction to nurturing and supportive life teachers.
	Ceres	Cancer	♋	8	Your Way of Meeting Your Needs manifests through your emotional and caring quest for and attraction to nurturing and supportive intimate relationships.
	Ceres	Cancer	♋	9	Your Way of Meeting Your Needs manifests through your emotional and caring quest for and attraction to nurturing and supportive mastership of a body of knowledge.
	Ceres	Cancer	♋	10	Your Way of Meeting Your Needs manifests through your emotional and caring quest for and attraction to nurturing and supportive accomplishments.
	Ceres	Cancer	♋	11	Your Way of Meeting Your Needs manifests through your emotional and caring quest for and attraction to nurturing and supportive community.
	Ceres	Cancer	♋	12	Your Way of Meeting Your Needs manifests through your emotional and caring quest for and attraction to nurturing and supportive spirituality.

♀ (Ceres glyph)	Ceres	Leo	♌	1	Your Way of Meeting Your Needs manifests through your energetic and dramatic quest for and attraction to creative and romantic identity development.
♀ (Ceres glyph)	Ceres	Leo	♌	2	Your Way of Meeting Your Needs manifests through your energetic and dramatic quest for and attraction to creative and romantic values and ways to meet your needs.
♀ (Ceres glyph)	Ceres	Leo	♌	3	Your Way of Meeting Your Needs manifests through your energetic and dramatic quest for and attraction to creative and romantic understanding of the world around you.
♀ (Ceres glyph)	Ceres	Leo	♌	4	Your Way of Meeting Your Needs manifests through your energetic and dramatic quest for and attraction to creative and romantic emotional caretaking and traditions.
♀ (Ceres glyph)	Ceres	Leo	♌	5	Your Way of Meeting Your Needs manifests through your energetic and dramatic quest for and attraction to creative and romantic creative expression.
♀ (Ceres glyph)	Ceres	Leo	♌	6	Your Way of Meeting Your Needs manifests through your energetic and dramatic quest for and attraction to creative and romantic service for others.
♀ (Ceres glyph)	Ceres	Leo	♌	7	Your Way of Meeting Your Needs manifests through your energetic and dramatic quest for and attraction to creative and romantic life teachers.
♀ (Ceres glyph)	Ceres	Leo	♌	8	Your Way of Meeting Your Needs manifests through your energetic and dramatic quest for and attraction to creative and romantic intimate relationships.
♀ (Ceres glyph)	Ceres	Leo	♌	9	Your Way of Meeting Your Needs manifests through your energetic and dramatic quest for and attraction to creative and romantic mastership of a body of knowledge.
♀ (Ceres glyph)	Ceres	Leo	♌	10	Your Way of Meeting Your Needs manifests through your energetic and dramatic quest for and attraction to creative and romantic accomplishments.
♀ (Ceres glyph)	Ceres	Leo	♌	11	Your Way of Meeting Your Needs manifests through your energetic and dramatic quest for and attraction to creative and romantic community.
♀ (Ceres glyph)	Ceres	Leo	♌	12	Your Way of Meeting Your Needs manifests through your energetic and dramatic quest for and attraction to creative and romantic spirituality.

♀	Ceres	Virgo	♍	1	Your Way of Meeting Your Needs manifests through your critically-minded and methodical quest for and attraction to meticulous and practical identity development.
♀	Ceres	Virgo	♍	2	Your Way of Meeting Your Needs manifests through your critically-minded and methodical quest for and attraction to meticulous and practical values and ways to meet your needs.
♀	Ceres	Virgo	♍	3	Your Way of Meeting Your Needs manifests through your critically-minded and methodical quest for and attraction to meticulous and practical understanding of the world around you.
♀	Ceres	Virgo	♍	4	Your Way of Meeting Your Needs manifests through your critically-minded and methodical quest for and attraction to meticulous and practical emotional caretaking and traditions.
♀	Ceres	Virgo	♍	5	Your Way of Meeting Your Needs manifests through your critically-minded and methodical quest for and attraction to meticulous and practical creative expression.
♀	Ceres	Virgo	♍	6	Your Way of Meeting Your Needs manifests through your critically-minded and methodical quest for and attraction to meticulous and practical service for others.
♀	Ceres	Virgo	♍	7	Your Way of Meeting Your Needs manifests through your critically-minded and methodical quest for and attraction to meticulous and practical life teachers.
♀	Ceres	Virgo	♍	8	Your Way of Meeting Your Needs manifests through your critically-minded and methodical quest for and attraction to meticulous and practical intimate relationships.
♀	Ceres	Virgo	♍	9	Your Way of Meeting Your Needs manifests through your critically-minded and methodical quest for and attraction to meticulous and practical mastership of a body of knowledge.
♀	Ceres	Virgo	♍	10	Your Way of Meeting Your Needs manifests through your critically-minded and methodical quest for and attraction to meticulous and practical accomplishments.
♀	Ceres	Virgo	♍	11	Your Way of Meeting Your Needs manifests through your critically-minded and methodical quest for and attraction to meticulous and practical community.
♀	Ceres	Virgo	♍	12	Your Way of Meeting Your Needs manifests through your critically-minded and methodical quest for and attraction to meticulous and practical spirituality.

Astrology Unlocked by Philip Young, PhD

♀	Ceres	Libra	♎	1	Your Way of Meeting Your Needs manifests through your analytical and balanced quest for and attraction to harmonious and logical identity development.
♀	Ceres	Libra	♎	2	Your Way of Meeting Your Needs manifests through your analytical and balanced quest for and attraction to harmonious and logical values and ways to meet your needs.
♀	Ceres	Libra	♎	3	Your Way of Meeting Your Needs manifests through your analytical and balanced quest for and attraction to harmonious and logical understanding of the world around you.
♀	Ceres	Libra	♎	4	Your Way of Meeting Your Needs manifests through your analytical and balanced quest for and attraction to harmonious and logical emotional caretaking and traditions.
♀	Ceres	Libra	♎	5	Your Way of Meeting Your Needs manifests through your analytical and balanced quest for and attraction to harmonious and logical creative expression.
♀	Ceres	Libra	♎	6	Your Way of Meeting Your Needs manifests through your analytical and balanced quest for and attraction to harmonious and logical service for others.
♀	Ceres	Libra	♎	7	Your Way of Meeting Your Needs manifests through your analytical and balanced quest for and attraction to harmonious and logical life teachers.
♀	Ceres	Libra	♎	8	Your Way of Meeting Your Needs manifests through your analytical and balanced quest for and attraction to harmonious and logical intimate relationships.
♀	Ceres	Libra	♎	9	Your Way of Meeting Your Needs manifests through your analytical and balanced quest for and attraction to harmonious and logical mastership of a body of knowledge.
♀	Ceres	Libra	♎	10	Your Way of Meeting Your Needs manifests through your analytical and balanced quest for and attraction to harmonious and logical accomplishments.
♀	Ceres	Libra	♎	11	Your Way of Meeting Your Needs manifests through your analytical and balanced quest for and attraction to harmonious and logical community.
♀	Ceres	Libra	♎	12	Your Way of Meeting Your Needs manifests through your analytical and balanced quest for and attraction to harmonious and logical spirituality.

♀	Ceres	Scorpio	♏	1	Your Way of Meeting Your Needs manifests through your intense and truth seeking quest for and attraction to penetrating and emotionally transformative identity development.
♀	Ceres	Scorpio	♏	2	Your Way of Meeting Your Needs manifests through your intense and truth seeking quest for and attraction to penetrating and emotionally transformative values and ways to meet your needs.
♀	Ceres	Scorpio	♏	3	Your Way of Meeting Your Needs manifests through your intense and truth seeking quest for and attraction to penetrating and emotionally transformative understanding of the world around you.
♀	Ceres	Scorpio	♏	4	Your Way of Meeting Your Needs manifests through your intense and truth seeking quest for and attraction to penetrating and emotionally transformative emotional caretaking and traditions.
♀	Ceres	Scorpio	♏	5	Your Way of Meeting Your Needs manifests through your intense and truth seeking quest for and attraction to penetrating and emotionally transformative creative expression.
♀	Ceres	Scorpio	♏	6	Your Way of Meeting Your Needs manifests through your intense and truth seeking quest for and attraction to penetrating and emotionally transformative service for others.
♀	Ceres	Scorpio	♏	7	Your Way of Meeting Your Needs manifests through your intense and truth seeking quest for and attraction to penetrating and emotionally transformative life teachers.
♀	Ceres	Scorpio	♏	8	Your Way of Meeting Your Needs manifests through your intense and truth seeking quest for and attraction to penetrating and emotionally transformative intimate relationships.
♀	Ceres	Scorpio	♏	9	Your Way of Meeting Your Needs manifests through your intense and truth seeking quest for and attraction to penetrating and emotionally transformative mastership of a body of knowledge.
♀	Ceres	Scorpio	♏	10	Your Way of Meeting Your Needs manifests through your intense and truth seeking quest for and attraction to penetrating and emotionally transformative accomplishments.
♀	Ceres	Scorpio	♏	11	Your Way of Meeting Your Needs manifests through your intense and truth seeking quest for and attraction to penetrating and emotionally transformative community.
♀	Ceres	Scorpio	♏	12	Your Way of Meeting Your Needs manifests through your intense and truth seeking quest for and attraction to penetrating and emotionally transformative spirituality.

	Ceres	Sagittarius	♐	1	Your Way of Meeting Your Needs manifests through your wide-ranging and open-minded quest for and attraction to experiential and risk-taking identity development.
⚳	Ceres	Sagittarius	♐	2	Your Way of Meeting Your Needs manifests through your wide-ranging and open-minded quest for and attraction to experiential and risk-taking values and ways to meet your needs.
⚳	Ceres	Sagittarius	♐	3	Your Way of Meeting Your Needs manifests through your wide-ranging and open-minded quest for and attraction to experiential and risk-taking understanding of the world around you.
⚳	Ceres	Sagittarius	♐	4	Your Way of Meeting Your Needs manifests through your wide-ranging and open-minded quest for and attraction to experiential and risk-taking emotional caretaking and traditions.
⚳	Ceres	Sagittarius	♐	5	Your Way of Meeting Your Needs manifests through your wide-ranging and open-minded quest for and attraction to experiential and risk-taking creative expression.
⚳	Ceres	Sagittarius	♐	6	Your Way of Meeting Your Needs manifests through your wide-ranging and open-minded quest for and attraction to experiential and risk-taking service for others.
⚳	Ceres	Sagittarius	♐	7	Your Way of Meeting Your Needs manifests through your wide-ranging and open-minded quest for and attraction to experiential and risk-taking life teachers.
⚳	Ceres	Sagittarius	♐	8	Your Way of Meeting Your Needs manifests through your wide-ranging and open-minded quest for and attraction to experiential and risk-taking intimate relationships.
⚳	Ceres	Sagittarius	♐	9	Your Way of Meeting Your Needs manifests through your wide-ranging and open-minded quest for and attraction to experiential and risk-taking mastership of a body of knowledge.
⚳	Ceres	Sagittarius	♐	10	Your Way of Meeting Your Needs manifests through your wide-ranging and open-minded quest for and attraction to experiential and risk-taking accomplishments.
⚳	Ceres	Sagittarius	♐	11	Your Way of Meeting Your Needs manifests through your wide-ranging and open-minded quest for and attraction to experiential and risk-taking community.
⚳	Ceres	Sagittarius	♐	12	Your Way of Meeting Your Needs manifests through your wide-ranging and open-minded quest for and attraction to experiential and risk-taking spirituality.

225

♀	Ceres	Capricorn	♑	1	Your Way of Meeting Your Needs manifests through your goal-driven and focused quest for and attraction to results-oriented and successful identity development.
♀	Ceres	Capricorn	♑	2	Your Way of Meeting Your Needs manifests through your goal-driven and focused quest for and attraction to results-oriented and successful values and ways to meet your needs.
♀	Ceres	Capricorn	♑	3	Your Way of Meeting Your Needs manifests through your goal-driven and focused quest for and attraction to results-oriented and successful understanding of the world around you.
♀	Ceres	Capricorn	♑	4	Your Way of Meeting Your Needs manifests through your goal-driven and focused quest for and attraction to results-oriented and successful emotional caretaking and traditions.
♀	Ceres	Capricorn	♑	5	Your Way of Meeting Your Needs manifests through your goal-driven and focused quest for and attraction to results-oriented and successful creative expression.
♀	Ceres	Capricorn	♑	6	Your Way of Meeting Your Needs manifests through your goal-driven and focused quest for and attraction to results-oriented and successful service for others.
♀	Ceres	Capricorn	♑	7	Your Way of Meeting Your Needs manifests through your goal-driven and focused quest for and attraction to results-oriented and successful life teachers.
♀	Ceres	Capricorn	♑	8	Your Way of Meeting Your Needs manifests through your goal-driven and focused quest for and attraction to results-oriented and successful intimate relationships.
♀	Ceres	Capricorn	♑	9	Your Way of Meeting Your Needs manifests through your goal-driven and focused quest for and attraction to results-oriented and successful mastership of a body of knowledge.
♀	Ceres	Capricorn	♑	10	Your Way of Meeting Your Needs manifests through your goal-driven and focused quest for and attraction to results-oriented and successful accomplishments.
♀	Ceres	Capricorn	♑	11	Your Way of Meeting Your Needs manifests through your goal-driven and focused quest for and attraction to results-oriented and successful community.
♀	Ceres	Capricorn	♑	12	Your Way of Meeting Your Needs manifests through your goal-driven and focused quest for and attraction to results-oriented and successful spirituality.

	Ceres	Aquarius	♒	1	Your Way of Meeting Your Needs manifests through your unconventional and idealistic quest for and attraction to authentic and non-traditional identity development.
♀	Ceres	Aquarius	♒	2	Your Way of Meeting Your Needs manifests through your unconventional and idealistic quest for and attraction to authentic and non-traditional values and ways to meet your needs.
♀	Ceres	Aquarius	♒	3	Your Way of Meeting Your Needs manifests through your unconventional and idealistic quest for and attraction to authentic and non-traditional understanding of the world around you.
♀	Ceres	Aquarius	♒	4	Your Way of Meeting Your Needs manifests through your unconventional and idealistic quest for and attraction to authentic and non-traditional emotional caretaking and traditions.
♀	Ceres	Aquarius	♒	5	Your Way of Meeting Your Needs manifests through your unconventional and idealistic quest for and attraction to authentic and non-traditional creative expression.
♀	Ceres	Aquarius	♒	6	Your Way of Meeting Your Needs manifests through your unconventional and idealistic quest for and attraction to authentic and non-traditional service for others.
♀	Ceres	Aquarius	♒	7	Your Way of Meeting Your Needs manifests through your unconventional and idealistic quest for and attraction to authentic and non-traditional life teachers.
♀	Ceres	Aquarius	♒	8	Your Way of Meeting Your Needs manifests through your unconventional and idealistic quest for and attraction to authentic and non-traditional intimate relationships.
♀	Ceres	Aquarius	♒	9	Your Way of Meeting Your Needs manifests through your unconventional and idealistic quest for and attraction to authentic and non-traditional mastership of a body of knowledge.
♀	Ceres	Aquarius	♒	10	Your Way of Meeting Your Needs manifests through your unconventional and idealistic quest for and attraction to authentic and non-traditional accomplishments.
♀	Ceres	Aquarius	♒	11	Your Way of Meeting Your Needs manifests through your unconventional and idealistic quest for and attraction to authentic and non-traditional community.
♀	Ceres	Aquarius	♒	12	Your Way of Meeting Your Needs manifests through your unconventional and idealistic quest for and attraction to authentic and non-traditional spirituality.

♀	Ceres	Pisces	♓	1	Your Way of Meeting Your Needs manifests through your imaginative and faithful quest for and attraction to consciousness-raising and soulful identity development.
♀	Ceres	Pisces	♓	2	Your Way of Meeting Your Needs manifests through your imaginative and faithful quest for and attraction to consciousness-raising and soulful values and ways to meet your needs.
♀	Ceres	Pisces	♓	3	Your Way of Meeting Your Needs manifests through your imaginative and faithful quest for and attraction to consciousness-raising and soulful understanding of the world around you.
♀	Ceres	Pisces	♓	4	Your Way of Meeting Your Needs manifests through your imaginative and faithful quest for and attraction to consciousness-raising and soulful emotional caretaking and traditions.
♀	Ceres	Pisces	♓	5	Your Way of Meeting Your Needs manifests through your imaginative and faithful quest for and attraction to consciousness-raising and soulful creative expression.
♀	Ceres	Pisces	♓	6	Your Way of Meeting Your Needs manifests through your imaginative and faithful quest for and attraction to consciousness-raising and soulful service for others.
♀	Ceres	Pisces	♓	7	Your Way of Meeting Your Needs manifests through your imaginative and faithful quest for and attraction to consciousness-raising and soulful life teachers.
♀	Ceres	Pisces	♓	8	Your Way of Meeting Your Needs manifests through your imaginative and faithful quest for and attraction to consciousness-raising and soulful intimate relationships.
♀	Ceres	Pisces	♓	9	Your Way of Meeting Your Needs manifests through your imaginative and faithful quest for and attraction to consciousness-raising and soulful mastership of a body of knowledge.
♀	Ceres	Pisces	♓	10	Your Way of Meeting Your Needs manifests through your imaginative and faithful quest for and attraction to consciousness-raising and soulful accomplishments.
♀	Ceres	Pisces	♓	11	Your Way of Meeting Your Needs manifests through your imaginative and faithful quest for and attraction to consciousness-raising and soulful community.
♀	Ceres	Pisces	♓	12	Your Way of Meeting Your Needs manifests through your imaginative and faithful quest for and attraction to consciousness-raising and soulful spirituality.

Pallas | ⚴

Energy Point Type: **Asteroid**

Co-Rules Sign: **Libra**

Co-Rules House: **7ᵗʰ**

Element: **Air**

Key Phrase: **Way of Strategy**

Pallas (Athena) represents your Way of Strategy. Its placement in Sign and House reveals how we strategize to solve problems and where we are best able to reason critically. In my case my Way of Strategy is expressed through Earth (Virgo) in my quest for community (11ᵗʰ House). Earth's expression is accomplished, persistent, and practical. In Virgo the Element acts critically, meticulously, and pragmatically. So, my key phrase is *"Your Way of Strategy manifests through your critically-minded and methodical quest for and attraction to meticulous and practical community."* In short, I am a practical problem solver for my community or group. As it turns out I have a lot of handy man experience, having worked on the top of Houses and underneath them, a solid reflection of this energy in my chart.

When you consider your Pallas placement, think about how you try to problem solve and where you will need to do the work most to evolve the energy to its highest expression. Keep in mind that the type of strategies you employ will take on the nature of the Sign, so a person with an Aries Pallas would enjoy and employ martial strategies while a person with a Libra Pallas would enjoy and employ negotiation strategies. Now consider Pallas in Sagittarius in the 4ᵗʰ House, *"Your Way of Strategy manifests through your wide-ranging and open-minded quest for and attraction to experiential and risky emotional caretaking and traditions."* Here is an individual whose strategic approach excels through the family and culture (4ᵗʰ House), expressing the process creatively and energetically (Fire). A Sagittarius Pallas prefers to use life experience as his or her critical tool; this individual develops "street smarts" and uses them to work on family issues and his or her inner life development. The 4ᵗʰ House represents the deepest part of the chart, where we learn our most important lessons before we are out in the world as adults. This placement will make those lessons the critical tools the individual uses to resolve problems throughout his or her life.

229

For more in depth reading about Pallas (Athena), I recommend purchasing and reading:

- *Asteroid Goddesses: The Mythology, Psychology and Astrology of the Reemerging Feminine* by Demetra George, with Douglas Bloch (ISBN: 00935127151)
- *The Ultimate Asteroid Book* by J. Lee Lehman, PhD (ISBN: 0914918788)

	Pallas	Aries	♈	1	Your Way of Strategy manifests through your independent and heroic quest for and attraction to maverick and individualistic identity development.
♀	Pallas	Aries	♈	2	Your Way of Strategy manifests through your independent and heroic quest for and attraction to maverick and individualistic values and ways to meet your needs.
♀	Pallas	Aries	♈	3	Your Way of Strategy manifests through your independent and heroic quest for and attraction to maverick and individualistic understanding of the world around you.
♀	Pallas	Aries	♈	4	Your Way of Strategy manifests through your independent and heroic quest for and attraction to maverick and individualistic emotional caretaking and traditions.
♀	Pallas	Aries	♈	5	Your Way of Strategy manifests through your independent and heroic quest for and attraction to maverick and individualistic creative expression.
♀	Pallas	Aries	♈	6	Your Way of Strategy manifests through your independent and heroic quest for and attraction to maverick and individualistic service for others.
♀	Pallas	Aries	♈	7	Your Way of Strategy manifests through your independent and heroic quest for and attraction to maverick and individualistic life teachers.
♀	Pallas	Aries	♈	8	Your Way of Strategy manifests through your independent and heroic quest for and attraction to maverick and individualistic intimate relationships.
♀	Pallas	Aries	♈	9	Your Way of Strategy manifests through your independent and heroic quest for and attraction to maverick and individualistic mastership of a body of knowledge.
♀	Pallas	Aries	♈	10	Your Way of Strategy manifests through your independent and heroic quest for and attraction to maverick and individualistic accomplishments.
♀	Pallas	Aries	♈	11	Your Way of Strategy manifests through your independent and heroic quest for and attraction to maverick and individualistic community.
♀	Pallas	Aries	♈	12	Your Way of Strategy manifests through your independent and heroic quest for and attraction to maverick and individualistic spirituality.

♀	Pallas	Taurus	♉	1	Your Way of Strategy manifests through your steadfast and persistent quest for and attraction to enduring and secure identity development.
♀	Pallas	Taurus	♉	2	Your Way of Strategy manifests through your steadfast and persistent quest for and attraction to enduring and secure values and ways to meet your needs.
♀	Pallas	Taurus	♉	3	Your Way of Strategy manifests through your steadfast and persistent quest for and attraction to enduring and secure understanding of the world around you.
♀	Pallas	Taurus	♉	4	Your Way of Strategy manifests through your steadfast and persistent quest for and attraction to enduring and secure emotional caretaking and traditions.
♀	Pallas	Taurus	♉	5	Your Way of Strategy manifests through your steadfast and persistent quest for and attraction to enduring and secure creative expression.
♀	Pallas	Taurus	♉	6	Your Way of Strategy manifests through your steadfast and persistent quest for and attraction to enduring and secure service for others.
♀	Pallas	Taurus	♉	7	Your Way of Strategy manifests through your steadfast and persistent quest for and attraction to enduring and secure life teachers.
♀	Pallas	Taurus	♉	8	Your Way of Strategy manifests through your steadfast and persistent quest for and attraction to enduring and secure intimate relationships.
♀	Pallas	Taurus	♉	9	Your Way of Strategy manifests through your steadfast and persistent quest for and attraction to enduring and secure mastership of a body of knowledge.
♀	Pallas	Taurus	♉	10	Your Way of Strategy manifests through your steadfast and persistent quest for and attraction to enduring and secure accomplishments.
♀	Pallas	Taurus	♉	11	Your Way of Strategy manifests through your steadfast and persistent quest for and attraction to enduring and secure community.
♀	Pallas	Taurus	♉	12	Your Way of Strategy manifests through your steadfast and persistent quest for and attraction to enduring and secure spirituality.

232

	Pallas	Gemini	♊	1	Your Way of Strategy manifests through your inquisitive and mentally agile quest for and attraction to ever changing and adaptable identity development.
	Pallas	Gemini	♊	2	Your Way of Strategy manifests through your inquisitive and mentally agile quest for and attraction to ever changing and adaptable values and ways to meet your needs.
	Pallas	Gemini	♊	3	Your Way of Strategy manifests through your inquisitive and mentally agile quest for and attraction to ever changing and adaptable understanding of the world around you.
	Pallas	Gemini	♊	4	Your Way of Strategy manifests through your inquisitive and mentally agile quest for and attraction to ever changing and adaptable emotional caretaking and traditions.
	Pallas	Gemini	♊	5	Your Way of Strategy manifests through your inquisitive and mentally agile quest for and attraction to ever changing and adaptable creative expression.
	Pallas	Gemini	♊	6	Your Way of Strategy manifests through your inquisitive and mentally agile quest for and attraction to ever changing and adaptable service for others.
	Pallas	Gemini	♊	7	Your Way of Strategy manifests through your inquisitive and mentally agile quest for and attraction to ever changing and adaptable life teachers.
	Pallas	Gemini	♊	8	Your Way of Strategy manifests through your inquisitive and mentally agile quest for and attraction to ever changing and adaptable intimate relationships.
	Pallas	Gemini	♊	9	Your Way of Strategy manifests through your inquisitive and mentally agile quest for and attraction to ever changing and adaptable mastership of a body of knowledge.
	Pallas	Gemini	♊	10	Your Way of Strategy manifests through your inquisitive and mentally agile quest for and attraction to ever changing and adaptable accomplishments.
	Pallas	Gemini	♊	11	Your Way of Strategy manifests through your inquisitive and mentally agile quest for and attraction to ever changing and adaptable community.
	Pallas	Gemini	♊	12	Your Way of Strategy manifests through your inquisitive and mentally agile quest for and attraction to ever changing and adaptable spirituality.

♀ (Pallas symbol)	Pallas	Cancer	♋	1	Your Way of Strategy manifests through your emotional and caring quest for and attraction to nurturing and supportive identity development.
♀ (Pallas symbol)	Pallas	Cancer	♋	2	Your Way of Strategy manifests through your emotional and caring quest for and attraction to nurturing and supportive values and ways to meet your needs.
♀ (Pallas symbol)	Pallas	Cancer	♋	3	Your Way of Strategy manifests through your emotional and caring quest for and attraction to nurturing and supportive understanding of the world around you.
♀ (Pallas symbol)	Pallas	Cancer	♋	4	Your Way of Strategy manifests through your emotional and caring quest for and attraction to nurturing and supportive emotional caretaking and traditions.
♀ (Pallas symbol)	Pallas	Cancer	♋	5	Your Way of Strategy manifests through your emotional and caring quest for and attraction to nurturing and supportive creative expression.
♀ (Pallas symbol)	Pallas	Cancer	♋	6	Your Way of Strategy manifests through your emotional and caring quest for and attraction to nurturing and supportive service for others.
♀ (Pallas symbol)	Pallas	Cancer	♋	7	Your Way of Strategy manifests through your emotional and caring quest for and attraction to nurturing and supportive life teachers.
♀ (Pallas symbol)	Pallas	Cancer	♋	8	Your Way of Strategy manifests through your emotional and caring quest for and attraction to nurturing and supportive intimate relationships.
♀ (Pallas symbol)	Pallas	Cancer	♋	9	Your Way of Strategy manifests through your emotional and caring quest for and attraction to nurturing and supportive mastership of a body of knowledge.
♀ (Pallas symbol)	Pallas	Cancer	♋	10	Your Way of Strategy manifests through your emotional and caring quest for and attraction to nurturing and supportive accomplishments.
♀ (Pallas symbol)	Pallas	Cancer	♋	11	Your Way of Strategy manifests through your emotional and caring quest for and attraction to nurturing and supportive community.
♀ (Pallas symbol)	Pallas	Cancer	♋	12	Your Way of Strategy manifests through your emotional and caring quest for and attraction to nurturing and supportive spirituality.

Astrology Unlocked by Philip Young, PhD

	Pallas	Leo	♌	1	Your Way of Strategy manifests through your energetic and dramatic quest for and attraction to creative and romantic identity development.
♀	Pallas	Leo	♌	2	Your Way of Strategy manifests through your energetic and dramatic quest for and attraction to creative and romantic values and ways to meet your needs.
♀	Pallas	Leo	♌	3	Your Way of Strategy manifests through your energetic and dramatic quest for and attraction to creative and romantic understanding of the world around you.
♀	Pallas	Leo	♌	4	Your Way of Strategy manifests through your energetic and dramatic quest for and attraction to creative and romantic emotional caretaking and traditions.
♀	Pallas	Leo	♌	5	Your Way of Strategy manifests through your energetic and dramatic quest for and attraction to creative and romantic creative expression.
♀	Pallas	Leo	♌	6	Your Way of Strategy manifests through your energetic and dramatic quest for and attraction to creative and romantic service for others.
♀	Pallas	Leo	♌	7	Your Way of Strategy manifests through your energetic and dramatic quest for and attraction to creative and romantic life teachers.
♀	Pallas	Leo	♌	8	Your Way of Strategy manifests through your energetic and dramatic quest for and attraction to creative and romantic intimate relationships.
♀	Pallas	Leo	♌	9	Your Way of Strategy manifests through your energetic and dramatic quest for and attraction to creative and romantic mastership of a body of knowledge.
♀	Pallas	Leo	♌	10	Your Way of Strategy manifests through your energetic and dramatic quest for and attraction to creative and romantic accomplishments.
♀	Pallas	Leo	♌	11	Your Way of Strategy manifests through your energetic and dramatic quest for and attraction to creative and romantic community.
♀	Pallas	Leo	♌	12	Your Way of Strategy manifests through your energetic and dramatic quest for and attraction to creative and romantic spirituality.

	Pallas	Virgo	♍	1	Your Way of Strategy manifests through your critically-minded and methodical quest for and attraction to meticulous and practical identity development.
	Pallas	Virgo	♍	2	Your Way of Strategy manifests through your critically-minded and methodical quest for and attraction to meticulous and practical values and ways to meet your needs.
	Pallas	Virgo	♍	3	Your Way of Strategy manifests through your critically-minded and methodical quest for and attraction to meticulous and practical understanding of the world around you.
	Pallas	Virgo	♍	4	Your Way of Strategy manifests through your critically-minded and methodical quest for and attraction to meticulous and practical emotional caretaking and traditions.
	Pallas	Virgo	♍	5	Your Way of Strategy manifests through your critically-minded and methodical quest for and attraction to meticulous and practical creative expression.
	Pallas	Virgo	♍	6	Your Way of Strategy manifests through your critically-minded and methodical quest for and attraction to meticulous and practical service for others.
	Pallas	Virgo	♍	7	Your Way of Strategy manifests through your critically-minded and methodical quest for and attraction to meticulous and practical life teachers.
	Pallas	Virgo	♍	8	Your Way of Strategy manifests through your critically-minded and methodical quest for and attraction to meticulous and practical intimate relationships.
	Pallas	Virgo	♍	9	Your Way of Strategy manifests through your critically-minded and methodical quest for and attraction to meticulous and practical mastership of a body of knowledge.
	Pallas	Virgo	♍	10	Your Way of Strategy manifests through your critically-minded and methodical quest for and attraction to meticulous and practical accomplishments.
	Pallas	Virgo	♍	11	Your Way of Strategy manifests through your critically-minded and methodical quest for and attraction to meticulous and practical community.
	Pallas	Virgo	♍	12	Your Way of Strategy manifests through your critically-minded and methodical quest for and attraction to meticulous and practical spirituality.

Astrology Unlocked by Philip Young, PhD

	Pallas	Libra	♎	1	Your Way of Strategy manifests through your analytical and balanced quest for and attraction to harmonious and logical identity development.
	Pallas	Libra	♎	2	Your Way of Strategy manifests through your analytical and balanced quest for and attraction to harmonious and logical values and ways to meet your needs.
	Pallas	Libra	♎	3	Your Way of Strategy manifests through your analytical and balanced quest for and attraction to harmonious and logical understanding of the world around you.
	Pallas	Libra	♎	4	Your Way of Strategy manifests through your analytical and balanced quest for and attraction to harmonious and logical emotional caretaking and traditions.
	Pallas	Libra	♎	5	Your Way of Strategy manifests through your analytical and balanced quest for and attraction to harmonious and logical creative expression.
	Pallas	Libra	♎	6	Your Way of Strategy manifests through your analytical and balanced quest for and attraction to harmonious and logical service for others.
	Pallas	Libra	♎	7	Your Way of Strategy manifests through your analytical and balanced quest for and attraction to harmonious and logical life teachers.
	Pallas	Libra	♎	8	Your Way of Strategy manifests through your analytical and balanced quest for and attraction to harmonious and logical intimate relationships.
	Pallas	Libra	♎	9	Your Way of Strategy manifests through your analytical and balanced quest for and attraction to harmonious and logical mastership of a body of knowledge.
	Pallas	Libra	♎	10	Your Way of Strategy manifests through your analytical and balanced quest for and attraction to harmonious and logical accomplishments.
	Pallas	Libra	♎	11	Your Way of Strategy manifests through your analytical and balanced quest for and attraction to harmonious and logical community.
	Pallas	Libra	♎	12	Your Way of Strategy manifests through your analytical and balanced quest for and attraction to harmonious and logical spirituality.

	Pallas	Scorpio	♏	1	Your Way of Strategy manifests through your intense and truth seeking quest for and attraction to penetrating and emotionally transformative identity development.
	Pallas	Scorpio	♏	2	Your Way of Strategy manifests through your intense and truth seeking quest for and attraction to penetrating and emotionally transformative values.
	Pallas	Scorpio	♏	3	Your Way of Strategy manifests through your intense and truth seeking quest for and attraction to penetrating and emotionally transformative understanding of the world around you.
	Pallas	Scorpio	♏	4	Your Way of Strategy manifests through your intense and truth seeking quest for and attraction to penetrating and emotionally transformative emotional caretaking and traditions.
	Pallas	Scorpio	♏	5	Your Way of Strategy manifests through your intense and truth seeking quest for and attraction to penetrating and emotionally transformative creative expression.
	Pallas	Scorpio	♏	6	Your Way of Strategy manifests through your intense and truth seeking quest for and attraction to penetrating and emotionally transformative service for others.
	Pallas	Scorpio	♏	7	Your Way of Strategy manifests through your intense and truth seeking quest for and attraction to penetrating and emotionally transformative life teachers.
	Pallas	Scorpio	♏	8	Your Way of Strategy manifests through your intense and truth seeking quest for and attraction to penetrating and emotionally transformative intimate relationships.
	Pallas	Scorpio	♏	9	Your Way of Strategy manifests through your intense and truth seeking quest for and attraction to penetrating and emotionally transformative mastership of a body of knowledge.
	Pallas	Scorpio	♏	10	Your Way of Strategy manifests through your intense and truth seeking quest for and attraction to penetrating and emotionally transformative accomplishments.
	Pallas	Scorpio	♏	11	Your Way of Strategy manifests through your intense and truth seeking quest for and attraction to penetrating and emotionally transformative community.
	Pallas	Scorpio	♏	12	Your Way of Strategy manifests through your intense and truth seeking quest for and attraction to penetrating and emotionally transformative spirituality.

	Pallas	Sagittarius	↗	1	Your Way of Strategy manifests through your wide-ranging and open-minded quest for and attraction to experiential and risk-taking identity development.
	Pallas	Sagittarius	↗	2	Your Way of Strategy manifests through your wide-ranging and open-minded quest for and attraction to experiential and risk-taking values and ways to meet your needs.
	Pallas	Sagittarius	↗	3	Your Way of Strategy manifests through your wide-ranging and open-minded quest for and attraction to experiential and risk-taking understanding of the world around you.
	Pallas	Sagittarius	↗	4	Your Way of Strategy manifests through your wide-ranging and open-minded quest for and attraction to experiential and risk-taking emotional caretaking and traditions.
	Pallas	Sagittarius	↗	5	Your Way of Strategy manifests through your wide-ranging and open-minded quest for and attraction to experiential and risk-taking creative expression.
	Pallas	Sagittarius	↗	6	Your Way of Strategy manifests through your wide-ranging and open-minded quest for and attraction to experiential and risk-taking service for others.
	Pallas	Sagittarius	↗	7	Your Way of Strategy manifests through your wide-ranging and open-minded quest for and attraction to experiential and risk-taking life teachers.
	Pallas	Sagittarius	↗	8	Your Way of Strategy manifests through your wide-ranging and open-minded quest for and attraction to experiential and risk-taking intimate relationships.
	Pallas	Sagittarius	↗	9	Your Way of Strategy manifests through your wide-ranging and open-minded quest for and attraction to experiential and risk-taking mastership of a body of knowledge.
	Pallas	Sagittarius	↗	10	Your Way of Strategy manifests through your wide-ranging and open-minded quest for and attraction to experiential and risk-taking accomplishments.
	Pallas	Sagittarius	↗	11	Your Way of Strategy manifests through your wide-ranging and open-minded quest for and attraction to experiential and risk-taking community.
	Pallas	Sagittarius	↗	12	Your Way of Strategy manifests through your wide-ranging and open-minded quest for and attraction to experiential and risk-taking spirituality.

♀	Pallas	Capricorn	♑	1	Your Way of Strategy manifests through your goal-driven and focused quest for and attraction to results-oriented and successful identity development.
♀	Pallas	Capricorn	♑	2	Your Way of Strategy manifests through your goal-driven and focused quest for and attraction to results-oriented and successful values and ways to meet your needs.
♀	Pallas	Capricorn	♑	3	Your Way of Strategy manifests through your goal-driven and focused quest for and attraction to results-oriented and successful understanding of the world around you.
♀	Pallas	Capricorn	♑	4	Your Way of Strategy manifests through your goal-driven and focused quest for and attraction to results-oriented and successful emotional caretaking and traditions.
♀	Pallas	Capricorn	♑	5	Your Way of Strategy manifests through your goal-driven and focused quest for and attraction to results-oriented and successful creative expression.
♀	Pallas	Capricorn	♑	6	Your Way of Strategy manifests through your goal-driven and focused quest for and attraction to results-oriented and successful service for others.
♀	Pallas	Capricorn	♑	7	Your Way of Strategy manifests through your goal-driven and focused quest for and attraction to results-oriented and successful life teachers.
♀	Pallas	Capricorn	♑	8	Your Way of Strategy manifests through your goal-driven and focused quest for and attraction to results-oriented and successful intimate relationships.
♀	Pallas	Capricorn	♑	9	Your Way of Strategy manifests through your goal-driven and focused quest for and attraction to results-oriented and successful mastership of a body of knowledge.
♀	Pallas	Capricorn	♑	10	Your Way of Strategy manifests through your goal-driven and focused quest for and attraction to results-oriented and successful accomplishments.
♀	Pallas	Capricorn	♑	11	Your Way of Strategy manifests through your goal-driven and focused quest for and attraction to results-oriented and successful community.
♀	Pallas	Capricorn	♑	12	Your Way of Strategy manifests through your goal-driven and focused quest for and attraction to results-oriented and successful spirituality.

	Pallas	Aquarius	♒	1	Your Way of Strategy manifests through your unconventional and idealistic quest for and attraction to authentic and non-traditional identity development.
	Pallas	Aquarius	♒	2	Your Way of Strategy manifests through your unconventional and idealistic quest for and attraction to authentic and non-traditional values and ways to meet your needs.
	Pallas	Aquarius	♒	3	Your Way of Strategy manifests through your unconventional and idealistic quest for and attraction to authentic and non-traditional understanding of the world around you.
	Pallas	Aquarius	♒	4	Your Way of Strategy manifests through your unconventional and idealistic quest for and attraction to authentic and non-traditional emotional caretaking and traditions.
	Pallas	Aquarius	♒	5	Your Way of Strategy manifests through your unconventional and idealistic quest for and attraction to authentic and non-traditional creative expression.
	Pallas	Aquarius	♒	6	Your Way of Strategy manifests through your unconventional and idealistic quest for and attraction to authentic and non-traditional service for others.
	Pallas	Aquarius	♒	7	Your Way of Strategy manifests through your unconventional and idealistic quest for and attraction to authentic and non-traditional life teachers.
	Pallas	Aquarius	♒	8	Your Way of Strategy manifests through your unconventional and idealistic quest for and attraction to authentic and non-traditional intimate relationships.
	Pallas	Aquarius	♒	9	Your Way of Strategy manifests through your unconventional and idealistic quest for and attraction to authentic and non-traditional mastership of a body of knowledge.
	Pallas	Aquarius	♒	10	Your Way of Strategy manifests through your unconventional and idealistic quest for and attraction to authentic and non-traditional accomplishments.
	Pallas	Aquarius	♒	11	Your Way of Strategy manifests through your unconventional and idealistic quest for and attraction to authentic and non-traditional community.
	Ceres	Aquarius	♒	12	Your Way of Meeting Your Needs manifests through your unconventional and idealistic quest for and attraction to authentic and non-traditional spirituality.

241

	Pallas	Pisces	♓	1	Your Way of Strategy manifests through your imaginative and faithful quest for and attraction to consciousness-raising and soulful identity development.
	Pallas	Pisces	♓	2	Your Way of Strategy manifests through your imaginative and faithful quest for and attraction to consciousness-raising and soulful values and ways to meet your needs.
	Pallas	Pisces	♓	3	Your Way of Strategy manifests through your imaginative and faithful quest for and attraction to consciousness-raising and soulful understanding of the world around you.
	Pallas	Pisces	♓	4	Your Way of Strategy manifests through your imaginative and faithful quest for and attraction to consciousness-raising and soulful emotional caretaking and traditions.
	Pallas	Pisces	♓	5	Your Way of Strategy manifests through your imaginative and faithful quest for and attraction to consciousness-raising and soulful creative expression.
	Pallas	Pisces	♓	6	Your Way of Strategy manifests through your imaginative and faithful quest for and attraction to consciousness-raising and soulful service for others.
	Pallas	Pisces	♓	7	Your Way of Strategy manifests through your imaginative and faithful quest for and attraction to consciousness-raising and soulful life teachers.
	Pallas	Pisces	♓	8	Your Way of Strategy manifests through your imaginative and faithful quest for and attraction to consciousness-raising and soulful intimate relationships.
	Pallas	Pisces	♓	9	Your Way of Strategy manifests through your imaginative and faithful quest for and attraction to consciousness-raising and soulful mastership of a body of knowledge.
	Pallas	Pisces	♓	10	Your Way of Strategy manifests through your imaginative and faithful quest for and attraction to consciousness-raising and soulful accomplishments.
	Pallas	Pisces	♓	11	Your Way of Strategy manifests through your imaginative and faithful quest for and attraction to consciousness-raising and soulful community.
	Pallas	Pisces	♓	12	Your Way of Strategy manifests through your imaginative and faithful quest for and attraction to consciousness-raising and soulful spirituality.

Vesta | ⚶

Energy Point Type: **Asteroid**

Co-Rules Sign: **Taurus**

Co-Rules House: **2ⁿᵈ**

Element: **Earth**

Key Phrase: **Way of Sanctuary**

Vesta represents your Way of Sanctuary. Its placement in Sign and House reveals how we want to feel safe and stable, what we want in and from our home environment. In my case my Way of Sanctuary is expressed through Water (Pisces) in my quest for creative self-expression (5ᵗʰ House). Water's expression is emotional, intense, and imaginative. In Pisces the Element acts empathically, spiritually, and sensitively. So, my key phrase is *"Your Way of Sanctuary manifests through your imaginative and faithful quest for and attraction to consciousness-raising and soulful creative expression."* In short, I want my home to be a place where I can find spiritual comfort and express my spiritual creativity.

When considering your own Vesta placement, think about where you feel most "at home" and the place you prefer when you need to retreat from the world and recharge. The House placement will tell you where you decided to "spiritually" build your sanctuary in this lifetime. Consider Vesta in Virgo in the 11ᵗʰ House, *"Your Way of Sanctuary manifests through your critically-minded and methodical quest for and attraction to meticulous and practical community."* Here is an individual who, at the extreme, would appreciate a home in a commune (11ᵗʰ House), where everyone was doing their work and using their skills (Virgo) to support the group. Less dramatically, this person would find it enjoyable to have a home in a friendly neighborhood with practical and helpful neighbors, who enjoyed keeping their homes and neighborhood well-maintained (Virgo). He or she would rejuvenate by coming home to such a community and having a modest, but efficient home to meet his or her needs.

For more in depth reading about Vesta, I recommend purchasing and reading:

- *Asteroid Goddesses: The Mythology, Psychology and Astrology of the Reemerging Feminine* by Demetra George, with Douglas Bloch (ISBN: 00935127151)
- *The Ultimate Asteroid Book* by J. Lee Lehman, PhD (ISBN: 0914918788)

	Vesta	Aries	♈	1	Your Way of Sanctuary manifests through your independent and heroic quest for and attraction to maverick and individualistic identity development.
	Vesta	Aries	♈	2	Your Way of Sanctuary manifests through your independent and heroic quest for and attraction to maverick and individualistic values and ways to meet your needs.
	Vesta	Aries	♈	3	Your Way of Sanctuary manifests through your independent and heroic quest for and attraction to maverick and individualistic understanding of the world around you.
	Vesta	Aries	♈	4	Your Way of Sanctuary manifests through your independent and heroic quest for and attraction to maverick and individualistic emotional caretaking and traditions.
	Vesta	Aries	♈	5	Your Way of Sanctuary manifests through your independent and heroic quest for and attraction to maverick and individualistic creative expression.
	Vesta	Aries	♈	6	Your Way of Sanctuary manifests through your independent and heroic quest for and attraction to maverick and individualistic service for others.
	Vesta	Aries	♈	7	Your Way of Sanctuary manifests through your independent and heroic quest for and attraction to maverick and individualistic life teachers.
	Vesta	Aries	♈	8	Your Way of Sanctuary manifests through your independent and heroic quest for and attraction to maverick and individualistic relationships.
	Vesta	Aries	♈	9	Your Way of Sanctuary manifests through your independent and heroic quest for and attraction to maverick and individualistic mastership of a body of knowledge.
	Vesta	Aries	♈	10	Your Way of Sanctuary manifests through your independent and heroic quest for and attraction to maverick and individualistic career or accomplishments.
	Vesta	Aries	♈	11	Your Way of Sanctuary manifests through your independent and heroic quest for and attraction to maverick and individualistic community.
	Vesta	Aries	♈	12	Your Way of Sanctuary manifests through your independent and heroic quest for and attraction to maverick and individualistic spirituality.

	Vesta	Taurus	♉	1	Your Way of Sanctuary manifests through your steadfast and persistent quest for and attraction to enduring and secure identity development.
	Vesta	Taurus	♉	2	Your Way of Sanctuary manifests through your steadfast and persistent quest for and attraction to enduring and secure values and ways to meet your needs.
	Vesta	Taurus	♉	3	Your Way of Sanctuary manifests through your steadfast and persistent quest for and attraction to enduring and secure understanding of the world around you.
	Vesta	Taurus	♉	4	Your Way of Sanctuary manifests through your steadfast and persistent quest for and attraction to enduring and secure emotional caretaking and traditions.
	Vesta	Taurus	♉	5	Your Way of Sanctuary manifests through your steadfast and persistent quest for and attraction to enduring and secure creative expression.
	Vesta	Taurus	♉	6	Your Way of Sanctuary manifests through your steadfast and persistent quest for and attraction to enduring and secure service for others.
	Vesta	Taurus	♉	7	Your Way of Sanctuary manifests through your steadfast and persistent quest for and attraction to enduring and secure life teachers.
	Vesta	Taurus	♉	8	Your Way of Sanctuary manifests through your steadfast and persistent quest for and attraction to enduring and secure relationships.
	Vesta	Taurus	♉	9	Your Way of Sanctuary manifests through your steadfast and persistent quest for and attraction to enduring and secure mastership of a body of knowledge.
	Vesta	Taurus	♉	10	Your Way of Sanctuary manifests through your steadfast and persistent quest for and attraction to enduring and secure career or accomplishments.
	Vesta	Taurus	♉	11	Your Way of Sanctuary manifests through your steadfast and persistent quest for and attraction to enduring and secure community.
	Vesta	Taurus	♉	12	Your Way of Sanctuary manifests through your steadfast and persistent quest for and attraction to enduring and secure spirituality.

	Vesta	Gemini	♊	1	Your Way of Sanctuary manifests through your inquisitive and mentally agile quest for and attraction to ever changing and adaptable identity development.
	Vesta	Gemini	♊	2	Your Way of Sanctuary manifests through your inquisitive and mentally agile quest for and attraction to ever changing and adaptable values and ways to meet your needs.
	Vesta	Gemini	♊	3	Your Way of Sanctuary manifests through your inquisitive and mentally agile quest for and attraction to ever changing and adaptable understanding of the world around you.
	Vesta	Gemini	♊	4	Your Way of Sanctuary manifests through your inquisitive and mentally agile quest for and attraction to ever changing and adaptable emotional caretaking and traditions.
	Vesta	Gemini	♊	5	Your Way of Sanctuary manifests through your inquisitive and mentally agile quest for and attraction to ever changing and adaptable creative expression.
	Vesta	Gemini	♊	6	Your Way of Sanctuary manifests through your inquisitive and mentally agile quest for and attraction to ever changing and adaptable service for others.
	Vesta	Gemini	♊	7	Your Way of Sanctuary manifests through your inquisitive and mentally agile quest for and attraction to ever changing and adaptable life teachers.
	Vesta	Gemini	♊	8	Your Way of Sanctuary manifests through your inquisitive and mentally agile quest for and attraction to ever changing and adaptable relationships.
	Vesta	Gemini	♊	9	Your Way of Sanctuary manifests through your inquisitive and mentally agile quest for and attraction to ever changing and adaptable mastership of a body of knowledge.
	Vesta	Gemini	♊	10	Your Way of Sanctuary manifests through your inquisitive and mentally agile quest for and attraction to ever changing and adaptable career or accomplishments.
	Vesta	Gemini	♊	11	Your Way of Sanctuary manifests through your inquisitive and mentally agile quest for and attraction to ever changing and adaptable community.
	Vesta	Gemini	♊	12	Your Way of Sanctuary manifests through your inquisitive and mentally agile quest for and attraction to ever changing and adaptable spirituality.

	Vesta	Cancer	♋	1	Your Way of Sanctuary manifests through your emotional and caring quest for and attraction to nurturing and supportive identity development.
	Vesta	Cancer	♋	2	Your Way of Sanctuary manifests through your emotional and caring quest for and attraction to nurturing and supportive values and ways to meet your needs.
	Vesta	Cancer	♋	3	Your Way of Sanctuary manifests through your emotional and caring quest for and attraction to nurturing and supportive understanding of the world around you.
	Vesta	Cancer	♋	4	Your Way of Sanctuary manifests through your emotional and caring quest for and attraction to nurturing and supportive emotional caretaking and traditions.
	Vesta	Cancer	♋	5	Your Way of Sanctuary manifests through your emotional and caring quest for and attraction to nurturing and supportive creative expression.
	Vesta	Cancer	♋	6	Your Way of Sanctuary manifests through your emotional and caring quest for and attraction to nurturing and supportive service for others.
	Vesta	Cancer	♋	7	Your Way of Sanctuary manifests through your emotional and caring quest for and attraction to nurturing and supportive life teachers.
	Vesta	Cancer	♋	8	Your Way of Sanctuary manifests through your emotional and caring quest for and attraction to nurturing and supportive relationships.
	Vesta	Cancer	♋	9	Your Way of Sanctuary manifests through your emotional and caring quest for and attraction to nurturing and supportive mastership of a body of knowledge.
	Vesta	Cancer	♋	10	Your Way of Sanctuary manifests through your emotional and caring quest for and attraction to nurturing and supportive career or accomplishments.
	Vesta	Cancer	♋	11	Your Way of Sanctuary manifests through your emotional and caring quest for and attraction to nurturing and supportive community.
	Vesta	Cancer	♋	12	Your Way of Sanctuary manifests through your emotional and caring quest for and attraction to nurturing and supportive spirituality.

Astrology Unlocked by Philip Young, PhD

	Vesta	Leo	♌	1	Your Way of Sanctuary manifests through your energetic and dramatic quest for and attraction to creative and romantic identity development.
	Vesta	Leo	♌	2	Your Way of Sanctuary manifests through your energetic and dramatic quest for and attraction to creative and romantic values and ways to meet your needs.
	Vesta	Leo	♌	3	Your Way of Sanctuary manifests through your energetic and dramatic quest for and attraction to creative and romantic understanding of the world around you.
	Vesta	Leo	♌	4	Your Way of Sanctuary manifests through your energetic and dramatic quest for and attraction to creative and romantic emotional caretaking and traditions.
	Vesta	Leo	♌	5	Your Way of Sanctuary manifests through your energetic and dramatic quest for and attraction to creative and romantic creative expression.
	Vesta	Leo	♌	6	Your Way of Sanctuary manifests through your energetic and dramatic quest for and attraction to creative and romantic service for others.
	Vesta	Leo	♌	7	Your Way of Sanctuary manifests through your energetic and dramatic quest for and attraction to creative and romantic life teachers.
	Vesta	Leo	♌	8	Your Way of Sanctuary manifests through your energetic and dramatic quest for and attraction to creative and romantic relationships.
	Vesta	Leo	♌	9	Your Way of Sanctuary manifests through your energetic and dramatic quest for and attraction to creative and romantic mastership of a body of knowledge.
	Vesta	Leo	♌	10	Your Way of Sanctuary manifests through your energetic and dramatic quest for and attraction to creative and romantic career or accomplishments.
	Vesta	Leo	♌	11	Your Way of Sanctuary manifests through your energetic and dramatic quest for and attraction to creative and romantic community.
	Vesta	Leo	♌	12	Your Way of Sanctuary manifests through your energetic and dramatic quest for and attraction to creative and romantic spirituality.

	Vesta	Virgo	♍	1	Your Way of Sanctuary manifests through your critically-minded and methodical quest for and attraction to meticulous and practical identity development.
	Vesta	Virgo	♍	2	Your Way of Sanctuary manifests through your critically-minded and methodical quest for and attraction to meticulous and practical values and ways to meet your needs.
	Vesta	Virgo	♍	3	Your Way of Sanctuary manifests through your critically-minded and methodical quest for and attraction to meticulous and practical understanding of the world around you.
	Vesta	Virgo	♍	4	Your Way of Sanctuary manifests through your critically-minded and methodical quest for and attraction to meticulous and practical emotional caretaking and traditions.
	Vesta	Virgo	♍	5	Your Way of Sanctuary manifests through your critically-minded and methodical quest for and attraction to meticulous and practical creative expression.
	Vesta	Virgo	♍	6	Your Way of Sanctuary manifests through your critically-minded and methodical quest for and attraction to meticulous and practical service for others.
	Vesta	Virgo	♍	7	Your Way of Sanctuary manifests through your critically-minded and methodical quest for and attraction to meticulous and practical life teachers.
	Vesta	Virgo	♍	8	Your Way of Sanctuary manifests through your critically-minded and methodical quest for and attraction to meticulous and practical relationships.
	Vesta	Virgo	♍	.9	Your Way of Sanctuary manifests through your critically-minded and methodical quest for and attraction to meticulous and practical mastership of a body of knowledge.
	Vesta	Virgo	♍	10	Your Way of Sanctuary manifests through your critically-minded and methodical quest for and attraction to meticulous and practical career or accomplishments.
	Vesta	Virgo	♍	11	Your Way of Sanctuary manifests through your critically-minded and methodical quest for and attraction to meticulous and practical community.
	Vesta	Virgo	♍	12	Your Way of Sanctuary manifests through your critically-minded and methodical quest for and attraction to meticulous and practical spirituality.

	Vesta	Libra	♎	1	Your Way of Sanctuary manifests through your analytical and balanced quest for and attraction to harmonious and logical identity development.
	Vesta	Libra	♎	2	Your Way of Sanctuary manifests through your analytical and balanced quest for and attraction to harmonious and logical values and ways to meet your needs.
	Vesta	Libra	♎	3	Your Way of Sanctuary manifests through your analytical and balanced quest for and attraction to harmonious and logical understanding of the world around you.
	Vesta	Libra	♎	4	Your Way of Sanctuary manifests through your analytical and balanced quest for and attraction to harmonious and logical emotional caretaking and traditions.
	Vesta	Libra	♎	5	Your Way of Sanctuary manifests through your analytical and balanced quest for and attraction to harmonious and logical creative expression.
	Vesta	Libra	♎	6	Your Way of Sanctuary manifests through your analytical and balanced quest for and attraction to harmonious and logical service for others.
	Vesta	Libra	♎	7	Your Way of Sanctuary manifests through your analytical and balanced quest for and attraction to harmonious and logical life teachers.
	Vesta	Libra	♎	8	Your Way of Sanctuary manifests through your analytical and balanced quest for and attraction to harmonious and logical relationships.
	Vesta	Libra	♎	9	Your Way of Sanctuary manifests through your analytical and balanced quest for and attraction to harmonious and logical mastership of a body of knowledge.
	Vesta	Libra	♎	10	Your Way of Sanctuary manifests through your analytical and balanced quest for and attraction to harmonious and logical career or accomplishments.
	Vesta	Libra	♎	11	Your Way of Sanctuary manifests through your analytical and balanced quest for and attraction to harmonious and logical community.
	Vesta	Libra	♎	12	Your Way of Sanctuary manifests through your analytical and balanced quest for and attraction to harmonious and logical spirituality.

	Vesta	Scorpio	♏	1	Your Way of Sanctuary manifests through your intense and truth seeking quest for and attraction to penetrating and emotionally transformative identity development.
	Vesta	Scorpio	♏	2	Your Way of Sanctuary manifests through your intense and truth seeking quest for and attraction to penetrating and emotionally transformative values and ways to meet your needs.
	Vesta	Scorpio	♏	3	Your Way of Sanctuary manifests through your intense and truth seeking quest for and attraction to penetrating and emotionally transformative understanding of the world around you.
	Vesta	Scorpio	♏	4	Your Way of Sanctuary manifests through your intense and truth seeking quest for and attraction to penetrating and emotionally transformative emotional caretaking and traditions.
	Vesta	Scorpio	♏	5	Your Way of Sanctuary manifests through your intense and truth seeking quest for and attraction to penetrating and emotionally transformative creative expression.
	Vesta	Scorpio	♏	6	Your Way of Sanctuary manifests through your intense and truth seeking quest for and attraction to penetrating and emotionally transformative service for others.
	Vesta	Scorpio	♏	7	Your Way of Sanctuary manifests through your intense and truth seeking quest for and attraction to penetrating and emotionally transformative life teachers.
	Vesta	Scorpio	♏	8	Your Way of Sanctuary manifests through your intense and truth seeking quest for and attraction to penetrating and emotionally transformative relationships.
	Vesta	Scorpio	♏	9	Your Way of Sanctuary manifests through your intense and truth seeking quest for and attraction to penetrating and emotionally transformative mastership of a body of knowledge.
	Vesta	Scorpio	♏	10	Your Way of Sanctuary manifests through your intense and truth seeking quest for and attraction to penetrating and emotionally transformative career or accomplishments.
	Vesta	Scorpio	♏	11	Your Way of Sanctuary manifests through your intense and truth seeking quest for and attraction to penetrating and emotionally transformative community.
	Vesta	Scorpio	♏	12	Your Way of Sanctuary manifests through your intense and truth seeking quest for and attraction to penetrating and emotionally transformative spirituality.

	Vesta	Sagittarius	↗	1	Your Way of Sanctuary manifests through your wide-ranging and open-minded quest for and attraction to experiential and risk-taking identity development.
	Vesta	Sagittarius	↗	2	Your Way of Sanctuary manifests through your wide-ranging and open-minded quest for and attraction to experiential and risk-taking values and ways to meet your needs.
	Vesta	Sagittarius	↗	3	Your Way of Sanctuary manifests through your wide-ranging and open-minded quest for and attraction to experiential and risk-taking understanding of the world around you.
	Vesta	Sagittarius	↗	4	Your Way of Sanctuary manifests through your wide-ranging and open-minded quest for and attraction to experiential and risk-taking emotional caretaking and traditions.
	Vesta	Sagittarius	↗	5	Your Way of Sanctuary manifests through your wide-ranging and open-minded quest for and attraction to experiential and risk-taking creative expression.
	Vesta	Sagittarius	↗	6	Your Way of Sanctuary manifests through your wide-ranging and open-minded quest for and attraction to experiential and risk-taking service for others.
	Vesta	Sagittarius	↗	7	Your Way of Sanctuary manifests through your wide-ranging and open-minded quest for and attraction to experiential and risk-taking life teachers.
	Vesta	Sagittarius	↗	8	Your Way of Sanctuary manifests through your wide-ranging and open-minded quest for and attraction to experiential and risk-taking relationships.
	Vesta	Sagittarius	↗	9	Your Way of Sanctuary manifests through your wide-ranging and open-minded quest for and attraction to experiential and risk-taking mastership of a body of knowledge.
	Vesta	Sagittarius	↗	10	Your Way of Sanctuary manifests through your wide-ranging and open-minded quest for and attraction to experiential and risk-taking career or accomplishments.
	Vesta	Sagittarius	↗	11	Your Way of Sanctuary manifests through your wide-ranging and open-minded quest for and attraction to experiential and risk-taking community.
	Vesta	Sagittarius	↗	12	Your Way of Sanctuary manifests through your wide-ranging and open-minded quest for and attraction to experiential and risk-taking spirituality.

	Vesta	Capricorn	♑	1	Your Way of Sanctuary manifests through your goal-driven and focused quest for and attraction to results-oriented and successful identity development.
	Vesta	Capricorn	♑	2	Your Way of Sanctuary manifests through your goal-driven and focused quest for and attraction to results-oriented and successful values and ways to meet your needs.
	Vesta	Capricorn	♑	3	Your Way of Sanctuary manifests through your goal-driven and focused quest for and attraction to results-oriented and successful understanding of the world around you.
	Vesta	Capricorn	♑	4	Your Way of Sanctuary manifests through your goal-driven and focused quest for and attraction to results-oriented and successful emotional caretaking and traditions.
	Vesta	Capricorn	♑	5	Your Way of Sanctuary manifests through your goal-driven and focused quest for and attraction to results-oriented and successful creative expression.
	Vesta	Capricorn	♑	6	Your Way of Sanctuary manifests through your goal-driven and focused quest for and attraction to results-oriented and successful service for others.
	Vesta	Capricorn	♑	7	Your Way of Sanctuary manifests through your goal-driven and focused quest for and attraction to results-oriented and successful life teachers.
	Vesta	Capricorn	♑	8	Your Way of Sanctuary manifests through your goal-driven and focused quest for and attraction to results-oriented and successful relationships.
	Vesta	Capricorn	♑	9	Your Way of Sanctuary manifests through your goal-driven and focused quest for and attraction to results-oriented and successful mastership of a body of knowledge.
	Vesta	Capricorn	♑	10	Your Way of Sanctuary manifests through your goal-driven and focused quest for and attraction to results-oriented and successful career or accomplishments.
	Vesta	Capricorn	♑	11	Your Way of Sanctuary manifests through your goal-driven and focused quest for and attraction to results-oriented and successful community.
	Vesta	Capricorn	♑	12	Your Way of Sanctuary manifests through your goal-driven and focused quest for and attraction to results-oriented and successful spirituality.

	Vesta	Aquarius	≋	1	Your Way of Sanctuary manifests through your unconventional and idealistic quest for and attraction to authentic and non-traditional identity development.
	Vesta	Aquarius	≋	2	Your Way of Sanctuary manifests through your unconventional and idealistic quest for and attraction to authentic and non-traditional values and ways to meet your needs.
	Vesta	Aquarius	≋	3	Your Way of Sanctuary manifests through your unconventional and idealistic quest for and attraction to authentic and non-traditional understanding of the world around you.
	Vesta	Aquarius	≋	4	Your Way of Sanctuary manifests through your unconventional and idealistic quest for and attraction to authentic and non-traditional emotional caretaking and traditions.
	Vesta	Aquarius	≋	5	Your Way of Sanctuary manifests through your unconventional and idealistic quest for and attraction to authentic and non-traditional creative expression.
	Vesta	Aquarius	≋	6	Your Way of Sanctuary manifests through your unconventional and idealistic quest for and attraction to authentic and non-traditional service for others.
	Vesta	Aquarius	≋	7	Your Way of Sanctuary manifests through your unconventional and idealistic quest for and attraction to authentic and non-traditional life teachers.
	Vesta	Aquarius	≋	8	Your Way of Sanctuary manifests through your unconventional and idealistic quest for and attraction to authentic and non-traditional relationships.
	Vesta	Aquarius	≋	9	Your Way of Sanctuary manifests through your unconventional and idealistic quest for and attraction to authentic and non-traditional mastership of a body of knowledge.
	Vesta	Aquarius	≋	10	Your Way of Sanctuary manifests through your unconventional and idealistic quest for and attraction to authentic and non-traditional career or accomplishments.
	Vesta	Aquarius	≋	11	Your Way of Sanctuary manifests through your unconventional and idealistic quest for and attraction to authentic and non-traditional community.
	Vesta	Aquarius	≋	12	Your Way of Sanctuary manifests through your unconventional and idealistic quest for and attraction to authentic and non-traditional spirituality.

	Vesta	Pisces	♓	1	Your Way of Sanctuary manifests through your imaginative and faithful quest for and attraction to consciousness-raising and soulful identity development.
	Vesta	Pisces	♓	2	Your Way of Sanctuary manifests through your imaginative and faithful quest for and attraction to consciousness-raising and soulful values and ways to meet your needs.
	Vesta	Pisces	♓	3	Your Way of Sanctuary manifests through your imaginative and faithful quest for and attraction to consciousness-raising and soulful understanding of the world around you.
	Vesta	Pisces	♓	4	Your Way of Sanctuary manifests through your imaginative and faithful quest for and attraction to consciousness-raising and soulful emotional caretaking and traditions.
	Vesta	Pisces	♓	5	Your Way of Sanctuary manifests through your imaginative and faithful quest for and attraction to consciousness-raising and soulful creative expression.
	Vesta	Pisces	♓	6	Your Way of Sanctuary manifests through your imaginative and faithful quest for and attraction to consciousness-raising and soulful service for others.
	Vesta	Pisces	♓	7	Your Way of Sanctuary manifests through your imaginative and faithful quest for and attraction to consciousness-raising and soulful life teachers.
	Vesta	Pisces	♓	8	Your Way of Sanctuary manifests through your imaginative and faithful quest for and attraction to consciousness-raising and soulful relationships.
	Vesta	Pisces	♓	9	Your Way of Sanctuary manifests through your imaginative and faithful quest for and attraction to consciousness-raising and soulful mastership of a body of knowledge.
	Vesta	Pisces	♓	10	Your Way of Sanctuary manifests through your imaginative and faithful quest for and attraction to consciousness-raising and soulful career or accomplishments.
	Vesta	Pisces	♓	11	Your Way of Sanctuary manifests through your imaginative and faithful quest for and attraction to consciousness-raising and soulful community.
	Vesta	Pisces	♓	12	Your Way of Sanctuary manifests through your imaginative and faithful quest for and attraction to consciousness-raising and soulful spirituality.

Juno | ⚳

Energy Point Type: **Asteroid**

Co-Rules Sign: **Sagittarius**

Co-Rules House: **9**th

Element: **Fire**

Key Phrase: **Way of Duty**

Juno represents your Way of Duty. Its placement in Sign and House reveals how we make commitments that we intend to endure and where we are willing to make sacrifices to see that they endure. In my case my Way of Duty is expressed through Water (Scorpio) in my quest for identity (1st House). Water's expression is emotional, intense, and imaginative. In Scorpio the Element acts intensely, transformatively, and unrelentingly. So, my key phrase is *"Your Way of Duty manifests through your intense and truth seeking quest for and attraction to penetrating and emotionally transformative identity development."* In short, I am committed to deep, powerful identity transformation and understanding about who I am and want to be. Also, I make strong emotional commitments to romantic partners, enduring even after the relationship has ended.

When considering the placement of your own Juno, think about the way you commit and where you face your need to sacrifice and make commitments. Consider Juno in Taurus in the 7th House, *"Your Way of Duty manifests through your steadfast and persistent quest for and attraction to enduring and secure life teachers."* Here is an individual who either really needs to commit to any type of partnership (friend, lover, co-worker, and so on) or learn the lesson of proper commitments to others. This placement is especially strong since the energy of Taurus is all about enduring and persisting and the 7th House is all about making connections. Juno in this placement a powerful energy alignment, but strength of the placement is also its greatest weakness. If healthy, this individual will be steadfast and doggedly reliable; but if the responsibility is not appropriate or balanced, this individual can sacrifice too much and "over" commit.

257

For more in depth reading about Juno, I recommend purchasing and reading:

- *Asteroid Goddesses: The Mythology, Psychology and Astrology of the Reemerging Feminine* by Demetra George, with Douglas Bloch (ISBN: 00935127151)
- *The Ultimate Asteroid Book* by J. Lee Lehman, PhD (ISBN: 0914918788)

	Juno	Aries	♈	1	Your Way of Duty manifests through your independent and heroic quest for and attraction to maverick and individualistic identity development.
	Juno	Aries	♈	2	Your Way of Duty manifests through your independent and heroic quest for and attraction to maverick and individualistic values and ways to meet your needs.
	Juno	Aries	♈	3	Your Way of Duty manifests through your independent and heroic quest for and attraction to maverick and individualistic understanding of the world around you.
	Juno	Aries	♈	4	Your Way of Duty manifests through your independent and heroic quest for and attraction to maverick and individualistic emotional caretaking and traditions.
	Juno	Aries	♈	5	Your Way of Duty manifests through your independent and heroic quest for and attraction to maverick and individualistic creative expression.
	Juno	Aries	♈	6	Your Way of Duty manifests through your independent and heroic quest for and attraction to maverick and individualistic services for others.
	Juno	Aries	♈	7	Your Way of Duty manifests through your independent and heroic quest for and attraction to maverick and individualistic life teachers.
	Juno	Aries	♈	8	Your Way of Duty manifests through your independent and heroic quest for and attraction to maverick and individualistic intimate relationships.
	Juno	Aries	♈	9	Your Way of Duty manifests through your independent and heroic quest for and attraction to maverick and individualistic mastership of a body of life experience.
	Juno	Aries	♈	10	Your Way of Duty manifests through your independent and heroic quest for and attraction to maverick and individualistic accomplishments.
	Juno	Aries	♈	11	Your Way of Duty manifests through your independent and heroic quest for and attraction to maverick and individualistic community.
	Juno	Aries	♈	12	Your Way of Duty manifests through your independent and heroic quest for and attraction to maverick and individualistic spirituality.

⚹	Juno	Taurus	♉	I	Your Way of Duty manifests through your steadfast and persistent quest for and attraction to enduring and secure identity development.
⚹	Juno	Taurus	♉	2	Your Way of Duty manifests through your steadfast and persistent quest for and attraction to enduring and secure values and ways to meet your needs.
⚹	Juno	Taurus	♉	3	Your Way of Duty manifests through your steadfast and persistent quest for and attraction to enduring and secure understanding of the world around you.
⚹	Juno	Taurus	♉	4	Your Way of Duty manifests through your steadfast and persistent quest for and attraction to enduring and secure emotional caretaking and traditions.
⚹	Juno	Taurus	♉	5	Your Way of Duty manifests through your steadfast and persistent quest for and attraction to enduring and secure creative expression.
⚹	Juno	Taurus	♉	6	Your Way of Duty manifests through your steadfast and persistent quest for and attraction to enduring and secure services for others.
⚹	Juno	Taurus	♉	7	Your Way of Duty manifests through your steadfast and persistent quest for and attraction to enduring and secure life teachers.
⚹	Juno	Taurus	♉	8	Your Way of Duty manifests through your steadfast and persistent quest for and attraction to enduring and secure intimate relationships.
⚹	Juno	Taurus	♉	9	Your Way of Duty manifests through your steadfast and persistent quest for and attraction to enduring and secure mastership of a body of life experience.
⚹	Juno	Taurus	♉	10	Your Way of Duty manifests through your steadfast and persistent quest for and attraction to enduring and secure accomplishments.
⚹	Juno	Taurus	♉	11	Your Way of Duty manifests through your steadfast and persistent quest for and attraction to enduring and secure community.
⚹	Juno	Taurus	♉	12	Your Way of Duty manifests through your steadfast and persistent quest for and attraction to enduring and secure spirituality.

⚵	Juno	Gemini	♊	1	Your Way of Duty manifests through your inquisitive and mentally agile quest for and attraction to ever changing and adaptable identity development.
⚵	Juno	Gemini	♊	2	Your Way of Duty manifests through your inquisitive and mentally agile quest for and attraction to ever changing and adaptable values and ways to meet your needs.
⚵	Juno	Gemini	♊	3	Your Way of Duty manifests through your inquisitive and mentally agile quest for and attraction to ever changing and adaptable understanding of the world around you.
⚵	Juno	Gemini	♊	4	Your Way of Duty manifests through your inquisitive and mentally agile quest for and attraction to ever changing and adaptable emotional caretaking and traditions.
⚵	Juno	Gemini	♊	5	Your Way of Duty manifests through your inquisitive and mentally agile quest for and attraction to ever changing and adaptable creative expression.
⚵	Juno	Gemini	♊	6	Your Way of Duty manifests through your inquisitive and mentally agile quest for and attraction to ever changing and adaptable services for others.
⚵	Juno	Gemini	♊	7	Your Way of Duty manifests through your inquisitive and mentally agile quest for and attraction to ever changing and adaptable life teachers.
⚵	Juno	Gemini	♊	8	Your Way of Duty manifests through your inquisitive and mentally agile quest for and attraction to ever changing and adaptable intimate relationships.
⚵	Juno	Gemini	♊	9	Your Way of Duty manifests through your inquisitive and mentally agile quest for and attraction to ever changing and adaptable mastership of a body of life experience.
⚵	Juno	Gemini	♊	10	Your Way of Duty manifests through your inquisitive and mentally agile quest for and attraction to ever changing and adaptable accomplishments.
⚵	Juno	Gemini	♊	11	Your Way of Duty manifests through your inquisitive and mentally agile quest for and attraction to ever changing and adaptable community.
⚵	Juno	Gemini	♊	12	Your Way of Duty manifests through your inquisitive and mentally agile quest for and attraction to ever changing and adaptable spirituality.

261

✳	Juno	Cancer	♋	1	Your Way of Duty manifests through your emotional and caring quest for and attraction to nurturing and supportive identity development.
✳	Juno	Cancer	♋	2	Your Way of Duty manifests through your emotional and caring quest for and attraction to nurturing and supportive values and ways to meet your needs.
✳	Juno	Cancer	♋	3	Your Way of Duty manifests through your emotional and caring quest for and attraction to nurturing and supportive understanding of the world around you.
✳	Juno	Cancer	♋	4	Your Way of Duty manifests through your emotional and caring quest for and attraction to nurturing and supportive emotional caretaking and traditions.
✳	Juno	Cancer	♋	5	Your Way of Duty manifests through your emotional and caring quest for and attraction to nurturing and supportive creative expression.
✳	Juno	Cancer	♋	6	Your Way of Duty manifests through your emotional and caring quest for and attraction to nurturing and supportive services for others.
✳	Juno	Cancer	♋	7	Your Way of Duty manifests through your emotional and caring quest for and attraction to nurturing and supportive life teachers.
✳	Juno	Cancer	♋	8	Your Way of Duty manifests through your emotional and caring quest for and attraction to nurturing and supportive intimate relationships.
✳	Juno	Cancer	♋	9	Your Way of Duty manifests through your emotional and caring quest for and attraction to nurturing and supportive mastership of a body of life experience.
✳	Juno	Cancer	♋	10	Your Way of Duty manifests through your emotional and caring quest for and attraction to nurturing and supportive accomplishments.
✳	Juno	Cancer	♋	11	Your Way of Duty manifests through your emotional and caring quest for and attraction to nurturing and supportive community.
✳	Juno	Cancer	♋	12	Your Way of Duty manifests through your emotional and caring quest for and attraction to nurturing and supportive spirituality.

⚹	Juno	Leo	♌	1	Your Way of Duty manifests through your energetic and dramatic quest for and attraction to creative and romantic identity development.
⚹	Juno	Leo	♌	2	Your Way of Duty manifests through your energetic and dramatic quest for and attraction to creative and romantic values and ways to meet your needs.
⚹	Juno	Leo	♌	3	Your Way of Duty manifests through your energetic and dramatic quest for and attraction to creative and romantic understanding of the world around you.
⚹	Juno	Leo	♌	4	Your Way of Duty manifests through your energetic and dramatic quest for and attraction to creative and romantic emotional caretaking and traditions.
⚹	Juno	Leo	♌	5	Your Way of Duty manifests through your energetic and dramatic quest for and attraction to creative and romantic creative expression.
⚹	Juno	Leo	♌	6	Your Way of Duty manifests through your energetic and dramatic quest for and attraction to creative and romantic services for others.
⚹	Juno	Leo	♌	7	Your Way of Duty manifests through your energetic and dramatic quest for and attraction to creative and romantic life teachers.
⚹	Juno	Leo	♌	8	Your Way of Duty manifests through your energetic and dramatic quest for and attraction to creative and romantic intimate relationships.
⚹	Juno	Leo	♌	9	Your Way of Duty manifests through your energetic and dramatic quest for and attraction to creative and romantic mastership of a body of life experience.
⚹	Juno	Leo	♌	10	Your Way of Duty manifests through your energetic and dramatic quest for and attraction to creative and romantic accomplishments.
⚹	Juno	Leo	♌	11	Your Way of Duty manifests through your energetic and dramatic quest for and attraction to creative and romantic community.
⚹	Juno	Leo	♌	12	Your Way of Duty manifests through your energetic and dramatic quest for and attraction to creative and romantic spirituality.

263

⚹	Juno	Virgo	♍	1	Your Way of Duty manifests through your critically-minded and methodical quest for and attraction to meticulous and practical identity development.
⚹	Juno	Virgo	♍	2	Your Way of Duty manifests through your critically-minded and methodical quest for and attraction to meticulous and practical values and ways to meet your needs.
⚹	Juno	Virgo	♍	3	Your Way of Duty manifests through your critically-minded and methodical quest for and attraction to meticulous and practical understanding of the world around you.
⚹	Juno	Virgo	♍	4	Your Way of Duty manifests through your critically-minded and methodical quest for and attraction to meticulous and practical emotional caretaking and traditions.
⚹	Juno	Virgo	♍	5	Your Way of Duty manifests through your critically-minded and methodical quest for and attraction to meticulous and practical creative expression.
⚹	Juno	Virgo	♍	6	Your Way of Duty manifests through your critically-minded and methodical quest for and attraction to meticulous and practical services for others.
⚹	Juno	Virgo	♍	7	Your Way of Duty manifests through your critically-minded and methodical quest for and attraction to meticulous and practical life teachers.
⚹	Juno	Virgo	♍	8	Your Way of Duty manifests through your critically-minded and methodical quest for and attraction to meticulous and practical intimate relationships.
⚹	Juno	Virgo	♍	9	Your Way of Duty manifests through your critically-minded and methodical quest for and attraction to meticulous and practical mastership of a body of life experience.
⚹	Juno	Virgo	♍	10	Your Way of Duty manifests through your critically-minded and methodical quest for and attraction to meticulous and practical accomplishments.
⚹	Juno	Virgo	♍	11	Your Way of Duty manifests through your critically-minded and methodical quest for and attraction to meticulous and practical community.
⚹	Juno	Virgo	♍	12	Your Way of Duty manifests through your critically-minded and methodical quest for and attraction to meticulous and practical spirituality.

✳	Juno	Libra	♎	1	Your Way of Duty manifests through your analytical and balanced quest for and attraction to harmonious and logical identity development.
✳	Juno	Libra	♎	2	Your Way of Duty manifests through your analytical and balanced quest for and attraction to harmonious and logical values and ways to meet your needs.
✳	Juno	Libra	♎	3	Your Way of Duty manifests through your analytical and balanced quest for and attraction to harmonious and logical understanding of the world around you.
✳	Juno	Libra	♎	4	Your Way of Duty manifests through your analytical and balanced quest for and attraction to harmonious and logical emotional caretaking and traditions.
✳	Juno	Libra	♎	5	Your Way of Duty manifests through your analytical and balanced quest for and attraction to harmonious and logical creative expression.
✳	Juno	Libra	♎	6	Your Way of Duty manifests through your analytical and balanced quest for and attraction to harmonious and logical services for others.
✳	Juno	Libra	♎	7	Your Way of Duty manifests through your analytical and balanced quest for and attraction to harmonious and logical life teachers.
✳	Juno	Libra	♎	8	Your Way of Duty manifests through your analytical and balanced quest for and attraction to harmonious and logical intimate relationships.
✳	Juno	Libra	♎	9	Your Way of Duty manifests through your analytical and balanced quest for and attraction to harmonious and logical mastership of a body of life experience.
✳	Juno	Libra	♎	10	Your Way of Duty manifests through your analytical and balanced quest for and attraction to harmonious and logical accomplishments.
✳	Juno	Libra	♎	11	Your Way of Duty manifests through your analytical and balanced quest for and attraction to harmonious and logical community.
✳	Juno	Libra	♎	12	Your Way of Duty manifests through your analytical and balanced quest for and attraction to harmonious and logical spirituality.

	Juno	Scorpio	♏	1	Your Way of Duty manifests through your intense and truth seeking quest for and attraction to penetrating and emotionally transformative identity development.
	Juno	Scorpio	♏	2	Your Way of Duty manifests through your intense and truth seeking quest for and attraction to penetrating and emotionally transformative values and ways to meet your needs.
	Juno	Scorpio	♏	3	Your Way of Duty manifests through your intense and truth seeking quest for and attraction to penetrating and emotionally transformative understanding of the world around you.
	Juno	Scorpio	♏	4	Your Way of Duty manifests through your intense and truth seeking quest for and attraction to penetrating and emotionally transformative emotional caretaking and traditions.
	Juno	Scorpio	♏	5	Your Way of Duty manifests through your intense and truth seeking quest for and attraction to penetrating and emotionally transformative creative expression.
	Juno	Scorpio	♏	6	Your Way of Duty manifests through your intense and truth seeking quest for and attraction to penetrating and emotionally transformative services for others.
	Juno	Scorpio	♏	7	Your Way of Duty manifests through your intense and truth seeking quest for and attraction to penetrating and emotionally transformative life teachers.
	Juno	Scorpio	♏	8	Your Way of Duty manifests through your intense and truth seeking quest for and attraction to penetrating and emotionally transformative intimate relationships.
	Juno	Scorpio	♏	9	Your Way of Duty manifests through your intense and truth seeking quest for and attraction to penetrating and emotionally transformative mastership of a body of life experience.
	Juno	Scorpio	♏	10	Your Way of Duty manifests through your intense and truth seeking quest for and attraction to penetrating and emotionally transformative accomplishments.
	Juno	Scorpio	♏	11	Your Way of Duty manifests through your intense and truth seeking quest for and attraction to penetrating and emotionally transformative community.
	Juno	Scorpio	♏	12	Your Way of Duty manifests through your intense and truth seeking quest for and attraction to penetrating and emotionally transformative spirituality.

	Juno	Sagittarius	⚷	1	Your Way of Duty manifests through your wide-ranging and open-minded quest for and attraction to experiential and risk-taking identity development.
	Juno	Sagittarius	⚷	2	Your Way of Duty manifests through your wide-ranging and open-minded quest for and attraction to experiential and risk-taking values and ways to meet your needs.
	Juno	Sagittarius	⚷	3	Your Way of Duty manifests through your wide-ranging and open-minded quest for and attraction to experiential and risk-taking understanding of the world around you.
	Juno	Sagittarius	⚷	4	Your Way of Duty manifests through your wide-ranging and open-minded quest for and attraction to experiential and risk-taking emotional caretaking and traditions.
	Juno	Sagittarius	⚷	5	Your Way of Duty manifests through your wide-ranging and open-minded quest for and attraction to experiential and risk-taking creative expression.
	Juno	Sagittarius	⚷	6	Your Way of Duty manifests through your wide-ranging and open-minded quest for and attraction to experiential and risk-taking services for others.
	Juno	Sagittarius	⚷	7	Your Way of Duty manifests through your wide-ranging and open-minded quest for and attraction to experiential and risk-taking life teachers.
	Juno	Sagittarius	⚷	8	Your Way of Duty manifests through your wide-ranging and open-minded quest for and attraction to experiential and risk-taking intimate relationships.
	Juno	Sagittarius	⚷	9	Your Way of Duty manifests through your wide-ranging and open-minded quest for and attraction to experiential and risk-taking mastership of a body of life experience.
	Juno	Sagittarius	⚷	10	Your Way of Duty manifests through your wide-ranging and open-minded quest for and attraction to experiential and risk-taking accomplishments.
	Juno	Sagittarius	⚷	11	Your Way of Duty manifests through your wide-ranging and open-minded quest for and attraction to experiential and risk-taking community.
	Juno	Sagittarius	⚷	12	Your Way of Duty manifests through your wide-ranging and open-minded quest for and attraction to experiential and risk-taking spirituality.

✷	Juno	Capricorn	♑	1	Your Way of Duty manifests through your goal-driven and focused quest for and attraction to results-oriented and successful identity development.
✷	Juno	Capricorn	♑	2	Your Way of Duty manifests through your goal-driven and focused quest for and attraction to results-oriented and successful values and ways to meet your needs.
✷	Juno	Capricorn	♑	3	Your Way of Duty manifests through your goal-driven and focused quest for and attraction to results-oriented and successful understanding of the world around you.
✷	Juno	Capricorn	♑	4	Your Way of Duty manifests through your goal-driven and focused quest for and attraction to results-oriented and successful emotional caretaking and traditions.
✷	Juno	Capricorn	♑	5	Your Way of Duty manifests through your goal-driven and focused quest for and attraction to results-oriented and successful creative expression.
✷	Juno	Capricorn	♑	6	Your Way of Duty manifests through your goal-driven and focused quest for and attraction to results-oriented and successful services for others.
✷	Juno	Capricorn	♑	7	Your Way of Duty manifests through your goal-driven and focused quest for and attraction to results-oriented and successful life teachers.
✷	Juno	Capricorn	♑	8	Your Way of Duty manifests through your goal-driven and focused quest for and attraction to results-oriented and successful intimate relationships.
✷	Juno	Capricorn	♑	9	Your Way of Duty manifests through your goal-driven and focused quest for and attraction to results-oriented and successful mastership of a body of life experience.
✷	Juno	Capricorn	♑	10	Your Way of Duty manifests through your goal-driven and focused quest for and attraction to results-oriented and successful accomplishments.
✷	Juno	Capricorn	♑	11	Your Way of Duty manifests through your goal-driven and focused quest for and attraction to results-oriented and successful community.
✷	Juno	Capricorn	♑	12	Your Way of Duty manifests through your goal-driven and focused quest for and attraction to results-oriented and successful spirituality.

	Juno	Aquarius	♒	1	Your Way of Duty manifests through your unconventional and idealistic quest for and attraction to authentic and non-traditional identity development.
	Juno	Aquarius	♒	2	Your Way of Duty manifests through your unconventional and idealistic quest for and attraction to authentic and non-traditional values and ways to meet your needs.
	Juno	Aquarius	♒	3	Your Way of Duty manifests through your unconventional and idealistic quest for and attraction to authentic and non-traditional understanding of the world around you.
	Juno	Aquarius	♒	4	Your Way of Duty manifests through your unconventional and idealistic quest for and attraction to authentic and non-traditional emotional caretaking and traditions.
	Juno	Aquarius	♒	5	Your Way of Duty manifests through your unconventional and idealistic quest for and attraction to authentic and non-traditional creative expression.
	Juno	Aquarius	♒	6	Your Way of Duty manifests through your unconventional and idealistic quest for and attraction to authentic and non-traditional services for others.
	Juno	Aquarius	♒	7	Your Way of Duty manifests through your unconventional and idealistic quest for and attraction to authentic and non-traditional life teachers.
	Juno	Aquarius	♒	8	Your Way of Duty manifests through your unconventional and idealistic quest for and attraction to authentic and non-traditional intimate relationships.
	Juno	Aquarius	♒	9	Your Way of Duty manifests through your unconventional and idealistic quest for and attraction to authentic and non-traditional mastership of a body of life experience.
	Juno	Aquarius	♒	10	Your Way of Duty manifests through your unconventional and idealistic quest for and attraction to authentic and non-traditional accomplishments.
	Juno	Aquarius	♒	11	Your Way of Duty manifests through your unconventional and idealistic quest for and attraction to authentic and non-traditional community.
	Juno	Aquarius	♒	12	Your Way of Duty manifests through your unconventional and idealistic quest for and attraction to authentic and non-traditional spirituality.

	Juno	Pisces	♓	1	Your Way of Duty manifests through your imaginative and faithful quest for and attraction to consciousness-raising and soulful identity development.
	Juno	Pisces	♓	2	Your Way of Duty manifests through your imaginative and faithful quest for and attraction to consciousness-raising and soulful values and ways to meet your needs.
	Juno	Pisces	♓	3	Your Way of Duty manifests through your imaginative and faithful quest for and attraction to consciousness-raising and soulful understanding of the world around you.
	Juno	Pisces	♓	4	Your Way of Duty manifests through your imaginative and faithful quest for and attraction to consciousness-raising and soulful emotional caretaking and traditions.
	Juno	Pisces	♓	5	Your Way of Duty manifests through your imaginative and faithful quest for and attraction to consciousness-raising and soulful creative expression.
	Juno	Pisces	♓	6	Your Way of Duty manifests through your imaginative and faithful quest for and attraction to consciousness-raising and soulful services for others.
	Juno	Pisces	♓	7	Your Way of Duty manifests through your imaginative and faithful quest for and attraction to consciousness-raising and soulful life teachers.
	Juno	Pisces	♓	8	Your Way of Duty manifests through your imaginative and faithful quest for and attraction to consciousness-raising and soulful intimate relationships.
	Juno	Pisces	♓	9	Your Way of Duty manifests through your imaginative and faithful quest for and attraction to consciousness-raising and soulful mastership of a body of life experience.
	Juno	Pisces	♓	10	Your Way of Duty manifests through your imaginative and faithful quest for and attraction to consciousness-raising and soulful accomplishments.
	Juno	Pisces	♓	11	Your Way of Duty manifests through your imaginative and faithful quest for and attraction to consciousness-raising and soulful community.
	Juno	Pisces	♓	12	Your Way of Duty manifests through your imaginative and faithful quest for and attraction to consciousness-raising and soulful spirituality.

Lilith (The Black Moon) | ☽

Energy Point Type: **Calculated Point**
Co-Rules Sign: **Aries**
Co-Rules House: **1st**
Element: **Fire**
Key Phrase: **Way of Unyielding**

Lilith represents your Way of Unyielding. Its placement in Sign and House reveals how and where we stand on principle, how and where we will not bend or give in. In my case my Way of Unyielding is expressed through Earth (Taurus) in my quest for life teachers (7th House). Earth's expression is accomplished, persistent, and practical. In Taurus the Element acts protectively, conservatively, and reliably. So, my key phrase is *"Your Way of Unyielding manifests through your steadfast and persistent quest for and attraction to enduring and secure life teachers."* In short, I idealize the nature of partnerships and hold people to the standard I expect in terms of the partner I need and the partner I intend to be, whether it is a business commitment, friendship, or love relationship.

The story of Lilith used to identify the Quality assigned to the Energy Point comes from "the Babylonian Talmud, the *Zohar*, and the Alphabet of *Ben Sira*, all of which were written or compiled outside of Eretz Isreal, presumably after 70 CE, although they draw upon earlier oral and written tales."[26] In the story Lilith is created, like Adam, from the Earth, introducing the "subversive concept of woman's equality,"[27] which she expresses by refusing to submit to Adam. Since she would not submit and Adam would not allow her equal status, she chose instead to flee the Garden of Eden.[28] Summarily:

The legend concerning the wife of Adam, who preceded the creation of Eve, merged with the earlier legend of Lilith as a demon who killed infants and endangered women in childbirth. When the story of creation was being written

---

[26] Demetra George, *Mysteries of the Dark Moon* (New York: Harper Collins, 1992), 179.
[27] Ibid.
[28] Ibid, 180.

down, mention of Lilith was exorcised from scripture, with the one exception of Isaiah. The biblical patriarchs did not want to give the world a model of a wife who demanded equality and defied and left her husband; instead they extolled the virtues of Eve, who had no such ideas but instead would be subservient, enabling her husband in all ways.[29]

When you consider the placement of Lilith in your chart, think about how and where you need to stand firm in your beliefs, keeping in mind that this energy is not simple stubbornness, but rather an issue of integrity. Now consider Lilith in Cancer in the 1st House, *"Your Way of Unyielding manifests through your emotional and caring quest for and attraction to nurturing and supportive identity development."* First and foremost, this individual will feel compelled to follow his or her identity development on his or her own terms. The spiritual goal is the right kind of relationships that will properly nurture his or her identity, accepting no lesser substitute. This person will be very cautious about opening up (Cancer) and will not accept interactions that do not make him or her feel secure when sharing his or her trials and concerns about who he or she is and who he or she is becoming.

For additional information on Lilith, I recommend buying and reading:

- *Mysteries of the Dark Moon* by Demetra George (ISBN: 0062503707)

---

[29] Ibid, 181.

Astrology Unlocked by Philip Young, PhD

	Lilith	Aries	♈	1	Your Way of Unyielding manifests through your independent and heroic quest for and attraction to maverick and individualistic identity development.
	Lilith	Aries	♈	2	Your Way of Unyielding manifests through your independent and heroic quest for and attraction to maverick and individualistic values and ways to meet your needs.
	Lilith	Aries	♈	3	Your Way of Unyielding manifests through your independent and heroic quest for and attraction to maverick and individualistic understanding of the world around you.
	Lilith	Aries	♈	4	Your Way of Unyielding manifests through your independent and heroic quest for and attraction to maverick and individualistic emotional caretaking and traditions.
	Lilith	Aries	♈	5	Your Way of Unyielding manifests through your independent and heroic quest for and attraction to maverick and individualistic creative expression.
	Lilith	Aries	♈	6	Your Way of Unyielding manifests through your independent and heroic quest for and attraction to maverick and individualistic service for others.
	Lilith	Aries	♈	7	Your Way of Unyielding manifests through your independent and heroic quest for and attraction to maverick and individualistic life teachers.
	Lilith	Aries	♈	8	Your Way of Unyielding manifests through your independent and heroic quest for and attraction to maverick and individualistic intimate relationships.
	Lilith	Aries	♈	9	Your Way of Unyielding manifests through your independent and heroic quest for and attraction to maverick and individualistic mastership of a body of knowledge.
	Lilith	Aries	♈	10	Your Way of Unyielding manifests through your independent and heroic quest for and attraction to maverick and individualistic accomplishments.
	Lilith	Aries	♈	11	Your Way of Unyielding manifests through your independent and heroic quest for and attraction to maverick and individualistic community.
	Lilith	Aries	♈	12	Your Way of Unyielding manifests through your independent and heroic quest for and attraction to maverick and individualistic spirituality.

	Lilith	Taurus	♉	1	Your Way of Unyielding manifests through your steadfast and persistent quest for and attraction to enduring and secure identity development.
	Lilith	Taurus	♉	2	Your Way of Unyielding manifests through your steadfast and persistent quest for and attraction to enduring and secure values and ways to meet your needs.
	Lilith	Taurus	♉	3	Your Way of Unyielding manifests through your steadfast and persistent quest for and attraction to enduring and secure understanding of the world around you.
	Lilith	Taurus	♉	4	Your Way of Unyielding manifests through your steadfast and persistent quest for and attraction to enduring and secure emotional caretaking and traditions.
	Lilith	Taurus	♉	5	Your Way of Unyielding manifests through your steadfast and persistent quest for and attraction to enduring and secure creative expression.
	Lilith	Taurus	♉	6	Your Way of Unyielding manifests through your steadfast and persistent quest for and attraction to enduring and secure service for others.
	Lilith	Taurus	♉	7	Your Way of Unyielding manifests through your steadfast and persistent quest for and attraction to enduring and secure life teachers.
	Lilith	Taurus	♉	8	Your Way of Unyielding manifests through your steadfast and persistent quest for and attraction to enduring and secure intimate relationships.
	Lilith	Taurus	♉	9	Your Way of Unyielding manifests through your steadfast and persistent quest for and attraction to enduring and secure mastership of a body of knowledge.
	Lilith	Taurus	♉	10	Your Way of Unyielding manifests through your steadfast and persistent quest for and attraction to enduring and secure accomplishments.
	Lilith	Taurus	♉	11	Your Way of Unyielding manifests through your steadfast and persistent quest for and attraction to enduring and secure community.
	Lilith	Taurus	♉	12	Your Way of Unyielding manifests through your steadfast and persistent quest for and attraction to enduring and secure spirituality.

☽	Lilith	Gemini	♊	1	Your Way of Unyielding manifests through your inquisitive and mentally agile quest for and attraction to ever changing and adaptable identity development.
☽	Lilith	Gemini	♊	2	Your Way of Unyielding manifests through your inquisitive and mentally agile quest for and attraction to ever changing and adaptable values and ways to meet your needs.
☽	Lilith	Gemini	♊	3	Your Way of Unyielding manifests through your inquisitive and mentally agile quest for and attraction to ever changing and adaptable understanding of the world around you.
☽	Lilith	Gemini	♊	4	Your Way of Unyielding manifests through your inquisitive and mentally agile quest for and attraction to ever changing and adaptable emotional caretaking and traditions.
☽	Lilith	Gemini	♊	5	Your Way of Unyielding manifests through your inquisitive and mentally agile quest for and attraction to ever changing and adaptable creative expression.
☽	Lilith	Gemini	♊	6	Your Way of Unyielding manifests through your inquisitive and mentally agile quest for and attraction to ever changing and adaptable service for others.
☽	Lilith	Gemini	♊	7	Your Way of Unyielding manifests through your inquisitive and mentally agile quest for and attraction to ever changing and adaptable life teachers.
☽	Lilith	Gemini	♊	8	Your Way of Unyielding manifests through your inquisitive and mentally agile quest for and attraction to ever changing and adaptable intimate relationships.
☽	Lilith	Gemini	♊	9	Your Way of Unyielding manifests through your inquisitive and mentally agile quest for and attraction to ever changing and adaptable mastership of a body of knowledge.
☽	Lilith	Gemini	♊	10	Your Way of Unyielding manifests through your inquisitive and mentally agile quest for and attraction to ever changing and adaptable accomplishments.
☽	Lilith	Gemini	♊	11	Your Way of Unyielding manifests through your inquisitive and mentally agile quest for and attraction to ever changing and adaptable community.
☽	Lilith	Gemini	♊	12	Your Way of Unyielding manifests through your inquisitive and mentally agile quest for and attraction to ever changing and adaptable spirituality.

⚸	Lilith	Cancer	♋	1	Your Way of Unyielding manifests through your emotional and caring quest for and attraction to nurturing and supportive identity development.
⚸	Lilith	Cancer	♋	2	Your Way of Unyielding manifests through your emotional and caring quest for and attraction to nurturing and supportive values and ways to meet your needs.
⚸	Lilith	Cancer	♋	3	Your Way of Unyielding manifests through your emotional and caring quest for and attraction to nurturing and supportive understanding of the world around you.
⚸	Lilith	Cancer	♋	4	Your Way of Unyielding manifests through your emotional and caring quest for and attraction to nurturing and supportive emotional caretaking and traditions.
⚸	Lilith	Cancer	♋	5	Your Way of Unyielding manifests through your emotional and caring quest for and attraction to nurturing and supportive creative expression.
⚸	Lilith	Cancer	♋	6	Your Way of Unyielding manifests through your emotional and caring quest for and attraction to nurturing and supportive service for others.
⚸	Lilith	Cancer	♋	7	Your Way of Unyielding manifests through your emotional and caring quest for and attraction to nurturing and supportive life teachers.
⚸	Lilith	Cancer	♋	8	Your Way of Unyielding manifests through your emotional and caring quest for and attraction to nurturing and supportive intimate relationships.
⚸	Lilith	Cancer	♋	9	Your Way of Unyielding manifests through your emotional and caring quest for and attraction to nurturing and supportive mastership of a body of knowledge.
⚸	Lilith	Cancer	♋	10	Your Way of Unyielding manifests through your emotional and caring quest for and attraction to nurturing and supportive accomplishments.
⚸	Lilith	Cancer	♋	11	Your Way of Unyielding manifests through your emotional and caring quest for and attraction to nurturing and supportive community.
⚸	Lilith	Cancer	♋	12	Your Way of Unyielding manifests through your emotional and caring quest for and attraction to nurturing and supportive spirituality.

Astrology Unlocked by Philip Young, PhD

☽	Lilith	Leo	♌	1	Your Way of Unyielding manifests through your energetic and dramatic quest for and attraction to creative and romantic identity development.
☽	Lilith	Leo	♌	2	Your Way of Unyielding manifests through your energetic and dramatic quest for and attraction to creative and romantic values and ways to meet your needs.
☽	Lilith	Leo	♌	3	Your Way of Unyielding manifests through your energetic and dramatic quest for and attraction to creative and romantic understanding of the world around you.
☽	Lilith	Leo	♌	4	Your Way of Unyielding manifests through your energetic and dramatic quest for and attraction to creative and romantic emotional caretaking and traditions.
☽	Lilith	Leo	♌	5	Your Way of Unyielding manifests through your energetic and dramatic quest for and attraction to creative and romantic creative expression.
☽	Lilith	Leo	♌	6	Your Way of Unyielding manifests through your energetic and dramatic quest for and attraction to creative and romantic service for others.
☽	Lilith	Leo	♌	7	Your Way of Unyielding manifests through your energetic and dramatic quest for and attraction to creative and romantic life teachers.
☽	Lilith	Leo	♌	8	Your Way of Unyielding manifests through your energetic and dramatic quest for and attraction to creative and romantic intimate relationships.
☽	Lilith	Leo	♌	9	Your Way of Unyielding manifests through your energetic and dramatic quest for and attraction to creative and romantic mastership of a body of knowledge.
☽	Lilith	Leo	♌	10	Your Way of Unyielding manifests through your energetic and dramatic quest for and attraction to creative and romantic accomplishments.
☽	Lilith	Leo	♌	11	Your Way of Unyielding manifests through your energetic and dramatic quest for and attraction to creative and romantic community.
☽	Lilith	Leo	♌	12	Your Way of Unyielding manifests through your energetic and dramatic quest for and attraction to creative and romantic spirituality.

☽	Lilith	Virgo	♍	1	Your Way of Unyielding manifests through your critically-minded and methodical quest for and attraction to meticulous and practical identity development.
☽	Lilith	Virgo	♍	2	Your Way of Unyielding manifests through your critically-minded and methodical quest for and attraction to meticulous and practical values and ways to meet your needs.
☽	Lilith	Virgo	♍	3	Your Way of Unyielding manifests through your critically-minded and methodical quest for and attraction to meticulous and practical understanding of the world around you.
☽	Lilith	Virgo	♍	4	Your Way of Unyielding manifests through your critically-minded and methodical quest for and attraction to meticulous and practical emotional caretaking and traditions.
☽	Lilith	Virgo	♍	5	Your Way of Unyielding manifests through your critically-minded and methodical quest for and attraction to meticulous and practical creative expression.
☽	Lilith	Virgo	♍	6	Your Way of Unyielding manifests through your critically-minded and methodical quest for and attraction to meticulous and practical service for others.
☽	Lilith	Virgo	♍	7	Your Way of Unyielding manifests through your critically-minded and methodical quest for and attraction to meticulous and practical life teachers.
☽	Lilith	Virgo	♍	8	Your Way of Unyielding manifests through your critically-minded and methodical quest for and attraction to meticulous and practical intimate relationships.
☽	Lilith	Virgo	♍	9	Your Way of Unyielding manifests through your critically-minded and methodical quest for and attraction to meticulous and practical mastership of a body of knowledge.
☽	Lilith	Virgo	♍	10	Your Way of Unyielding manifests through your critically-minded and methodical quest for and attraction to meticulous and practical accomplishments.
☽	Lilith	Virgo	♍	11	Your Way of Unyielding manifests through your critically-minded and methodical quest for and attraction to meticulous and practical community.
☽	Lilith	Virgo	♍	12	Your Way of Unyielding manifests through your critically-minded and methodical quest for and attraction to meticulous and practical spirituality.

	Lilith	Libra	♎	1	Your Way of Unyielding manifests through your analytical and balanced quest for and attraction to harmonious and logical identity development.
⚸	Lilith	Libra	♎	2	Your Way of Unyielding manifests through your analytical and balanced quest for and attraction to harmonious and logical values and ways to meet your needs.
⚸	Lilith	Libra	♎	3	Your Way of Unyielding manifests through your analytical and balanced quest for and attraction to harmonious and logical understanding of the world around you.
⚸	Lilith	Libra	♎	4	Your Way of Unyielding manifests through your analytical and balanced quest for and attraction to harmonious and logical emotional caretaking and traditions.
⚸	Lilith	Libra	♎	5	Your Way of Unyielding manifests through your analytical and balanced quest for and attraction to harmonious and logical creative expression.
⚸	Lilith	Libra	♎	6	Your Way of Unyielding manifests through your analytical and balanced quest for and attraction to harmonious and logical service for others.
⚸	Lilith	Libra	♎	7	Your Way of Unyielding manifests through your analytical and balanced quest for and attraction to harmonious and logical life teachers.
⚸	Lilith	Libra	♎	8	Your Way of Unyielding manifests through your analytical and balanced quest for and attraction to harmonious and logical intimate relationships.
⚸	Lilith	Libra	♎	9	Your Way of Unyielding manifests through your analytical and balanced quest for and attraction to harmonious and logical mastership of a body of knowledge.
⚸	Lilith	Libra	♎	10	Your Way of Unyielding manifests through your analytical and balanced quest for and attraction to harmonious and logical accomplishments.
⚸	Lilith	Libra	♎	11	Your Way of Unyielding manifests through your analytical and balanced quest for and attraction to harmonious and logical community.
⚸	Lilith	Libra	♎	12	Your Way of Unyielding manifests through your analytical and balanced quest for and attraction to harmonious and logical spirituality.

⚸	Lilith	Scorpio	♏	1	Your Way of Unyielding manifests through your intense and truth seeking quest for and attraction to penetrating and emotionally transformative identity development.
⚸	Lilith	Scorpio	♏	2	Your Way of Unyielding manifests through your intense and truth seeking quest for and attraction to penetrating and emotionally transformative values and ways to meet your needs.
⚸	Lilith	Scorpio	♏	3	Your Way of Unyielding manifests through your intense and truth seeking quest for and attraction to penetrating and emotionally transformative understanding of the world around you.
⚸	Lilith	Scorpio	♏	4	Your Way of Unyielding manifests through your intense and truth seeking quest for and attraction to penetrating and emotionally transformative emotional caretaking and traditions.
⚸	Lilith	Scorpio	♏	5	Your Way of Unyielding manifests through your intense and truth seeking quest for and attraction to penetrating and emotionally transformative creative expression.
⚸	Lilith	Scorpio	♏	6	Your Way of Unyielding manifests through your intense and truth seeking quest for and attraction to penetrating and emotionally transformative service for others.
⚸	Lilith	Scorpio	♏	7	Your Way of Unyielding manifests through your intense and truth seeking quest for and attraction to penetrating and emotionally transformative life teachers.
⚸	Lilith	Scorpio	♏	8	Your Way of Unyielding manifests through your intense and truth seeking quest for and attraction to penetrating and emotionally transformative intimate relationships.
⚸	Lilith	Scorpio	♏	9	Your Way of Unyielding manifests through your intense and truth seeking quest for and attraction to penetrating and emotionally transformative mastership of a body of knowledge.
⚸	Lilith	Scorpio	♏	10	Your Way of Unyielding manifests through your intense and truth seeking quest for and attraction to penetrating and emotionally transformative accomplishments.
⚸	Lilith	Scorpio	♏	11	Your Way of Unyielding manifests through your intense and truth seeking quest for and attraction to penetrating and emotionally transformative community.
⚸	Lilith	Scorpio	♏	12	Your Way of Unyielding manifests through your intense and truth seeking quest for and attraction to penetrating and emotionally transformative spirituality.

	Lilith	Sagittarius	♐	1	Your Way of Unyielding manifests through your wide-ranging and open-minded quest for and attraction to experiential and risk-taking identity development.
	Lilith	Sagittarius	♐	2	Your Way of Unyielding manifests through your wide-ranging and open-minded quest for and attraction to experiential and risk-taking values and ways to meet your needs.
	Lilith	Sagittarius	♐	3	Your Way of Unyielding manifests through your wide-ranging and open-minded quest for and attraction to experiential and risk-taking understanding of the world around you.
	Lilith	Sagittarius	♐	4	Your Way of Unyielding manifests through your wide-ranging and open-minded quest for and attraction to experiential and risk-taking emotional caretaking and traditions.
	Lilith	Sagittarius	♐	5	Your Way of Unyielding manifests through your wide-ranging and open-minded quest for and attraction to experiential and risk-taking creative expression.
	Lilith	Sagittarius	♐	6	Your Way of Unyielding manifests through your wide-ranging and open-minded quest for and attraction to experiential and risk-taking service for others.
	Lilith	Sagittarius	♐	7	Your Way of Unyielding manifests through your wide-ranging and open-minded quest for and attraction to experiential and risk-taking life teachers.
	Lilith	Sagittarius	♐	8	Your Way of Unyielding manifests through your wide-ranging and open-minded quest for and attraction to experiential and risk-taking intimate relationships.
	Lilith	Sagittarius	♐	9	Your Way of Unyielding manifests through your wide-ranging and open-minded quest for and attraction to experiential and risk-taking mastership of a body of knowledge.
	Lilith	Sagittarius	♐	10	Your Way of Unyielding manifests through your wide-ranging and open-minded quest for and attraction to experiential and risk-taking accomplishments.
	Lilith	Sagittarius	♐	11	Your Way of Unyielding manifests through your wide-ranging and open-minded quest for and attraction to experiential and risk-taking community.
	Lilith	Sagittarius	♐	12	Your Way of Unyielding manifests through your wide-ranging and open-minded quest for and attraction to experiential and risk-taking spirituality.

☾	Lilith	Capricorn	♑	1	Your Way of Unyielding manifests through your goal-driven and focused quest for and attraction to results-oriented and successful identity development.
☾	Lilith	Capricorn	♑	2	Your Way of Unyielding manifests through your goal-driven and focused quest for and attraction to results-oriented and successful values and ways to meet your needs.
☾	Lilith	Capricorn	♑	3	Your Way of Unyielding manifests through your goal-driven and focused quest for and attraction to results-oriented and successful understanding of the world around you.
☾	Lilith	Capricorn	♑	4	Your Way of Unyielding manifests through your goal-driven and focused quest for and attraction to results-oriented and successful emotional caretaking and traditions.
☾	Lilith	Capricorn	♑	5	Your Way of Unyielding manifests through your goal-driven and focused quest for and attraction to results-oriented and successful creative expression.
☾	Lilith	Capricorn	♑	6	Your Way of Unyielding manifests through your goal-driven and focused quest for and attraction to results-oriented and successful service for others.
☾	Lilith	Capricorn	♑	7	Your Way of Unyielding manifests through your goal-driven and focused quest for and attraction to results-oriented and successful life teachers.
☾	Lilith	Capricorn	♑	8	Your Way of Unyielding manifests through your goal-driven and focused quest for and attraction to results-oriented and successful intimate relationships.
☾	Lilith	Capricorn	♑	9	Your Way of Unyielding manifests through your goal-driven and focused quest for and attraction to results-oriented and successful mastership of a body of knowledge.
☾	Lilith	Capricorn	♑	10	Your Way of Unyielding manifests through your goal-driven and focused quest for and attraction to results-oriented and successful accomplishments.
☾	Lilith	Capricorn	♑	11	Your Way of Unyielding manifests through your goal-driven and focused quest for and attraction to results-oriented and successful community.
☾	Lilith	Capricorn	♑	12	Your Way of Unyielding manifests through your goal-driven and focused quest for and attraction to results-oriented and successful spirituality.

☾	Lilith	Aquarius	♒	1	Your Way of Unyielding manifests through your unconventional and idealistic quest for and attraction to authentic and non-traditional identity development.
☾	Lilith	Aquarius	♒	2	Your Way of Unyielding manifests through your unconventional and idealistic quest for and attraction to authentic and non-traditional values and ways to meet your needs.
☾	Lilith	Aquarius	♒	3	Your Way of Unyielding manifests through your unconventional and idealistic quest for and attraction to authentic and non-traditional understanding of the world around you.
☾	Lilith	Aquarius	♒	4	Your Way of Unyielding manifests through your unconventional and idealistic quest for and attraction to authentic and non-traditional emotional caretaking and traditions.
☾	Lilith	Aquarius	♒	5	Your Way of Unyielding manifests through your unconventional and idealistic quest for and attraction to authentic and non-traditional creative expression.
☾	Lilith	Aquarius	♒	6	Your Way of Unyielding manifests through your unconventional and idealistic quest for and attraction to authentic and non-traditional service for others.
☾	Lilith	Aquarius	♒	7	Your Way of Unyielding manifests through your unconventional and idealistic quest for and attraction to authentic and non-traditional life teachers.
☾	Lilith	Aquarius	♒	8	Your Way of Unyielding manifests through your unconventional and idealistic quest for and attraction to authentic and non-traditional intimate relationships.
☾	Lilith	Aquarius	♒	9	Your Way of Unyielding manifests through your unconventional and idealistic quest for and attraction to authentic and non-traditional mastership of a body of knowledge.
☾	Lilith	Aquarius	♒	10	Your Way of Unyielding manifests through your unconventional and idealistic quest for and attraction to authentic and non-traditional accomplishments.
☾	Lilith	Aquarius	♒	11	Your Way of Unyielding manifests through your unconventional and idealistic quest for and attraction to authentic and non-traditional community.
☾	Lilith	Aquarius	♒	12	Your Way of Unyielding manifests through your unconventional and idealistic quest for and attraction to authentic and non-traditional spirituality.

☾	Lilith	Pisces	♓	1	Your Way of Unyielding manifests through your imaginative and faithful quest for and attraction to consciousness-raising and soulful identity development.
☾	Lilith	Pisces	♓	2	Your Way of Unyielding manifests through your imaginative and faithful quest for and attraction to consciousness-raising and soulful values and ways to meet your needs.
☾	Lilith	Pisces	♓	3	Your Way of Unyielding manifests through your imaginative and faithful quest for and attraction to consciousness-raising and soulful understanding of the world around you.
☾	Lilith	Pisces	♓	4	Your Way of Unyielding manifests through your imaginative and faithful quest for and attraction to consciousness-raising and soulful emotional caretaking and traditions.
☾	Lilith	Pisces	♓	5	Your Way of Unyielding manifests through your imaginative and faithful quest for and attraction to consciousness-raising and soulful creative expression.
☾	Lilith	Pisces	♓	6	Your Way of Unyielding manifests through your imaginative and faithful quest for and attraction to consciousness-raising and soulful service for others.
☾	Lilith	Pisces	♓	7	Your Way of Unyielding manifests through your imaginative and faithful quest for and attraction to consciousness-raising and soulful life teachers.
☾	Lilith	Pisces	♓	8	Your Way of Unyielding manifests through your imaginative and faithful quest for and attraction to consciousness-raising and soulful intimate relationships.
☾	Lilith	Pisces	♓	9	Your Way of Unyielding manifests through your imaginative and faithful quest for and attraction to consciousness-raising and soulful mastership of a body of knowledge.
☾	Lilith	Pisces	♓	10	Your Way of Unyielding manifests through your imaginative and faithful quest for and attraction to consciousness-raising and soulful accomplishments.
☾	Lilith	Pisces	♓	11	Your Way of Unyielding manifests through your imaginative and faithful quest for and attraction to consciousness-raising and soulful community.
☾	Lilith	Pisces	♓	12	Your Way of Unyielding manifests through your imaginative and faithful quest for and attraction to consciousness-raising and soulful spirituality.

Vulcan[30] | ↓

Energy Point Type: **Hypothetical Planet (calculated between the Sun and Mercury)**

Co-Rules Sign: **Taurus**

Co-Rules House: **2nd**

Element: **Earth**

Key Phrase: **Way of Productivity**

Vulcan represents your Way of Productivity. Its placement in Sign and House reveals the activity and skills that reflect our values and provide us with the means to be productive to be able to get our needs met. In my case my Way of Productivity is expressed through Fire (Aries) in my quest for service (6th House). Fire's expression is pioneering, creative, and exploratory. In Aries the Element acts independently, heroically, and aggressively. So, my key phrase is *"Your Way of Building manifests through your independent and heroic quest for and attraction to maverick and individualistic service for others."* In short, I am most productive when I am able to work independently and break new ground with my efforts.

When you look up your own Vulcan in the Sign and House formula, think about the skills you enjoy and put to use that help you get resources. If you could have any kind of workshop, what would it look like and how would it reflect your Vulcan placement? Consider Vulcan in Gemini in the 12th House: *"Your Way of Building manifests through your inquisitive and mentally agile quest for and attraction to ever changing and adaptable spirituality."* This individual builds with his or her mind and would prefer a workshop filled with books and electronic devices. His or her spiritual quest and values would reflect the Gemini curiosity with books and artifacts from religions and belief systems from around the world. Or, he or she may worship video games.

---

[30]Vulcan is an unusual point in astrology because it represents, oddly enough, a failed idea in astronomy. At the time (19th Century) no one had been able to explain the peculiarities of Mercury's orbit, so French mathematician Urbain Le Vierrer proposed that the erratic orbit was caused by another planet, which he named Vulcan. It was not until Einstein's Theory of Relativity that the orbit of Mercury was understood and explained, eliminating the possible existence of Vulcan. Still, other calculated points are used effectively in astrology and I have chosen to incorporate this one as a counterpoint to Vesta, co-ruling Taurus and the 2nd House.

Astrology Unlocked by Philip Young, PhD

↓	Vulcan	Aries	♈	1	Your Way of Productivity manifests through your independent and heroic quest for and attraction to maverick and individualistic identity development.
↓	Vulcan	Aries	♈	2	Your Way of Productivity manifests through your independent and heroic quest for and attraction to maverick and individualistic values and ways to meet your needs.
↓	Vulcan	Aries	♈	3	Your Way of Productivity manifests through your independent and heroic quest for and attraction to maverick and individualistic understanding of the world around you.
↓	Vulcan	Aries	♈	4	Your Way of Productivity manifests through your independent and heroic quest for and attraction to maverick and individualistic emotional caretaking and traditions.
↓	Vulcan	Aries	♈	5	Your Way of Productivity manifests through your independent and heroic quest for and attraction to maverick and individualistic creative expression.
↓	Vulcan	Aries	♈	6	Your Way of Productivity manifests through your independent and heroic quest for and attraction to maverick and individualistic service for others.
↓	Vulcan	Aries	♈	7	Your Way of Productivity manifests through your independent and heroic quest for and attraction to maverick and individualistic life teachers.
↓	Vulcan	Aries	♈	8	Your Way of Productivity manifests through your independent and heroic quest for and attraction to maverick and individualistic intimate relationships.
↓	Vulcan	Aries	♈	9	Your Way of Productivity manifests through your independent and heroic quest for and attraction to maverick and individualistic mastership of a body of life experience.
↓	Vulcan	Aries	♈	10	Your Way of Productivity manifests through your independent and heroic quest for and attraction to maverick and individualistic accomplishments.
↓	Vulcan	Aries	♈	11	Your Way of Productivity manifests through your independent and heroic quest for and attraction to maverick and individualistic community.
↓	Vulcan	Aries	♈	12	Your Way of Productivity manifests through your independent and heroic quest for and attraction to maverick and individualistic spirituality.

	Vulcan	Taurus	♉	1	Your Way of Productivity manifests through your steadfast and persistent quest for and attraction to enduring and secure identity development.
↓	Vulcan	Taurus	♉	2	Your Way of Productivity manifests through your steadfast and persistent quest for and attraction to enduring and secure values and ways to meet your needs.
↓	Vulcan	Taurus	♉	3	Your Way of Productivity manifests through your steadfast and persistent quest for and attraction to enduring and secure understanding of the world around you.
↓	Vulcan	Taurus	♉	4	Your Way of Productivity manifests through your steadfast and persistent quest for and attraction to enduring and secure emotional caretaking and traditions.
↓	Vulcan	Taurus	♉	5	Your Way of Productivity manifests through your steadfast and persistent quest for and attraction to enduring and secure creative expression.
↓	Vulcan	Taurus	♉	6	Your Way of Productivity manifests through your steadfast and persistent quest for and attraction to enduring and secure service for others.
↓	Vulcan	Taurus	♉	7	Your Way of Productivity manifests through your steadfast and persistent quest for and attraction to enduring and secure life teachers.
↓	Vulcan	Taurus	♉	8	Your Way of Productivity manifests through your steadfast and persistent quest for and attraction to enduring and secure intimate relationships.
↓	Vulcan	Taurus	♉	9	Your Way of Productivity manifests through your steadfast and persistent quest for and attraction to enduring and secure mastership of a body of life experience.
↓	Vulcan	Taurus	♉	10	Your Way of Productivity manifests through your steadfast and persistent quest for and attraction to enduring and secure accomplishments.
↓	Vulcan	Taurus	♉	11	Your Way of Productivity manifests through your steadfast and persistent quest for and attraction to enduring and secure community.
↓	Vulcan	Taurus	♉	12	Your Way of Productivity manifests through your steadfast and persistent quest for and attraction to enduring and secure spirituality.

↓	Vulcan	Gemini	♊	1	Your Way of Productivity manifests through your inquisitive and mentally agile quest for and attraction to ever changing and adaptable identity development.
↓	Vulcan	Gemini	♊	2	Your Way of Productivity manifests through your inquisitive and mentally agile quest for and attraction to ever changing and adaptable values and ways to meet your needs.
↓	Vulcan	Gemini	♊	3	Your Way of Productivity manifests through your inquisitive and mentally agile quest for and attraction to ever changing and adaptable understanding of the world around you.
↓	Vulcan	Gemini	♊	4	Your Way of Productivity manifests through your inquisitive and mentally agile quest for and attraction to ever changing and adaptable emotional caretaking and traditions.
↓	Vulcan	Gemini	♊	5	Your Way of Productivity manifests through your inquisitive and mentally agile quest for and attraction to ever changing and adaptable creative expression.
↓	Vulcan	Gemini	♊	6	Your Way of Productivity manifests through your inquisitive and mentally agile quest for and attraction to ever changing and adaptable service for others.
↓	Vulcan	Gemini	♊	7	Your Way of Productivity manifests through your inquisitive and mentally agile quest for and attraction to ever changing and adaptable life teachers.
↓	Vulcan	Gemini	♊	8	Your Way of Productivity manifests through your inquisitive and mentally agile quest for and attraction to ever changing and adaptable intimate relationships.
↓	Vulcan	Gemini	♊	9	Your Way of Productivity manifests through your inquisitive and mentally agile quest for and attraction to ever changing and adaptable mastership of a body of life experience.
↓	Vulcan	Gemini	♊	10	Your Way of Productivity manifests through your inquisitive and mentally agile quest for and attraction to ever changing and adaptable accomplishments.
↓	Vulcan	Gemini	♊	11	Your Way of Productivity manifests through your inquisitive and mentally agile quest for and attraction to ever changing and adaptable community.
↓	Vulcan	Gemini	♊	12	Your Way of Productivity manifests through your inquisitive and mentally agile quest for and attraction to ever changing and adaptable spirituality.

288

	Vulcan	Cancer	♋	1	Your Way of Productivity manifests through your emotional and caring quest for and attraction to nurturing and supportive identity development.
↓	Vulcan	Cancer	♋	2	Your Way of Productivity manifests through your emotional and caring quest for and attraction to nurturing and supportive values and ways to meet your needs.
↓	Vulcan	Cancer	♋	3	Your Way of Productivity manifests through your emotional and caring quest for and attraction to nurturing and supportive understanding of the world around you.
↓	Vulcan	Cancer	♋	4	Your Way of Productivity manifests through your emotional and caring quest for and attraction to nurturing and supportive emotional caretaking and traditions.
↓	Vulcan	Cancer	♋	5	Your Way of Productivity manifests through your emotional and caring quest for and attraction to nurturing and supportive creative expression.
↓	Vulcan	Cancer	♋	6	Your Way of Productivity manifests through your emotional and caring quest for and attraction to nurturing and supportive service for others.
↓	Vulcan	Cancer	♋	7	Your Way of Productivity manifests through your emotional and caring quest for and attraction to nurturing and supportive life teachers.
↓	Vulcan	Cancer	♋	8	Your Way of Productivity manifests through your emotional and caring quest for and attraction to nurturing and supportive intimate relationships.
↓	Vulcan	Cancer	♋	9	Your Way of Productivity manifests through your emotional and caring quest for and attraction to nurturing and supportive mastership of a body of life experience.
↓	Vulcan	Cancer	♋	10	Your Way of Productivity manifests through your emotional and caring quest for and attraction to nurturing and supportive accomplishments.
↓	Vulcan	Cancer	♋	11	Your Way of Productivity manifests through your emotional and caring quest for and attraction to nurturing and supportive community.
↓	Vulcan	Cancer	♋	12	Your Way of Productivity manifests through your emotional and caring quest for and attraction to nurturing and supportive spirituality.

↓	Vulcan	Leo	♌	1	Your Way of Productivity manifests through your energetic and dramatic quest for and attraction to creative and romantic identity development.
↓	Vulcan	Leo	♌	2	Your Way of Productivity manifests through your energetic and dramatic quest for and attraction to creative and romantic values and ways to meet your needs.
↓	Vulcan	Leo	♌	3	Your Way of Productivity manifests through your energetic and dramatic quest for and attraction to creative and romantic understanding of the world around you.
↓	Vulcan	Leo	♌	4	Your Way of Productivity manifests through your energetic and dramatic quest for and attraction to creative and romantic emotional caretaking and traditions.
↓	Vulcan	Leo	♌	5	Your Way of Productivity manifests through your energetic and dramatic quest for and attraction to creative and romantic creative expression.
↓	Vulcan	Leo	♌	6	Your Way of Productivity manifests through your energetic and dramatic quest for and attraction to creative and romantic service for others.
↓	Vulcan	Leo	♌	7	Your Way of Productivity manifests through your energetic and dramatic quest for and attraction to creative and romantic life teachers.
↓	Vulcan	Leo	♌	8	Your Way of Productivity manifests through your energetic and dramatic quest for and attraction to creative and romantic intimate relationships.
↓	Vulcan	Leo	♌	9	Your Way of Productivity manifests through your energetic and dramatic quest for and attraction to creative and romantic mastership of a body of life experience.
↓	Vulcan	Leo	♌	10	Your Way of Productivity manifests through your energetic and dramatic quest for and attraction to creative and romantic accomplishments.
↓	Vulcan	Leo	♌	11	Your Way of Productivity manifests through your energetic and dramatic quest for and attraction to creative and romantic community.
↓	Vulcan	Leo	♌	12	Your Way of Productivity manifests through your energetic and dramatic quest for and attraction to creative and romantic spirituality.

↓	Vulcan	Virgo	♍	1	Your Way of Productivity manifests through your critically-minded and methodical quest for and attraction to meticulous and practical identity development.
↓	Vulcan	Virgo	♍	2	Your Way of Productivity manifests through your critically-minded and methodical quest for and attraction to meticulous and practical values and ways to meet your needs.
↓	Vulcan	Virgo	♍	3	Your Way of Productivity manifests through your critically-minded and methodical quest for and attraction to meticulous and practical understanding of the world around you.
↓	Vulcan	Virgo	♍	4	Your Way of Productivity manifests through your critically-minded and methodical quest for and attraction to meticulous and practical emotional caretaking and traditions.
↓	Vulcan	Virgo	♍	5	Your Way of Productivity manifests through your critically-minded and methodical quest for and attraction to meticulous and practical creative expression.
↓	Vulcan	Virgo	♍	6	Your Way of Productivity manifests through your critically-minded and methodical quest for and attraction to meticulous and practical service for others.
↓	Vulcan	Virgo	♍	7	Your Way of Productivity manifests through your critically-minded and methodical quest for and attraction to meticulous and practical life teachers.
↓	Vulcan	Virgo	♍	8	Your Way of Productivity manifests through your critically-minded and methodical quest for and attraction to meticulous and practical intimate relationships.
↓	Vulcan	Virgo	♍	9	Your Way of Productivity manifests through your critically-minded and methodical quest for and attraction to meticulous and practical mastership of a body of life experience.
↓	Vulcan	Virgo	♍	10	Your Way of Productivity manifests through your critically-minded and methodical quest for and attraction to meticulous and practical accomplishments.
↓	Vulcan	Virgo	♍	11	Your Way of Productivity manifests through your critically-minded and methodical quest for and attraction to meticulous and practical community.
↓	Vulcan	Virgo	♍	12	Your Way of Productivity manifests through your critically-minded and methodical quest for and attraction to meticulous and practical spirituality.

↓	Vulcan	Libra	♎	1	Your Way of Productivity manifests through your analytical and balanced quest for and attraction to harmonious and logical identity development.
↓	Vulcan	Libra	♎	2	Your Way of Productivity manifests through your analytical and balanced quest for and attraction to harmonious and logical values and ways to meet your needs.
↓	Vulcan	Libra	♎	3	Your Way of Productivity manifests through your analytical and balanced quest for and attraction to harmonious and logical understanding of the world around you.
↓	Vulcan	Libra	♎	4	Your Way of Productivity manifests through your analytical and balanced quest for and attraction to harmonious and logical emotional caretaking and traditions.
↓	Vulcan	Libra	♎	5	Your Way of Productivity manifests through your analytical and balanced quest for and attraction to harmonious and logical creative expression.
↓	Vulcan	Libra	♎	6	Your Way of Productivity manifests through your analytical and balanced quest for and attraction to harmonious and logical service for others.
↓	Vulcan	Libra	♎	7	Your Way of Productivity manifests through your analytical and balanced quest for and attraction to harmonious and logical life teachers.
↓	Vulcan	Libra	♎	8	Your Way of Productivity manifests through your analytical and balanced quest for and attraction to harmonious and logical intimate relationships.
↓	Vulcan	Libra	♎	9	Your Way of Productivity manifests through your analytical and balanced quest for and attraction to harmonious and logical mastership of a body of life experience.
↓	Vulcan	Libra	♎	10	Your Way of Productivity manifests through your analytical and balanced quest for and attraction to harmonious and logical accomplishments.
↓	Vulcan	Libra	♎	11	Your Way of Productivity manifests through your analytical and balanced quest for and attraction to harmonious and logical community.
↓	Vulcan	Libra	♎	12	Your Way of Productivity manifests through your analytical and balanced quest for and attraction to harmonious and logical spirituality.

↓	Vulcan	Scorpio	♏	1	Your Way of Productivity manifests through your intense and truth seeking quest for and attraction to penetrating and emotionally transformative identity development.
↓	Vulcan	Scorpio	♏	2	Your Way of Productivity manifests through your intense and truth seeking quest for and attraction to penetrating and emotionally transformative values and ways to meet your needs.
↓	Vulcan	Scorpio	♏	3	Your Way of Productivity manifests through your intense and truth seeking quest for and attraction to penetrating and emotionally transformative understanding of the world around you.
↓	Vulcan	Scorpio	♏	4	Your Way of Productivity manifests through your intense and truth seeking quest for and attraction to penetrating and emotionally transformative emotional caretaking and traditions.
↓	Vulcan	Scorpio	♏	5	Your Way of Productivity manifests through your intense and truth seeking quest for and attraction to penetrating and emotionally transformative creative expression.
↓	Vulcan	Scorpio	♏	6	Your Way of Productivity manifests through your intense and truth seeking quest for and attraction to penetrating and emotionally transformative service for others.
↓	Vulcan	Scorpio	♏	7	Your Way of Productivity manifests through your intense and truth seeking quest for and attraction to penetrating and emotionally transformative life teachers.
↓	Vulcan	Scorpio	♏	8	Your Way of Productivity manifests through your intense and truth seeking quest for and attraction to penetrating and emotionally transformative intimate relationships.
↓	Vulcan	Scorpio	♏	9	Your Way of Productivity manifests through your intense and truth seeking quest for and attraction to penetrating and emotionally transformative mastership of a body of life experience.
↓	Vulcan	Scorpio	♏	10	Your Way of Productivity manifests through your intense and truth seeking quest for and attraction to penetrating and emotionally transformative accomplishments.
↓	Vulcan	Scorpio	♏	11	Your Way of Productivity manifests through your intense and truth seeking quest for and attraction to penetrating and emotionally transformative community.
↓	Vulcan	Scorpio	♏	12	Your Way of Productivity manifests through your intense and truth seeking quest for and attraction to penetrating and emotionally transformative spirituality.

	Vulcan	Sagittarius	↗	1	Your Way of Productivity manifests through your wide-ranging and open-minded quest for and attraction to experiential and risk-taking identity development.
↓	Vulcan	Sagittarius	↗	2	Your Way of Productivity manifests through your wide-ranging and open-minded quest for and attraction to experiential and risk-taking values and ways to meet your needs.
↓	Vulcan	Sagittarius	↗	3	Your Way of Productivity manifests through your wide-ranging and open-minded quest for and attraction to experiential and risk-taking understanding of the world around you.
↓	Vulcan	Sagittarius	↗	4	Your Way of Productivity manifests through your wide-ranging and open-minded quest for and attraction to experiential and risk-taking emotional caretaking and traditions.
↓	Vulcan	Sagittarius	↗	5	Your Way of Productivity manifests through your wide-ranging and open-minded quest for and attraction to experiential and risk-taking creative expression.
↓	Vulcan	Sagittarius	↗	6	Your Way of Productivity manifests through your wide-ranging and open-minded quest for and attraction to experiential and risk-taking service for others.
↓	Vulcan	Sagittarius	↗	7	Your Way of Productivity manifests through your wide-ranging and open-minded quest for and attraction to experiential and risk-taking life teachers.
↓	Vulcan	Sagittarius	↗	8	Your Way of Productivity manifests through your wide-ranging and open-minded quest for and attraction to experiential and risk-taking intimate relationships.
↓	Vulcan	Sagittarius	↗	9	Your Way of Productivity manifests through your wide-ranging and open-minded quest for and attraction to experiential and risk-taking mastership of a body of life experience.
↓	Vulcan	Sagittarius	↗	10	Your Way of Productivity manifests through your wide-ranging and open-minded quest for and attraction to experiential and risk-taking accomplishments.
↓	Vulcan	Sagittarius	↗	11	Your Way of Productivity manifests through your wide-ranging and open-minded quest for and attraction to experiential and risk-taking community.
↓	Vulcan	Sagittarius	↗	12	Your Way of Productivity manifests through your wide-ranging and open-minded quest for and attraction to experiential and risk-taking spirituality.

↓	Vulcan	Capricorn	♑	1	Your Way of Productivity manifests through your goal-driven and focused quest for and attraction to results-oriented and successful identity development.
↓	Vulcan	Capricorn	♑	2	Your Way of Productivity manifests through your goal-driven and focused quest for and attraction to results-oriented and successful values and ways to meet your needs.
↓	Vulcan	Capricorn	♑	3	Your Way of Productivity manifests through your goal-driven and focused quest for and attraction to results-oriented and successful understanding of the world around you.
↓	Vulcan	Capricorn	♑	4	Your Way of Productivity manifests through your goal-driven and focused quest for and attraction to results-oriented and successful emotional caretaking and traditions.
↓	Vulcan	Capricorn	♑	5	Your Way of Productivity manifests through your goal-driven and focused quest for and attraction to results-oriented and successful creative expression.
↓	Vulcan	Capricorn	♑	6	Your Way of Productivity manifests through your goal-driven and focused quest for and attraction to results-oriented and successful service for others.
↓	Vulcan	Capricorn	♑	7	Your Way of Productivity manifests through your goal-driven and focused quest for and attraction to results-oriented and successful life teachers.
↓	Vulcan	Capricorn	♑	8	Your Way of Productivity manifests through your goal-driven and focused quest for and attraction to results-oriented and successful intimate relationships.
↓	Vulcan	Capricorn	♑	9	Your Way of Productivity manifests through your goal-driven and focused quest for and attraction to results-oriented and successful mastership of a body of life experience.
↓	Vulcan	Capricorn	♑	10	Your Way of Productivity manifests through your goal-driven and focused quest for and attraction to results-oriented and successful accomplishments.
↓	Vulcan	Capricorn	♑	11	Your Way of Productivity manifests through your goal-driven and focused quest for and attraction to results-oriented and successful community.
↓	Vulcan	Capricorn	♑	12	Your Way of Productivity manifests through your goal-driven and focused quest for and attraction to results-oriented and successful spirituality.

	Vulcan	Aquarius	♒	1	Your Way of Productivity manifests through your unconventional and idealistic quest for and attraction to authentic and non-traditional identity development.
↓	Vulcan	Aquarius	♒	2	Your Way of Productivity manifests through your unconventional and idealistic quest for and attraction to authentic and non-traditional values and ways to meet your needs.
↓	Vulcan	Aquarius	♒	3	Your Way of Productivity manifests through your unconventional and idealistic quest for and attraction to authentic and non-traditional understanding of the world around you.
↓	Vulcan	Aquarius	♒	4	Your Way of Productivity manifests through your unconventional and idealistic quest for and attraction to authentic and non-traditional emotional caretaking and traditions.
↓	Vulcan	Aquarius	♒	5	Your Way of Productivity manifests through your unconventional and idealistic quest for and attraction to authentic and non-traditional creative expression.
↓	Vulcan	Aquarius	♒	6	Your Way of Productivity manifests through your unconventional and idealistic quest for and attraction to authentic and non-traditional service for others.
↓	Vulcan	Aquarius	♒	7	Your Way of Productivity manifests through your unconventional and idealistic quest for and attraction to authentic and non-traditional life teachers.
↓	Vulcan	Aquarius	♒	8	Your Way of Productivity manifests through your unconventional and idealistic quest for and attraction to authentic and non-traditional intimate relationships.
↓	Vulcan	Aquarius	♒	9	Your Way of Productivity manifests through your unconventional and idealistic quest for and attraction to authentic and non-traditional mastership of a body of life experience.
↓	Vulcan	Aquarius	♒	10	Your Way of Productivity manifests through your unconventional and idealistic quest for and attraction to authentic and non-traditional accomplishments.
↓	Vulcan	Aquarius	♒	11	Your Way of Productivity manifests through your unconventional and idealistic quest for and attraction to authentic and non-traditional community.
↓	Vulcan	Aquarius	♒	12	Your Way of Productivity manifests through your unconventional and idealistic quest for and attraction to authentic and non-traditional spirituality.

↓	Vulcan	Pisces	♓	1	Your Way of Productivity manifests through your imaginative and faithful quest for and attraction to consciousness-raising and soulful identity development.
↓	Vulcan	Pisces	♓	2	Your Way of Productivity manifests through your imaginative and faithful quest for and attraction to consciousness-raising and soulful values and ways to meet your needs.
↓	Vulcan	Pisces	♓	3	Your Way of Productivity manifests through your imaginative and faithful quest for and attraction to consciousness-raising and soulful understanding of the world around you.
↓	Vulcan	Pisces	♓	4	Your Way of Productivity manifests through your imaginative and faithful quest for and attraction to consciousness-raising and soulful emotional caretaking and traditions.
↓	Vulcan	Pisces	♓	5	Your Way of Productivity manifests through your imaginative and faithful quest for and attraction to consciousness-raising and soulful creative expression.
↓	Vulcan	Pisces	♓	6	Your Way of Productivity manifests through your imaginative and faithful quest for and attraction to consciousness-raising and soulful service for others.
↓	Vulcan	Pisces	♓	7	Your Way of Productivity manifests through your imaginative and faithful quest for and attraction to consciousness-raising and soulful life teachers.
↓	Vulcan	Pisces	♓	8	Your Way of Productivity manifests through your imaginative and faithful quest for and attraction to consciousness-raising and soulful intimate relationships.
↓	Vulcan	Pisces	♓	9	Your Way of Productivity manifests through your imaginative and faithful quest for and attraction to consciousness-raising and soulful mastership of a body of life experience.
↓	Vulcan	Pisces	♓	10	Your Way of Productivity manifests through your imaginative and faithful quest for and attraction to consciousness-raising and soulful accomplishments.
↓	Vulcan	Pisces	♓	11	Your Way of Productivity manifests through your imaginative and faithful quest for and attraction to consciousness-raising and soulful community.
↓	Vulcan	Pisces	♓	12	Your Way of Productivity manifests through your imaginative and faithful quest for and attraction to consciousness-raising and soulful spirituality.

Urania | U

Energy Point Type: **Asteroid**

Co-Rules Sign: **Gemini**

Co-Rules House: **3rd**

Element: **Air**

Key Phrase: **Thirst for Knowledge**

Urania represents your Thirst for Knowledge. Its placement in Sign and House reveals our curiosity about the world and where and how we thirst for knowledge. In my case my Thirst for Knowledge is expressed through Earth (Taurus) in my quest for knowledge from others (7th House). Earth's expression is accomplished, persistent, and practical. In Taurus the Element acts protectively, conservatively, and reliably. So, my key phrase is *"Your Thirst for Knowledge manifests through your steadfast and persistent quest for and attraction to enduring and secure life teachers."* In short, I am fascinated with how people connect and interact with one another. My favorite astrology charts to work on are synastry (relationship) charts.

When you look up your Urania in the Sign and House formula, consider how and where you thirst for knowledge. If the energy is in Earth, you will want to understand a subject practically; if Air, intellectually; if Water, emotionally; and if Fire, energetically. Consider Urania in Cancer in the 4th House, *"Your Thirst for Knowledge manifests through your emotional and caring quest for and attraction to nurturing and supportive emotional caretaking and traditions."* This individual will want to know all there is to know about his or her family and the caretaking necessary to help the family. Expect to find him or her in the child psychology section or holiday cookbook sections of the bookstore. He or she may be especially interested in the family genealogy.

For more in depth reading about Urania, I recommend purchasing and reading:

- *The Ultimate Asteroid Book* by J. Lee Lehman, PhD (ISBN: 0914918788)

U	Urania	Aries	♈	1	Your Thirst for Knowledge manifests through your independent and heroic quest for and attraction to maverick and individualistic identity development.
U	Urania	Aries	♈	2	Your Thirst for Knowledge manifests through your independent and heroic quest for and attraction to maverick and individualistic values and ways to meet your needs.
U	Urania	Aries	♈	3	Your Thirst for Knowledge manifests through your independent and heroic quest for and attraction to maverick and individualistic understanding of the world around you.
U	Urania	Aries	♈	4	Your Thirst for Knowledge manifests through your independent and heroic quest for and attraction to maverick and individualistic emotional caretaking and traditions.
U	Urania	Aries	♈	5	Your Thirst for Knowledge manifests through your independent and heroic quest for and attraction to maverick and individualistic creative expression.
U	Urania	Aries	♈	6	Your Thirst for Knowledge manifests through your independent and heroic quest for and attraction to maverick and individualistic service for others.
U	Urania	Aries	♈	7	Your Thirst for Knowledge manifests through your independent and heroic quest for and attraction to maverick and individualistic life teachers.
U	Urania	Aries	♈	8	Your Thirst for Knowledge manifests through your independent and heroic quest for and attraction to maverick and individualistic intimate relationships.
U	Urania	Aries	♈	9	Your Thirst for Knowledge manifests through your independent and heroic quest for and attraction to maverick and individualistic mastership of a body of knowledge.
U	Urania	Aries	♈	10	Your Thirst for Knowledge manifests through your independent and heroic quest for and attraction to maverick and individualistic accomplishments.
U	Urania	Aries	♈	11	Your Thirst for Knowledge manifests through your independent and heroic quest for and attraction to maverick and individualistic community.
U	Urania	Aries	♈	12	Your Thirst for Knowledge manifests through your independent and heroic quest for and attraction to maverick and individualistic spirituality.

U	Urania	Taurus	♉	1	Your Thirst for Knowledge manifests through your steadfast and persistent quest for and attraction to enduring and secure identity development.
U	Urania	Taurus	♉	2	Your Thirst for Knowledge manifests through your steadfast and persistent quest for and attraction to enduring and secure values and ways to meet your needs.
U	Urania	Taurus	♉	3	Your Thirst for Knowledge manifests through your steadfast and persistent quest for and attraction to enduring and secure understanding of the world around you.
U	Urania	Taurus	♉	4	Your Thirst for Knowledge manifests through your steadfast and persistent quest for and attraction to enduring and secure emotional caretaking and traditions.
U	Urania	Taurus	♉	5	Your Thirst for Knowledge manifests through your steadfast and persistent quest for and attraction to enduring and secure creative expression.
U	Urania	Taurus	♉	6	Your Thirst for Knowledge manifests through your steadfast and persistent quest for and attraction to enduring and secure service for others.
U	Urania	Taurus	♉	7	Your Thirst for Knowledge manifests through your steadfast and persistent quest for and attraction to enduring and secure life teachers.
U	Urania	Taurus	♉	8	Your Thirst for Knowledge manifests through your steadfast and persistent quest for and attraction to enduring and secure intimate relationships.
U	Urania	Taurus	♉	9	Your Thirst for Knowledge manifests through your steadfast and persistent quest for and attraction to enduring and secure mastership of a body of knowledge.
U	Urania	Taurus	♉	10	Your Thirst for Knowledge manifests through your steadfast and persistent quest for and attraction to enduring and secure accomplishments.
U	Urania	Taurus	♉	11	Your Thirst for Knowledge manifests through your steadfast and persistent quest for and attraction to enduring and secure community.
U	Urania	Taurus	♉	12	Your Thirst for Knowledge manifests through your steadfast and persistent quest for and attraction to enduring and secure spirituality.

U	Urania	Gemini	Ⅱ	1	Your Thirst for Knowledge manifests through your inquisitive and mentally agile quest for and attraction to ever changing and adaptable identity development.
U	Urania	Gemini	Ⅱ	2	Your Thirst for Knowledge manifests through your inquisitive and mentally agile quest for and attraction to ever changing and adaptable values and ways to meet your needs.
U	Urania	Gemini	Ⅱ	3	Your Thirst for Knowledge manifests through your inquisitive and mentally agile quest for and attraction to ever changing and adaptable understanding of the world around you.
U	Urania	Gemini	Ⅱ	4	Your Thirst for Knowledge manifests through your inquisitive and mentally agile quest for and attraction to ever changing and adaptable emotional caretaking and traditions.
U	Urania	Gemini	Ⅱ	5	Your Thirst for Knowledge manifests through your inquisitive and mentally agile quest for and attraction to ever changing and adaptable creative expression.
U	Urania	Gemini	Ⅱ	6	Your Thirst for Knowledge manifests through your inquisitive and mentally agile quest for and attraction to ever changing and adaptable service for others.
U	Urania	Gemini	Ⅱ	7	Your Thirst for Knowledge manifests through your inquisitive and mentally agile quest for and attraction to ever changing and adaptable life teachers.
U	Urania	Gemini	Ⅱ	8	Your Thirst for Knowledge manifests through your inquisitive and mentally agile quest for and attraction to ever changing and adaptable intimate relationships.
U	Urania	Gemini	Ⅱ	9	Your Thirst for Knowledge manifests through your inquisitive and mentally agile quest for and attraction to ever changing and adaptable mastership of a body of knowledge.
U	Urania	Gemini	Ⅱ	10	Your Thirst for Knowledge manifests through your inquisitive and mentally agile quest for and attraction to ever changing and adaptable accomplishments.
U	Urania	Gemini	Ⅱ	11	Your Thirst for Knowledge manifests through your inquisitive and mentally agile quest for and attraction to ever changing and adaptable community.
U	Urania	Gemini	Ⅱ	12	Your Thirst for Knowledge manifests through your inquisitive and mentally agile quest for and attraction to ever changing and adaptable spirituality.

U	Urania	Cancer	♋	1	Your Thirst for Knowledge manifests through your emotional and caring quest for and attraction to nurturing and supportive identity development.
U	Urania	Cancer	♋	2	Your Thirst for Knowledge manifests through your emotional and caring quest for and attraction to nurturing and supportive values and ways to meet your needs.
U	Urania	Cancer	♋	3	Your Thirst for Knowledge manifests through your emotional and caring quest for and attraction to nurturing and supportive understanding of the world around you.
U	Urania	Cancer	♋	4	Your Thirst for Knowledge manifests through your emotional and caring quest for and attraction to nurturing and supportive emotional caretaking and traditions.
U	Urania	Cancer	♋	5	Your Thirst for Knowledge manifests through your emotional and caring quest for and attraction to nurturing and supportive creative expression.
U	Urania	Cancer	♋	6	Your Thirst for Knowledge manifests through your emotional and caring quest for and attraction to nurturing and supportive service for others.
U	Urania	Cancer	♋	7	Your Thirst for Knowledge manifests through your emotional and caring quest for and attraction to nurturing and supportive life teachers.
U	Urania	Cancer	♋	8	Your Thirst for Knowledge manifests through your emotional and caring quest for and attraction to nurturing and supportive intimate relationships.
U	Urania	Cancer	♋	9	Your Thirst for Knowledge manifests through your emotional and caring quest for and attraction to nurturing and supportive mastership of a body of knowledge.
U	Urania	Cancer	♋	10	Your Thirst for Knowledge manifests through your emotional and caring quest for and attraction to nurturing and supportive accomplishments.
U	Urania	Cancer	♋	11	Your Thirst for Knowledge manifests through your emotional and caring quest for and attraction to nurturing and supportive community.
U	Urania	Cancer	♋	12	Your Thirst for Knowledge manifests through your emotional and caring quest for and attraction to nurturing and supportive spirituality.

U	Urania	Leo	♌	1	Your Thirst for Knowledge manifests through your energetic and dramatic quest for and attraction to creative and romantic identity development.
U	Urania	Leo	♌	2	Your Thirst for Knowledge manifests through your energetic and dramatic quest for and attraction to creative and romantic values and ways to meet your needs.
U	Urania	Leo	♌	3	Your Thirst for Knowledge manifests through your energetic and dramatic quest for and attraction to creative and romantic understanding of the world around you.
U	Urania	Leo	♌	4	Your Thirst for Knowledge manifests through your energetic and dramatic quest for and attraction to creative and romantic emotional caretaking and traditions.
U	Urania	Leo	♌	5	Your Thirst for Knowledge manifests through your energetic and dramatic quest for and attraction to creative and romantic creative expression.
U	Urania	Leo	♌	6	Your Thirst for Knowledge manifests through your energetic and dramatic quest for and attraction to creative and romantic service for others.
U	Urania	Leo	♌	7	Your Thirst for Knowledge manifests through your energetic and dramatic quest for and attraction to creative and romantic life teachers.
U	Urania	Leo	♌	8	Your Thirst for Knowledge manifests through your energetic and dramatic quest for and attraction to creative and romantic intimate relationships.
U	Urania	Leo	♌	9	Your Thirst for Knowledge manifests through your energetic and dramatic quest for and attraction to creative and romantic mastership of a body of knowledge.
U	Urania	Leo	♌	10	Your Thirst for Knowledge manifests through your energetic and dramatic quest for and attraction to creative and romantic accomplishments.
U	Urania	Leo	♌	11	Your Thirst for Knowledge manifests through your energetic and dramatic quest for and attraction to creative and romantic community.
U	Urania	Leo	♌	12	Your Thirst for Knowledge manifests through your energetic and dramatic quest for and attraction to creative and romantic spirituality.

U	Urania	Virgo	♍	1	Your Thirst for Knowledge manifests through your critically-minded and methodical quest for and attraction to meticulous and practical identity development.
U	Urania	Virgo	♍	2	Your Thirst for Knowledge manifests through your critically-minded and methodical quest for and attraction to meticulous and practical values and ways to meet your needs.
U	Urania	Virgo	♍	3	Your Thirst for Knowledge manifests through your critically-minded and methodical quest for and attraction to meticulous and practical understanding of the world around you.
U	Urania	Virgo	♍	4	Your Thirst for Knowledge manifests through your critically-minded and methodical quest for and attraction to meticulous and practical emotional caretaking and traditions.
U	Urania	Virgo	♍	5	Your Thirst for Knowledge manifests through your critically-minded and methodical quest for and attraction to meticulous and practical creative expression.
U	Urania	Virgo	♍	6	Your Thirst for Knowledge manifests through your critically-minded and methodical quest for and attraction to meticulous and practical service for others.
U	Urania	Virgo	♍	7	Your Thirst for Knowledge manifests through your critically-minded and methodical quest for and attraction to meticulous and practical life teachers.
U	Urania	Virgo	♍	8	Your Thirst for Knowledge manifests through your critically-minded and methodical quest for and attraction to meticulous and practical intimate relationships.
U	Urania	Virgo	♍	9	Your Thirst for Knowledge manifests through your critically-minded and methodical quest for and attraction to meticulous and practical mastership of a body of knowledge.
U	Urania	Virgo	♍	10	Your Thirst for Knowledge manifests through your critically-minded and methodical quest for and attraction to meticulous and practical accomplishments.
U	Urania	Virgo	♍	11	Your Thirst for Knowledge manifests through your critically-minded and methodical quest for and attraction to meticulous and practical community.
U	Urania	Virgo	♍	12	Your Thirst for Knowledge manifests through your critically-minded and methodical quest for and attraction to meticulous and practical spirituality.

U	Urania	Libra	♎	1	Your Thirst for Knowledge manifests through your analytical and balanced quest for and attraction to harmonious and logical identity development.
U	Urania	Libra	♎	2	Your Thirst for Knowledge manifests through your analytical and balanced quest for and attraction to harmonious and logical values and ways to meet your needs.
U	Urania	Libra	♎	3	Your Thirst for Knowledge manifests through your analytical and balanced quest for and attraction to harmonious and logical understanding of the world around you.
U	Urania	Libra	♎	4	Your Thirst for Knowledge manifests through your analytical and balanced quest for and attraction to harmonious and logical emotional caretaking and traditions.
U	Urania	Libra	♎	5	Your Thirst for Knowledge manifests through your analytical and balanced quest for and attraction to harmonious and logical creative expression.
U	Urania	Libra	♎	6	Your Thirst for Knowledge manifests through your analytical and balanced quest for and attraction to harmonious and logical service for others.
U	Urania	Libra	♎	7	Your Thirst for Knowledge manifests through your analytical and balanced quest for and attraction to harmonious and logical life teachers.
U	Urania	Libra	♎	8	Your Thirst for Knowledge manifests through your analytical and balanced quest for and attraction to harmonious and logical intimate relationships.
U	Urania	Libra	♎	9	Your Thirst for Knowledge manifests through your analytical and balanced quest for and attraction to harmonious and logical mastership of a body of knowledge.
U	Urania	Libra	♎	10	Your Thirst for Knowledge manifests through your analytical and balanced quest for and attraction to harmonious and logical accomplishments.
U	Urania	Libra	♎	11	Your Thirst for Knowledge manifests through your analytical and balanced quest for and attraction to harmonious and logical community.
U	Urania	Libra	♎	12	Your Thirst for Knowledge manifests through your analytical and balanced quest for and attraction to harmonious and logical spirituality.

U	Urania	Scorpio	♏	1	Your Thirst for Knowledge manifests through your intense and truth seeking quest for and attraction to penetrating and emotionally transformative identity development.
U	Urania	Scorpio	♏	2	Your Thirst for Knowledge manifests through your intense and truth seeking quest for and attraction to penetrating and emotionally transformative values and ways to meet your needs.
U	Urania	Scorpio	♏	3	Your Thirst for Knowledge manifests through your intense and truth seeking quest for and attraction to penetrating and emotionally transformative understanding of the world around you.
U	Urania	Scorpio	♏	4	Your Thirst for Knowledge manifests through your intense and truth seeking quest for and attraction to penetrating and emotionally transformative emotional caretaking and traditions.
U	Urania	Scorpio	♏	5	Your Thirst for Knowledge manifests through your intense and truth seeking quest for and attraction to penetrating and emotionally transformative creative expression.
U	Urania	Scorpio	♏	6	Your Thirst for Knowledge manifests through your intense and truth seeking quest for and attraction to penetrating and emotionally transformative service for others.
U	Urania	Scorpio	♏	7	Your Thirst for Knowledge manifests through your intense and truth seeking quest for and attraction to penetrating and emotionally transformative life teachers.
U	Urania	Scorpio	♏	8	Your Thirst for Knowledge manifests through your intense and truth seeking quest for and attraction to penetrating and emotionally transformative intimate relationships.
U	Urania	Scorpio	♏	9	Your Thirst for Knowledge manifests through your intense and truth seeking quest for and attraction to penetrating and emotionally transformative mastership of a body of knowledge.
U	Urania	Scorpio	♏	10	Your Thirst for Knowledge manifests through your intense and truth seeking quest for and attraction to penetrating and emotionally transformative accomplishments.
U	Urania	Scorpio	♏	11	Your Thirst for Knowledge manifests through your intense and truth seeking quest for and attraction to penetrating and emotionally transformative community.
U	Urania	Scorpio	♏	12	Your Thirst for Knowledge manifests through your intense and truth seeking quest for and attraction to penetrating and emotionally transformative spirituality.

U	Urania	Sagittarius	↗	I	Your Thirst for Knowledge manifests through your wide-ranging and open-minded quest for and attraction to experiential and risk-taking identity development.
U	Urania	Sagittarius	↗	2	Your Thirst for Knowledge manifests through your wide-ranging and open-minded quest for and attraction to experiential and risk-taking values and ways to meet your needs.
U	Urania	Sagittarius	↗	3	Your Thirst for Knowledge manifests through your wide-ranging and open-minded quest for and attraction to experiential and risk-taking understanding of the world around you.
U	Urania	Sagittarius	↗	4	Your Thirst for Knowledge manifests through your wide-ranging and open-minded quest for and attraction to experiential and risk-taking emotional caretaking and traditions.
U	Urania	Sagittarius	↗	5	Your Thirst for Knowledge manifests through your wide-ranging and open-minded quest for and attraction to experiential and risk-taking creative expression.
U	Urania	Sagittarius	↗	6	Your Thirst for Knowledge manifests through your wide-ranging and open-minded quest for and attraction to experiential and risk-taking service for others.
U	Urania	Sagittarius	↗	7	Your Thirst for Knowledge manifests through your wide-ranging and open-minded quest for and attraction to experiential and risk-taking life teachers.
U	Urania	Sagittarius	↗	8	Your Thirst for Knowledge manifests through your wide-ranging and open-minded quest for and attraction to experiential and risk-taking intimate relationships.
U	Urania	Sagittarius	↗	9	Your Thirst for Knowledge manifests through your wide-ranging and open-minded quest for and attraction to experiential and risk-taking mastership of a body of knowledge.
U	Urania	Sagittarius	↗	10	Your Thirst for Knowledge manifests through your wide-ranging and open-minded quest for and attraction to experiential and risk-taking accomplishments.
U	Urania	Sagittarius	↗	11	Your Thirst for Knowledge manifests through your wide-ranging and open-minded quest for and attraction to experiential and risk-taking community.
U	Urania	Sagittarius	↗	12	Your Thirst for Knowledge manifests through your wide-ranging and open-minded quest for and attraction to experiential and risk-taking spirituality.

U	Urania	Capricorn	♑	1	Your Thirst for Knowledge manifests through your goal-driven and focused quest for and attraction to results-oriented and successful identity development.
U	Urania	Capricorn	♑	2	Your Thirst for Knowledge manifests through your goal-driven and focused quest for and attraction to results-oriented and successful values and ways to meet your needs.
U	Urania	Capricorn	♑	3	Your Thirst for Knowledge manifests through your goal-driven and focused quest for and attraction to results-oriented and successful understanding of the world around you.
U	Urania	Capricorn	♑	4	Your Thirst for Knowledge manifests through your goal-driven and focused quest for and attraction to results-oriented and successful emotional caretaking and traditions.
U	Urania	Capricorn	♑	5	Your Thirst for Knowledge manifests through your goal-driven and focused quest for and attraction to results-oriented and successful creative expression.
U	Urania	Capricorn	♑	6	Your Thirst for Knowledge manifests through your goal-driven and focused quest for and attraction to results-oriented and successful service for others.
U	Urania	Capricorn	♑	7	Your Thirst for Knowledge manifests through your goal-driven and focused quest for and attraction to results-oriented and successful life teachers.
U	Urania	Capricorn	♑	8	Your Thirst for Knowledge manifests through your goal-driven and focused quest for and attraction to results-oriented and successful intimate relationships.
U	Urania	Capricorn	♑	9	Your Thirst for Knowledge manifests through your goal-driven and focused quest for and attraction to results-oriented and successful mastership of a body of knowledge.
U	Urania	Capricorn	♑	10	Your Thirst for Knowledge manifests through your goal-driven and focused quest for and attraction to results-oriented and successful accomplishments.
U	Urania	Capricorn	♑	11	Your Thirst for Knowledge manifests through your goal-driven and focused quest for and attraction to results-oriented and successful community.
U	Urania	Capricorn	♑	12	Your Thirst for Knowledge manifests through your goal-driven and focused quest for and attraction to results-oriented and successful spirituality.

U	Urania	Aquarius	♒	1	Your Thirst for Knowledge manifests through your unconventional and idealistic quest for and attraction to authentic and non-traditional identity development.
U	Urania	Aquarius	♒	2	Your Thirst for Knowledge manifests through your unconventional and idealistic quest for and attraction to authentic and non-traditional values and ways to meet your needs.
U	Urania	Aquarius	♒	3	Your Thirst for Knowledge manifests through your unconventional and idealistic quest for and attraction to authentic and non-traditional understanding of the world around you.
U	Urania	Aquarius	♒	4	Your Thirst for Knowledge manifests through your unconventional and idealistic quest for and attraction to authentic and non-traditional emotional caretaking and traditions.
U	Urania	Aquarius	♒	5	Your Thirst for Knowledge manifests through your unconventional and idealistic quest for and attraction to authentic and non-traditional creative expression.
U	Urania	Aquarius	♒	6	Your Thirst for Knowledge manifests through your unconventional and idealistic quest for and attraction to authentic and non-traditional service for others.
U	Urania	Aquarius	♒	7	Your Thirst for Knowledge manifests through your unconventional and idealistic quest for and attraction to authentic and non-traditional life teachers.
U	Urania	Aquarius	♒	8	Your Thirst for Knowledge manifests through your unconventional and idealistic quest for and attraction to authentic and non-traditional intimate relationships.
U	Urania	Aquarius	♒	9	Your Thirst for Knowledge manifests through your unconventional and idealistic quest for and attraction to authentic and non-traditional mastership of a body of knowledge.
U	Urania	Aquarius	♒	10	Your Thirst for Knowledge manifests through your unconventional and idealistic quest for and attraction to authentic and non-traditional accomplishments.
U	Urania	Aquarius	♒	11	Your Thirst for Knowledge manifests through your unconventional and idealistic quest for and attraction to authentic and non-traditional community.
U	Urania	Aquarius	♒	12	Your Thirst for Knowledge manifests through your unconventional and idealistic quest for and attraction to authentic and non-traditional spirituality.

U	Urania	Pisces	♓	1	Your Thirst for Knowledge manifests through your imaginative and faithful quest for and attraction to consciousness-raising and soulful identity development.
U	Urania	Pisces	♓	2	Your Thirst for Knowledge manifests through your imaginative and faithful quest for and attraction to consciousness-raising and soulful values and ways to meet your needs.
U	Urania	Pisces	♓	3	Your Thirst for Knowledge manifests through your imaginative and faithful quest for and attraction to consciousness-raising and soulful understanding of the world around you.
U	Urania	Pisces	♓	4	Your Thirst for Knowledge manifests through your imaginative and faithful quest for and attraction to consciousness-raising and soulful emotional caretaking and traditions.
U	Urania	Pisces	♓	5	Your Thirst for Knowledge manifests through your imaginative and faithful quest for and attraction to consciousness-raising and soulful creative expression.
U	Urania	Pisces	♓	6	Your Thirst for Knowledge manifests through your imaginative and faithful quest for and attraction to consciousness-raising and soulful service for others.
U	Urania	Pisces	♓	7	Your Thirst for Knowledge manifests through your imaginative and faithful quest for and attraction to consciousness-raising and soulful life teachers.
U	Urania	Pisces	♓	8	Your Thirst for Knowledge manifests through your imaginative and faithful quest for and attraction to consciousness-raising and soulful intimate relationships.
U	Urania	Pisces	♓	9	Your Thirst for Knowledge manifests through your imaginative and faithful quest for and attraction to consciousness-raising and soulful mastership of a body of knowledge.
U	Urania	Pisces	♓	10	Your Thirst for Knowledge manifests through your imaginative and faithful quest for and attraction to consciousness-raising and soulful accomplishments.
U	Urania	Pisces	♓	11	Your Thirst for Knowledge manifests through your imaginative and faithful quest for and attraction to consciousness-raising and soulful community.
U	Urania	Pisces	♓	12	Your Thirst for Knowledge manifests through your imaginative and faithful quest for and attraction to consciousness-raising and soulful spirituality.

Hygeia | ⚕

Energy Point Type: **Asteroid**

Co-Rules Sign: **Virgo**

Co-Rules House: **6**th

Element: **Earth**

Key Phrase: **Way of Health**

Hygeia represents your Way of Health. Its placement in Sign and House reveals the type of energy that best supports our spiritual health, and thus our physical health, and in what area it is most important for us to maintain our health. In my case my Way of Health is expressed through Earth (Virgo) in my quest for community (11th House). Earth's expression is accomplished, persistent, and practical. In Virgo the Element acts critically, meticulously, and pragmatically. So, my key phrase is *"Your Way of Health manifests through your critically-minded and methodical quest for and attraction to meticulous and practical community."* In short, my mental and physical health both thrive when I take practical and meticulous care of my body and surround myself with people who do the same. Regular exercise (I cycle almost daily) and a strict diet (gluten free and organic foods) have proven necessary for my continued good health.

When you look up your Hygeia in the Sign and House formula, consider how and where you can best manage your health, both mental and physical. If the energy is Water, then you should focus on your emotional needs and well-being; if Earth, nutrition and physical activity for your body; if Air, keeping your mind in a healthy state; and if Fire, that you are using and protecting your energy properly. Consider Hygeia in Sagittarius in the 5th House, *"Your Way of Health manifests through your wide-ranging and open-minded quest for and attraction to experiential and risk-taking creative expression."* The individual with this placement will enjoy the best state of health if he or she can expand and explore through creative engagement. This energy could find its best resonance in writing, an artistic field, performance, or some form of creative travel. A nearly perfect expression would be living life as a circus performer!

Astrology Unlocked by Philip Young, PhD

	Hygeia	Aries	♈	1	Your Way of Health manifests through your independent and heroic quest for and attraction to maverick and individualistic identity development.
	Hygeia	Aries	♈	2	Your Way of Health manifests through your independent and heroic quest for and attraction to maverick and individualistic values and ways to meet your needs.
	Hygeia	Aries	♈	3	Your Way of Health manifests through your independent and heroic quest for and attraction to maverick and individualistic understanding of the world around you.
	Hygeia	Aries	♈	4	Your Way of Health manifests through your independent and heroic quest for and attraction to maverick and individualistic emotional caretaking and traditions.
	Hygeia	Aries	♈	5	Your Way of Health manifests through your independent and heroic quest for and attraction to maverick and individualistic creative expression.
	Hygeia	Aries	♈	6	Your Way of Health manifests through your independent and heroic quest for and attraction to maverick and individualistic service for others.
	Hygeia	Aries	♈	7	Your Way of Health manifests through your independent and heroic quest for and attraction to maverick and individualistic life teachers.
	Hygeia	Aries	♈	8	Your Way of Health manifests through your independent and heroic quest for and attraction to maverick and individualistic intimate relationships.
	Hygeia	Aries	♈	9	Your Way of Health manifests through your independent and heroic quest for and attraction to maverick and individualistic mastership of a body of knowledge.
	Hygeia	Aries	♈	10	Your Way of Health manifests through your independent and heroic quest for and attraction to maverick and individualistic accomplishments.
	Hygeia	Aries	♈	11	Your Way of Health manifests through your independent and heroic quest for and attraction to maverick and individualistic community.
	Hygeia	Aries	♈	12	Your Way of Health manifests through your independent and heroic quest for and attraction to maverick and individualistic spirituality.

	Hygeia	Taurus	♉	1	Your Way of Health manifests through your steadfast and persistent quest for and attraction to enduring and secure identity development.
	Hygeia	Taurus	♉	2	Your Way of Health manifests through your steadfast and persistent quest for and attraction to enduring and secure values and ways to meet your needs.
	Hygeia	Taurus	♉	3	Your Way of Health manifests through your steadfast and persistent quest for and attraction to enduring and secure understanding of the world around you.
	Hygeia	Taurus	♉	4	Your Way of Health manifests through your steadfast and persistent quest for and attraction to enduring and secure emotional caretaking and traditions.
	Hygeia	Taurus	♉	5	Your Way of Health manifests through your steadfast and persistent quest for and attraction to enduring and secure creative expression.
	Hygeia	Taurus	♉	6	Your Way of Health manifests through your steadfast and persistent quest for and attraction to enduring and secure service for others.
	Hygeia	Taurus	♉	7	Your Way of Health manifests through your steadfast and persistent quest for and attraction to enduring and secure life teachers.
	Hygeia	Taurus	♉	8	Your Way of Health manifests through your steadfast and persistent quest for and attraction to enduring and secure intimate relationships.
	Hygeia	Taurus	♉	9	Your Way of Health manifests through your steadfast and persistent quest for and attraction to enduring and secure mastership of a body of knowledge.
	Hygeia	Taurus	♉	10	Your Way of Health manifests through your steadfast and persistent quest for and attraction to enduring and secure accomplishments.
	Hygeia	Taurus	♉	11	Your Way of Health manifests through your steadfast and persistent quest for and attraction to enduring and secure community.
	Hygeia	Taurus	♉	12	Your Way of Health manifests through your steadfast and persistent quest for and attraction to enduring and secure spirituality.

313

	Hygeia	Gemini	♊	1	Your Way of Health manifests through your inquisitive and mentally agile quest for and attraction to ever changing and adaptable identity development.
	Hygeia	Gemini	♊	2	Your Way of Health manifests through your inquisitive and mentally agile quest for and attraction to ever changing and adaptable values and ways to meet your needs.
	Hygeia	Gemini	♊	3	Your Way of Health manifests through your inquisitive and mentally agile quest for and attraction to ever changing and adaptable understanding of the world around you.
	Hygeia	Gemini	♊	4	Your Way of Health manifests through your inquisitive and mentally agile quest for and attraction to ever changing and adaptable emotional caretaking and traditions.
	Hygeia	Gemini	♊	5	Your Way of Health manifests through your inquisitive and mentally agile quest for and attraction to ever changing and adaptable creative expression.
	Hygeia	Gemini	♊	6	Your Way of Health manifests through your inquisitive and mentally agile quest for and attraction to ever changing and adaptable service for others.
	Hygeia	Gemini	♊	7	Your Way of Health manifests through your inquisitive and mentally agile quest for and attraction to ever changing and adaptable life teachers.
	Hygeia	Gemini	♊	8	Your Way of Health manifests through your inquisitive and mentally agile quest for and attraction to ever changing and adaptable intimate relationships.
	Hygeia	Gemini	♊	9	Your Way of Health manifests through your inquisitive and mentally agile quest for and attraction to ever changing and adaptable mastership of a body of knowledge.
	Hygeia	Gemini	♊	10	Your Way of Health manifests through your inquisitive and mentally agile quest for and attraction to ever changing and adaptable accomplishments.
	Hygeia	Gemini	♊	11	Your Way of Health manifests through your inquisitive and mentally agile quest for and attraction to ever changing and adaptable community.
	Hygeia	Gemini	♊	12	Your Way of Health manifests through your inquisitive and mentally agile quest for and attraction to ever changing and adaptable spirituality.

	Hygeia	Cancer	♋	1	Your Way of Health manifests through your emotional and caring quest for and attraction to nurturing and supportive identity development.
	Hygeia	Cancer	♋	2	Your Way of Health manifests through your emotional and caring quest for and attraction to nurturing and supportive values and ways to meet your needs.
	Hygeia	Cancer	♋	3	Your Way of Health manifests through your emotional and caring quest for and attraction to nurturing and supportive understanding of the world around you.
	Hygeia	Cancer	♋	4	Your Way of Health manifests through your emotional and caring quest for and attraction to nurturing and supportive emotional caretaking and traditions.
	Hygeia	Cancer	♋	5	Your Way of Health manifests through your emotional and caring quest for and attraction to nurturing and supportive creative expression.
	Hygeia	Cancer	♋	6	Your Way of Health manifests through your emotional and caring quest for and attraction to nurturing and supportive service for others.
	Hygeia	Cancer	♋	7	Your Way of Health manifests through your emotional and caring quest for and attraction to nurturing and supportive life teachers.
	Hygeia	Cancer	♋	8	Your Way of Health manifests through your emotional and caring quest for and attraction to nurturing and supportive intimate relationships.
	Hygeia	Cancer	♋	9	Your Way of Health manifests through your emotional and caring quest for and attraction to nurturing and supportive mastership of a body of knowledge.
	Hygeia	Cancer	♋	10	Your Way of Health manifests through your emotional and caring quest for and attraction to nurturing and supportive accomplishments.
	Hygeia	Cancer	♋	11	Your Way of Health manifests through your emotional and caring quest for and attraction to nurturing and supportive community.
	Hygeia	Cancer	♋	12	Your Way of Health manifests through your emotional and caring quest for and attraction to nurturing and supportive spirituality.

	Hygeia	Leo	♌	1	Your Way of Health manifests through your energetic and dramatic quest for and attraction to creative and romantic identity development.
	Hygeia	Leo	♌	2	Your Way of Health manifests through your energetic and dramatic quest for and attraction to creative and romantic values and ways to meet your needs.
	Hygeia	Leo	♌	3	Your Way of Health manifests through your energetic and dramatic quest for and attraction to creative and romantic understanding of the world around you.
	Hygeia	Leo	♌	4	Your Way of Health manifests through your energetic and dramatic quest for and attraction to creative and romantic emotional caretaking and traditions.
	Hygeia	Leo	♌	5	Your Way of Health manifests through your energetic and dramatic quest for and attraction to creative and romantic creative expression.
	Hygeia	Leo	♌	6	Your Way of Health manifests through your energetic and dramatic quest for and attraction to creative and romantic service for others.
	Hygeia	Leo	♌	7	Your Way of Health manifests through your energetic and dramatic quest for and attraction to creative and romantic life teachers.
	Hygeia	Leo	♌	8	Your Way of Health manifests through your energetic and dramatic quest for and attraction to creative and romantic intimate relationships.
	Hygeia	Leo	♌	9	Your Way of Health manifests through your energetic and dramatic quest for and attraction to creative and romantic mastership of a body of knowledge.
	Hygeia	Leo	♌	10	Your Way of Health manifests through your energetic and dramatic quest for and attraction to creative and romantic accomplishments.
	Hygeia	Leo	♌	11	Your Way of Health manifests through your energetic and dramatic quest for and attraction to creative and romantic community.
	Hygeia	Leo	♌	12	Your Way of Health manifests through your energetic and dramatic quest for and attraction to creative and romantic spirituality.

	Hygeia	Virgo	♍	1	Your Way of Health manifests through your critically-minded and methodical quest for and attraction to meticulous and practical identity development.
	Hygeia	Virgo	♍	2	Your Way of Health manifests through your critically-minded and methodical quest for and attraction to meticulous and practical values and ways to meet your needs.
	Hygeia	Virgo	♍	3	Your Way of Health manifests through your critically-minded and methodical quest for and attraction to meticulous and practical understanding of the world around you.
	Hygeia	Virgo	♍	4	Your Way of Health manifests through your critically-minded and methodical quest for and attraction to meticulous and practical emotional caretaking and traditions.
	Hygeia	Virgo	♍	5	Your Way of Health manifests through your critically-minded and methodical quest for and attraction to meticulous and practical creative expression.
	Hygeia	Virgo	♍	6	Your Way of Health manifests through your critically-minded and methodical quest for and attraction to meticulous and practical service for others.
	Hygeia	Virgo	♍	7	Your Way of Health manifests through your critically-minded and methodical quest for and attraction to meticulous and practical life teachers.
	Hygeia	Virgo	♍	8	Your Way of Health manifests through your critically-minded and methodical quest for and attraction to meticulous and practical intimate relationships.
	Hygeia	Virgo	♍	9	Your Way of Health manifests through your critically-minded and methodical quest for and attraction to meticulous and practical mastership of a body of knowledge.
	Hygeia	Virgo	♍	10	Your Way of Health manifests through your critically-minded and methodical quest for and attraction to meticulous and practical accomplishments.
	Hygeia	Virgo	♍	11	Your Way of Health manifests through your critically-minded and methodical quest for and attraction to meticulous and practical community.
	Hygeia	Virgo	♍	12	Your Way of Health manifests through your critically-minded and methodical quest for and attraction to meticulous and practical spirituality.

	Hygeia	Libra	♎	1	Your Way of Health manifests through your analytical and balanced quest for and attraction to harmonious and logical identity development.
	Hygeia	Libra	♎	2	Your Way of Health manifests through your analytical and balanced quest for and attraction to harmonious and logical values and ways to meet your needs.
	Hygeia	Libra	♎	3	Your Way of Health manifests through your analytical and balanced quest for and attraction to harmonious and logical understanding of the world around you.
	Hygeia	Libra	♎	4	Your Way of Health manifests through your analytical and balanced quest for and attraction to harmonious and logical emotional caretaking and traditions.
	Hygeia	Libra	♎	5	Your Way of Health manifests through your analytical and balanced quest for and attraction to harmonious and logical creative expression.
	Hygeia	Libra	♎	6	Your Way of Health manifests through your analytical and balanced quest for and attraction to harmonious and logical service for others.
	Hygeia	Libra	♎	7	Your Way of Health manifests through your analytical and balanced quest for and attraction to harmonious and logical life teachers.
	Hygeia	Libra	♎	8	Your Way of Health manifests through your analytical and balanced quest for and attraction to harmonious and logical intimate relationships.
	Hygeia	Libra	♎	9	Your Way of Health manifests through your analytical and balanced quest for and attraction to harmonious and logical mastership of a body of knowledge.
	Hygeia	Libra	♎	10	Your Way of Health manifests through your analytical and balanced quest for and attraction to harmonious and logical accomplishments.
	Hygeia	Libra	♎	11	Your Way of Health manifests through your analytical and balanced quest for and attraction to harmonious and logical community.
	Hygeia	Libra	♎	12	Your Way of Health manifests through your analytical and balanced quest for and attraction to harmonious and logical spirituality.

318

	Hygeia	Scorpio	♏	1	Your Way of Health manifests through your intense and truth seeking quest for and attraction to penetrating and emotionally transformative identity development.
	Hygeia	Scorpio	♏	2	Your Way of Health manifests through your intense and truth seeking quest for and attraction to penetrating and emotionally transformative values and ways to meet your needs.
	Hygeia	Scorpio	♏	3	Your Way of Health manifests through your intense and truth seeking quest for and attraction to penetrating and emotionally transformative understanding of the world around you.
	Hygeia	Scorpio	♏	4	Your Way of Health manifests through your intense and truth seeking quest for and attraction to penetrating and emotionally transformative emotional caretaking and traditions.
	Hygeia	Scorpio	♏	5	Your Way of Health manifests through your intense and truth seeking quest for and attraction to penetrating and emotionally transformative creative expression.
	Hygeia	Scorpio	♏	6	Your Way of Health manifests through your intense and truth seeking quest for and attraction to penetrating and emotionally transformative service for others.
	Hygeia	Scorpio	♏	7	Your Way of Health manifests through your intense and truth seeking quest for and attraction to penetrating and emotionally transformative life teachers.
	Hygeia	Scorpio	♏	8	Your Way of Health manifests through your intense and truth seeking quest for and attraction to penetrating and emotionally transformative intimate relationships.
	Hygeia	Scorpio	♏	9	Your Way of Health manifests through your intense and truth seeking quest for and attraction to penetrating and emotionally transformative mastership of a body of knowledge.
	Hygeia	Scorpio	♏	10	Your Way of Health manifests through your intense and truth seeking quest for and attraction to penetrating and emotionally transformative accomplishments.
	Hygeia	Scorpio	♏	11	Your Way of Health manifests through your intense and truth seeking quest for and attraction to penetrating and emotionally transformative community.
	Hygeia	Scorpio	♏	12	Your Way of Health manifests through your intense and truth seeking quest for and attraction to penetrating and emotionally transformative spirituality.

	Hygeia	Sagittarius	↗	1	Your Way of Health manifests through your wide-ranging and open-minded quest for and attraction to experiential and risk-taking identity development.
	Hygeia	Sagittarius	↗	2	Your Way of Health manifests through your wide-ranging and open-minded quest for and attraction to experiential and risk-taking values and ways to meet your needs.
	Hygeia	Sagittarius	↗	3	Your Way of Health manifests through your wide-ranging and open-minded quest for and attraction to experiential and risk-taking understanding of the world around you.
	Hygeia	Sagittarius	↗	4	Your Way of Health manifests through your wide-ranging and open-minded quest for and attraction to experiential and risk-taking emotional caretaking and traditions.
	Hygeia	Sagittarius	↗	5	Your Way of Health manifests through your wide-ranging and open-minded quest for and attraction to experiential and risk-taking creative expression.
	Hygeia	Sagittarius	↗	6	Your Way of Health manifests through your wide-ranging and open-minded quest for and attraction to experiential and risk-taking service for others.
	Hygeia	Sagittarius	↗	7	Your Way of Health manifests through your wide-ranging and open-minded quest for and attraction to experiential and risk-taking life teachers.
	Hygeia	Sagittarius	↗	8	Your Way of Health manifests through your wide-ranging and open-minded quest for and attraction to experiential and risk-taking intimate relationships.
	Hygeia	Sagittarius	↗	9	Your Way of Health manifests through your wide-ranging and open-minded quest for and attraction to experiential and risk-taking mastership of a body of knowledge.
	Hygeia	Sagittarius	↗	10	Your Way of Health manifests through your wide-ranging and open-minded quest for and attraction to experiential and risk-taking accomplishments.
	Hygeia	Sagittarius	↗	11	Your Way of Health manifests through your wide-ranging and open-minded quest for and attraction to experiential and risk-taking community.
	Hygeia	Sagittarius	↗	12	Your Way of Health manifests through your wide-ranging and open-minded quest for and attraction to experiential and risk-taking spirituality.

	Hygeia	Capricorn	♑	1	Your Way of Health manifests through your goal-driven and focused quest for and attraction to results-oriented and successful identity development.
	Hygeia	Capricorn	♑	2	Your Way of Health manifests through your goal-driven and focused quest for and attraction to results-oriented and successful values and ways to meet your needs.
	Hygeia	Capricorn	♑	3	Your Way of Health manifests through your goal-driven and focused quest for and attraction to results-oriented and successful understanding of the world around you.
	Hygeia	Capricorn	♑	4	Your Way of Health manifests through your goal-driven and focused quest for and attraction to results-oriented and successful emotional caretaking and traditions.
	Hygeia	Capricorn	♑	5	Your Way of Health manifests through your goal-driven and focused quest for and attraction to results-oriented and successful creative expression.
	Hygeia	Capricorn	♑	6	Your Way of Health manifests through your goal-driven and focused quest for and attraction to results-oriented and successful service for others.
	Hygeia	Capricorn	♑	7	Your Way of Health manifests through your goal-driven and focused quest for and attraction to results-oriented and successful life teachers.
	Hygeia	Capricorn	♑	8	Your Way of Health manifests through your goal-driven and focused quest for and attraction to results-oriented and successful intimate relationships.
	Hygeia	Capricorn	♑	9	Your Way of Health manifests through your goal-driven and focused quest for and attraction to results-oriented and successful mastership of a body of knowledge.
	Hygeia	Capricorn	♑	10	Your Way of Health manifests through your goal-driven and focused quest for and attraction to results-oriented and successful accomplishments.
	Hygeia	Capricorn	♑	11	Your Way of Health manifests through your goal-driven and focused quest for and attraction to results-oriented and successful community.
	Hygeia	Capricorn	♑	12	Your Way of Health manifests through your goal-driven and focused quest for and attraction to results-oriented and successful spirituality.

321

	Hygeia	Aquarius	♒	1	Your Way of Health manifests through your unconventional and idealistic quest for and attraction to authentic and non-traditional identity development.
	Hygeia	Aquarius	♒	2	Your Way of Health manifests through your unconventional and idealistic quest for and attraction to authentic and non-traditional values and ways to meet your needs.
	Hygeia	Aquarius	♒	3	Your Way of Health manifests through your unconventional and idealistic quest for and attraction to authentic and non-traditional understanding of the world around you.
	Hygeia	Aquarius	♒	4	Your Way of Health manifests through your unconventional and idealistic quest for and attraction to authentic and non-traditional emotional caretaking and traditions.
	Hygeia	Aquarius	♒	5	Your Way of Health manifests through your unconventional and idealistic quest for and attraction to authentic and non-traditional creative expression.
	Hygeia	Aquarius	♒	6	Your Way of Health manifests through your unconventional and idealistic quest for and attraction to authentic and non-traditional service for others.
	Hygeia	Aquarius	♒	7	Your Way of Health manifests through your unconventional and idealistic quest for and attraction to authentic and non-traditional life teachers.
	Hygeia	Aquarius	♒	8	Your Way of Health manifests through your unconventional and idealistic quest for and attraction to authentic and non-traditional intimate relationships.
	Hygeia	Aquarius	♒	9	Your Way of Health manifests through your unconventional and idealistic quest for and attraction to authentic and non-traditional mastership of a body of knowledge.
	Hygeia	Aquarius	♒	10	Your Way of Health manifests through your unconventional and idealistic quest for and attraction to authentic and non-traditional accomplishments.
	Hygeia	Aquarius	♒	11	Your Way of Health manifests through your unconventional and idealistic quest for and attraction to authentic and non-traditional community.
	Hygeia	Aquarius	♒	12	Your Way of Health manifests through your unconventional and idealistic quest for and attraction to authentic and non-traditional spirituality.

	Hygeia	Pisces	♓	1	Your Way of Health manifests through your imaginative and faithful quest for and attraction to consciousness-raising and soulful identity development.
	Hygeia	Pisces	♓	2	Your Way of Health manifests through your imaginative and faithful quest for and attraction to consciousness-raising and soulful values and ways to meet your needs.
	Hygeia	Pisces	♓	3	Your Way of Health manifests through your imaginative and faithful quest for and attraction to consciousness-raising and soulful understanding of the world around you.
	Hygeia	Pisces	♓	4	Your Way of Health manifests through your imaginative and faithful quest for and attraction to consciousness-raising and soulful emotional caretaking and traditions.
	Hygeia	Pisces	♓	5	Your Way of Health manifests through your imaginative and faithful quest for and attraction to consciousness-raising and soulful creative expression.
	Hygeia	Pisces	♓	6	Your Way of Health manifests through your imaginative and faithful quest for and attraction to consciousness-raising and soulful service for others.
	Hygeia	Pisces	♓	7	Your Way of Health manifests through your imaginative and faithful quest for and attraction to consciousness-raising and soulful life teachers.
	Hygeia	Pisces	♓	8	Your Way of Health manifests through your imaginative and faithful quest for and attraction to consciousness-raising and soulful intimate relationships.
	Hygeia	Pisces	♓	9	Your Way of Health manifests through your imaginative and faithful quest for and attraction to consciousness-raising and soulful mastership of a body of knowledge.
	Hygeia	Pisces	♓	10	Your Way of Health manifests through your imaginative and faithful quest for and attraction to consciousness-raising and soulful accomplishments.
	Hygeia	Pisces	♓	11	Your Way of Health manifests through your imaginative and faithful quest for and attraction to consciousness-raising and soulful community.
	Hygeia	Pisces	♓	12	Your Way of Health manifests through your imaginative and faithful quest for and attraction to consciousness-raising and soulful spirituality.

Zeus | ⚡

Energy Point Type: **Asteroid**
Co-Rules Sign: **Libra**
Co-Rules House: **7ᵗʰ**
Element: **Air**
Key Phrase: **Way of Authority**

Zeus represents your Way of Authority. Its placement in Sign and House reveals the type of energy that you use to lead and decide based on some form or combination of power, usually expressed through great ability, extensive knowledge, or tremendous success. In my case my Way of Authority is expressed through Earth (Virgo) in my quest for community (11ᵗʰ House). Earth's expression is accomplished, persistent, and practical. In Virgo the Element acts critically, meticulously, and pragmatically. So, my key phrase is *"Your Way of Authority manifests through your critically-minded and methodical quest for and attraction to meticulous and practical community."* In short, I am comfortable and easily seek out a leadership or authoritarian role in my community based on extensive knowledge gained from practical experience. And I am "given power" when I demonstrate my usefulness in my community.

When you look up your Zeus in the Sign and House formula, consider how and where you may be called upon or desire to take a leadership role where you act as the "final" decision maker. If the energy is in Water, then you will want to "Rule" your emotions and use them in your decision making process; if Earth, you will want power over the world around you; if Air, you will want to "Rule" your mind and use logic; and if Fire, you will want to "Rule" your passion and use inspiration. Consider Zeus in Capricorn in the 7ᵗʰ House, *"Your Way of Authority manifests through your goal-driven and focused quest for and attraction to results-oriented and successful life teachers."* The individual with this placement will need to be in a high level or powerful place of authority, where his or her decision making impacts the goals and outcomes of his or her partnerships.

	Zeus	Aries	♈	1	Your Way of Authority manifests through your independent and heroic quest for and attraction to maverick and individualistic identity development.
	Zeus	Aries	♈	2	Your Way of Authority manifests through your independent and heroic quest for and attraction to maverick and individualistic values and ways to meet your needs.
	Zeus	Aries	♈	3	Your Way of Authority manifests through your independent and heroic quest for and attraction to maverick and individualistic understanding of the world around you.
	Zeus	Aries	♈	4	Your Way of Authority manifests through your independent and heroic quest for and attraction to maverick and individualistic emotional caretaking and traditions.
	Zeus	Aries	♈	5	Your Way of Authority manifests through your independent and heroic quest for and attraction to maverick and individualistic creative expression.
	Zeus	Aries	♈	6	Your Way of Authority manifests through your independent and heroic quest for and attraction to maverick and individualistic service for others.
	Zeus	Aries	♈	7	Your Way of Authority manifests through your independent and heroic quest for and attraction to maverick and individualistic life teachers.
	Zeus	Aries	♈	8	Your Way of Authority manifests through your independent and heroic quest for and attraction to maverick and individualistic intimate relationships.
	Zeus	Aries	♈	9	Your Way of Authority manifests through your independent and heroic quest for and attraction to maverick and individualistic mastership of a body of knowledge.
	Zeus	Aries	♈	10	Your Way of Authority manifests through your independent and heroic quest for and attraction to maverick and individualistic accomplishments.
	Zeus	Aries	♈	11	Your Way of Authority manifests through your independent and heroic quest for and attraction to maverick and individualistic community.
	Zeus	Aries	♈	12	Your Way of Authority manifests through your independent and heroic quest for and attraction to maverick and individualistic spirituality.

⚼	Zeus	Taurus	♉	1	Your Way of Authority manifests through your steadfast and persistent quest for and attraction to enduring and secure identity development.
⚼	Zeus	Taurus	♉	2	Your Way of Authority manifests through your steadfast and persistent quest for and attraction to enduring and secure values and ways to meet your needs.
⚼	Zeus	Taurus	♉	3	Your Way of Authority manifests through your steadfast and persistent quest for and attraction to enduring and secure understanding of the world around you.
⚼	Zeus	Taurus	♉	4	Your Way of Authority manifests through your steadfast and persistent quest for and attraction to enduring and secure emotional caretaking and traditions.
⚼	Zeus	Taurus	♉	5	Your Way of Authority manifests through your steadfast and persistent quest for and attraction to enduring and secure creative expression.
⚼	Zeus	Taurus	♉	6	Your Way of Authority manifests through your steadfast and persistent quest for and attraction to enduring and secure service for others.
⚼	Zeus	Taurus	♉	7	Your Way of Authority manifests through your steadfast and persistent quest for and attraction to enduring and secure life teachers.
⚼	Zeus	Taurus	♉	8	Your Way of Authority manifests through your steadfast and persistent quest for and attraction to enduring and secure intimate relationships.
⚼	Zeus	Taurus	♉	9	Your Way of Authority manifests through your steadfast and persistent quest for and attraction to enduring and secure mastership of a body of knowledge.
⚼	Zeus	Taurus	♉	10	Your Way of Authority manifests through your steadfast and persistent quest for and attraction to enduring and secure accomplishments.
⚼	Zeus	Taurus	♉	11	Your Way of Authority manifests through your steadfast and persistent quest for and attraction to enduring and secure community.
⚼	Zeus	Taurus	♉	12	Your Way of Authority manifests through your steadfast and persistent quest for and attraction to enduring and secure spirituality.

Astrology Unlocked by Philip Young, PhD

	Zeus	Gemini	♊	1	Your Way of Authority manifests through your inquisitive and mentally agile quest for and attraction to ever changing and adaptable identity development.
	Zeus	Gemini	♊	2	Your Way of Authority manifests through your inquisitive and mentally agile quest for and attraction to ever changing and adaptable values and ways to meet your needs.
	Zeus	Gemini	♊	3	Your Way of Authority manifests through your inquisitive and mentally agile quest for and attraction to ever changing and adaptable understanding of the world around you.
	Zeus	Gemini	♊	4	Your Way of Authority manifests through your inquisitive and mentally agile quest for and attraction to ever changing and adaptable emotional caretaking and traditions.
	Zeus	Gemini	♊	5	Your Way of Authority manifests through your inquisitive and mentally agile quest for and attraction to ever changing and adaptable creative expression.
	Zeus	Gemini	♊	6	Your Way of Authority manifests through your inquisitive and mentally agile quest for and attraction to ever changing and adaptable service for others.
	Zeus	Gemini	♊	7	Your Way of Authority manifests through your inquisitive and mentally agile quest for and attraction to ever changing and adaptable life teachers.
	Zeus	Gemini	♊	8	Your Way of Authority manifests through your inquisitive and mentally agile quest for and attraction to ever changing and adaptable intimate relationships.
	Zeus	Gemini	♊	9	Your Way of Authority manifests through your inquisitive and mentally agile quest for and attraction to ever changing and adaptable mastership of a body of knowledge.
	Zeus	Gemini	♊	10	Your Way of Authority manifests through your inquisitive and mentally agile quest for and attraction to ever changing and adaptable accomplishments.
	Zeus	Gemini	♊	11	Your Way of Authority manifests through your inquisitive and mentally agile quest for and attraction to ever changing and adaptable community.
	Zeus	Gemini	♊	12	Your Way of Authority manifests through your inquisitive and mentally agile quest for and attraction to ever changing and adaptable spirituality.

	Zeus	Cancer	♋	1	Your Way of Authority manifests through your emotional and caring quest for and attraction to nurturing and supportive identity development.
	Zeus	Cancer	♋	2	Your Way of Authority manifests through your emotional and caring quest for and attraction to nurturing and supportive values and ways to meet your needs.
	Zeus	Cancer	♋	3	Your Way of Authority manifests through your emotional and caring quest for and attraction to nurturing and supportive understanding of the world around you.
	Zeus	Cancer	♋	4	Your Way of Authority manifests through your emotional and caring quest for and attraction to nurturing and supportive emotional caretaking and traditions.
	Zeus	Cancer	♋	5	Your Way of Authority manifests through your emotional and caring quest for and attraction to nurturing and supportive creative expression.
	Zeus	Cancer	♋	6	Your Way of Authority manifests through your emotional and caring quest for and attraction to nurturing and supportive service for others.
	Zeus	Cancer	♋	7	Your Way of Authority manifests through your emotional and caring quest for and attraction to nurturing and supportive life teachers.
	Zeus	Cancer	♋	8	Your Way of Authority manifests through your emotional and caring quest for and attraction to nurturing and supportive intimate relationships.
	Zeus	Cancer	♋	9	Your Way of Authority manifests through your emotional and caring quest for and attraction to nurturing and supportive mastership of a body of knowledge.
	Zeus	Cancer	♋	10	Your Way of Authority manifests through your emotional and caring quest for and attraction to nurturing and supportive accomplishments.
	Zeus	Cancer	♋	11	Your Way of Authority manifests through your emotional and caring quest for and attraction to nurturing and supportive community.
	Zeus	Cancer	♋	12	Your Way of Authority manifests through your emotional and caring quest for and attraction to nurturing and supportive spirituality.

⚥	Zeus	Leo	♌	1	Your Way of Authority manifests through your energetic and dramatic quest for and attraction to creative and romantic identity development.
⚥	Zeus	Leo	♌	2	Your Way of Authority manifests through your energetic and dramatic quest for and attraction to creative and romantic values and ways to meet your needs.
⚥	Zeus	Leo	♌	3	Your Way of Authority manifests through your energetic and dramatic quest for and attraction to creative and romantic understanding of the world around you.
⚥	Zeus	Leo	♌	4	Your Way of Authority manifests through your energetic and dramatic quest for and attraction to creative and romantic emotional caretaking and traditions.
⚥	Zeus	Leo	♌	5	Your Way of Authority manifests through your energetic and dramatic quest for and attraction to creative and romantic creative expression.
⚥	Zeus	Leo	♌	6	Your Way of Authority manifests through your energetic and dramatic quest for and attraction to creative and romantic service for others.
⚥	Zeus	Leo	♌	7	Your Way of Authority manifests through your energetic and dramatic quest for and attraction to creative and romantic life teachers.
⚥	Zeus	Leo	♌	8	Your Way of Authority manifests through your energetic and dramatic quest for and attraction to creative and romantic intimate relationships.
⚥	Zeus	Leo	♌	9	Your Way of Authority manifests through your energetic and dramatic quest for and attraction to creative and romantic mastership of a body of knowledge.
⚥	Zeus	Leo	♌	10	Your Way of Authority manifests through your energetic and dramatic quest for and attraction to creative and romantic accomplishments.
⚥	Zeus	Leo	♌	11	Your Way of Authority manifests through your energetic and dramatic quest for and attraction to creative and romantic community.
⚥	Zeus	Leo	♌	12	Your Way of Authority manifests through your energetic and dramatic quest for and attraction to creative and romantic spirituality.

	Zeus	Virgo	♍	1	Your Way of Authority manifests through your critically-minded and methodical quest for and attraction to meticulous and practical identity development.
	Zeus	Virgo	♍	2	Your Way of Authority manifests through your critically-minded and methodical quest for and attraction to meticulous and practical values and ways to meet your needs.
	Zeus	Virgo	♍	3	Your Way of Authority manifests through your critically-minded and methodical quest for and attraction to meticulous and practical understanding of the world around you.
	Zeus	Virgo	♍	4	Your Way of Authority manifests through your critically-minded and methodical quest for and attraction to meticulous and practical emotional caretaking and traditions.
	Zeus	Virgo	♍	5	Your Way of Authority manifests through your critically-minded and methodical quest for and attraction to meticulous and practical creative expression.
	Zeus	Virgo	♍	6	Your Way of Authority manifests through your critically-minded and methodical quest for and attraction to meticulous and practical service for others.
	Zeus	Virgo	♍	7	Your Way of Authority manifests through your critically-minded and methodical quest for and attraction to meticulous and practical life teachers.
	Zeus	Virgo	♍	8	Your Way of Authority manifests through your critically-minded and methodical quest for and attraction to meticulous and practical intimate relationships.
	Zeus	Virgo	♍	9	Your Way of Authority manifests through your critically-minded and methodical quest for and attraction to meticulous and practical mastership of a body of knowledge.
	Zeus	Virgo	♍	10	Your Way of Authority manifests through your critically-minded and methodical quest for and attraction to meticulous and practical accomplishments.
	Zeus	Virgo	♍	11	Your Way of Authority manifests through your critically-minded and methodical quest for and attraction to meticulous and practical community.
	Zeus	Virgo	♍	12	Your Way of Authority manifests through your critically-minded and methodical quest for and attraction to meticulous and practical spirituality.

	Zeus	Libra	♎	1	Your Way of Authority manifests through your analytical and balanced quest for and attraction to harmonious and logical identity development.
	Zeus	Libra	♎	2	Your Way of Authority manifests through your analytical and balanced quest for and attraction to harmonious and logical values and ways to meet your needs.
	Zeus	Libra	♎	3	Your Way of Authority manifests through your analytical and balanced quest for and attraction to harmonious and logical understanding of the world around you.
	Zeus	Libra	♎	4	Your Way of Authority manifests through your analytical and balanced quest for and attraction to harmonious and logical emotional caretaking and traditions.
	Zeus	Libra	♎	5	Your Way of Authority manifests through your analytical and balanced quest for and attraction to harmonious and logical creative expression.
	Zeus	Libra	♎	6	Your Way of Authority manifests through your analytical and balanced quest for and attraction to harmonious and logical service for others.
	Zeus	Libra	♎	7	Your Way of Authority manifests through your analytical and balanced quest for and attraction to harmonious and logical life teachers.
	Zeus	Libra	♎	8	Your Way of Authority manifests through your analytical and balanced quest for and attraction to harmonious and logical intimate relationships.
	Zeus	Libra	♎	9	Your Way of Authority manifests through your analytical and balanced quest for and attraction to harmonious and logical mastership of a body of knowledge.
	Zeus	Libra	♎	10	Your Way of Authority manifests through your analytical and balanced quest for and attraction to harmonious and logical accomplishments.
	Zeus	Libra	♎	11	Your Way of Authority manifests through your analytical and balanced quest for and attraction to harmonious and logical community.
	Zeus	Libra	♎	12	Your Way of Authority manifests through your analytical and balanced quest for and attraction to harmonious and logical spirituality.

⚡	Zeus	Scorpio	♏	1	Your Way of Authority manifests through your intense and truth seeking quest for and attraction to penetrating and emotionally transformative identity development.
⚡	Zeus	Scorpio	♏	2	Your Way of Authority manifests through your intense and truth seeking quest for and attraction to penetrating and emotionally transformative values and ways to meet your needs.
⚡	Zeus	Scorpio	♏	3	Your Way of Authority manifests through your intense and truth seeking quest for and attraction to penetrating and emotionally transformative understanding of the world around you.
⚡	Zeus	Scorpio	♏	4	Your Way of Authority manifests through your intense and truth seeking quest for and attraction to penetrating and emotionally transformative emotional caretaking and traditions.
⚡	Zeus	Scorpio	♏	5	Your Way of Authority manifests through your intense and truth seeking quest for and attraction to penetrating and emotionally transformative creative expression.
⚡	Zeus	Scorpio	♏	6	Your Way of Authority manifests through your intense and truth seeking quest for and attraction to penetrating and emotionally transformative service for others.
⚡	Zeus	Scorpio	♏	7	Your Way of Authority manifests through your intense and truth seeking quest for and attraction to penetrating and emotionally transformative life teachers.
⚡	Zeus	Scorpio	♏	8	Your Way of Authority manifests through your intense and truth seeking quest for and attraction to penetrating and emotionally transformative intimate relationships.
⚡	Zeus	Scorpio	♏	9	Your Way of Authority manifests through your intense and truth seeking quest for and attraction to penetrating and emotionally transformative mastership of a body of knowledge.
⚡	Zeus	Scorpio	♏	10	Your Way of Authority manifests through your intense and truth seeking quest for and attraction to penetrating and emotionally transformative accomplishments.
⚡	Zeus	Scorpio	♏	11	Your Way of Authority manifests through your intense and truth seeking quest for and attraction to penetrating and emotionally transformative community.
⚡	Zeus	Scorpio	♏	12	Your Way of Authority manifests through your intense and truth seeking quest for and attraction to penetrating and emotionally transformative spirituality.

⇕✳	Zeus	Sagittarius	↗	1	Your Way of Authority manifests through your wide-ranging and open-minded quest for and attraction to experiential and risk-taking identity development.
⇕✳	Zeus	Sagittarius	↗	2	Your Way of Authority manifests through your wide-ranging and open-minded quest for and attraction to experiential and risk-taking values and ways to meet your needs.
⇕✳	Zeus	Sagittarius	↗	3	Your Way of Authority manifests through your wide-ranging and open-minded quest for and attraction to experiential and risk-taking understanding of the world around you.
⇕✳	Zeus	Sagittarius	↗	4	Your Way of Authority manifests through your wide-ranging and open-minded quest for and attraction to experiential and risk-taking emotional caretaking and traditions.
⇕✳	Zeus	Sagittarius	↗	5	Your Way of Authority manifests through your wide-ranging and open-minded quest for and attraction to experiential and risk-taking creative expression.
⇕✳	Zeus	Sagittarius	↗	6	Your Way of Authority manifests through your wide-ranging and open-minded quest for and attraction to experiential and risk-taking service for others.
⇕✳	Zeus	Sagittarius	↗	7	Your Way of Authority manifests through your wide-ranging and open-minded quest for and attraction to experiential and risk-taking life teachers.
⇕✳	Zeus	Sagittarius	↗	8	Your Way of Authority manifests through your wide-ranging and open-minded quest for and attraction to experiential and risk-taking intimate relationships.
⇕✳	Zeus	Sagittarius	↗	9	Your Way of Authority manifests through your wide-ranging and open-minded quest for and attraction to experiential and risk-taking mastership of a body of knowledge.
⇕✳	Zeus	Sagittarius	↗	10	Your Way of Authority manifests through your wide-ranging and open-minded quest for and attraction to experiential and risk-taking accomplishments.
⇕✳	Zeus	Sagittarius	↗	11	Your Way of Authority manifests through your wide-ranging and open-minded quest for and attraction to experiential and risk-taking community.
⇕✳	Zeus	Sagittarius	↗	12	Your Way of Authority manifests through your wide-ranging and open-minded quest for and attraction to experiential and risk-taking spirituality.

	Zeus	Capricorn	♑	1	Your Way of Authority manifests through your goal-driven and focused quest for and attraction to results-oriented and successful identity development.
	Zeus	Capricorn	♑	2	Your Way of Authority manifests through your goal-driven and focused quest for and attraction to results-oriented and successful values and ways to meet your needs.
	Zeus	Capricorn	♑	3	Your Way of Authority manifests through your goal-driven and focused quest for and attraction to results-oriented and successful understanding of the world around you.
	Zeus	Capricorn	♑	4	Your Way of Authority manifests through your goal-driven and focused quest for and attraction to results-oriented and successful emotional caretaking and traditions.
	Zeus	Capricorn	♑	5	Your Way of Authority manifests through your goal-driven and focused quest for and attraction to results-oriented and successful creative expression.
	Zeus	Capricorn	♑	6	Your Way of Authority manifests through your goal-driven and focused quest for and attraction to results-oriented and successful service for others.
	Zeus	Capricorn	♑	7	Your Way of Authority manifests through your goal-driven and focused quest for and attraction to results-oriented and successful life teachers.
	Zeus	Capricorn	♑	8	Your Way of Authority manifests through your goal-driven and focused quest for and attraction to results-oriented and successful intimate relationships.
	Zeus	Capricorn	♑	9	Your Way of Authority manifests through your goal-driven and focused quest for and attraction to results-oriented and successful mastership of a body of knowledge.
	Zeus	Capricorn	♑	10	Your Way of Authority manifests through your goal-driven and focused quest for and attraction to results-oriented and successful accomplishments.
	Zeus	Capricorn	♑	11	Your Way of Authority manifests through your goal-driven and focused quest for and attraction to results-oriented and successful community.
	Zeus	Capricorn	♑	12	Your Way of Authority manifests through your goal-driven and focused quest for and attraction to results-oriented and successful spirituality.

	Zeus	Aquarius	♒	1	Your Way of Authority manifests through your unconventional and idealistic quest for and attraction to authentic and non-traditional identity development.
	Zeus	Aquarius	♒	2	Your Way of Authority manifests through your unconventional and idealistic quest for and attraction to authentic and non-traditional values and ways to meet your needs.
	Zeus	Aquarius	♒	3	Your Way of Authority manifests through your unconventional and idealistic quest for and attraction to authentic and non-traditional understanding of the world around you.
	Zeus	Aquarius	♒	4	Your Way of Authority manifests through your unconventional and idealistic quest for and attraction to authentic and non-traditional emotional caretaking and traditions.
	Zeus	Aquarius	♒	5	Your Way of Authority manifests through your unconventional and idealistic quest for and attraction to authentic and non-traditional creative expression.
	Zeus	Aquarius	♒	6	Your Way of Authority manifests through your unconventional and idealistic quest for and attraction to authentic and non-traditional service for others.
	Zeus	Aquarius	♒	7	Your Way of Authority manifests through your unconventional and idealistic quest for and attraction to authentic and non-traditional life teachers.
	Zeus	Aquarius	♒	8	Your Way of Authority manifests through your unconventional and idealistic quest for and attraction to authentic and non-traditional intimate relationships.
	Zeus	Aquarius	♒	9	Your Way of Authority manifests through your unconventional and idealistic quest for and attraction to authentic and non-traditional mastership of a body of knowledge.
	Zeus	Aquarius	♒	10	Your Way of Authority manifests through your unconventional and idealistic quest for and attraction to authentic and non-traditional accomplishments.
	Zeus	Aquarius	♒	11	Your Way of Authority manifests through your unconventional and idealistic quest for and attraction to authentic and non-traditional community.
	Zeus	Aquarius	♒	12	Your Way of Authority manifests through your unconventional and idealistic quest for and attraction to authentic and non-traditional spirituality.

	Zeus	Pisces	♓	1	Your Way of Authority manifests through your imaginative and faithful quest for and attraction to consciousness-raising and soulful identity development.
	Zeus	Pisces	♓	2	Your Way of Authority manifests through your imaginative and faithful quest for and attraction to consciousness-raising and soulful values and ways to meet your needs.
	Zeus	Pisces	♓	3	Your Way of Authority manifests through your imaginative and faithful quest for and attraction to consciousness-raising and soulful understanding of the world around you.
	Zeus	Pisces	♓	4	Your Way of Authority manifests through your imaginative and faithful quest for and attraction to consciousness-raising and soulful emotional caretaking and traditions.
	Zeus	Pisces	♓	5	Your Way of Authority manifests through your imaginative and faithful quest for and attraction to consciousness-raising and soulful creative expression.
	Zeus	Pisces	♓	6	Your Way of Authority manifests through your imaginative and faithful quest for and attraction to consciousness-raising and soulful service for others.
	Zeus	Pisces	♓	7	Your Way of Authority manifests through your imaginative and faithful quest for and attraction to consciousness-raising and soulful life teachers.
	Zeus	Pisces	♓	8	Your Way of Authority manifests through your imaginative and faithful quest for and attraction to consciousness-raising and soulful intimate relationships.
	Zeus	Pisces	♓	9	Your Way of Authority manifests through your imaginative and faithful quest for and attraction to consciousness-raising and soulful mastership of a body of knowledge.
	Zeus	Pisces	♓	10	Your Way of Authority manifests through your imaginative and faithful quest for and attraction to consciousness-raising and soulful accomplishments.
	Zeus	Pisces	♓	11	Your Way of Authority manifests through your imaginative and faithful quest for and attraction to consciousness-raising and soulful community.
	Zeus	Pisces	♓	12	Your Way of Authority manifests through your imaginative and faithful quest for and attraction to consciousness-raising and soulful spirituality.

Astrology Unlocked by Philip Young, PhD

Eris | ♀

Energy Point Type: **Dwarf Planet**
Co-Rules Sign: **Scorpio**
Co-Rules House: **8**th
Element: **Water**
Key Phrase: **Way of Disruption**

Eris represents your Way of Disruption. Its placement in Sign and House reveals how and where we bring about and attract discord and disruption necessary for our spiritual growth. In my case my Way of Discord is expressed through Fire (Aries) in my quest for service (11th House). Fire's expression is pioneering, creative, and exploratory. In Aries the Element acts independently, heroically, and aggressively. So my key phrase is *"Your Way of Discord manifests through your independent and heroic quest for and attraction to maverick and individualistic community."* In essence, I prefer work where I can be spiritually disruptive and shake the status quo. Being a professional astrologer certainly gives me plenty of opportunities to "throw a Golden Apple"[31] into the flow of people's lives to help them wake up and consider sometimes difficult, but necessary alternatives to their current path.

When you look up your Eris in the Sign and House formula, think about how and where you cause and attract spiritual disruption in your life to bring about necessary change. Eris is the energy that prods you to "upset the apple cart" in order to learn an important lesson in your spiritual development. Now consider Eris in Aries in the 12th House, *"Your Way of Discord manifests through your independent and heroic quest for and attraction to maverick and individualistic spirituality."* This individual needs to challenge the status quo of spiritual beliefs (12th House) and will feel disrupted when forced to adhere to any belief system that demands obedience. He or

---

[31] The most famous story involving Eris tells how she was left off the invitation list to the wedding of Thetis and Peleus on Mount Olympus. All the other Gods and Goddesses had been invited. Living up to her name, she tossed a Golden Apple into the gathering with the words "To the Most Beautiful" inscribed on it. Hera, Aphrodite, and Athena immediately claimed the apple, which may have been the prize that created the first beauty contest. They turned to Zeus to make the judgment. He may have been a philanderer, but he was no fool. So he gave the task to a schmuck human, Paris, who decided in favor of Aphrodite, so he could get the most beautiful woman in the world. Helen, that woman, happened to be married and became "the face that launched a thousand ships" (from Greece to Troy). Helen was married to a Greek King, Menalaus, who did not take kindly to having his wife stolen. Thus, the Judgment of Paris became the beauty contest decision that started the Trojan War.

she could be a spiritual activist, but one without the agenda to create a following. His or her spiritual independence will likely bother, or disrupt, those people around him or her so they can be charged to do the necessary spiritual work they need at the time.

♀⃗	Eris	Aries	♈	1	Your Way of Disruption manifests through your independent and heroic quest for and attraction to maverick and individualistic identity development.
♀⃗	Eris	Aries	♈	2	Your Way of Disruption manifests through your independent and heroic quest for and attraction to maverick and individualistic values and ways to meet your needs.
♀⃗	Eris	Aries	♈	3	Your Way of Disruption manifests through your independent and heroic quest for and attraction to maverick and individualistic understanding of the world around you.
♀⃗	Eris	Aries	♈	4	Your Way of Disruption manifests through your independent and heroic quest for and attraction to maverick and individualistic emotional caretaking and traditions.
♀⃗	Eris	Aries	♈	5	Your Way of Disruption manifests through your independent and heroic quest for and attraction to maverick and individualistic creative expression.
♀⃗	Eris	Aries	♈	6	Your Way of Disruption manifests through your independent and heroic quest for and attraction to maverick and individualistic service for others.
♀⃗	Eris	Aries	♈	7	Your Way of Disruption manifests through your independent and heroic quest for and attraction to maverick and individualistic life teachers.
♀⃗	Eris	Aries	♈	8	Your Way of Disruption manifests through your independent and heroic quest for and attraction to maverick and individualistic intimate relationships.
♀⃗	Eris	Aries	♈	9	Your Way of Disruption manifests through your independent and heroic quest for and attraction to maverick and individualistic mastership of a body of knowledge.
♀⃗	Eris	Aries	♈	10	Your Way of Disruption manifests through your independent and heroic quest for and attraction to maverick and individualistic accomplishments.
♀⃗	Eris	Aries	♈	11	Your Way of Disruption manifests through your independent and heroic quest for and attraction to maverick and individualistic community.
♀⃗	Eris	Aries	♈	12	Your Way of Disruption manifests through your independent and heroic quest for and attraction to maverick and individualistic spirituality.

♀↓	Eris	Taurus	♉	1	Your Way of Disruption manifests through your steadfast and persistent quest for and attraction to enduring and secure identity development.
♀↓	Eris	Taurus	♉	2	Your Way of Disruption manifests through your steadfast and persistent quest for and attraction to enduring and secure values and ways to meet your needs.
♀↓	Eris	Taurus	♉	3	Your Way of Disruption manifests through your steadfast and persistent quest for and attraction to enduring and secure understanding of the world around you.
♀↓	Eris	Taurus	♉	4	Your Way of Disruption manifests through your steadfast and persistent quest for and attraction to enduring and secure emotional caretaking and traditions.
♀↓	Eris	Taurus	♉	5	Your Way of Disruption manifests through your steadfast and persistent quest for and attraction to enduring and secure creative expression.
♀↓	Eris	Taurus	♉	6	Your Way of Disruption manifests through your steadfast and persistent quest for and attraction to enduring and secure service for others.
♀↓	Eris	Taurus	♉	7	Your Way of Disruption manifests through your steadfast and persistent quest for and attraction to enduring and secure life teachers.
♀↓	Eris	Taurus	♉	8	Your Way of Disruption manifests through your steadfast and persistent quest for and attraction to enduring and secure intimate relationships.
♀↓	Eris	Taurus	♉	9	Your Way of Disruption manifests through your steadfast and persistent quest for and attraction to enduring and secure mastership of a body of knowledge.
♀↓	Eris	Taurus	♉	10	Your Way of Disruption manifests through your steadfast and persistent quest for and attraction to enduring and secure accomplishments.
♀↓	Eris	Taurus	♉	11	Your Way of Disruption manifests through your steadfast and persistent quest for and attraction to enduring and secure community.
♀↓	Eris	Taurus	♉	12	Your Way of Disruption manifests through your steadfast and persistent quest for and attraction to enduring and secure spirituality.

♀	Eris	Gemini	♊	1	Your Way of Disruption manifests through your inquisitive and mentally agile quest for and attraction to ever changing and adaptable identity development.
♀	Eris	Gemini	♊	2	Your Way of Disruption manifests through your inquisitive and mentally agile quest for and attraction to ever changing and adaptable values and ways to meet your needs.
♀	Eris	Gemini	♊	3	Your Way of Disruption manifests through your inquisitive and mentally agile quest for and attraction to ever changing and adaptable understanding of the world around you.
♀	Eris	Gemini	♊	4	Your Way of Disruption manifests through your inquisitive and mentally agile quest for and attraction to ever changing and adaptable emotional caretaking and traditions.
♀	Eris	Gemini	♊	5	Your Way of Disruption manifests through your inquisitive and mentally agile quest for and attraction to ever changing and adaptable creative expression.
♀	Eris	Gemini	♊	6	Your Way of Disruption manifests through your inquisitive and mentally agile quest for and attraction to ever changing and adaptable service for others.
♀	Eris	Gemini	♊	7	Your Way of Disruption manifests through your inquisitive and mentally agile quest for and attraction to ever changing and adaptable life teachers.
♀	Eris	Gemini	♊	8	Your Way of Disruption manifests through your inquisitive and mentally agile quest for and attraction to ever changing and adaptable intimate relationships.
♀	Eris	Gemini	♊	9	Your Way of Disruption manifests through your inquisitive and mentally agile quest for and attraction to ever changing and adaptable mastership of a body of knowledge.
♀	Eris	Gemini	♊	10	Your Way of Disruption manifests through your inquisitive and mentally agile quest for and attraction to ever changing and adaptable accomplishments.
♀	Eris	Gemini	♊	11	Your Way of Disruption manifests through your inquisitive and mentally agile quest for and attraction to ever changing and adaptable community.
♀	Eris	Gemini	♊	12	Your Way of Disruption manifests through your inquisitive and mentally agile quest for and attraction to ever changing and adaptable spirituality.

♀ (Eris)	Eris	Cancer	♋	1	Your Way of Disruption manifests through your emotional and caring quest for and attraction to nurturing and supportive identity development.
♀ (Eris)	Eris	Cancer	♋	2	Your Way of Disruption manifests through your emotional and caring quest for and attraction to nurturing and supportive values and ways to meet your needs.
♀ (Eris)	Eris	Cancer	♋	3	Your Way of Disruption manifests through your emotional and caring quest for and attraction to nurturing and supportive understanding of the world around you.
♀ (Eris)	Eris	Cancer	♋	4	Your Way of Disruption manifests through your emotional and caring quest for and attraction to nurturing and supportive emotional caretaking and traditions.
♀ (Eris)	Eris	Cancer	♋	5	Your Way of Disruption manifests through your emotional and caring quest for and attraction to nurturing and supportive creative expression.
♀ (Eris)	Eris	Cancer	♋	6	Your Way of Disruption manifests through your emotional and caring quest for and attraction to nurturing and supportive service for others.
♀ (Eris)	Eris	Cancer	♋	7	Your Way of Disruption manifests through your emotional and caring quest for and attraction to nurturing and supportive life teachers.
♀ (Eris)	Eris	Cancer	♋	8	Your Way of Disruption manifests through your emotional and caring quest for and attraction to nurturing and supportive intimate relationships.
♀ (Eris)	Eris	Cancer	♋	9	Your Way of Disruption manifests through your emotional and caring quest for and attraction to nurturing and supportive mastership of a body of knowledge.
♀ (Eris)	Eris	Cancer	♋	10	Your Way of Disruption manifests through your emotional and caring quest for and attraction to nurturing and supportive accomplishments.
♀ (Eris)	Eris	Cancer	♋	11	Your Way of Disruption manifests through your emotional and caring quest for and attraction to nurturing and supportive community.
♀ (Eris)	Eris	Cancer	♋	12	Your Way of Disruption manifests through your emotional and caring quest for and attraction to nurturing and supportive spirituality.

♀↓	Eris	Leo	♌	1	Your Way of Disruption manifests through your energetic and dramatic quest for and attraction to creative and romantic identity development.
♀↓	Eris	Leo	♌	2	Your Way of Disruption manifests through your energetic and dramatic quest for and attraction to creative and romantic values and ways to meet your needs.
♀↓	Eris	Leo	♌	3	Your Way of Disruption manifests through your energetic and dramatic quest for and attraction to creative and romantic understanding of the world around you.
♀↓	Eris	Leo	♌	4	Your Way of Disruption manifests through your energetic and dramatic quest for and attraction to creative and romantic emotional caretaking and traditions.
♀↓	Eris	Leo	♌	5	Your Way of Disruption manifests through your energetic and dramatic quest for and attraction to creative and romantic creative expression.
♀↓	Eris	Leo	♌	6	Your Way of Disruption manifests through your energetic and dramatic quest for and attraction to creative and romantic service for others.
♀↓	Eris	Leo	♌	7	Your Way of Disruption manifests through your energetic and dramatic quest for and attraction to creative and romantic life teachers.
♀↓	Eris	Leo	♌	8	Your Way of Disruption manifests through your energetic and dramatic quest for and attraction to creative and romantic intimate relationships.
♀↓	Eris	Leo	♌	9	Your Way of Disruption manifests through your energetic and dramatic quest for and attraction to creative and romantic mastership of a body of knowledge.
♀↓	Eris	Leo	♌	10	Your Way of Disruption manifests through your energetic and dramatic quest for and attraction to creative and romantic accomplishments.
♀↓	Eris	Leo	♌	11	Your Way of Disruption manifests through your energetic and dramatic quest for and attraction to creative and romantic community.
♀↓	Eris	Leo	♌	12	Your Way of Disruption manifests through your energetic and dramatic quest for and attraction to creative and romantic spirituality.

	Eris	Virgo	♍	1	Your Way of Disruption manifests through your critically-minded and methodical quest for and attraction to meticulous and practical identity development.
	Eris	Virgo	♍	2	Your Way of Disruption manifests through your critically-minded and methodical quest for and attraction to meticulous and practical values and ways to meet your needs.
	Eris	Virgo	♍	3	Your Way of Disruption manifests through your critically-minded and methodical quest for and attraction to meticulous and practical understanding of the world around you.
	Eris	Virgo	♍	4	Your Way of Disruption manifests through your critically-minded and methodical quest for and attraction to meticulous and practical emotional caretaking and traditions.
	Eris	Virgo	♍	5	Your Way of Disruption manifests through your critically-minded and methodical quest for and attraction to meticulous and practical creative expression.
	Eris	Virgo	♍	6	Your Way of Disruption manifests through your critically-minded and methodical quest for and attraction to meticulous and practical service for others.
	Eris	Virgo	♍	7	Your Way of Disruption manifests through your critically-minded and methodical quest for and attraction to meticulous and practical life teachers.
	Eris	Virgo	♍	8	Your Way of Disruption manifests through your critically-minded and methodical quest for and attraction to meticulous and practical intimate relationships.
	Eris	Virgo	♍	9	Your Way of Disruption manifests through your critically-minded and methodical quest for and attraction to meticulous and practical mastership of a body of knowledge.
	Eris	Virgo	♍	10	Your Way of Disruption manifests through your critically-minded and methodical quest for and attraction to meticulous and practical accomplishments.
	Eris	Virgo	♍	11	Your Way of Disruption manifests through your critically-minded and methodical quest for and attraction to meticulous and practical community.
	Eris	Virgo	♍	12	Your Way of Disruption manifests through your critically-minded and methodical quest for and attraction to meticulous and practical spirituality.

Astrology Unlocked by Philip Young, PhD

♀	Eris	Libra	♎	1	Your Way of Disruption manifests through your analytical and balanced quest for and attraction to harmonious and logical identity development.
♀	Eris	Libra	♎	2	Your Way of Disruption manifests through your analytical and balanced quest for and attraction to harmonious and logical values and ways to meet your needs.
♀	Eris	Libra	♎	3	Your Way of Disruption manifests through your analytical and balanced quest for and attraction to harmonious and logical understanding of the world around you.
♀	Eris	Libra	♎	4	Your Way of Disruption manifests through your analytical and balanced quest for and attraction to harmonious and logical emotional caretaking and traditions.
♀	Eris	Libra	♎	5	Your Way of Disruption manifests through your analytical and balanced quest for and attraction to harmonious and logical creative expression.
♀	Eris	Libra	♎	6	Your Way of Disruption manifests through your analytical and balanced quest for and attraction to harmonious and logical service for others.
♀	Eris	Libra	♎	7	Your Way of Disruption manifests through your analytical and balanced quest for and attraction to harmonious and logical life teachers.
♀	Eris	Libra	♎	8	Your Way of Disruption manifests through your analytical and balanced quest for and attraction to harmonious and logical intimate relationships.
♀	Eris	Libra	♎	9	Your Way of Disruption manifests through your analytical and balanced quest for and attraction to harmonious and logical mastership of a body of knowledge.
♀	Eris	Libra	♎	10	Your Way of Disruption manifests through your analytical and balanced quest for and attraction to harmonious and logical accomplishments.
♀	Eris	Libra	♎	11	Your Way of Disruption manifests through your analytical and balanced quest for and attraction to harmonious and logical community.
♀	Eris	Libra	♎	12	Your Way of Disruption manifests through your analytical and balanced quest for and attraction to harmonious and logical spirituality.

♀	Eris	Scorpio	♏	1	Your Way of Disruption manifests through your intense and truth seeking quest for and attraction to penetrating and emotionally transformative identity development.
♀	Eris	Scorpio	♏	2	Your Way of Disruption manifests through your intense and truth seeking quest for and attraction to penetrating and emotionally transformative values and ways to meet your needs.
♀	Eris	Scorpio	♏	3	Your Way of Disruption manifests through your intense and truth seeking quest for and attraction to penetrating and emotionally transformative understanding of the world around you.
♀	Eris	Scorpio	♏	4	Your Way of Disruption manifests through your intense and truth seeking quest for and attraction to penetrating and emotionally transformative emotional caretaking and traditions.
♀	Eris	Scorpio	♏	5	Your Way of Disruption manifests through your intense and truth seeking quest for and attraction to penetrating and emotionally transformative creative expression.
♀	Eris	Scorpio	♏	6	Your Way of Disruption manifests through your intense and truth seeking quest for and attraction to penetrating and emotionally transformative service for others.
♀	Eris	Scorpio	♏	7	Your Way of Disruption manifests through your intense and truth seeking quest for and attraction to penetrating and emotionally transformative life teachers.
♀	Eris	Scorpio	♏	8	Your Way of Disruption manifests through your intense and truth seeking quest for and attraction to penetrating and emotionally transformative intimate relationships.
♀	Eris	Scorpio	♏	9	Your Way of Disruption manifests through your intense and truth seeking quest for and attraction to penetrating and emotionally transformative mastership of a body of knowledge.
♀	Eris	Scorpio	♏	10	Your Way of Disruption manifests through your intense and truth seeking quest for and attraction to penetrating and emotionally transformative accomplishments.
♀	Eris	Scorpio	♏	11	Your Way of Disruption manifests through your intense and truth seeking quest for and attraction to penetrating and emotionally transformative community.
♀	Eris	Scorpio	♏	12	Your Way of Disruption manifests through your intense and truth seeking quest for and attraction to penetrating and emotionally transformative spirituality.

♀ (Eris)	Eris	Sagittarius	↗	1	Your Way of Disruption manifests through your wide-ranging and open-minded quest for and attraction to experiential and risk-taking identity development.
♀ (Eris)	Eris	Sagittarius	↗	2	Your Way of Disruption manifests through your wide-ranging and open-minded quest for and attraction to experiential and risk-taking values and ways to meet your needs.
♀ (Eris)	Eris	Sagittarius	↗	3	Your Way of Disruption manifests through your wide-ranging and open-minded quest for and attraction to experiential and risk-taking understanding of the world around you.
♀ (Eris)	Eris	Sagittarius	↗	4	Your Way of Disruption manifests through your wide-ranging and open-minded quest for and attraction to experiential and risk-taking emotional caretaking and traditions.
♀ (Eris)	Eris	Sagittarius	↗	5	Your Way of Disruption manifests through your wide-ranging and open-minded quest for and attraction to experiential and risk-taking creative expression.
♀ (Eris)	Eris	Sagittarius	↗	6	Your Way of Disruption manifests through your wide-ranging and open-minded quest for and attraction to experiential and risk-taking service for others.
♀ (Eris)	Eris	Sagittarius	↗	7	Your Way of Disruption manifests through your wide-ranging and open-minded quest for and attraction to experiential and risk-taking life teachers.
♀ (Eris)	Eris	Sagittarius	↗	8	Your Way of Disruption manifests through your wide-ranging and open-minded quest for and attraction to experiential and risk-taking intimate relationships.
♀ (Eris)	Eris	Sagittarius	↗	9	Your Way of Disruption manifests through your wide-ranging and open-minded quest for and attraction to experiential and risk-taking mastership of a body of knowledge.
♀ (Eris)	Eris	Sagittarius	↗	10	Your Way of Disruption manifests through your wide-ranging and open-minded quest for and attraction to experiential and risk-taking accomplishments.
♀ (Eris)	Eris	Sagittarius	↗	11	Your Way of Disruption manifests through your wide-ranging and open-minded quest for and attraction to experiential and risk-taking community.
♀ (Eris)	Eris	Sagittarius	↗	12	Your Way of Disruption manifests through your wide-ranging and open-minded quest for and attraction to experiential and risk-taking spirituality.

	Eris	Capricorn	♑	1	Your Way of Disruption manifests through your goal-driven and focused quest for and attraction to results-oriented and successful identity development.
♀	Eris	Capricorn	♑	2	Your Way of Disruption manifests through your goal-driven and focused quest for and attraction to results-oriented and successful values and ways to meet your needs.
♀	Eris	Capricorn	♑	3	Your Way of Disruption manifests through your goal-driven and focused quest for and attraction to results-oriented and successful understanding of the world around you.
♀	Eris	Capricorn	♑	4	Your Way of Disruption manifests through your goal-driven and focused quest for and attraction to results-oriented and successful emotional caretaking and traditions.
♀	Eris	Capricorn	♑	5	Your Way of Disruption manifests through your goal-driven and focused quest for and attraction to results-oriented and successful creative expression.
♀	Eris	Capricorn	♑	6	Your Way of Disruption manifests through your goal-driven and focused quest for and attraction to results-oriented and successful service for others.
♀	Eris	Capricorn	♑	7	Your Way of Disruption manifests through your goal-driven and focused quest for and attraction to results-oriented and successful life teachers.
♀	Eris	Capricorn	♑	8	Your Way of Disruption manifests through your goal-driven and focused quest for and attraction to results-oriented and successful intimate relationships.
♀	Eris	Capricorn	♑	9	Your Way of Disruption manifests through your goal-driven and focused quest for and attraction to results-oriented and successful mastership of a body of knowledge.
♀	Eris	Capricorn	♑	10	Your Way of Disruption manifests through your goal-driven and focused quest for and attraction to results-oriented and successful accomplishments.
♀	Eris	Capricorn	♑	11	Your Way of Disruption manifests through your goal-driven and focused quest for and attraction to results-oriented and successful community.
♀	Eris	Capricorn	♑	12	Your Way of Disruption manifests through your goal-driven and focused quest for and attraction to results-oriented and successful spirituality.

	Eris	Aquarius	♒	1	Your Way of Disruption manifests through your unconventional and idealistic quest for and attraction to authentic and non-traditional identity development.
♀	Eris	Aquarius	♒	2	Your Way of Disruption manifests through your unconventional and idealistic quest for and attraction to authentic and non-traditional values and ways to meet your needs.
♀	Eris	Aquarius	♒	3	Your Way of Disruption manifests through your unconventional and idealistic quest for and attraction to authentic and non-traditional understanding of the world around you.
♀	Eris	Aquarius	♒	4	Your Way of Disruption manifests through your unconventional and idealistic quest for and attraction to authentic and non-traditional emotional caretaking and traditions.
♀	Eris	Aquarius	♒	5	Your Way of Disruption manifests through your unconventional and idealistic quest for and attraction to authentic and non-traditional creative expression.
♀	Eris	Aquarius	♒	6	Your Way of Disruption manifests through your unconventional and idealistic quest for and attraction to authentic and non-traditional service for others.
♀	Eris	Aquarius	♒	7	Your Way of Disruption manifests through your unconventional and idealistic quest for and attraction to authentic and non-traditional life teachers.
♀	Eris	Aquarius	♒	8	Your Way of Disruption manifests through your unconventional and idealistic quest for and attraction to authentic and non-traditional intimate relationships.
♀	Eris	Aquarius	♒	9	Your Way of Disruption manifests through your unconventional and idealistic quest for and attraction to authentic and non-traditional mastership of a body of knowledge.
♀	Eris	Aquarius	♒	10	Your Way of Disruption manifests through your unconventional and idealistic quest for and attraction to authentic and non-traditional accomplishments.
♀	Eris	Aquarius	♒	11	Your Way of Disruption manifests through your unconventional and idealistic quest for and attraction to authentic and non-traditional community.
♀	Eris	Aquarius	♒	12	Your Way of Disruption manifests through your unconventional and idealistic quest for and attraction to authentic and non-traditional spirituality.

♀↓	Eris	Pisces	♓	1	Your Way of Disruption manifests through your imaginative and faithful quest for and attraction to consciousness-raising and soulful identity development.
♀↓	Eris	Pisces	♓	2	Your Way of Disruption manifests through your imaginative and faithful quest for and attraction to consciousness-raising and soulful values and ways to meet your needs.
♀↓	Eris	Pisces	♓	3	Your Way of Disruption manifests through your imaginative and faithful quest for and attraction to consciousness-raising and soulful understanding of the world around you.
♀↓	Eris	Pisces	♓	4	Your Way of Disruption manifests through your imaginative and faithful quest for and attraction to consciousness-raising and soulful emotional caretaking and traditions.
♀↓	Eris	Pisces	♓	5	Your Way of Disruption manifests through your imaginative and faithful quest for and attraction to consciousness-raising and soulful creative expression.
♀↓	Eris	Pisces	♓	6	Your Way of Disruption manifests through your imaginative and faithful quest for and attraction to consciousness-raising and soulful service for others.
♀↓	Eris	Pisces	♓	7	Your Way of Disruption manifests through your imaginative and faithful quest for and attraction to consciousness-raising and soulful life teachers.
♀↓	Eris	Pisces	♓	8	Your Way of Disruption manifests through your imaginative and faithful quest for and attraction to consciousness-raising and soulful intimate relationships.
♀↓	Eris	Pisces	♓	9	Your Way of Disruption manifests through your imaginative and faithful quest for and attraction to consciousness-raising and soulful mastership of a body of knowledge.
♀↓	Eris	Pisces	♓	10	Your Way of Disruption manifests through your imaginative and faithful quest for and attraction to consciousness-raising and soulful accomplishments.
♀↓	Eris	Pisces	♓	11	Your Way of Disruption manifests through your imaginative and faithful quest for and attraction to consciousness-raising and soulful community.
♀↓	Eris	Pisces	♓	12	Your Way of Disruption manifests through your imaginative and faithful quest for and attraction to consciousness-raising and soulful spirituality.

Astraea | $\frac{0}{0}$

Energy Point Type: **Asteroid**

Co-Rules Sign: **Libra**

Co-Rules House: **7th**

Element: **Air**

Key Phrase: **Way of Community**

Astraea represents your Way of Community. Its placement in Sign and House reveals the type of energy that you use to find your community and how you best fit in with the community you seek. In my case my Way of Community is expressed through Air (Aquarius) in my quest for my roots (4th House). Air's expression is analytical, strategic, and curious. In Aquarius the Element acts unconventionally, authentically, and scientifically. So, my key phrase is *"Your Way of Community manifests through your unconventional and idealistic quest for and attraction to authentic and non-traditional emotional caretaking and traditions."* In short, I am seeking an unconventional family to give me the opportunity to express my authentic self and build my community.

When you look up your Astraea in the Sign and House formula, consider how and where you want to belong and how you want to be part of a group. If the energy is in Water, then you should connect mainly through your feelings; if Earth, connect through doing for others; if Air, connect through intellect and verbal communication; and if Fire, connect through creativity and activity. Consider Astraea in Capricorn in the 9th House, *"Your Way of Community manifests through your goal-driven and focused quest for and attraction to results-oriented and successful mastership of a body of knowledge."* The individual with this placement will be well-suited to be part of the academic, university (9th House) world, not so much as a professor, but more as a manager/administrator (Capricorn).

	Astraea	Aries	♈	1	Your Way of Community manifests through your independent and heroic quest for and attraction to maverick and individualistic identity development.
	Astraea	Aries	♈	2	Your Way of Community manifests through your independent and heroic quest for and attraction to maverick and individualistic values and ways to meet your needs.
	Astraea	Aries	♈	3	Your Way of Community manifests through your independent and heroic quest for and attraction to maverick and individualistic understanding of the world around you.
	Astraea	Aries	♈	4	Your Way of Community manifests through your independent and heroic quest for and attraction to maverick and individualistic emotional caretaking and traditions.
	Astraea	Aries	♈	5	Your Way of Community manifests through your independent and heroic quest for and attraction to maverick and individualistic creative expression.
	Astraea	Aries	♈	6	Your Way of Community manifests through your independent and heroic quest for and attraction to maverick and individualistic service for others.
	Astraea	Aries	♈	7	Your Way of Community manifests through your independent and heroic quest for and attraction to maverick and individualistic life teachers.
	Astraea	Aries	♈	8	Your Way of Community manifests through your independent and heroic quest for and attraction to maverick and individualistic intimate relationships.
	Astraea	Aries	♈	9	Your Way of Community manifests through your independent and heroic quest for and attraction to maverick and individualistic mastership of a body of knowledge.
	Astraea	Aries	♈	10	Your Way of Community manifests through your independent and heroic quest for and attraction to maverick and individualistic accomplishments.
	Astraea	Aries	♈	11	Your Way of Community manifests through your independent and heroic quest for and attraction to maverick and individualistic community.
	Astraea	Aries	♈	12	Your Way of Community manifests through your independent and heroic quest for and attraction to maverick and individualistic spirituality.

	Astraea	Taurus	♉	1	Your Way of Community manifests through your steadfast and persistent quest for and attraction to enduring and secure identity development.
	Astraea	Taurus	♉	2	Your Way of Community manifests through your steadfast and persistent quest for and attraction to enduring and secure values and ways to meet your needs.
	Astraea	Taurus	♉	3	Your Way of Community manifests through your steadfast and persistent quest for and attraction to enduring and secure understanding of the world around you.
	Astraea	Taurus	♉	4	Your Way of Community manifests through your steadfast and persistent quest for and attraction to enduring and secure emotional caretaking and traditions.
	Astraea	Taurus	♉	5	Your Way of Community manifests through your steadfast and persistent quest for and attraction to enduring and secure creative expression.
	Astraea	Taurus	♉	6	Your Way of Community manifests through your steadfast and persistent quest for and attraction to enduring and secure service for others.
	Astraea	Taurus	♉	7	Your Way of Community manifests through your steadfast and persistent quest for and attraction to enduring and secure life teachers.
	Astraea	Taurus	♉	8	Your Way of Community manifests through your steadfast and persistent quest for and attraction to enduring and secure intimate relationships.
	Astraea	Taurus	♉	9	Your Way of Community manifests through your steadfast and persistent quest for and attraction to enduring and secure mastership of a body of knowledge.
	Astraea	Taurus	♉	10	Your Way of Community manifests through your steadfast and persistent quest for and attraction to enduring and secure accomplishments.
	Astraea	Taurus	♉	11	Your Way of Community manifests through your steadfast and persistent quest for and attraction to enduring and secure community.
	Astraea	Taurus	♉	12	Your Way of Community manifests through your steadfast and persistent quest for and attraction to enduring and secure spirituality.

	Astraea	Gemini	♊	1	Your Way of Community manifests through your inquisitive and mentally agile quest for and attraction to ever changing and adaptable identity development.
	Astraea	Gemini	♊	2	Your Way of Community manifests through your inquisitive and mentally agile quest for and attraction to ever changing and adaptable values and ways to meet your needs.
	Astraea	Gemini	♊	3	Your Way of Community manifests through your inquisitive and mentally agile quest for and attraction to ever changing and adaptable understanding of the world around you.
	Astraea	Gemini	♊	4	Your Way of Community manifests through your inquisitive and mentally agile quest for and attraction to ever changing and adaptable emotional caretaking and traditions.
	Astraea	Gemini	♊	5	Your Way of Community manifests through your inquisitive and mentally agile quest for and attraction to ever changing and adaptable creative expression.
	Astraea	Gemini	♊	6	Your Way of Community manifests through your inquisitive and mentally agile quest for and attraction to ever changing and adaptable service for others.
	Astraea	Gemini	♊	7	Your Way of Community manifests through your inquisitive and mentally agile quest for and attraction to ever changing and adaptable life teachers.
	Astraea	Gemini	♊	8	Your Way of Community manifests through your inquisitive and mentally agile quest for and attraction to ever changing and adaptable intimate relationships.
	Astraea	Gemini	♊	9	Your Way of Community manifests through your inquisitive and mentally agile quest for and attraction to ever changing and adaptable mastership of a body of knowledge.
	Astraea	Gemini	♊	10	Your Way of Community manifests through your inquisitive and mentally agile quest for and attraction to ever changing and adaptable accomplishments.
	Astraea	Gemini	♊	11	Your Way of Community manifests through your inquisitive and mentally agile quest for and attraction to ever changing and adaptable community.
	Astraea	Gemini	♊	12	Your Way of Community manifests through your inquisitive and mentally agile quest for and attraction to ever changing and adaptable spirituality.

	Astraea	Cancer	♋	1	Your Way of Community manifests through your emotional and caring quest for and attraction to nurturing and supportive identity development.
	Astraea	Cancer	♋	2	Your Way of Community manifests through your emotional and caring quest for and attraction to nurturing and supportive values and ways to meet your needs.
	Astraea	Cancer	♋	3	Your Way of Community manifests through your emotional and caring quest for and attraction to nurturing and supportive understanding of the world around you.
	Astraea	Cancer	♋	4	Your Way of Community manifests through your emotional and caring quest for and attraction to nurturing and supportive emotional caretaking and traditions.
	Astraea	Cancer	♋	5	Your Way of Community manifests through your emotional and caring quest for and attraction to nurturing and supportive creative expression.
	Astraea	Cancer	♋	6	Your Way of Community manifests through your emotional and caring quest for and attraction to nurturing and supportive service for others.
	Astraea	Cancer	♋	7	Your Way of Community manifests through your emotional and caring quest for and attraction to nurturing and supportive life teachers.
	Astraea	Cancer	♋	8	Your Way of Community manifests through your emotional and caring quest for and attraction to nurturing and supportive intimate relationships.
	Astraea	Cancer	♋	9	Your Way of Community manifests through your emotional and caring quest for and attraction to nurturing and supportive mastership of a body of knowledge.
	Astraea	Cancer	♋	10	Your Way of Community manifests through your emotional and caring quest for and attraction to nurturing and supportive accomplishments.
	Astraea	Cancer	♋	11	Your Way of Community manifests through your emotional and caring quest for and attraction to nurturing and supportive community.
	Astraea	Cancer	♋	12	Your Way of Community manifests through your emotional and caring quest for and attraction to nurturing and supportive spirituality.

355

	Astraea	Leo	♌	1	Your Way of Community manifests through your energetic and dramatic quest for and attraction to creative and romantic identity development.
	Astraea	Leo	♌	2	Your Way of Community manifests through your energetic and dramatic quest for and attraction to creative and romantic values and ways to meet your needs.
	Astraea	Leo	♌	3	Your Way of Community manifests through your energetic and dramatic quest for and attraction to creative and romantic understanding of the world around you.
	Astraea	Leo	♌	4	Your Way of Community manifests through your energetic and dramatic quest for and attraction to creative and romantic emotional caretaking and traditions.
	Astraea	Leo	♌	5	Your Way of Community manifests through your energetic and dramatic quest for and attraction to creative and romantic creative expression.
	Astraea	Leo	♌	6	Your Way of Community manifests through your energetic and dramatic quest for and attraction to creative and romantic service for others.
	Astraea	Leo	♌	7	Your Way of Community manifests through your energetic and dramatic quest for and attraction to creative and romantic life teachers.
	Astraea	Leo	♌	8	Your Way of Community manifests through your energetic and dramatic quest for and attraction to creative and romantic intimate relationships.
	Astraea	Leo	♌	9	Your Way of Community manifests through your energetic and dramatic quest for and attraction to creative and romantic mastership of a body of knowledge.
	Astraea	Leo	♌	10	Your Way of Community manifests through your energetic and dramatic quest for and attraction to creative and romantic accomplishments.
	Astraea	Leo	♌	11	Your Way of Community manifests through your energetic and dramatic quest for and attraction to creative and romantic community.
	Astraea	Leo	♌	12	Your Way of Community manifests through your energetic and dramatic quest for and attraction to creative and romantic spirituality.

	Astraea	Virgo	♍	1	Your Way of Community manifests through your critically-minded and methodical quest for and attraction to meticulous and practical identity development.
	Astraea	Virgo	♍	2	Your Way of Community manifests through your critically-minded and methodical quest for and attraction to meticulous and practical values and ways to meet your needs.
	Astraea	Virgo	♍	3	Your Way of Community manifests through your critically-minded and methodical quest for and attraction to meticulous and practical understanding of the world around you.
	Astraea	Virgo	♍	4	Your Way of Community manifests through your critically-minded and methodical quest for and attraction to meticulous and practical emotional caretaking and traditions.
	Astraea	Virgo	♍	5	Your Way of Community manifests through your critically-minded and methodical quest for and attraction to meticulous and practical creative expression.
	Astraea	Virgo	♍	6	Your Way of Community manifests through your critically-minded and methodical quest for and attraction to meticulous and practical service for others.
	Astraea	Virgo	♍	7	Your Way of Community manifests through your critically-minded and methodical quest for and attraction to meticulous and practical life teachers.
	Astraea	Virgo	♍	8	Your Way of Community manifests through your critically-minded and methodical quest for and attraction to meticulous and practical intimate relationships.
	Astraea	Virgo	♍	9	Your Way of Community manifests through your critically-minded and methodical quest for and attraction to meticulous and practical mastership of a body of knowledge.
	Astraea	Virgo	♍	10	Your Way of Community manifests through your critically-minded and methodical quest for and attraction to meticulous and practical accomplishments.
	Astraea	Virgo	♍	11	Your Way of Community manifests through your critically-minded and methodical quest for and attraction to meticulous and practical community.
	Astraea	Virgo	♍	12	Your Way of Community manifests through your critically-minded and methodical quest for and attraction to meticulous and practical spirituality.

357

	Astraea	Libra	♎	1	Your Way of Community manifests through your analytical and balanced quest for and attraction to harmonious and logical identity development.
	Astraea	Libra	♎	2	Your Way of Community manifests through your analytical and balanced quest for and attraction to harmonious and logical values and ways to meet your needs.
	Astraea	Libra	♎	3	Your Way of Community manifests through your analytical and balanced quest for and attraction to harmonious and logical understanding of the world around you.
	Astraea	Libra	♎	4	Your Way of Community manifests through your analytical and balanced quest for and attraction to harmonious and logical emotional caretaking and traditions.
	Astraea	Libra	♎	5	Your Way of Community manifests through your analytical and balanced quest for and attraction to harmonious and logical creative expression.
	Astraea	Libra	♎	6	Your Way of Community manifests through your analytical and balanced quest for and attraction to harmonious and logical service for others.
	Astraea	Libra	♎	7	Your Way of Community manifests through your analytical and balanced quest for and attraction to harmonious and logical life teachers.
	Astraea	Libra	♎	8	Your Way of Community manifests through your analytical and balanced quest for and attraction to harmonious and logical intimate relationships.
	Astraea	Libra	♎	9	Your Way of Community manifests through your analytical and balanced quest for and attraction to harmonious and logical mastership of a body of knowledge.
	Astraea	Libra	♎	10	Your Way of Community manifests through your analytical and balanced quest for and attraction to harmonious and logical accomplishments.
	Astraea	Libra	♎	11	Your Way of Community manifests through your analytical and balanced quest for and attraction to harmonious and logical community.
	Astraea	Libra	♎	12	Your Way of Community manifests through your analytical and balanced quest for and attraction to harmonious and logical spirituality.

⅙	Astraea	Scorpio	♏	1	Your Way of Community manifests through your intense and truth seeking quest for and attraction to penetrating and emotionally transformative identity development.
⅙	Astraea	Scorpio	♏	2	Your Way of Community manifests through your intense and truth seeking quest for and attraction to penetrating and emotionally transformative values and ways to meet your needs.
⅙	Astraea	Scorpio	♏	3	Your Way of Community manifests through your intense and truth seeking quest for and attraction to penetrating and emotionally transformative understanding of the world around you.
⅙	Astraea	Scorpio	♏	4	Your Way of Community manifests through your intense and truth seeking quest for and attraction to penetrating and emotionally transformative emotional caretaking and traditions.
⅙	Astraea	Scorpio	♏	5	Your Way of Community manifests through your intense and truth seeking quest for and attraction to penetrating and emotionally transformative creative expression.
⅙	Astraea	Scorpio	♏	6	Your Way of Community manifests through your intense and truth seeking quest for and attraction to penetrating and emotionally transformative service for others.
⅙	Astraea	Scorpio	♏	7	Your Way of Community manifests through your intense and truth seeking quest for and attraction to penetrating and emotionally transformative life teachers.
⅙	Astraea	Scorpio	♏	8	Your Way of Community manifests through your intense and truth seeking quest for and attraction to penetrating and emotionally transformative intimate relationships.
⅙	Astraea	Scorpio	♏	9	Your Way of Community manifests through your intense and truth seeking quest for and attraction to penetrating and emotionally transformative mastership of a body of knowledge.
⅙	Astraea	Scorpio	♏	10	Your Way of Community manifests through your intense and truth seeking quest for and attraction to penetrating and emotionally transformative accomplishments.
⅙	Astraea	Scorpio	♏	11	Your Way of Community manifests through your intense and truth seeking quest for and attraction to penetrating and emotionally transformative community.
⅙	Astraea	Scorpio	♏	12	Your Way of Community manifests through your intense and truth seeking quest for and attraction to penetrating and emotionally transformative spirituality.

	Astraea	Sagittarius	♐	1	Your Way of Community manifests through your wide-ranging and open-minded quest for and attraction to experiential and risk-taking identity development.
	Astraea	Sagittarius	♐	2	Your Way of Community manifests through your wide-ranging and open-minded quest for and attraction to experiential and risk-taking values and ways to meet your needs.
	Astraea	Sagittarius	♐	3	Your Way of Community manifests through your wide-ranging and open-minded quest for and attraction to experiential and risk-taking understanding of the world around you.
	Astraea	Sagittarius	♐	4	Your Way of Community manifests through your wide-ranging and open-minded quest for and attraction to experiential and risk-taking emotional caretaking and traditions.
	Astraea	Sagittarius	♐	5	Your Way of Community manifests through your wide-ranging and open-minded quest for and attraction to experiential and risk-taking creative expression.
	Astraea	Sagittarius	♐	6	Your Way of Community manifests through your wide-ranging and open-minded quest for and attraction to experiential and risk-taking service for others.
	Astraea	Sagittarius	♐	7	Your Way of Community manifests through your wide-ranging and open-minded quest for and attraction to experiential and risk-taking life teachers.
	Astraea	Sagittarius	♐	8	Your Way of Community manifests through your wide-ranging and open-minded quest for and attraction to experiential and risk-taking intimate relationships.
	Astraea	Sagittarius	♐	9	Your Way of Community manifests through your wide-ranging and open-minded quest for and attraction to experiential and risk-taking mastership of a body of knowledge.
	Astraea	Sagittarius	♐	10	Your Way of Community manifests through your wide-ranging and open-minded quest for and attraction to experiential and risk-taking accomplishments.
	Astraea	Sagittarius	♐	11	Your Way of Community manifests through your wide-ranging and open-minded quest for and attraction to experiential and risk-taking community.
	Astraea	Sagittarius	♐	12	Your Way of Community manifests through your wide-ranging and open-minded quest for and attraction to experiential and risk-taking spirituality.

Astrology Unlocked by Philip Young, PhD

	Astraea	Capricorn	♑	1	Your Way of Community manifests through your goal-driven and focused quest for and attraction to results-oriented and successful identity development.
	Astraea	Capricorn	♑	2	Your Way of Community manifests through your goal-driven and focused quest for and attraction to results-oriented and successful values and ways to meet your needs.
	Astraea	Capricorn	♑	3	Your Way of Community manifests through your goal-driven and focused quest for and attraction to results-oriented and successful understanding of the world around you.
	Astraea	Capricorn	♑	4	Your Way of Community manifests through your goal-driven and focused quest for and attraction to results-oriented and successful emotional caretaking and traditions.
	Astraea	Capricorn	♑	5	Your Way of Community manifests through your goal-driven and focused quest for and attraction to results-oriented and successful creative expression.
	Astraea	Capricorn	♑	6	Your Way of Community manifests through your goal-driven and focused quest for and attraction to results-oriented and successful service for others.
	Astraea	Capricorn	♑	7	Your Way of Community manifests through your goal-driven and focused quest for and attraction to results-oriented and successful life teachers.
	Astraea	Capricorn	♑	8	Your Way of Community manifests through your goal-driven and focused quest for and attraction to results-oriented and successful intimate relationships.
	Astraea	Capricorn	♑	9	Your Way of Community manifests through your goal-driven and focused quest for and attraction to results-oriented and successful mastership of a body of knowledge.
	Astraea	Capricorn	♑	10	Your Way of Community manifests through your goal-driven and focused quest for and attraction to results-oriented and successful accomplishments.
	Astraea	Capricorn	♑	11	Your Way of Community manifests through your goal-driven and focused quest for and attraction to results-oriented and successful community.
	Astraea	Capricorn	♑	12	Your Way of Community manifests through your goal-driven and focused quest for and attraction to results-oriented and successful spirituality.

0∫0	Astraea	Aquarius	♒	1	Your Way of Community manifests through your unconventional and idealistic quest for and attraction to authentic and non-traditional identity development.
0∫0	Astraea	Aquarius	♒	2	Your Way of Community manifests through your unconventional and idealistic quest for and attraction to authentic and non-traditional values and ways to meet your needs.
0∫0	Astraea	Aquarius	♒	3	Your Way of Community manifests through your unconventional and idealistic quest for and attraction to authentic and non-traditional understanding of the world around you.
0∫0	Astraea	Aquarius	♒	4	Your Way of Community manifests through your unconventional and idealistic quest for and attraction to authentic and non-traditional emotional caretaking and traditions.
0∫0	Astraea	Aquarius	♒	5	Your Way of Community manifests through your unconventional and idealistic quest for and attraction to authentic and non-traditional creative expression.
0∫0	Astraea	Aquarius	♒	6	Your Way of Community manifests through your unconventional and idealistic quest for and attraction to authentic and non-traditional service for others.
0∫0	Astraea	Aquarius	♒	7	Your Way of Community manifests through your unconventional and idealistic quest for and attraction to authentic and non-traditional life teachers.
0∫0	Astraea	Aquarius	♒	8	Your Way of Community manifests through your unconventional and idealistic quest for and attraction to authentic and non-traditional intimate relationships.
0∫0	Astraea	Aquarius	♒	9	Your Way of Community manifests through your unconventional and idealistic quest for and attraction to authentic and non-traditional mastership of a body of knowledge.
0∫0	Astraea	Aquarius	♒	10	Your Way of Community manifests through your unconventional and idealistic quest for and attraction to authentic and non-traditional accomplishments.
0∫0	Astraea	Aquarius	♒	11	Your Way of Community manifests through your unconventional and idealistic quest for and attraction to authentic and non-traditional community.
0∫0	Astraea	Aquarius	♒	12	Your Way of Community manifests through your unconventional and idealistic quest for and attraction to authentic and non-traditional spirituality.

⚵ $^0/_0$	Astraea	Pisces	♓	1	Your Way of Community manifests through your imaginative and faithful quest for and attraction to consciousness-raising and soulful identity development.
⚵ $^0/_0$	Astraea	Pisces	♓	2	Your Way of Community manifests through your imaginative and faithful quest for and attraction to consciousness-raising and soulful values and ways to meet your needs.
⚵ $^0/_0$	Astraea	Pisces	♓	3	Your Way of Community manifests through your imaginative and faithful quest for and attraction to consciousness-raising and soulful understanding of the world around you.
⚵ $^0/_0$	Astraea	Pisces	♓	4	Your Way of Community manifests through your imaginative and faithful quest for and attraction to consciousness-raising and soulful emotional caretaking and traditions.
⚵ $^0/_0$	Astraea	Pisces	♓	5	Your Way of Community manifests through your imaginative and faithful quest for and attraction to consciousness-raising and soulful creative expression.
⚵ $^0/_0$	Astraea	Pisces	♓	6	Your Way of Community manifests through your imaginative and faithful quest for and attraction to consciousness-raising and soulful service for others.
⚵ $^0/_0$	Astraea	Pisces	♓	7	Your Way of Community manifests through your imaginative and faithful quest for and attraction to consciousness-raising and soulful life teachers.
⚵ $^0/_0$	Astraea	Pisces	♓	8	Your Way of Community manifests through your imaginative and faithful quest for and attraction to consciousness-raising and soulful intimate relationships.
⚵ $^0/_0$	Astraea	Pisces	♓	9	Your Way of Community manifests through your imaginative and faithful quest for and attraction to consciousness-raising and soulful mastership of a body of knowledge.
⚵ $^0/_0$	Astraea	Pisces	♓	10	Your Way of Community manifests through your imaginative and faithful quest for and attraction to consciousness-raising and soulful accomplishments.
⚵ $^0/_0$	Astraea	Pisces	♓	11	Your Way of Community manifests through your imaginative and faithful quest for and attraction to consciousness-raising and soulful community.
⚵ $^0/_0$	Astraea	Pisces	♓	12	Your Way of Community manifests through your imaginative and faithful quest for and attraction to consciousness-raising and soulful spirituality.

363

North Node | ☊

Energy Point Type: **Calculated Point**

No Rulership

Key Phrase: **Stretch Goal**

The North Node represents your Stretch Goal in this lifetime. Its placement in Sign and House reveals how and where we need to grow and engage in new energy and experiences. In my case my Stretch Goal is expressed through Fire (Aries) in my quest for service (6th House). Fire's expression is pioneering, creative, and exploratory. In Aries the Element acts independently, heroically, and aggressively. So, my key phrase is "*Your Stretch Goal manifests through your independent and heroic quest for and attraction to maverick and individualistic service for others.*" In short, I am learning to be an Aries in this lifetime. Even with all the energy I have in Aries in my chart, I am still, "karmicly speaking," an Aries in training.

When you think of the placement of the North Node in your chart, you almost have to think of the goal you fear the most, but know, deep down, you need to face. Your comfort energy will flow from an opposite Element, forcing you to exert real effort to get going properly in the direction of the North Node. Depending on other energy relationships, the effort may be greatly supported or severely challenged. Now consider the North Node in Pisces in the 5th House, "*Your Stretch Goal manifests through your imaginative and faithful quest for and attraction to consciousness-raising and soulful creative expression.*" This individual will need to stretch in the direction of his or her own creativity (5th House), allowing the process to be imaginative, divinely inspired, and full of faith (Pisces). Since this House represents Self-expression, he or she will need to pull away from peer input/pressure and community activities (11th House Virgo). The lesson is to make time for creative work that puts the individual in touch with the divine and his or her dreams.

For more in depth reading about North Node, I recommend purchasing and reading:

- *Karmic Astrology: The Moon's Nodes and Reincarnation (Volume 1)* by Martin Schulman (ISBN: 0877282889)
- *Karmic Astrology: Past Lives, Present Loves* by Ruth Aharoni (ISBN: 9780738709673)
- *Lunar Nodes: Discover Your Soul's Karmic Mission* by Celeste Teal (ISBN: 9780738713373)
- *Yesterday's Sky: Astrology and Reincarnation* by Steven Forrest (ISBN: 0979067731)

♌	North Node	Aries	♈	1	Your Stretch Goal manifests through your independent and heroic quest for and attraction to maverick and individualistic identity development.
♌	North Node	Aries	♈	2	Your Stretch Goal manifests through your independent and heroic quest for and attraction to maverick and individualistic values and ways to meet your needs.
♌	North Node	Aries	♈	3	Your Stretch Goal manifests through your independent and heroic quest for and attraction to maverick and individualistic understanding of the world around you.
♌	North Node	Aries	♈	4	Your Stretch Goal manifests through your independent and heroic quest for and attraction to maverick and individualistic emotional caretaking and traditions.
♌	North Node	Aries	♈	5	Your Stretch Goal manifests through your independent and heroic quest for and attraction to maverick and individualistic creative expression.
♌	North Node	Aries	♈	6	Your Stretch Goal manifests through your independent and heroic quest for and attraction to maverick and individualistic service for others.
♌	North Node	Aries	♈	7	Your Stretch Goal manifests through your independent and heroic quest for and attraction to maverick and individualistic life teachers.
♌	North Node	Aries	♈	8	Your Stretch Goal manifests through your independent and heroic quest for and attraction to maverick and individualistic intimate relationships.
♌	North Node	Aries	♈	9	Your Stretch Goal manifests through your independent and heroic quest for and attraction to maverick and individualistic mastership of a body of knowledge.
♌	North Node	Aries	♈	10	Your Stretch Goal manifests through your independent and heroic quest for and attraction to maverick and individualistic accomplishments.
♌	North Node	Aries	♈	11	Your Stretch Goal manifests through your independent and heroic quest for and attraction to maverick and individualistic community.
♌	North Node	Aries	♈	12	Your Stretch Goal manifests through your independent and heroic quest for and attraction to maverick and individualistic spirituality.

☊	North Node	Taurus	♉	1	Your Stretch Goal manifests through your steadfast and persistent quest for and attraction to enduring and secure identity development.
☊	North Node	Taurus	♉	2	Your Stretch Goal manifests through your steadfast and persistent quest for and attraction to enduring and secure values and ways to meet your needs.
☊	North Node	Taurus	♉	3	Your Stretch Goal manifests through your steadfast and persistent quest for and attraction to enduring and secure understanding of the world around you.
☊	North Node	Taurus	♉	4	Your Stretch Goal manifests through your steadfast and persistent quest for and attraction to enduring and secure emotional caretaking and traditions.
☊	North Node	Taurus	♉	5	Your Stretch Goal manifests through your steadfast and persistent quest for and attraction to enduring and secure creative expression.
☊	North Node	Taurus	♉	6	Your Stretch Goal manifests through your steadfast and persistent quest for and attraction to enduring and secure service for others.
☊	North Node	Taurus	♉	7	Your Stretch Goal manifests through your steadfast and persistent quest for and attraction to enduring and secure life teachers.
☊	North Node	Taurus	♉	8	Your Stretch Goal manifests through your steadfast and persistent quest for and attraction to enduring and secure intimate relationships.
☊	North Node	Taurus	♉	9	Your Stretch Goal manifests through your steadfast and persistent quest for and attraction to enduring and secure mastership of a body of knowledge.
☊	North Node	Taurus	♉	10	Your Stretch Goal manifests through your steadfast and persistent quest for and attraction to enduring and secure accomplishments.
☊	North Node	Taurus	♉	11	Your Stretch Goal manifests through your steadfast and persistent quest for and attraction to enduring and secure community.
☊	North Node	Taurus	♉	12	Your Stretch Goal manifests through your steadfast and persistent quest for and attraction to enduring and secure spirituality.

♌	North Node	Gemini	♊	1	Your Stretch Goal manifests through your inquisitive and mentally agile quest for and attraction to ever changing and adaptable identity development.
♌	North Node	Gemini	♊	2	Your Stretch Goal manifests through your inquisitive and mentally agile quest for and attraction to ever changing and adaptable values and ways to meet your needs.
♌	North Node	Gemini	♊	3	Your Stretch Goal manifests through your inquisitive and mentally agile quest for and attraction to ever changing and adaptable understanding of the world around you.
♌	North Node	Gemini	♊	4	Your Stretch Goal manifests through your inquisitive and mentally agile quest for and attraction to ever changing and adaptable emotional caretaking and traditions.
♌	North Node	Gemini	♊	5	Your Stretch Goal manifests through your inquisitive and mentally agile quest for and attraction to ever changing and adaptable creative expression.
♌	North Node	Gemini	♊	6	Your Stretch Goal manifests through your inquisitive and mentally agile quest for and attraction to ever changing and adaptable service for others.
♌	North Node	Gemini	♊	7	Your Stretch Goal manifests through your inquisitive and mentally agile quest for and attraction to ever changing and adaptable life teachers.
♌	North Node	Gemini	♊	8	Your Stretch Goal manifests through your inquisitive and mentally agile quest for and attraction to ever changing and adaptable intimate relationships.
♌	North Node	Gemini	♊	9	Your Stretch Goal manifests through your inquisitive and mentally agile quest for and attraction to ever changing and adaptable mastership of a body of knowledge.
♌	North Node	Gemini	♊	10	Your Stretch Goal manifests through your inquisitive and mentally agile quest for and attraction to ever changing and adaptable accomplishments.
♌	North Node	Gemini	♊	11	Your Stretch Goal manifests through your inquisitive and mentally agile quest for and attraction to ever changing and adaptable community.
♌	North Node	Gemini	♊	12	Your Stretch Goal manifests through your inquisitive and mentally agile quest for and attraction to ever changing and adaptable spirituality.

♌	North Node	Cancer	♋	1	Your Stretch Goal manifests through your emotional and caring quest for and attraction to nurturing and supportive identity development.
♌	North Node	Cancer	♋	2	Your Stretch Goal manifests through your emotional and caring quest for and attraction to nurturing and supportive values and ways to meet your needs.
♌	North Node	Cancer	♋	3	Your Stretch Goal manifests through your emotional and caring quest for and attraction to nurturing and supportive understanding of the world around you.
♌	North Node	Cancer	♋	4	Your Stretch Goal manifests through your emotional and caring quest for and attraction to nurturing and supportive emotional caretaking and traditions.
♌	North Node	Cancer	♋	5	Your Stretch Goal manifests through your emotional and caring quest for and attraction to nurturing and supportive creative expression.
♌	North Node	Cancer	♋	6	Your Stretch Goal manifests through your emotional and caring quest for and attraction to nurturing and supportive service for others.
♌	North Node	Cancer	♋	7	Your Stretch Goal manifests through your emotional and caring quest for and attraction to nurturing and supportive life teachers.
♌	North Node	Cancer	♋	8	Your Stretch Goal manifests through your emotional and caring quest for and attraction to nurturing and supportive intimate relationships.
♌	North Node	Cancer	♋	9	Your Stretch Goal manifests through your emotional and caring quest for and attraction to nurturing and supportive mastership of a body of knowledge.
♌	North Node	Cancer	♋	10	Your Stretch Goal manifests through your emotional and caring quest for and attraction to nurturing and supportive accomplishments.
♌	North Node	Cancer	♋	11	Your Stretch Goal manifests through your emotional and caring quest for and attraction to nurturing and supportive community.
♌	North Node	Cancer	♋	12	Your Stretch Goal manifests through your emotional and caring quest for and attraction to nurturing and supportive spirituality.

♌	North Node	Leo	♌	1	Your Stretch Goal manifests through your energetic and dramatic quest for and attraction to creative and romantic identity development.
♌	North Node	Leo	♌	2	Your Stretch Goal manifests through your energetic and dramatic quest for and attraction to creative and romantic values and ways to meet your needs.
♌	North Node	Leo	♌	3	Your Stretch Goal manifests through your energetic and dramatic quest for and attraction to creative and romantic understanding of the world around you.
♌	North Node	Leo	♌	4	Your Stretch Goal manifests through your energetic and dramatic quest for and attraction to creative and romantic emotional caretaking and traditions.
♌	North Node	Leo	♌	5	Your Stretch Goal manifests through your energetic and dramatic quest for and attraction to creative and romantic creative expression.
♌	North Node	Leo	♌	6	Your Stretch Goal manifests through your energetic and dramatic quest for and attraction to creative and romantic service for others.
♌	North Node	Leo	♌	7	Your Stretch Goal manifests through your energetic and dramatic quest for and attraction to creative and romantic life teachers.
♌	North Node	Leo	♌	8	Your Stretch Goal manifests through your energetic and dramatic quest for and attraction to creative and romantic intimate relationships.
♌	North Node	Leo	♌	9	Your Stretch Goal manifests through your energetic and dramatic quest for and attraction to creative and romantic mastership of a body of knowledge.
♌	North Node	Leo	♌	10	Your Stretch Goal manifests through your energetic and dramatic quest for and attraction to creative and romantic accomplishments.
♌	North Node	Leo	♌	11	Your Stretch Goal manifests through your energetic and dramatic quest for and attraction to creative and romantic community.
♌	North Node	Leo	♌	12	Your Stretch Goal manifests through your energetic and dramatic quest for and attraction to creative and romantic spirituality.

♌	North Node	Virgo	♍	1	Your Stretch Goal manifests through your critically-minded and methodical quest for and attraction to meticulous and practical identity development.
♌	North Node	Virgo	♍	2	Your Stretch Goal manifests through your critically-minded and methodical quest for and attraction to meticulous and practical values and ways to meet your needs.
♌	North Node	Virgo	♍	3	Your Stretch Goal manifests through your critically-minded and methodical quest for and attraction to meticulous and practical understanding of the world around you.
♌	North Node	Virgo	♍	4	Your Stretch Goal manifests through your critically-minded and methodical quest for and attraction to meticulous and practical emotional caretaking and traditions.
♌	North Node	Virgo	♍	5	Your Stretch Goal manifests through your critically-minded and methodical quest for and attraction to meticulous and practical creative expression.
♌	North Node	Virgo	♍	6	Your Stretch Goal manifests through your critically-minded and methodical quest for and attraction to meticulous and practical service for others.
♌	North Node	Virgo	♍	7	Your Stretch Goal manifests through your critically-minded and methodical quest for and attraction to meticulous and practical life teachers.
♌	North Node	Virgo	♍	8	Your Stretch Goal manifests through your critically-minded and methodical quest for and attraction to meticulous and practical intimate relationships.
♌	North Node	Virgo	♍	9	Your Stretch Goal manifests through your critically-minded and methodical quest for and attraction to meticulous and practical mastership of a body of knowledge.
♌	North Node	Virgo	♍	10	Your Stretch Goal manifests through your critically-minded and methodical quest for and attraction to meticulous and practical accomplishments.
♌	North Node	Virgo	♍	11	Your Stretch Goal manifests through your critically-minded and methodical quest for and attraction to meticulous and practical community.
♌	North Node	Virgo	♍	12	Your Stretch Goal manifests through your critically-minded and methodical quest for and attraction to meticulous and practical spirituality.

☊	North Node	Libra	♎	1	Your Stretch Goal manifests through your analytical and balanced quest for and attraction to harmonious and logical identity development.
☊	North Node	Libra	♎	2	Your Stretch Goal manifests through your analytical and balanced quest for and attraction to harmonious and logical values and ways to meet your needs.
☊	North Node	Libra	♎	3	Your Stretch Goal manifests through your analytical and balanced quest for and attraction to harmonious and logical understanding of the world around you.
☊	North Node	Libra	♎	4	Your Stretch Goal manifests through your analytical and balanced quest for and attraction to harmonious and logical emotional caretaking and traditions.
☊	North Node	Libra	♎	5	Your Stretch Goal manifests through your analytical and balanced quest for and attraction to harmonious and logical creative expression.
☊	North Node	Libra	♎	6	Your Stretch Goal manifests through your analytical and balanced quest for and attraction to harmonious and logical service for others.
☊	North Node	Libra	♎	7	Your Stretch Goal manifests through your analytical and balanced quest for and attraction to harmonious and logical life teachers.
☊	North Node	Libra	♎	8	Your Stretch Goal manifests through your analytical and balanced quest for and attraction to harmonious and logical intimate relationships.
☊	North Node	Libra	♎	9	Your Stretch Goal manifests through your analytical and balanced quest for and attraction to harmonious and logical mastership of a body of knowledge.
☊	North Node	Libra	♎	10	Your Stretch Goal manifests through your analytical and balanced quest for and attraction to harmonious and logical accomplishments.
☊	North Node	Libra	♎	11	Your Stretch Goal manifests through your analytical and balanced quest for and attraction to harmonious and logical community.
☊	North Node	Libra	♎	12	Your Stretch Goal manifests through your analytical and balanced quest for and attraction to harmonious and logical spirituality.

♌	North Node	Scorpio	♏	1	Your Stretch Goal manifests through your intense and truth seeking quest for and attraction to penetrating and emotionally transformative identity development.
♌	North Node	Scorpio	♏	2	Your Stretch Goal manifests through your intense and truth seeking quest for and attraction to penetrating and emotionally transformative values and ways to meet your needs.
♌	North Node	Scorpio	♏	3	Your Stretch Goal manifests through your intense and truth seeking quest for and attraction to penetrating and emotionally transformative understanding of the world around you.
♌	North Node	Scorpio	♏	4	Your Stretch Goal manifests through your intense and truth seeking quest for and attraction to penetrating and emotionally transformative emotional caretaking and traditions.
♌	North Node	Scorpio	♏	5	Your Stretch Goal manifests through your intense and truth seeking quest for and attraction to penetrating and emotionally transformative creative expression.
♌	North Node	Scorpio	♏	6	Your Stretch Goal manifests through your intense and truth seeking quest for and attraction to penetrating and emotionally transformative service for others.
♌	North Node	Scorpio	♏	7	Your Stretch Goal manifests through your intense and truth seeking quest for and attraction to penetrating and emotionally transformative life teachers.
♌	North Node	Scorpio	♏	8	Your Stretch Goal manifests through your intense and truth seeking quest for and attraction to penetrating and emotionally transformative intimate relationships.
♌	North Node	Scorpio	♏	9	Your Stretch Goal manifests through your intense and truth seeking quest for and attraction to penetrating and emotionally transformative mastership of a body of knowledge.
♌	North Node	Scorpio	♏	10	Your Stretch Goal manifests through your intense and truth seeking quest for and attraction to penetrating and emotionally transformative accomplishments.
♌	North Node	Scorpio	♏	11	Your Stretch Goal manifests through your intense and truth seeking quest for and attraction to penetrating and emotionally transformative community.
♌	North Node	Scorpio	♏	12	Your Stretch Goal manifests through your intense and truth seeking quest for and attraction to penetrating and emotionally transformative spirituality.

♌	North Node	Sagittarius	♐	1	Your Stretch Goal manifests through your wide-ranging and open-minded quest for and attraction to experiential and risk-taking identity development.
♌	North Node	Sagittarius	♐	2	Your Stretch Goal manifests through your wide-ranging and open-minded quest for and attraction to experiential and risk-taking values and ways to meet your needs.
♌	North Node	Sagittarius	♐	3	Your Stretch Goal manifests through your wide-ranging and open-minded quest for and attraction to experiential and risk-taking understanding of the world around you.
♌	North Node	Sagittarius	♐	4	Your Stretch Goal manifests through your wide-ranging and open-minded quest for and attraction to experiential and risk-taking emotional caretaking and traditions.
♌	North Node	Sagittarius	♐	5	Your Stretch Goal manifests through your wide-ranging and open-minded quest for and attraction to experiential and risk-taking creative expression.
♌	North Node	Sagittarius	♐	6	Your Stretch Goal manifests through your wide-ranging and open-minded quest for and attraction to experiential and risk-taking service for others.
♌	North Node	Sagittarius	♐	7	Your Stretch Goal manifests through your wide-ranging and open-minded quest for and attraction to experiential and risk-taking life teachers.
♌	North Node	Sagittarius	♐	8	Your Stretch Goal manifests through your wide-ranging and open-minded quest for and attraction to experiential and risk-taking intimate relationships.
♌	North Node	Sagittarius	♐	9	Your Stretch Goal manifests through your wide-ranging and open-minded quest for and attraction to experiential and risk-taking mastership of a body of knowledge.
♌	North Node	Sagittarius	♐	10	Your Stretch Goal manifests through your wide-ranging and open-minded quest for and attraction to experiential and risk-taking accomplishments.
♌	North Node	Sagittarius	♐	11	Your Stretch Goal manifests through your wide-ranging and open-minded quest for and attraction to experiential and risk-taking community.
♌	North Node	Sagittarius	♐	12	Your Stretch Goal manifests through your wide-ranging and open-minded quest for and attraction to experiential and risk-taking spirituality.

Astrology Unlocked by Philip Young, PhD

♌	North Node	Capricorn	♑	1	Your Stretch Goal manifests through your goal-driven and focused quest for and attraction to results-oriented and successful identity development.
♌	North Node	Capricorn	♑	2	Your Stretch Goal manifests through your goal-driven and focused quest for and attraction to results-oriented and successful values and ways to meet your needs.
♌	North Node	Capricorn	♑	3	Your Stretch Goal manifests through your goal-driven and focused quest for and attraction to results-oriented and successful understanding of the world around you.
♌	North Node	Capricorn	♑	4	Your Stretch Goal manifests through your goal-driven and focused quest for and attraction to results-oriented and successful emotional caretaking and traditions.
♌	North Node	Capricorn	♑	5	Your Stretch Goal manifests through your goal-driven and focused quest for and attraction to results-oriented and successful creative expression.
♌	North Node	Capricorn	♑	6	Your Stretch Goal manifests through your goal-driven and focused quest for and attraction to results-oriented and successful service for others.
♌	North Node	Capricorn	♑	7	Your Stretch Goal manifests through your goal-driven and focused quest for and attraction to results-oriented and successful life teachers.
♌	North Node	Capricorn	♑	8	Your Stretch Goal manifests through your goal-driven and focused quest for and attraction to results-oriented and successful intimate relationships.
♌	North Node	Capricorn	♑	9	Your Stretch Goal manifests through your goal-driven and focused quest for and attraction to results-oriented and successful mastership of a body of knowledge.
♌	North Node	Capricorn	♑	10	Your Stretch Goal manifests through your goal-driven and focused quest for and attraction to results-oriented and successful accomplishments.
♌	North Node	Capricorn	♑	11	Your Stretch Goal manifests through your goal-driven and focused quest for and attraction to results-oriented and successful community.
♌	North Node	Capricorn	♑	12	Your Stretch Goal manifests through your goal-driven and focused quest for and attraction to results-oriented and successful spirituality.

♌ ☋	North Node	Aquarius	♒	1	Your Stretch Goal manifests through your unconventional and idealistic quest for and attraction to authentic and non-traditional identity development.
♌ ☋	North Node	Aquarius	♒	2	Your Stretch Goal manifests through your unconventional and idealistic quest for and attraction to authentic and non-traditional values and ways to meet your needs.
♌ ☋	North Node	Aquarius	♒	3	Your Stretch Goal manifests through your unconventional and idealistic quest for and attraction to authentic and non-traditional understanding of the world around you.
♌ ☋	North Node	Aquarius	♒	4	Your Stretch Goal manifests through your unconventional and idealistic quest for and attraction to authentic and non-traditional emotional caretaking and traditions.
♌ ☋	North Node	Aquarius	♒	5	Your Stretch Goal manifests through your unconventional and idealistic quest for and attraction to authentic and non-traditional creative expression.
♌ ☋	North Node	Aquarius	♒	6	Your Stretch Goal manifests through your unconventional and idealistic quest for and attraction to authentic and non-traditional service for others.
♌ ☋	North Node	Aquarius	♒	7	Your Stretch Goal manifests through your unconventional and idealistic quest for and attraction to authentic and non-traditional life teachers.
♌ ☋	North Node	Aquarius	♒	8	Your Stretch Goal manifests through your unconventional and idealistic quest for and attraction to authentic and non-traditional intimate relationships.
♌ ☋	North Node	Aquarius	♒	9	Your Stretch Goal manifests through your unconventional and idealistic quest for and attraction to authentic and non-traditional mastership of a body of knowledge.
♌ ☋	North Node	Aquarius	♒	10	Your Stretch Goal manifests through your unconventional and idealistic quest for and attraction to authentic and non-traditional accomplishments.
♌ ☋	North Node	Aquarius	♒	11	Your Stretch Goal manifests through your unconventional and idealistic quest for and attraction to authentic and non-traditional community.
♌ ☋	North Node	Aquarius	♒	12	Your Stretch Goal manifests through your unconventional and idealistic quest for and attraction to authentic and non-traditional spirituality.

☊	North Node	Pisces	♓	1	Your Stretch Goal manifests through your imaginative and faithful quest for and attraction to consciousness-raising and soulful identity development.
☊	North Node	Pisces	♓	2	Your Stretch Goal manifests through your imaginative and faithful quest for and attraction to consciousness-raising and soulful values and ways to meet your needs.
☊	North Node	Pisces	♓	3	Your Stretch Goal manifests through your imaginative and faithful quest for and attraction to consciousness-raising and soulful understanding of the world around you.
☊	North Node	Pisces	♓	4	Your Stretch Goal manifests through your imaginative and faithful quest for and attraction to consciousness-raising and soulful emotional caretaking and traditions.
☊	North Node	Pisces	♓	5	Your Stretch Goal manifests through your imaginative and faithful quest for and attraction to consciousness-raising and soulful creative expression.
☊	North Node	Pisces	♓	6	Your Stretch Goal manifests through your imaginative and faithful quest for and attraction to consciousness-raising and soulful service for others.
☊	North Node	Pisces	♓	7	Your Stretch Goal manifests through your imaginative and faithful quest for and attraction to consciousness-raising and soulful life teachers.
☊	North Node	Pisces	♓	8	Your Stretch Goal manifests through your imaginative and faithful quest for and attraction to consciousness-raising and soulful intimate relationships.
☊	North Node	Pisces	♓	9	Your Stretch Goal manifests through your imaginative and faithful quest for and attraction to consciousness-raising and soulful mastership of a body of knowledge.
☊	North Node	Pisces	♓	10	Your Stretch Goal manifests through your imaginative and faithful quest for and attraction to consciousness-raising and soulful accomplishments.
☊	North Node	Pisces	♓	11	Your Stretch Goal manifests through your imaginative and faithful quest for and attraction to consciousness-raising and soulful community.
☊	North Node	Pisces	♓	12	Your Stretch Goal manifests through your imaginative and faithful quest for and attraction to consciousness-raising and soulful spirituality.

South Node | ☋

Energy Point Type: **Calculated Point**

No Rulership

Key Phrase: **Energetic Habit to Release**

The South Node represents your Energetic Habit to Release in this lifetime. Its placement in Sign and House reveals how and where we have behaviors that feel the safest, but no longer need development. In fact we need to move away from those energies in order to grow. In my case my Energetic Habit to Release is expressed through Air (Libra) in my quest for spirituality (12th House). Air's expression is analytical, strategic, and curious. In Libra the Element acts judgmentally, decisively, and neutrally. So, my key phrase is *"Your Energetic Habit to Release manifests through your analytical and balanced quest for and attraction to harmonious and logical spirituality."* In short, I need to let go of my analytical view of spirituality in order to embrace a more independent and functional role in my life (Aries in the 6th House). I am too comfortable trying to maintain the peace at all times and must stretch myself in the opposite direction by asserting what I want even if it causes disruption.

When you consider the placement of your own South Node, consider how and where you have a behavioral habit that you fall back on or resist letting go of because you fear doing your North Node work. As you start out in life (birth to 29), you will find this habit useful and even rewarded, but eventually you recognize that you are not growing from repeating that behavior; you are merely "playing it safe." Now consider a South Node in Cancer in the 4th House, *"Your Energetic Habits to Release manifests through your emotional and caring quest for and attraction to nurturing and supportive emotional caretaking and traditions."* Here is an individual who will have a tough time breaking away from family and familial roles. The Stretch Goal is to get out in life and achieve (Capricorn, 10th House). In past lives the individual was rewarded for staying close to home and taking on a caretaking role. To learn and grow this individual must go out and earn and provide, leaving the caretaking to someone else.

For more in depth reading about South Node, I recommend purchasing and reading:

- *Karmic Astrology: The Moon's Nodes and Reincarnation (Volume 1)* by Martin Schulman (ISBN: 0877282889)

- *Karmic Astrology: Past Lives, Present Loves* by Ruth Aharoni (ISBN: 9780738709673)

- *Lunar Nodes: Discover Your Soul's Karmic Mission* by Celeste Teal (ISBN: 9780738713373)

- *Yesterday's Sky: Astrology and Reincarnation* by Steven Forrest (ISBN: 0979067731)

☋	South Node	Aries	♈	1	Your Habit to Release manifests through your independent and heroic quest for and attraction to maverick and individualistic identity development.
☋	South Node	Aries	♈	2	Your Habit to Release manifests through your independent and heroic quest for and attraction to maverick and individualistic values and ways to meet your needs.
☋	South Node	Aries	♈	3	Your Habit to Release manifests through your independent and heroic quest for and attraction to maverick and individualistic understanding of the world around you.
☋	South Node	Aries	♈	4	Your Habit to Release manifests through your independent and heroic quest for and attraction to maverick and individualistic emotional caretaking and traditions.
☋	South Node	Aries	♈	5	Your Habit to Release manifests through your independent and heroic quest for and attraction to maverick and individualistic creative expression.
☋	South Node	Aries	♈	6	Your Habit to Release manifests through your independent and heroic quest for and attraction to maverick and individualistic service for others.
☋	South Node	Aries	♈	7	Your Habit to Release manifests through your independent and heroic quest for and attraction to maverick and individualistic life teachers.
☋	South Node	Aries	♈	8	Your Habit to Release manifests through your independent and heroic quest for and attraction to maverick and individualistic intimate relationships.
☋	South Node	Aries	♈	9	Your Habit to Release manifests through your independent and heroic quest for and attraction to maverick and individualistic mastership of a body of knowledge.
☋	South Node	Aries	♈	10	Your Habit to Release manifests through your independent and heroic quest for and attraction to maverick and individualistic accomplishments.
☋	South Node	Aries	♈	11	Your Habit to Release manifests through your independent and heroic quest for and attraction to maverick and individualistic community.
☋	South Node	Aries	♈	12	Your Habit to Release manifests through your independent and heroic quest for and attraction to maverick and individualistic spirituality.

Astrology Unlocked by Philip Young, PhD

☊	South Node	Taurus	♉	1	Your Habit to Release manifests through your steadfast and persistent quest for and attraction to enduring and secure identity development.
☊	South Node	Taurus	♉	2	Your Habit to Release manifests through your steadfast and persistent quest for and attraction to enduring and secure values and ways to meet your needs.
☊	South Node	Taurus	♉	3	Your Habit to Release manifests through your steadfast and persistent quest for and attraction to enduring and secure understanding of the world around you.
☊	South Node	Taurus	♉	4	Your Habit to Release manifests through your steadfast and persistent quest for and attraction to enduring and secure emotional caretaking and traditions.
☊	South Node	Taurus	♉	5	Your Habit to Release manifests through your steadfast and persistent quest for and attraction to enduring and secure creative expression.
☊	South Node	Taurus	♉	6	Your Habit to Release manifests through your steadfast and persistent quest for and attraction to enduring and secure service for others.
☊	South Node	Taurus	♉	7	Your Habit to Release manifests through your steadfast and persistent quest for and attraction to enduring and secure life teachers.
☊	South Node	Taurus	♉	8	Your Habit to Release manifests through your steadfast and persistent quest for and attraction to enduring and secure intimate relationships.
☊	South Node	Taurus	♉	9	Your Habit to Release manifests through your steadfast and persistent quest for and attraction to enduring and secure mastership of a body of knowledge.
☊	South Node	Taurus	♉	10	Your Habit to Release manifests through your steadfast and persistent quest for and attraction to enduring and secure accomplishments.
☊	South Node	Taurus	♉	11	Your Habit to Release manifests through your steadfast and persistent quest for and attraction to enduring and secure community.
☊	South Node	Taurus	♉	12	Your Habit to Release manifests through your steadfast and persistent quest for and attraction to enduring and secure spirituality.

☋	South Node	Gemini	♊	1	Your Habit to Release manifests through your inquisitive and mentally agile quest for and attraction to ever changing and adaptable identity development.
☋	South Node	Gemini	♊	2	Your Habit to Release manifests through your inquisitive and mentally agile quest for and attraction to ever changing and adaptable values and ways to meet your needs.
☋	South Node	Gemini	♊	3	Your Habit to Release manifests through your inquisitive and mentally agile quest for and attraction to ever changing and adaptable understanding of the world around you.
☋	South Node	Gemini	♊	4	Your Habit to Release manifests through your inquisitive and mentally agile quest for and attraction to ever changing and adaptable emotional caretaking and traditions.
☋	South Node	Gemini	♊	5	Your Habit to Release manifests through your inquisitive and mentally agile quest for and attraction to ever changing and adaptable creative expression.
☋	South Node	Gemini	♊	6	Your Habit to Release manifests through your inquisitive and mentally agile quest for and attraction to ever changing and adaptable service for others.
☋	South Node	Gemini	♊	7	Your Habit to Release manifests through your inquisitive and mentally agile quest for and attraction to ever changing and adaptable life teachers.
☋	South Node	Gemini	♊	8	Your Habit to Release manifests through your inquisitive and mentally agile quest for and attraction to ever changing and adaptable intimate relationships.
☋	South Node	Gemini	♊	9	Your Habit to Release manifests through your inquisitive and mentally agile quest for and attraction to ever changing and adaptable mastership of a body of knowledge.
☋	South Node	Gemini	♊	10	Your Habit to Release manifests through your inquisitive and mentally agile quest for and attraction to ever changing and adaptable accomplishments.
☋	South Node	Gemini	♊	11	Your Habit to Release manifests through your inquisitive and mentally agile quest for and attraction to ever changing and adaptable community.
☋	South Node	Gemini	♊	12	Your Habit to Release manifests through your inquisitive and mentally agile quest for and attraction to ever changing and adaptable spirituality.

☋	South Node	Cancer	♋	1	Your Habit to Release manifests through your emotional and caring quest for and attraction to nurturing and supportive identity development.
☋	South Node	Cancer	♋	2	Your Habit to Release manifests through your emotional and caring quest for and attraction to nurturing and supportive values and ways to meet your needs.
☋	South Node	Cancer	♋	3	Your Habit to Release manifests through your emotional and caring quest for and attraction to nurturing and supportive understanding of the world around you.
☋	South Node	Cancer	♋	4	Your Habit to Release manifests through your emotional and caring quest for and attraction to nurturing and supportive emotional caretaking and traditions.
☋	South Node	Cancer	♋	5	Your Habit to Release manifests through your emotional and caring quest for and attraction to nurturing and supportive creative expression.
☋	South Node	Cancer	♋	6	Your Habit to Release manifests through your emotional and caring quest for and attraction to nurturing and supportive service for others.
☋	South Node	Cancer	♋	7	Your Habit to Release manifests through your emotional and caring quest for and attraction to nurturing and supportive life teachers.
☋	South Node	Cancer	♋	8	Your Habit to Release manifests through your emotional and caring quest for and attraction to nurturing and supportive intimate relationships.
☋	South Node	Cancer	♋	9	Your Habit to Release manifests through your emotional and caring quest for and attraction to nurturing and supportive mastership of a body of knowledge.
☋	South Node	Cancer	♋	10	Your Habit to Release manifests through your emotional and caring quest for and attraction to nurturing and supportive accomplishments.
☋	South Node	Cancer	♋	11	Your Habit to Release manifests through your emotional and caring quest for and attraction to nurturing and supportive community.
☋	South Node	Cancer	♋	12	Your Habit to Release manifests through your emotional and caring quest for and attraction to nurturing and supportive spirituality.

☋	South Node	Leo	♌	1	Your Habit to Release manifests through your energetic and dramatic quest for and attraction to creative and romantic identity development.
☋	South Node	Leo	♌	2	Your Habit to Release manifests through your energetic and dramatic quest for and attraction to creative and romantic values and ways to meet your needs.
☋	South Node	Leo	♌	3	Your Habit to Release manifests through your energetic and dramatic quest for and attraction to creative and romantic understanding of the world around you.
☋	South Node	Leo	♌	4	Your Habit to Release manifests through your energetic and dramatic quest for and attraction to creative and romantic emotional caretaking and traditions.
☋	South Node	Leo	♌	5	Your Habit to Release manifests through your energetic and dramatic quest for and attraction to creative and romantic creative expression.
☋	South Node	Leo	♌	6	Your Habit to Release manifests through your energetic and dramatic quest for and attraction to creative and romantic service for others.
☋	South Node	Leo	♌	7	Your Habit to Release manifests through your energetic and dramatic quest for and attraction to creative and romantic life teachers.
☋	South Node	Leo	♌	8	Your Habit to Release manifests through your energetic and dramatic quest for and attraction to creative and romantic intimate relationships.
☋	South Node	Leo	♌	9	Your Habit to Release manifests through your energetic and dramatic quest for and attraction to creative and romantic mastership of a body of knowledge.
☋	South Node	Leo	♌	10	Your Habit to Release manifests through your energetic and dramatic quest for and attraction to creative and romantic accomplishments.
☋	South Node	Leo	♌	11	Your Habit to Release manifests through your energetic and dramatic quest for and attraction to creative and romantic community.
☋	South Node	Leo	♌	12	Your Habit to Release manifests through your energetic and dramatic quest for and attraction to creative and romantic spirituality.

☊	South Node	Virgo	♍	1	Your Habit to Release manifests through your critically-minded and methodical quest for and attraction to meticulous and practical identity development.
☊	South Node	Virgo	♍	2	Your Habit to Release manifests through your critically-minded and methodical quest for and attraction to meticulous and practical values and ways to meet your needs.
☊	South Node	Virgo	♍	3	Your Habit to Release manifests through your critically-minded and methodical quest for and attraction to meticulous and practical understanding of the world around you.
☊	South Node	Virgo	♍	4	Your Habit to Release manifests through your critically-minded and methodical quest for and attraction to meticulous and practical emotional caretaking and traditions.
☊	South Node	Virgo	♍	5	Your Habit to Release manifests through your critically-minded and methodical quest for and attraction to meticulous and practical creative expression.
☊	South Node	Virgo	♍	6	Your Habit to Release manifests through your critically-minded and methodical quest for and attraction to meticulous and practical service for others.
☊	South Node	Virgo	♍	7	Your Habit to Release manifests through your critically-minded and methodical quest for and attraction to meticulous and practical life teachers.
☊	South Node	Virgo	♍	8	Your Habit to Release manifests through your critically-minded and methodical quest for and attraction to meticulous and practical intimate relationships.
☊	South Node	Virgo	♍	9	Your Habit to Release manifests through your critically-minded and methodical quest for and attraction to meticulous and practical mastership of a body of knowledge.
☊	South Node	Virgo	♍	10	Your Habit to Release manifests through your critically-minded and methodical quest for and attraction to meticulous and practical accomplishments.
☊	South Node	Virgo	♍	11	Your Habit to Release manifests through your critically-minded and methodical quest for and attraction to meticulous and practical community.
☊	South Node	Virgo	♍	12	Your Habit to Release manifests through your critically-minded and methodical quest for and attraction to meticulous and practical spirituality.

☋	South Node	Libra	♎	1	Your Habit to Release manifests through your analytical and balanced quest for and attraction to harmonious and logical identity development.
☋	South Node	Libra	♎	2	Your Habit to Release manifests through your analytical and balanced quest for and attraction to harmonious and logical values and ways to meet your needs.
☋	South Node	Libra	♎	3	Your Habit to Release manifests through your analytical and balanced quest for and attraction to harmonious and logical understanding of the world around you.
☋	South Node	Libra	♎	4	Your Habit to Release manifests through your analytical and balanced quest for and attraction to harmonious and logical emotional caretaking and traditions.
☋	South Node	Libra	♎	5	Your Habit to Release manifests through your analytical and balanced quest for and attraction to harmonious and logical creative expression.
☋	South Node	Libra	♎	6	Your Habit to Release manifests through your analytical and balanced quest for and attraction to harmonious and logical service for others.
☋	South Node	Libra	♎	7	Your Habit to Release manifests through your analytical and balanced quest for and attraction to harmonious and logical life teachers.
☋	South Node	Libra	♎	8	Your Habit to Release manifests through your analytical and balanced quest for and attraction to harmonious and logical intimate relationships.
☋	South Node	Libra	♎	9	Your Habit to Release manifests through your analytical and balanced quest for and attraction to harmonious and logical mastership of a body of knowledge.
☋	South Node	Libra	♎	10	Your Habit to Release manifests through your analytical and balanced quest for and attraction to harmonious and logical accomplishments.
☋	South Node	Libra	♎	11	Your Habit to Release manifests through your analytical and balanced quest for and attraction to harmonious and logical community.
☋	South Node	Libra	♎	12	Your Habit to Release manifests through your analytical and balanced quest for and attraction to harmonious and logical spirituality.

☋	South Node	Scorpio	♏	1	Your Habit to Release manifests through your intense and truth seeking quest for and attraction to penetrating and emotionally transformative identity development.
☋	South Node	Scorpio	♏	2	Your Habit to Release manifests through your intense and truth seeking quest for and attraction to penetrating and emotionally transformative values and ways to meet your needs.
☋	South Node	Scorpio	♏	3	Your Habit to Release manifests through your intense and truth seeking quest for and attraction to penetrating and emotionally transformative understanding of the world around you.
☋	South Node	Scorpio	♏	4	Your Habit to Release manifests through your intense and truth seeking quest for and attraction to penetrating and emotionally transformative emotional caretaking and traditions.
☋	South Node	Scorpio	♏	5	Your Habit to Release manifests through your intense and truth seeking quest for and attraction to penetrating and emotionally transformative creative expression.
☋	South Node	Scorpio	♏	6	Your Habit to Release manifests through your intense and truth seeking quest for and attraction to penetrating and emotionally transformative service for others.
☋	South Node	Scorpio	♏	7	Your Habit to Release manifests through your intense and truth seeking quest for and attraction to penetrating and emotionally transformative life teachers.
☋	South Node	Scorpio	♏	8	Your Habit to Release manifests through your intense and truth seeking quest for and attraction to penetrating and emotionally transformative intimate relationships.
☋	South Node	Scorpio	♏	9	Your Habit to Release manifests through your intense and truth seeking quest for and attraction to penetrating and emotionally transformative mastership of a body of knowledge.
☋	South Node	Scorpio	♏	10	Your Habit to Release manifests through your intense and truth seeking quest for and attraction to penetrating and emotionally transformative accomplishments.
☋	South Node	Scorpio	♏	11	Your Habit to Release manifests through your intense and truth seeking quest for and attraction to penetrating and emotionally transformative community.
☋	South Node	Scorpio	♏	12	Your Habit to Release manifests through your intense and truth seeking quest for and attraction to penetrating and emotionally transformative spirituality.

☊	South Node	Sagittarius	♐	1	Your Habit to Release manifests through your wide-ranging and open-minded quest for and attraction to experiential and risk-taking identity development.
☊	South Node	Sagittarius	♐	2	Your Habit to Release manifests through your wide-ranging and open-minded quest for and attraction to experiential and risk-taking values and ways to meet your needs.
☊	South Node	Sagittarius	♐	3	Your Habit to Release manifests through your wide-ranging and open-minded quest for and attraction to experiential and risk-taking understanding of the world around you.
☊	South Node	Sagittarius	♐	4	Your Habit to Release manifests through your wide-ranging and open-minded quest for and attraction to experiential and risk-taking emotional caretaking and traditions.
☊	South Node	Sagittarius	♐	5	Your Habit to Release manifests through your wide-ranging and open-minded quest for and attraction to experiential and risk-taking creative expression.
☊	South Node	Sagittarius	♐	6	Your Habit to Release manifests through your wide-ranging and open-minded quest for and attraction to experiential and risk-taking service for others.
☊	South Node	Sagittarius	♐	7	Your Habit to Release manifests through your wide-ranging and open-minded quest for and attraction to experiential and risk-taking life teachers.
☊	South Node	Sagittarius	♐	8	Your Habit to Release manifests through your wide-ranging and open-minded quest for and attraction to experiential and risk-taking intimate relationships.
☊	South Node	Sagittarius	♐	9	Your Habit to Release manifests through your wide-ranging and open-minded quest for and attraction to experiential and risk-taking mastership of a body of knowledge.
☊	South Node	Sagittarius	♐	10	Your Habit to Release manifests through your wide-ranging and open-minded quest for and attraction to experiential and risk-taking accomplishments.
☊	South Node	Sagittarius	♐	11	Your Habit to Release manifests through your wide-ranging and open-minded quest for and attraction to experiential and risk-taking community.
☊	South Node	Sagittarius	♐	12	Your Habit to Release manifests through your wide-ranging and open-minded quest for and attraction to experiential and risk-taking spirituality.

☋	South Node	Capricorn	♑	1	Your Habit to Release manifests through your goal-driven and focused quest for and attraction to results-oriented and successful identity development.
☋	South Node	Capricorn	♑	2	Your Habit to Release manifests through your goal-driven and focused quest for and attraction to results-oriented and successful values and ways to meet your needs.
☋	South Node	Capricorn	♑	3	Your Habit to Release manifests through your goal-driven and focused quest for and attraction to results-oriented and successful understanding of the world around you.
☋	South Node	Capricorn	♑	4	Your Habit to Release manifests through your goal-driven and focused quest for and attraction to results-oriented and successful emotional caretaking and traditions.
☋	South Node	Capricorn	♑	5	Your Habit to Release manifests through your goal-driven and focused quest for and attraction to results-oriented and successful creative expression.
☋	South Node	Capricorn	♑	6	Your Habit to Release manifests through your goal-driven and focused quest for and attraction to results-oriented and successful service for others.
☋	South Node	Capricorn	♑	7	Your Habit to Release manifests through your goal-driven and focused quest for and attraction to results-oriented and successful life teachers.
☋	South Node	Capricorn	♑	8	Your Habit to Release manifests through your goal-driven and focused quest for and attraction to results-oriented and successful intimate relationships.
☋	South Node	Capricorn	♑	9	Your Habit to Release manifests through your goal-driven and focused quest for and attraction to results-oriented and successful mastership of a body of knowledge.
☋	South Node	Capricorn	♑	10	Your Habit to Release manifests through your goal-driven and focused quest for and attraction to results-oriented and successful accomplishments.
☋	South Node	Capricorn	♑	11	Your Habit to Release manifests through your goal-driven and focused quest for and attraction to results-oriented and successful community.
☋	South Node	Capricorn	♑	12	Your Habit to Release manifests through your goal-driven and focused quest for and attraction to results-oriented and successful spirituality.

☋	South Node	Aquarius	♒	1	Your Habit to Release manifests through your unconventional and idealistic quest for and attraction to authentic and non-traditional identity development.
☋	South Node	Aquarius	♒	2	Your Habit to Release manifests through your unconventional and idealistic quest for and attraction to authentic and non-traditional values and ways to meet your needs.
☋	South Node	Aquarius	♒	5	Your Habit to Release manifests through your unconventional and idealistic quest for and attraction to authentic and non-traditional creative expression.
☋	South Node	Aquarius	♒	6	Your Habit to Release manifests through your unconventional and idealistic quest for and attraction to authentic and non-traditional service for others.
☋	South Node	Aquarius	♒	7	Your Habit to Release manifests through your unconventional and idealistic quest for and attraction to authentic and non-traditional life teachers.
☋	South Node	Aquarius	♒	8	Your Habit to Release manifests through your unconventional and idealistic quest for and attraction to authentic and non-traditional intimate relationships.
☋	South Node	Aquarius	♒	9	Your Habit to Release manifests through your unconventional and idealistic quest for and attraction to authentic and non-traditional mastership of a body of knowledge.
☋	South Node	Aquarius	♒	10	Your Habit to Release manifests through your unconventional and idealistic quest for and attraction to authentic and non-traditional accomplishments.
☋	South Node	Aquarius	♒	11	Your Habit to Release manifests through your unconventional and idealistic quest for and attraction to authentic and non-traditional community.
☋	South Node	Aquarius	♒	12	Your Habit to Release manifests through your unconventional and idealistic quest for and attraction to authentic and non-traditional spirituality.

☋	South Node	Pisces	♓	1	Your Habit to Release manifests through your imaginative and faithful quest for and attraction to consciousness-raising and soulful identity development.
☋	South Node	Pisces	♓	2	Your Habit to Release manifests through your imaginative and faithful quest for and attraction to consciousness-raising and soulful values and ways to meet your needs.
☋	South Node	Pisces	♓	3	Your Habit to Release manifests through your imaginative and faithful quest for and attraction to consciousness-raising and soulful understanding of the world around you.
☋	South Node	Pisces	♓	4	Your Habit to Release manifests through your imaginative and faithful quest for and attraction to consciousness-raising and soulful emotional caretaking and traditions.
☋	South Node	Pisces	♓	5	Your Habit to Release manifests through your imaginative and faithful quest for and attraction to consciousness-raising and soulful creative expression.
☋	South Node	Pisces	♓	6	Your Habit to Release manifests through your imaginative and faithful quest for and attraction to consciousness-raising and soulful service for others.
☋	South Node	Pisces	♓	7	Your Habit to Release manifests through your imaginative and faithful quest for and attraction to consciousness-raising and soulful life teachers.
☋	South Node	Pisces	♓	8	Your Habit to Release manifests through your imaginative and faithful quest for and attraction to consciousness-raising and soulful intimate relationships.
☋	South Node	Pisces	♓	9	Your Habit to Release manifests through your imaginative and faithful quest for and attraction to consciousness-raising and soulful mastership of a body of knowledge.
☋	South Node	Pisces	♓	10	Your Habit to Release manifests through your imaginative and faithful quest for and attraction to consciousness-raising and soulful accomplishments.
☋	South Node	Pisces	♓	11	Your Habit to Release manifests through your imaginative and faithful quest for and attraction to consciousness-raising and soulful community.
☋	South Node	Pisces	♓	12	Your Habit to Release manifests through your imaginative and faithful quest for and attraction to consciousness-raising and soulful spirituality.

Part of Fortune[32] | ⊗

Energy Point Type: **Calculated Point**

No Rulership

Key Phrase: **Natural Good Luck**

The Part of Fortune represents your Natural Good Luck in this lifetime. Its placement in Sign and House reveals how and where we have benefits that help us in that area of life, a location and energy where we are charmed. In my case my Natural Good Luck is expressed through Earth (Taurus) in my quest for Life Teachers (7th House). Earth's expression is accomplished, persistent, and practical. In Taurus the Element acts protectively, conservatively, and reliably. So, my key phrase is *"Your Natural Good Luck manifests through your steadfast and persistent quest for and attraction to enduring and secure life teachers."* In short, I attract and benefit from partnerships where the other person is supportive and reliable, helping me in real and concrete ways, either with his or her time, money, or knowledge.

When considering the placement of the Part of Fortune in your chart, think about how and where you manifest good luck and support, how and where you find an easy flow. Now consider the Part of Fortune in Gemini in the 6th House, *"Your Natural Good Luck manifests through your inquisitive and mentally agile quest for and attraction to ever changing and adaptable service for others."* This individual should find it easy to learn new skills and multi-task (Gemini) at his or her day-to-day job (6th House). He or she will be the problem solver, the go-to person for information, and the one who can facilitate communication between co-workers, management and employees, and customers and staff. People will enjoy the stories, jokes, and gossip this person collects and shares; he or she will function as the communication hub in his or her work.

---

[32] The Part of Fortune is a calculated point based on one of two formulas. If you were born with your Sun above the horizon, the calculation is Ascendant + Moon − Sun. If you were born with your Sun below the horizon, the calculation is Ascendant + Sun − Moon. Using the 360 degrees of the dial, my Ascendant is at 28° of Scorpio and my Sun is at 23° of Aries (173°) in my 6th house, giving me 201°, minus my Moon at 22° of Libra (352°) in my 12th house for a total of -151°, which puts my Part of Fortune at 29° of Taurus in my 7th house.

⊗	Part of Fortune	Aries	♈	1	Your Natural Good Luck manifests through your independent and heroic quest for and attraction to maverick and individualistic identity development.
⊗	Part of Fortune	Aries	♈	2	Your Natural Good Luck manifests through your independent and heroic quest for and attraction to maverick and individualistic values and ways to meet your needs.
⊗	Part of Fortune	Aries	♈	3	Your Natural Good Luck manifests through your independent and heroic quest for and attraction to maverick and individualistic understanding of the world around you.
⊗	Part of Fortune	Aries	♈	4	Your Natural Good Luck manifests through your independent and heroic quest for and attraction to maverick and individualistic emotional caretaking and traditions.
⊗	Part of Fortune	Aries	♈	5	Your Natural Good Luck manifests through your independent and heroic quest for and attraction to maverick and individualistic creative expression.
⊗	Part of Fortune	Aries	♈	6	Your Natural Good Luck manifests through your independent and heroic quest for and attraction to maverick and individualistic service for others.
⊗	Part of Fortune	Aries	♈	7	Your Natural Good Luck manifests through your independent and heroic quest for and attraction to maverick and individualistic life teachers.
⊗	Part of Fortune	Aries	♈	8	Your Natural Good Luck manifests through your independent and heroic quest for and attraction to maverick and individualistic intimate relationships.
⊗	Part of Fortune	Aries	♈	9	Your Natural Good Luck manifests through your independent and heroic quest for and attraction to maverick and individualistic mastership of a body of knowledge.
⊗	Part of Fortune	Aries	♈	10	Your Natural Good Luck manifests through your independent and heroic quest for and attraction to maverick and individualistic accomplishments.
⊗	Part of Fortune	Aries	♈	11	Your Natural Good Luck manifests through your independent and heroic quest for and attraction to maverick and individualistic community.
⊗	Part of Fortune	Aries	♈	12	Your Natural Good Luck manifests through your independent and heroic quest for and attraction to maverick and individualistic spirituality.

⊗	Part of Fortune	Taurus	♉	1	Your Natural Good Luck manifests through your steadfast and persistent quest for and attraction to enduring and secure identity development.
⊗	Part of Fortune	Taurus	♉	2	Your Natural Good Luck manifests through your steadfast and persistent quest for and attraction to enduring and secure values and ways to meet your needs.
⊗	Part of Fortune	Taurus	♉	3	Your Natural Good Luck manifests through your steadfast and persistent quest for and attraction to enduring and secure understanding of the world around you.
⊗	Part of Fortune	Taurus	♉	4	Your Natural Good Luck manifests through your steadfast and persistent quest for and attraction to enduring and secure emotional caretaking and traditions.
⊗	Part of Fortune	Taurus	♉	5	Your Natural Good Luck manifests through your steadfast and persistent quest for and attraction to enduring and secure creative expression.
⊗	Part of Fortune	Taurus	♉	6	Your Natural Good Luck manifests through your steadfast and persistent quest for and attraction to enduring and secure service for others.
⊗	Part of Fortune	Taurus	♉	7	Your Natural Good Luck manifests through your steadfast and persistent quest for and attraction to enduring and secure life teachers.
⊗	Part of Fortune	Taurus	♉	8	Your Natural Good Luck manifests through your steadfast and persistent quest for and attraction to enduring and secure intimate relationships.
⊗	Part of Fortune	Taurus	♉	9	Your Natural Good Luck manifests through your steadfast and persistent quest for and attraction to enduring and secure mastership of a body of knowledge.
⊗	Part of Fortune	Taurus	♉	10	Your Natural Good Luck manifests through your steadfast and persistent quest for and attraction to enduring and secure accomplishments.
⊗	Part of Fortune	Taurus	♉	11	Your Natural Good Luck manifests through your steadfast and persistent quest for and attraction to enduring and secure community.
⊗	Part of Fortune	Taurus	♉	12	Your Natural Good Luck manifests through your steadfast and persistent quest for and attraction to enduring and secure spirituality.

⊗	Part of Fortune	Gemini	♊	1	Your Natural Good Luck manifests through your inquisitive and mentally agile quest for and attraction to ever changing and adaptable identity development.
⊗	Part of Fortune	Gemini	♊	2	Your Natural Good Luck manifests through your inquisitive and mentally agile quest for and attraction to ever changing and adaptable values and ways to meet your needs.
⊗	Part of Fortune	Gemini	♊	3	Your Natural Good Luck manifests through your inquisitive and mentally agile quest for and attraction to ever changing and adaptable understanding of the world around you.
⊗	Part of Fortune	Gemini	♊	4	Your Natural Good Luck manifests through your inquisitive and mentally agile quest for and attraction to ever changing and adaptable emotional caretaking and traditions.
⊗	Part of Fortune	Gemini	♊	5	Your Natural Good Luck manifests through your inquisitive and mentally agile quest for and attraction to ever changing and adaptable creative expression.
⊗	Part of Fortune	Gemini	♊	6	Your Natural Good Luck manifests through your inquisitive and mentally agile quest for and attraction to ever changing and adaptable service for others.
⊗	Part of Fortune	Gemini	♊	7	Your Natural Good Luck manifests through your inquisitive and mentally agile quest for and attraction to ever changing and adaptable life teachers.
⊗	Part of Fortune	Gemini	♊	8	Your Natural Good Luck manifests through your inquisitive and mentally agile quest for and attraction to ever changing and adaptable intimate relationships.
⊗	Part of Fortune	Gemini	♊	9	Your Natural Good Luck manifests through your inquisitive and mentally agile quest for and attraction to ever changing and adaptable mastership of a body of knowledge.
⊗	Part of Fortune	Gemini	♊	10	Your Natural Good Luck manifests through your inquisitive and mentally agile quest for and attraction to ever changing and adaptable accomplishments.
⊗	Part of Fortune	Gemini	♊	11	Your Natural Good Luck manifests through your inquisitive and mentally agile quest for and attraction to ever changing and adaptable community.
⊗	Part of Fortune	Gemini	♊	12	Your Natural Good Luck manifests through your inquisitive and mentally agile quest for and attraction to ever changing and adaptable spirituality.

	Part of Fortune	Cancer	♋	1	Your Natural Good Luck manifests through your emotional and caring quest for and attraction to nurturing and supportive identity development.
	Part of Fortune	Cancer	♋	2	Your Natural Good Luck manifests through your emotional and caring quest for and attraction to nurturing and supportive values and ways to meet your needs.
	Part of Fortune	Cancer	♋	3	Your Natural Good Luck manifests through your emotional and caring quest for and attraction to nurturing and supportive understanding of the world around you.
	Part of Fortune	Cancer	♋	4	Your Natural Good Luck manifests through your emotional and caring quest for and attraction to nurturing and supportive emotional caretaking and traditions.
	Part of Fortune	Cancer	♋	5	Your Natural Good Luck manifests through your emotional and caring quest for and attraction to nurturing and supportive creative expression.
	Part of Fortune	Cancer	♋	6	Your Natural Good Luck manifests through your emotional and caring quest for and attraction to nurturing and supportive service for others.
	Part of Fortune	Cancer	♋	7	Your Natural Good Luck manifests through your emotional and caring quest for and attraction to nurturing and supportive life teachers.
	Part of Fortune	Cancer	♋	8	Your Natural Good Luck manifests through your emotional and caring quest for and attraction to nurturing and supportive intimate relationships.
	Part of Fortune	Cancer	♋	9	Your Natural Good Luck manifests through your emotional and caring quest for and attraction to nurturing and supportive mastership of a body of knowledge.
	Part of Fortune	Cancer	♋	10	Your Natural Good Luck manifests through your emotional and caring quest for and attraction to nurturing and supportive accomplishments.
	Part of Fortune	Cancer	♋	11	Your Natural Good Luck manifests through your emotional and caring quest for and attraction to nurturing and supportive community.
	Part of Fortune	Cancer	♋	12	Your Natural Good Luck manifests through your emotional and caring quest for and attraction to nurturing and supportive spirituality.

Astrology Unlocked by Philip Young, PhD

⊗	Part of Fortune	Leo	♌	1	Your Natural Good Luck manifests through your energetic and dramatic quest for and attraction to creative and romantic identity development.
⊗	Part of Fortune	Leo	♌	2	Your Natural Good Luck manifests through your energetic and dramatic quest for and attraction to creative and romantic values and ways to meet your needs.
⊗	Part of Fortune	Leo	♌	3	Your Natural Good Luck manifests through your energetic and dramatic quest for and attraction to creative and romantic understanding of the world around you.
⊗	Part of Fortune	Leo	♌	4	Your Natural Good Luck manifests through your energetic and dramatic quest for and attraction to creative and romantic emotional caretaking and traditions.
⊗	Part of Fortune	Leo	♌	5	Your Natural Good Luck manifests through your energetic and dramatic quest for and attraction to creative and romantic creative expression.
⊗	Part of Fortune	Leo	♌	6	Your Natural Good Luck manifests through your energetic and dramatic quest for and attraction to creative and romantic service for others.
⊗	Part of Fortune	Leo	♌	7	Your Natural Good Luck manifests through your energetic and dramatic quest for and attraction to creative and romantic life teachers.
⊗	Part of Fortune	Leo	♌	8	Your Natural Good Luck manifests through your energetic and dramatic quest for and attraction to creative and romantic intimate relationships.
⊗	Part of Fortune	Leo	♌	9	Your Natural Good Luck manifests through your energetic and dramatic quest for and attraction to creative and romantic mastership of a body of knowledge.
⊗	Part of Fortune	Leo	♌	10	Your Natural Good Luck manifests through your energetic and dramatic quest for and attraction to creative and romantic accomplishments.
⊗	Part of Fortune	Leo	♌	11	Your Natural Good Luck manifests through your energetic and dramatic quest for and attraction to creative and romantic community.
⊗	Part of Fortune	Leo	♌	12	Your Natural Good Luck manifests through your energetic and dramatic quest for and attraction to creative and romantic spirituality.

⊗	Part of Fortune	Virgo	♍	1	Your Natural Good Luck manifests through your critically-minded and methodical quest for and attraction to meticulous and practical identity development.
⊗	Part of Fortune	Virgo	♍	2	Your Natural Good Luck manifests through your critically-minded and methodical quest for and attraction to meticulous and practical values and ways to meet your needs.
⊗	Part of Fortune	Virgo	♍	3	Your Natural Good Luck manifests through your critically-minded and methodical quest for and attraction to meticulous and practical understanding of the world around you.
⊗	Part of Fortune	Virgo	♍	4	Your Natural Good Luck manifests through your critically-minded and methodical quest for and attraction to meticulous and practical emotional caretaking and traditions.
⊗	Part of Fortune	Virgo	♍	5	Your Natural Good Luck manifests through your critically-minded and methodical quest for and attraction to meticulous and practical creative expression.
⊗	Part of Fortune	Virgo	♍	6	Your Natural Good Luck manifests through your critically-minded and methodical quest for and attraction to meticulous and practical service for others.
⊗	Part of Fortune	Virgo	♍	7	Your Natural Good Luck manifests through your critically-minded and methodical quest for and attraction to meticulous and practical life teachers.
⊗	Part of Fortune	Virgo	♍	8	Your Natural Good Luck manifests through your critically-minded and methodical quest for and attraction to meticulous and practical intimate relationships.
⊗	Part of Fortune	Virgo	♍	9	Your Natural Good Luck manifests through your critically-minded and methodical quest for and attraction to meticulous and practical mastership of a body of knowledge.
⊗	Part of Fortune	Virgo	♍	10	Your Natural Good Luck manifests through your critically-minded and methodical quest for and attraction to meticulous and practical accomplishments.
⊗	Part of Fortune	Virgo	♍	11	Your Natural Good Luck manifests through your critically-minded and methodical quest for and attraction to meticulous and practical community.
⊗	Part of Fortune	Virgo	♍	12	Your Natural Good Luck manifests through your critically-minded and methodical quest for and attraction to meticulous and practical spirituality.

⊗	Part of Fortune	Libra	♎	1	Your Natural Good Luck manifests through your analytical and balanced quest for and attraction to harmonious and logical identity development.
⊗	Part of Fortune	Libra	♎	2	Your Natural Good Luck manifests through your analytical and balanced quest for and attraction to harmonious and logical values and ways to meet your needs.
⊗	Part of Fortune	Libra	♎	3	Your Natural Good Luck manifests through your analytical and balanced quest for and attraction to harmonious and logical understanding of the world around you.
⊗	Part of Fortune	Libra	♎	4	Your Natural Good Luck manifests through your analytical and balanced quest for and attraction to harmonious and logical emotional caretaking and traditions.
⊗	Part of Fortune	Libra	♎	5	Your Natural Good Luck manifests through your analytical and balanced quest for and attraction to harmonious and logical creative expression.
⊗	Part of Fortune	Libra	♎	6	Your Natural Good Luck manifests through your analytical and balanced quest for and attraction to harmonious and logical service for others.
⊗	Part of Fortune	Libra	♎	7	Your Natural Good Luck manifests through your analytical and balanced quest for and attraction to harmonious and logical life teachers.
⊗	Part of Fortune	Libra	♎	8	Your Natural Good Luck manifests through your analytical and balanced quest for and attraction to harmonious and logical intimate relationships.
⊗	Part of Fortune	Libra	♎	9	Your Natural Good Luck manifests through your analytical and balanced quest for and attraction to harmonious and logical mastership of a body of knowledge.
⊗	Part of Fortune	Libra	♎	10	Your Natural Good Luck manifests through your analytical and balanced quest for and attraction to harmonious and logical accomplishments.
⊗	Part of Fortune	Libra	♎	11	Your Natural Good Luck manifests through your analytical and balanced quest for and attraction to harmonious and logical community.
⊗	Part of Fortune	Libra	♎	12	Your Natural Good Luck manifests through your analytical and balanced quest for and attraction to harmonious and logical spirituality.

399

⊗	Part of Fortune	Scorpio	♏	1	Your Natural Good Luck manifests through your intense and truth seeking quest for and attraction to penetrating and emotionally transformative identity development.
⊗	Part of Fortune	Scorpio	♏	2	Your Natural Good Luck manifests through your intense and truth seeking quest for and attraction to penetrating and emotionally transformative values and ways to meet your needs.
⊗	Part of Fortune	Scorpio	♏	3	Your Natural Good Luck manifests through your intense and truth seeking quest for and attraction to penetrating and emotionally transformative understanding of the world around you.
⊗	Part of Fortune	Scorpio	♏	4	Your Natural Good Luck manifests through your intense and truth seeking quest for and attraction to penetrating and emotionally transformative emotional caretaking and traditions.
⊗	Part of Fortune	Scorpio	♏	5	Your Natural Good Luck manifests through your intense and truth seeking quest for and attraction to penetrating and emotionally transformative creative expression.
⊗	Part of Fortune	Scorpio	♏	6	Your Natural Good Luck manifests through your intense and truth seeking quest for and attraction to penetrating and emotionally transformative service for others.
⊗	Part of Fortune	Scorpio	♏	7	Your Natural Good Luck manifests through your intense and truth seeking quest for and attraction to penetrating and emotionally transformative life teachers.
⊗	Part of Fortune	Scorpio	♏	8	Your Natural Good Luck manifests through your intense and truth seeking quest for and attraction to penetrating and emotionally transformative intimate relationships.
⊗	Part of Fortune	Scorpio	♏	9	Your Natural Good Luck manifests through your intense and truth seeking quest for and attraction to penetrating and emotionally transformative mastership of a body of knowledge.
⊗	Part of Fortune	Scorpio	♏	10	Your Natural Good Luck manifests through your intense and truth seeking quest for and attraction to penetrating and emotionally transformative accomplishments.
⊗	Part of Fortune	Scorpio	♏	11	Your Natural Good Luck manifests through your intense and truth seeking quest for and attraction to penetrating and emotionally transformative community.
⊗	Part of Fortune	Scorpio	♏	12	Your Natural Good Luck manifests through your intense and truth seeking quest for and attraction to penetrating and emotionally transformative spirituality.

⊗	Part of Fortune	Sagittarius	↗	1	Your Natural Good Luck manifests through your wide-ranging and open-minded quest for and attraction to experiential and risk-taking identity development.
⊗	Part of Fortune	Sagittarius	↗	2	Your Natural Good Luck manifests through your wide-ranging and open-minded quest for and attraction to experiential and risk-taking values and ways to meet your needs.
⊗	Part of Fortune	Sagittarius	↗	3	Your Natural Good Luck manifests through your wide-ranging and open-minded quest for and attraction to experiential and risk-taking understanding of the world around you.
⊗	Part of Fortune	Sagittarius	↗	4	Your Natural Good Luck manifests through your wide-ranging and open-minded quest for and attraction to experiential and risk-taking emotional caretaking and traditions.
⊗	Part of Fortune	Sagittarius	↗	5	Your Natural Good Luck manifests through your wide-ranging and open-minded quest for and attraction to experiential and risk-taking creative expression.
⊗	Part of Fortune	Sagittarius	↗	6	Your Natural Good Luck manifests through your wide-ranging and open-minded quest for and attraction to experiential and risk-taking service for others.
⊗	Part of Fortune	Sagittarius	↗	7	Your Natural Good Luck manifests through your wide-ranging and open-minded quest for and attraction to experiential and risk-taking life teachers.
⊗	Part of Fortune	Sagittarius	↗	8	Your Natural Good Luck manifests through your wide-ranging and open-minded quest for and attraction to experiential and risk-taking intimate relationships.
⊗	Part of Fortune	Sagittarius	↗	9	Your Natural Good Luck manifests through your wide-ranging and open-minded quest for and attraction to experiential and risk-taking mastership of a body of knowledge.
⊗	Part of Fortune	Sagittarius	↗	10	Your Natural Good Luck manifests through your wide-ranging and open-minded quest for and attraction to experiential and risk-taking accomplishments.
⊗	Part of Fortune	Sagittarius	↗	11	Your Natural Good Luck manifests through your wide-ranging and open-minded quest for and attraction to experiential and risk-taking community.
⊗	Part of Fortune	Sagittarius	↗	12	Your Natural Good Luck manifests through your wide-ranging and open-minded quest for and attraction to experiential and risk-taking spirituality.

⊗	Part of Fortune	Capricorn	♑	1	Your Natural Good Luck manifests through your goal-driven and focused quest for and attraction to results-oriented and successful identity development.
⊗	Part of Fortune	Capricorn	♑	2	Your Natural Good Luck manifests through your goal-driven and focused quest for and attraction to results-oriented and successful values and ways to meet your needs.
⊗	Part of Fortune	Capricorn	♑	3	Your Natural Good Luck manifests through your goal-driven and focused quest for and attraction to results-oriented and successful understanding of the world around you.
⊗	Part of Fortune	Capricorn	♑	4	Your Natural Good Luck manifests through your goal-driven and focused quest for and attraction to results-oriented and successful emotional caretaking and traditions.
⊗	Part of Fortune	Capricorn	♑	5	Your Natural Good Luck manifests through your goal-driven and focused quest for and attraction to results-oriented and successful creative expression.
⊗	Part of Fortune	Capricorn	♑	6	Your Natural Good Luck manifests through your goal-driven and focused quest for and attraction to results-oriented and successful service for others.
⊗	Part of Fortune	Capricorn	♑	7	Your Natural Good Luck manifests through your goal-driven and focused quest for and attraction to results-oriented and successful life teachers.
⊗	Part of Fortune	Capricorn	♑	8	Your Natural Good Luck manifests through your goal-driven and focused quest for and attraction to results-oriented and successful intimate relationships.
⊗	Part of Fortune	Capricorn	♑	9	Your Natural Good Luck manifests through your goal-driven and focused quest for and attraction to results-oriented and successful mastership of a body of knowledge.
⊗	Part of Fortune	Capricorn	♑	10	Your Natural Good Luck manifests through your goal-driven and focused quest for and attraction to results-oriented and successful accomplishments.
⊗	Part of Fortune	Capricorn	♑	11	Your Natural Good Luck manifests through your goal-driven and focused quest for and attraction to results-oriented and successful community.
⊗	Part of Fortune	Capricorn	♑	12	Your Natural Good Luck manifests through your goal-driven and focused quest for and attraction to results-oriented and successful spirituality.

Astrology Unlocked by Philip Young, PhD

⊗	Part of Fortune	Aquarius	♒	1	Your Natural Good Luck manifests through your unconventional and idealistic quest for and attraction to authentic and non-traditional identity development.
⊗	Part of Fortune	Aquarius	♒	2	Your Natural Good Luck manifests through your unconventional and idealistic quest for and attraction to authentic and non-traditional values and ways to meet your needs.
⊗	Part of Fortune	Aquarius	♒	3	Your Natural Good Luck manifests through your unconventional and idealistic quest for and attraction to authentic and non-traditional understanding of the world around you.
⊗	Part of Fortune	Aquarius	♒	4	Your Natural Good Luck manifests through your unconventional and idealistic quest for and attraction to authentic and non-traditional emotional caretaking and traditions.
⊗	Part of Fortune	Aquarius	♒	5	Your Natural Good Luck manifests through your unconventional and idealistic quest for and attraction to authentic and non-traditional creative expression.
⊗	Part of Fortune	Aquarius	♒	6	Your Natural Good Luck manifests through your unconventional and idealistic quest for and attraction to authentic and non-traditional service for others.
⊗	Part of Fortune	Aquarius	♒	7	Your Natural Good Luck manifests through your unconventional and idealistic quest for and attraction to authentic and non-traditional life teachers.
⊗	Part of Fortune	Aquarius	♒	8	Your Natural Good Luck manifests through your unconventional and idealistic quest for and attraction to authentic and non-traditional intimate relationships.
⊗	Part of Fortune	Aquarius	♒	9	Your Natural Good Luck manifests through your unconventional and idealistic quest for and attraction to authentic and non-traditional mastership of a body of knowledge.
⊗	Part of Fortune	Aquarius	♒	10	Your Natural Good Luck manifests through your unconventional and idealistic quest for and attraction to authentic and non-traditional accomplishments.
⊗	Part of Fortune	Aquarius	♒	11	Your Natural Good Luck manifests through your unconventional and idealistic quest for and attraction to authentic and non-traditional community.
⊗	Part of Fortune	Aquarius	♒	12	Your Natural Good Luck manifests through your unconventional and idealistic quest for and attraction to authentic and non-traditional spirituality.

⊗	Part of Fortune	Pisces	♓	1	Your Natural Good Luck manifests through your imaginative and faithful quest for and attraction to consciousness-raising and soulful identity development.
⊗	Part of Fortune	Pisces	♓	2	Your Natural Good Luck manifests through your imaginative and faithful quest for and attraction to consciousness-raising and soulful values and ways to meet your needs.
⊗	Part of Fortune	Pisces	♓	3	Your Natural Good Luck manifests through your imaginative and faithful quest for and attraction to consciousness-raising and soulful understanding of the world around you.
⊗	Part of Fortune	Pisces	♓	4	Your Natural Good Luck manifests through your imaginative and faithful quest for and attraction to consciousness-raising and soulful emotional caretaking and traditions.
⊗	Part of Fortune	Pisces	♓	5	Your Natural Good Luck manifests through your imaginative and faithful quest for and attraction to consciousness-raising and soulful creative expression.
⊗	Part of Fortune	Pisces	♓	6	Your Natural Good Luck manifests through your imaginative and faithful quest for and attraction to consciousness-raising and soulful service for others.
⊗	Part of Fortune	Pisces	♓	7	Your Natural Good Luck manifests through your imaginative and faithful quest for and attraction to consciousness-raising and soulful life teachers.
⊗	Part of Fortune	Pisces	♓	8	Your Natural Good Luck manifests through your imaginative and faithful quest for and attraction to consciousness-raising and soulful intimate relationships.
⊗	Part of Fortune	Pisces	♓	9	Your Natural Good Luck manifests through your imaginative and faithful quest for and attraction to consciousness-raising and soulful mastership of a body of knowledge.
⊗	Part of Fortune	Pisces	♓	10	Your Natural Good Luck manifests through your imaginative and faithful quest for and attraction to consciousness-raising and soulful accomplishments.
⊗	Part of Fortune	Pisces	♓	11	Your Natural Good Luck manifests through your imaginative and faithful quest for and attraction to consciousness-raising and soulful community.
⊗	Part of Fortune	Pisces	♓	12	Your Natural Good Luck manifests through your imaginative and faithful quest for and attraction to consciousness-raising and soulful spirituality.

Angular Points

In my practice I use the angles as Energy Points rather than House cusps. I use them this way because I cast charts using the Whole Sign House system as written about and practiced by Demetria George in her book *Astrology and the Authentic Self*. Using the Whole House system sets all the Houses at 0 degrees of a Sign, placing the Ascendant and Descendant within the 1st and 7th House. As a result, the Midheaven (Apex) and Imum Coeli (Nadir) can range from the 9th to the 11th and 4th to 6th Houses, respectively, due variations in the highest point of the Sun on the day you were born based on the time of year you were born and the distance from the equator. These four points naturally apply to the Cardinal Signs and Angular Houses (Aries/1st, Cancer/4th, Libra/7th, and Capricorn/10th); the places where we initiate action, emotional leadership, judgment, and goals.

Since the 1st House represents our quest for identity, the specific placement of the Ascendant indicates how a person presents and is perceived by the world. The Sign of the Ascendant is the spiritual garb of the individual, acting as the first impression others encounter when they meet you. In terms of relationships, the Ascendant tells another person what you bring to the relationship. My Ascendant is in Scorpio, so I present and am perceived as intense, focused, and emotionally deep.

Since the 7th House represents our quest for life teachers, the specific placement of the Descendant indicates the type of people you need to attract and learn from to fill out your identity work. The Sign of the Descendant is the spiritual handshake of the individual, acting as the charm you use, and others identify, to make the right connections with you. In terms of relationships, the Descendant tells you what you seek from a person to gain the most from a relationship. My Descendant is in Taurus, so I am seeking partnerships that will help me learn and express my values consistently, address my needs, and help promote and establish my security.

The Midheaven can occupy the 9th House of mastership, the 10th House of public responsibility, or the 11th House of community. The Midheaven indicates our public work for compensation (career). My Midheaven occupies my 11th House and is in Virgo. My best career path involves work that allows me to support my community in a practical way, taking action and completing tasks with tangible and measurable outcomes (Virgo).

405

The Imum Coeli can occupy the 3rd House of communication, the 4th House of roots and family, and the 5th House of creativity. The Imum Coeli indicates our most personal feelings and the energy of our inner world. My Imum Coeli occupies my 5th House and is in Pisces. My journey inward and my emotional sources activate, grow, and evolve when I express my dreams and spirituality creatively (Pisces). In the tables below you will find the same formula as the previous Energy Points, limited to the 1st, 3rd, 4th, 5th, 7th, 9th, 10th, and 11th Houses.

Astrology Unlocked by Philip Young, PhD

A^SC	Ascendant	Aries	♈	I	You Present To and Are Perceived By the Outside World as independent, maverick, and heroic.
A^SC	Ascendant	Taurus	♉	I	You Present To and Are Perceived By the Outside World as reliable, secure, and capable.
A^SC	Ascendant	Gemini	♊	I	You Present To and Are Perceived By the Outside World as inquisitive, mentally agile, and communicative.
A^SC	Ascendant	Cancer	♋	I	You Present To and Are Perceived By the Outside World as nurturing, protective, and sympathetic.
A^SC	Ascendant	Leo	♌	I	You Present To and Are Perceived By the Outside World as creative, playful, and passionate.
A^SC	Ascendant	Virgo	♍	I	You Present To and Are Perceived By the Outside World as practical, methodical, and patient.
A^SC	Ascendant	Libra	♎	I	You Present To and Are Perceived By the Outside World as analytical, objective, and neutral.
A^SC	Ascendant	Scorpio	♏	I	You Present To and Are Perceived By the Outside World as intense, transformative, and forceful.
A^SC	Ascendant	Sagittarius	♐	I	You Present To and Are Perceived By the Outside World as experimental, open-minded, and experience driven.
A^SC	Ascendant	Capricorn	♑	I	You Present To and Are Perceived By the Outside World as goal-oriented, accomplished, and mature.
A^SC	Ascendant	Aquarius	♒	I	You Present To and Are Perceived By the Outside World as unconventional, authentic, and idealistic.
A^SC	Ascendant	Pisces	♓	I	You Present To and Are Perceived By the Outside World as imaginative, empathic, and spiritual.

Astrology Unlocked by Philip Young, PhD

DSC	Descendant	Aries	♈	7	You Seek Life Teachers That Will Teach You how to be independent and discover your identity on your own terms.
DSC	Descendant	Taurus	♉	7	You Seek Life Teachers That Will Teach You how to express your values and do the work necessary to obtain the resources you want and need.
DSC	Descendant	Gemini	♊	7	You Seek Life Teachers That Will Teach You how to keep your mind active and successfully communicate with and understand others.
DSC	Descendant	Cancer	♋	7	You Seek Life Teachers That Will Teach You how to nurture and be nurtured by others.
DSC	Descendant	Leo	♌	7	You Seek Life Teachers That Will Teach You how to play and express your passions in life.
DSC	Descendant	Virgo	♍	7	You Seek Life Teachers That Will Teach You how to think critically and achieve practical goals through service to others.
DSC	Descendant	Libra	♎	7	You Seek Life Teachers That Will Teach You how to make successful and decisive judgments and achieve balance and harmony with others.
DSC	Descendant	Scorpio	♏	7	You Seek Life Teachers That Will Teach You how to go through transformations at deep emotional levels.
DSC	Descendant	Sagittarius	♐	7	You Seek Life Teachers That Will Teach You how to go out into the world and learn the lessons you need to grow through interactive experiences.
DSC	Descendant	Capricorn	♑	7	You Seek Life Teachers That Will Teach You how to set your goals and achieve your desired success(es) in this life.
DSC	Descendant	Aquarius	♒	7	You Seek Life Teachers That Will Teach You how to properly express your unconventional and authentic ideas about yourself and others.
DSC	Descendant	Pisces	♓	7	You Seek Life Teachers That Will Teach You how to express your imagination and connect with your spiritual lessons.

408

M^C	Midheaven	Aries	♈	9	Your Publically Outward Responsibility seeks mastership that earns you compensation by being a pioneer in a field of expert knowledge.
M^C	Midheaven	Taurus	♉	9	Your Publically Outward Responsibility seeks mastership that earns you compensation by being a stalwart in a field of expert knowledge.
M^C	Midheaven	Gemini	♊	9	Your Publically Outward Responsibility seeks mastership that earns you compensation by being a facilitator of communication and ideas in a field of expert knowledge.
M^C	Midheaven	Cancer	♋	9	Your Publically Outward Responsibility seeks mastership that earns you compensation by being a caretaker of expert knowledge.
M^C	Midheaven	Leo	♌	9	Your Publically Outward Responsibility seeks mastership that earns you compensation by being the shining star in your field of expert knowledge.
M^C	Midheaven	Virgo	♍	9	Your Publically Outward Responsibility seeks mastership that earns you compensation by being the critic in your field of expert knowledge.
M^C	Midheaven	Libra	♎	9	Your Publically Outward Responsibility seeks mastership that earns you compensation by being the judge and decision maker in your field of expert knowledge.
M^C	Midheaven	Scorpio	♏	9	Your Publically Outward Responsibility seeks mastership that earns you compensation by being the transformer in your field of expert knowledge.
M^C	Midheaven	Sagittarius	♐	9	Your Publically Outward Responsibility seeks mastership that earns you compensation by being the explorer in your field of expert knowledge.
M^C	Midheaven	Capricorn	♑	9	Your Publically Outward Responsibility seeks mastership that earns you compensation by being the most accomplished in your field of expert knowledge.
M^C	Midheaven	Aquarius	♒	9	Your Publically Outward Responsibility seeks mastership that earns you compensation by being unconventional in your field of expert knowledge.
M^C	Midheaven	Pisces	♓	9	Your Publically Outward Responsibility seeks mastership that earns you compensation by being imaginative in your field of expert knowledge.

M^C	Midheaven	Aries	♈	10	Your Publically Outward Responsibility seeks a career(s) that earns you compensation for your pioneering efforts in the world.
M^C	Midheaven	Taurus	♉	10	Your Publically Outward Responsibility seeks a career(s) that earns you compensation for your stalwart efforts in the world
M^C	Midheaven	Gemini	♊	10	Your Publically Outward Responsibility seeks a career(s) that earns you compensation for your facilitation of communication in the world.
M^C	Midheaven	Cancer	♋	10	Your Publically Outward Responsibility seeks a career(s) that earns you compensation for your caretaking efforts in the world.
M^C	Midheaven	Leo	♌	10	Your Publically Outward Responsibility seeks a career(s) that earns you compensation for your creative self-expression efforts in the world.
M^C	Midheaven	Virgo	♍	10	Your Publically Outward Responsibility seeks a career(s) that earns you compensation for your practical efforts in the world.
M^C	Midheaven	Libra	♎	10	Your Publically Outward Responsibility seeks a career(s) that earns you compensation for your decision making efforts in the world.
M^C	Midheaven	Scorpio	♏	10	Your Publically Outward Responsibility seeks a career(s) that earns you compensation for your transformative efforts in the world.
M^C	Midheaven	Sagittarius	♐	10	Your Publically Outward Responsibility seeks a career(s) that earns you compensation for your exploratory efforts in the world.
M^C	Midheaven	Capricorn	♑	10	Your Publically Outward Responsibility seeks a career(s) that earns you compensation for your goal-driven efforts in the world.
M^C	Midheaven	Aquarius	♒	10	Your Publically Outward Responsibility seeks a career(s) that earns you compensation for your unconventional efforts in the world.
M^C	Midheaven	Pisces	♓	10	Your Publically Outward Responsibility seeks a career(s) that earns you compensation for your imaginative efforts in the world.

M^C	Midheaven	Aries	♈	11	Your Publically Outward Responsibility seeks community involvement that earns you compensation for your pioneering vision for a group.
M^C	Midheaven	Taurus	♉	11	Your Publically Outward Responsibility seeks community involvement that earns you compensation for your stalwart vision for a group.
M^C	Midheaven	Gemini	♊	11	Your Publically Outward Responsibility seeks community involvement that earns you compensation for your interactive vision for a group.
M^C	Midheaven	Cancer	♋	11	Your Publically Outward Responsibility seeks community involvement that earns you compensation for your caretaking vision for a group.
M^C	Midheaven	Leo	♌	11	Your Publically Outward Responsibility seeks community involvement that earns you compensation for your creative vision for a group.
M^C	Midheaven	Virgo	♍	11	Your Publically Outward Responsibility seeks community involvement that earns you compensation for your critical vision of a group.
M^C	Midheaven	Libra	♎	11	Your Publically Outward Responsibility seeks community involvement that earns you compensation for your fair and just vision of a group.
M^C	Midheaven	Scorpio	♏	11	Your Publically Outward Responsibility seeks community involvement that earns you compensation for your transformative vision of a group.
M^C	Midheaven	Sagittarius	♐	11	Your Publically Outward Responsibility seeks community involvement that earns you compensation for your worldly vision of a group.
M^C	Midheaven	Capricorn	♑	11	Your Publically Outward Responsibility seeks community involvement that earns you compensation for your goal-oriented vision for a group.
M^C	Midheaven	Aquarius	♒	11	Your Publically Outward Responsibility seeks community involvement that earns you compensation for your unconventional vision for a group.
M^C	Descendant	Pisces	♓	11	Your Publically Outward Responsibility seeks community involvement that earns you compensation for your spiritual vision for a group.

I^C	Imum Coeli	Aries	♈	3	Your Foundation in Life seeks understanding about yourself through independent, maverick, and heroic thoughts.
I^C	Imum Coeli	Taurus	♉	3	Your Foundation in Life seeks understanding about yourself through reliable, secure, and capable thoughts.
I^C	Imum Coeli	Gemini	♊	3	Your Foundation in Life seeks understanding about yourself through inquisitive, mentally agile, and communicative thoughts.
I^C	Imum Coeli	Cancer	♋	3	Your Foundation in Life seeks understanding about yourself through nurturing, protective, and sympathetic thoughts.
I^C	Imum Coeli	Leo	♌	3	Your Foundation in Life seeks understanding about yourself through creative, playful, and passionate thoughts.
I^C	Imum Coeli	Virgo	♍	3	Your Foundation in Life seeks understanding about yourself through practical, methodical, and patient thoughts.
I^C	Imum Coeli	Libra	♎	3	Your Foundation in Life seeks understanding about yourself through analytical, objective, and neutral thoughts.
I^C	Imum Coeli	Scorpio	♏	3	Your Foundation in Life seeks understanding about yourself through intense, transformative, and forceful thoughts.
I^C	Imum Coeli	Sagittarius	♐	3	Your Foundation in Life seeks understanding about yourself through experimental, open-minded, and experience driven thoughts.
I^C	Imum Coeli	Capricorn	♑	3	Your Foundation in Life seeks understanding about yourself through goal-oriented, accomplished, and mature thoughts.
I^C	Imum Coeli	Aquarius	♒	3	Your Foundation in Life seeks understanding about yourself through unconventional, authentic, and idealistic thoughts.
I^C	Imum Coeli	Pisces	♓	3	Your Foundation in Life seeks understanding about yourself through imaginative, empathic, and spiritual thoughts.

Astrology Unlocked by Philip Young, PhD

I𝖢	Imum Coeli	Aries	♈	4	Your Foundation in Life seeks understanding about yourself through independent, maverick, and heroic feelings.
I𝖢	Imum Coeli	Taurus	♉	4	Your Foundation in Life seeks understanding about yourself through reliable, secure, and capable feelings.
I𝖢	Imum Coeli	Gemini	♊	4	Your Foundation in Life seeks understanding about yourself through inquisitive, mentally agile, and communicative feelings.
I𝖢	Imum Coeli	Cancer	♋	4	Your Foundation in Life seeks understanding about yourself through nurturing, protective, and sympathetic feelings.
I𝖢	Imum Coeli	Leo	♌	4	Your Foundation in Life seeks understanding about yourself through creative, playful, and passionate feelings.
I𝖢	Imum Coeli	Virgo	♍	4	Your Foundation in Life seeks understanding about yourself through practical, methodical, and patient feelings.
I𝖢	Imum Coeli	Libra	♎	4	Your Foundation in Life seeks understanding about yourself through analytical, objective, and neutral feelings.
I𝖢	Imum Coeli	Scorpio	♏	4	Your Foundation in Life seeks understanding about yourself through intense, transformative, and forceful feelings.
I𝖢	Imum Coeli	Sagittarius	♐	4	Your Foundation in Life seeks understanding about yourself through experimental, open-minded, and experience driven feelings.
I𝖢	Imum Coeli	Capricorn	♑	4	Your Foundation in Life seeks understanding about yourself through goal-oriented, accomplished, and mature feelings.
I𝖢	Imum Coeli	Aquarius	♒	4	Your Foundation in Life seeks understanding about yourself through unconventional, authentic, and idealistic feelings.
I𝖢	Imum Coeli	Pisces	♓	4	Your Foundation in Life seeks understanding about yourself through imaginative, empathic, and spiritual feelings.

I^c	Imum Coeli	Aries	♈	5	Your Foundation in Life seeks understanding about yourself through independent, maverick, and heroic creativity.
I^c	Imum Coeli	Taurus	♉	5	Your Foundation in Life seeks understanding about yourself through reliable, secure, and capable creativity.
I^c	Imum Coeli	Gemini	♊	5	Your Foundation in Life seeks understanding about yourself through inquisitive, mentally agile, and communicative creativity.
I^c	Imum Coeli	Cancer	♋	5	Your Foundation in Life seeks understanding about yourself nurturing, protective, and sympathetic creativity.
I^c	Imum Coeli	Leo	♌	5	Your Foundation in Life seeks understanding about yourself through energetic, playful, and passionate creativity.
I^c	Imum Coeli	Virgo	♍	5	Your Foundation in Life seeks understanding about yourself through practical, methodical, and patient creativity.
I^c	Imum Coeli	Libra	♎	5	Your Foundation in Life seeks understanding about yourself through analytical, objective, and neutral creativity.
I^c	Imum Coeli	Scorpio	♏	5	Your Foundation in Life seeks understanding about yourself through intense, transformative, and forceful creativity.
I^c	Imum Coeli	Sagittarius	♐	5	Your Foundation in Life seeks understanding about yourself through experimental, open-minded, and experience driven creativity.
I^c	Imum Coeli	Capricorn	♑	5	Your Foundation in Life seeks understanding about yourself through goal-oriented, accomplished, and mature creativity.
I^c	Imum Coeli	Aquarius	♒	5	Your Foundation in Life seeks understanding about yourself through unconventional, authentic, and idealistic creativity.
I^c	Imum Coeli	Pisces	♓	5	Your Foundation in Life seeks understanding about yourself through imaginative, empathic, and spiritual creativity.

House Meanings by Ascendant

When a chart is cast the Ascendant determines the Sign Rulership for all the Houses. Below are House meaning charts for all 12 Ascendants.

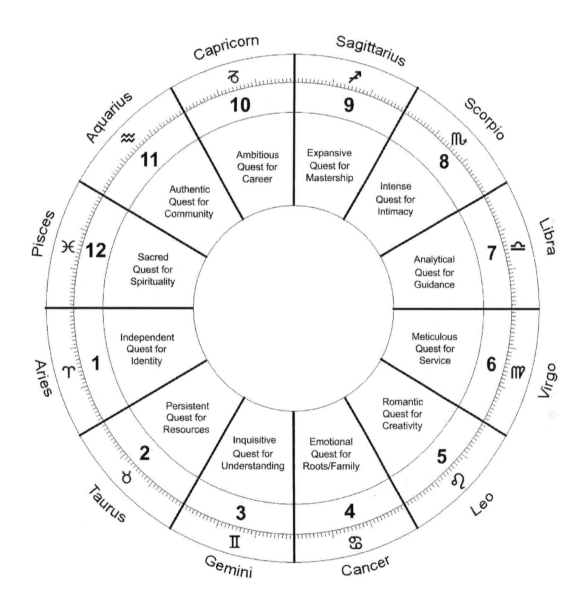

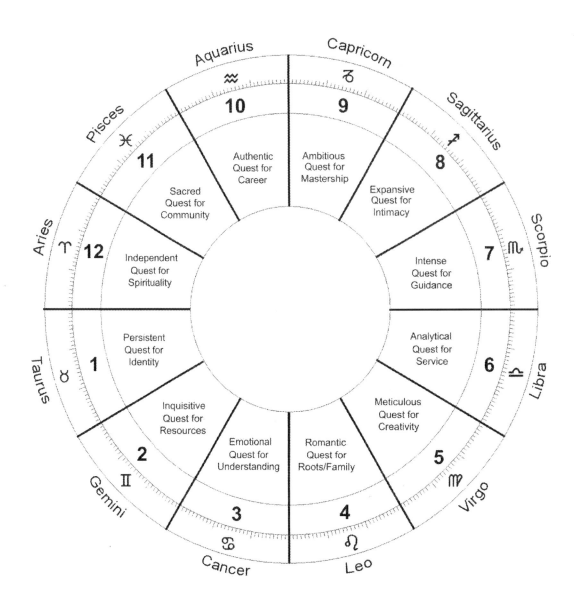

416

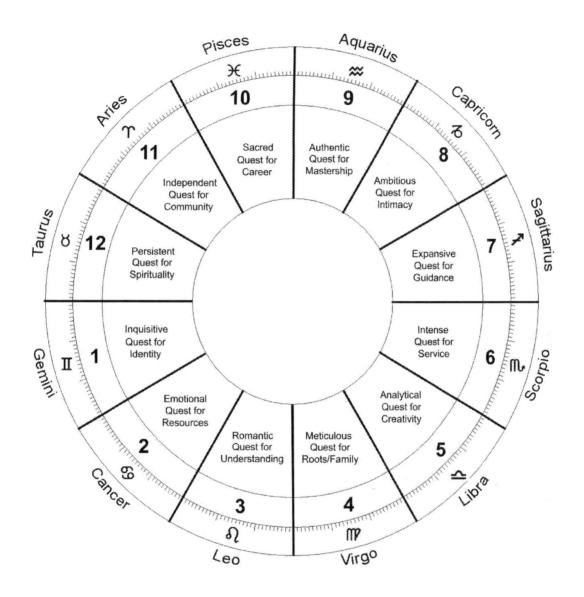

417

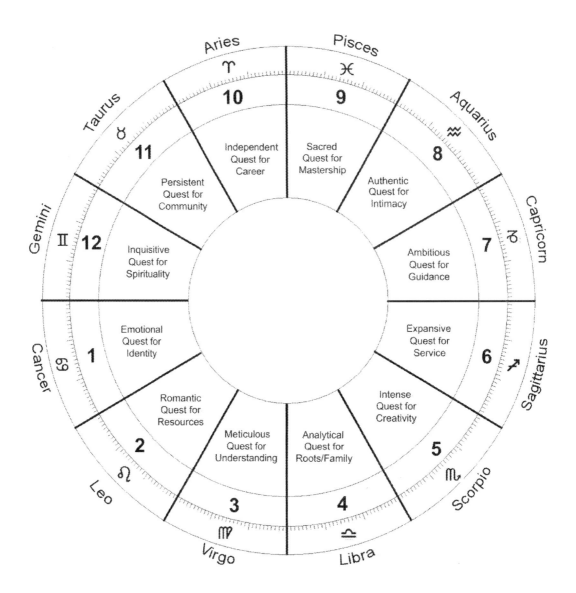

Astrology Unlocked by Philip Young, PhD

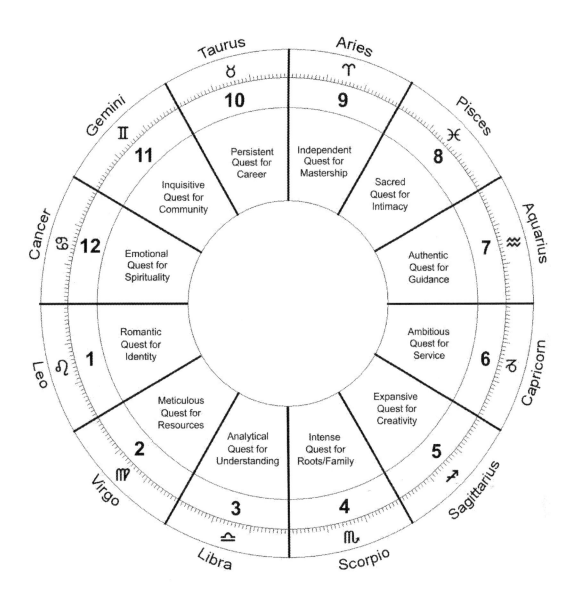

419

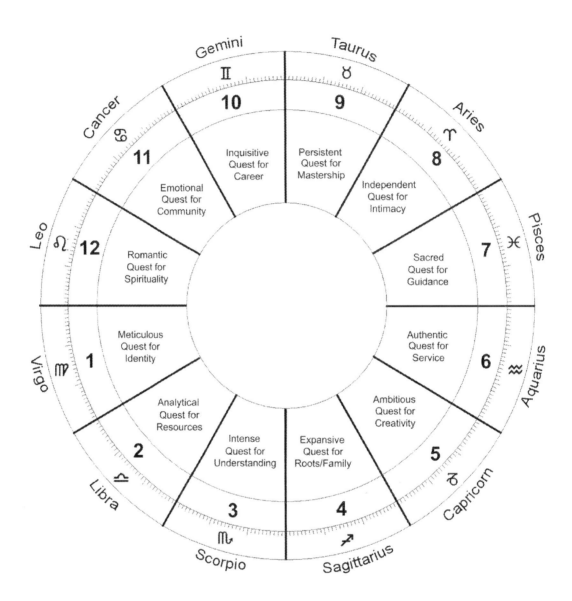

420

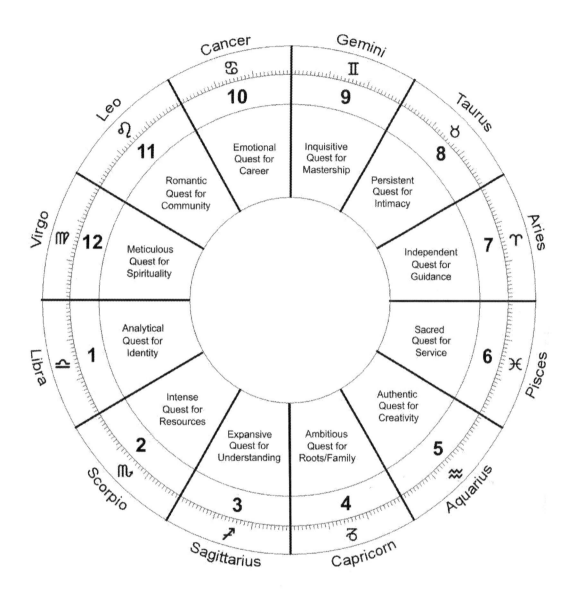

421

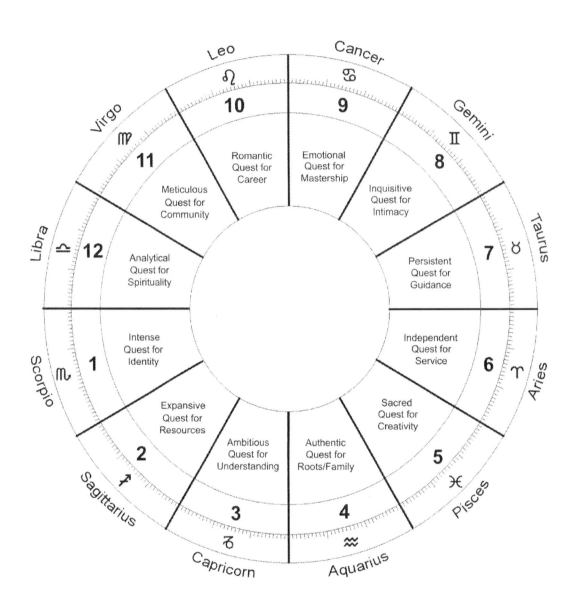

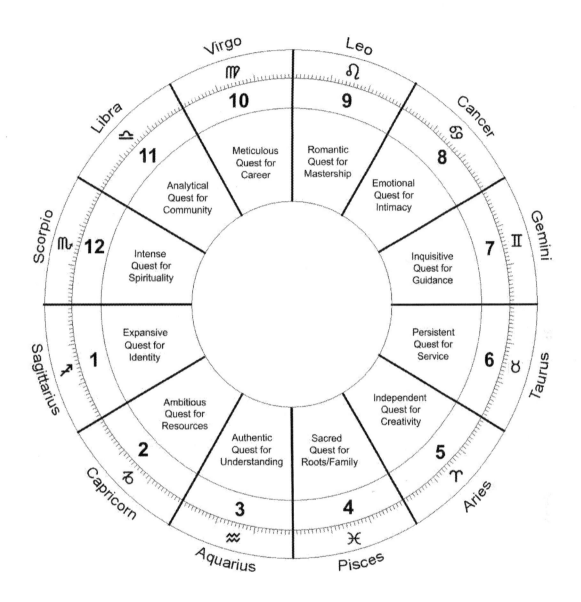

423

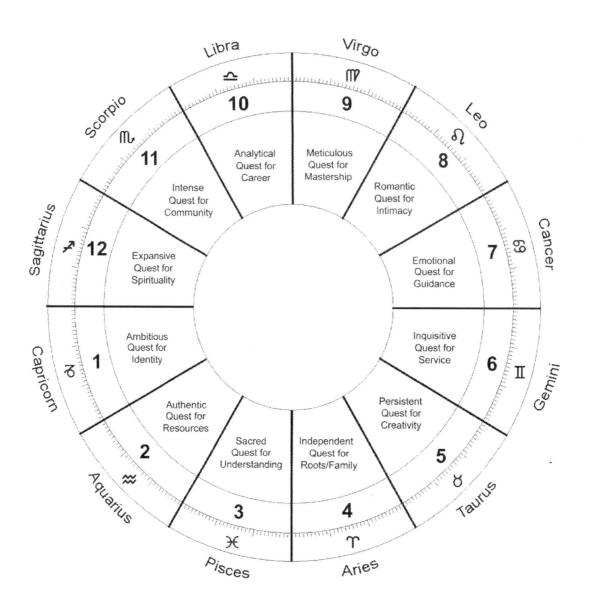

Astrology Unlocked by Philip Young, PhD

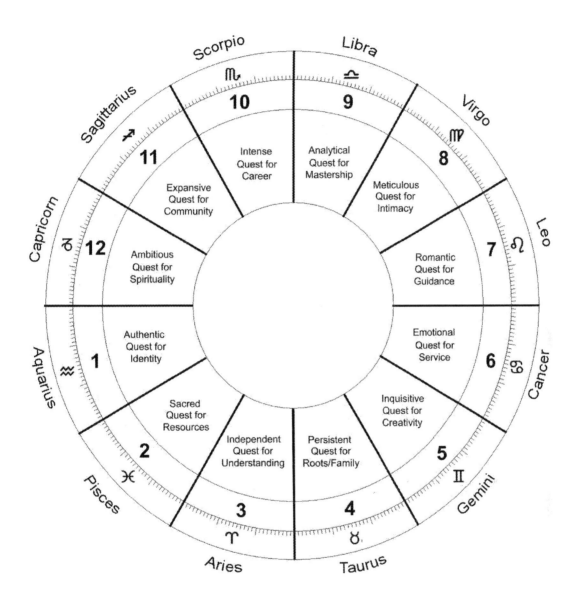

425

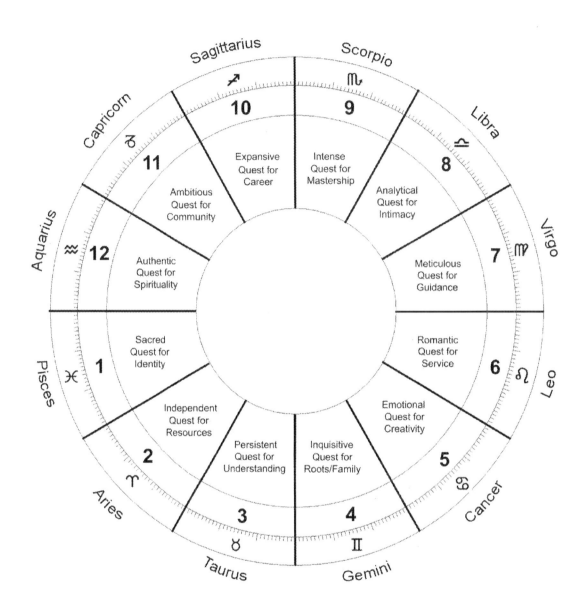

Sagittarius

Scorpio

Capricorn

Libra

Aquarius

Virgo

Pisces

Leo

Aries

Cancer

Taurus

Gemini

10 — Expansive Quest for Career

9 — Intense Quest for Mastership

11 — Ambitious Quest for Community

8 — Analytical Quest for Intimacy

12 — Authentic Quest for Spirituality

7 — Meticulous Quest for Guidance

1 — Sacred Quest for Identity

6 — Romantic Quest for Service

2 — Independent Quest for Resources

5 — Emotional Quest for Creativity

3 — Persistent Quest for Understanding

4 — Inquisitive Quest for Roots/Family

Astrology Unlocked by Philip Young, PhD

Energy Point	Energy Point Glyph	Energy Point Element	Sign	Sign Glyph	Sign Element	Sign Quality	House Number	House Element	House Quality	Interpretation
Sun (Example)	☉	Fire	Sagittarius	♐	Fire	Mutable	11	Air	Succedent	Your Primary Drive manifests through your wide-ranging and open-minded quest for and attraction to experiential and risk-taking community.
Classical Seven Energy Points and Angular House Points										
Sun										
Moon										
Mercury										
Venus										
Mars										
Jupiter										

Energy Point	Energy Point Glyph	Energy Point Element	Sign	Sign Glyph	Sign Element	Sign Quality	House Number	House Element	House Quality	Interpretation
Saturn										
Ascendant										
Descendant										
Midheaven										
Imum Coeli										
Modern Three Energy Points, Nodes of the Moon, and Part of Fortune										
Uranus										
Neptune										

Energy Point	Energy Point Glyph	Energy Point Element	Sign	Sign Glyph	Sign Element	Sign Quality	House Number	House Element	House Quality	Interpretation
Pluto										
North Node ℞										
South Node ℞										
Part of Fortune										
Most Written About Asteroids and the Black Moon Lilith										
Chiron										
Vesta										
Pallas										

Energy Point	Energy Point Glyph	Energy Point Element	Sign	Sign Glyph	Sign Element	Sign Quality	House Number	House Element	House Quality	Interpretation
Juno										
Ceres										
Lilith										

Asteroids and Vulcan to Balance Masculine and Feminine Chart Energies

Energy Point	Energy Point Glyph	Energy Point Element	Sign	Sign Glyph	Sign Element	Sign Quality	House Number	House Element	House Quality	Interpretation
Vulcan										
Zeus										
Astraea										
Eris										

Energy Point	Energy Point Glyph	Energy Point Element	Sign	Sign Glyph	Sign Element	Sign Quality	House Number	House Element	House Quality	Interpretation
Hygeia										
Urania										